First World War
and Army of Occupation
War Diary
France, Belgium and Germany

18 DIVISION
54 Infantry Brigade
Royal Fusiliers (City of London Regiment)
11th Battalion
26 July 1915 - 30 April 1919

WO95/2045/1

The Naval & Military Press Ltd
www.nmarchive.com
Published in association with The National Archives

Published by

The Naval & Military Press Ltd

Unit 10 Ridgewood Industrial Park,

Uckfield, East Sussex,

TN22 5QE England

Tel: +44 (0) 1825 749494

www.naval-military-press.com

www.nmarchive.com

This diary has been reprinted in facsimile from the original. Any imperfections are inevitably reproduced and the quality may fall short of modern type and cartographic standards.

© Crown Copyright
Images reproduced by permission of The National Archives, London, England, 2015.

Contents

Document type	Place/Title	Date From	Date To
Heading	2045/1 11th Battalion Royal		
Heading	18th Division 54th Infy Bde 11th Bn Royal Fus. Jly 1915-Apr 1919		
Miscellaneous	XVIII 11 R. Fus Vol 6		
Miscellaneous	11th (S) Bn. Royal Fusiliers		
Heading	18th Division 11th Royal Fusiliers Vol. 1 July to Oct 15		
Heading	War Diary of 11th (S) Bn. Royal Fusiliers. From 26th July 1915 To 31st October 1915		
War Diary	Codford	26/07/1915	26/07/1915
War Diary	France	27/07/1915	27/10/1915
Heading	18th Division 11th Royal Fusiliers Vol 2		
War Diary	Morlancourt	28/10/1915	18/11/1915
War Diary	Sector D1	18/11/1915	26/11/1915
War Diary	Morlancourt	26/11/1915	30/11/1915
War Diary	Sector D2	30/11/1915	30/11/1915
Heading	18th Div 11th Roy: Fus: Vol 3		
War Diary	D2	01/12/1915	04/12/1915
War Diary	Morlancourt	04/12/1915	15/12/1915
War Diary	D2	01/12/1915	01/01/1916
War Diary	Morlancourt	28/12/1915	30/12/1915
Miscellaneous	Appendix "A"		
Heading	11th Royal Fusiliers June 1916 Vol 4		
Miscellaneous	Officer i/c A.G's office Base	11/02/1916	11/02/1916
War Diary	D2	03/01/1916	11/01/1916
War Diary	Morlancourt	11/01/1916	18/01/1916
War Diary	D 2	19/01/1916	26/01/1916
War Diary	Morlancourt	31/01/1916	31/01/1916
War Diary	Franvillers	31/01/1916	31/01/1916
Miscellaneous	War Diaries The Office I/C GS Office Base	01/05/1916	01/05/1916
War Diary		29/02/1916	29/02/1916
War Diary	Franvillers.	01/03/1916	01/03/1916
War Diary	Corbie	06/03/1916	06/03/1916
War Diary	Bray	07/03/1916	07/03/1916
War Diary	Bronfay Fm Billon Wd	08/03/1916	08/03/1916
War Diary	A 1 Bronfay Farm Billon Wood	11/03/1916	11/03/1916
War Diary	A1	15/03/1916	15/03/1916
War Diary	Bray	19/03/1916	19/03/1916
War Diary	A 1	23/03/1916	23/03/1916
War Diary	Bronfay Fm And Billon Wd	27/03/1916	27/03/1916
War Diary	Billon Wood	01/04/1916	01/04/1916
War Diary	A 1	02/04/1916	07/04/1916
War Diary	Bray	08/04/1916	14/04/1916
War Diary	A 1	14/04/1916	14/04/1916
War Diary	Bronfay Farm Billon Wood	20/04/1916	26/04/1916
War Diary	A 1	27/04/1916	03/05/1916
War Diary	Chipilly	04/05/1916	31/05/1916
War Diary	Bois Celestine Chipilly	01/06/1916	03/06/1916
War Diary	Briquemesnil	04/06/1916	11/06/1916
War Diary	Picquigny	11/06/1916	23/06/1916
War Diary	Bray	24/06/1916	24/06/1916

Type	Location/Description	Start	End
War Diary	Carnoy	25/06/1916	30/06/1916
Heading	11th Battn. The Royal Fusiliers. July 1916		
Miscellaneous	War Diary		
War Diary		01/07/1916	02/07/1916
War Diary	Carnoy	03/07/1916	08/07/1916
War Diary	Bois Des Tailles	09/07/1916	13/07/1916
War Diary	Trigger Valley	14/07/1916	14/07/1916
War Diary	Maricourt Trenches	14/07/1916	18/07/1916
War Diary	Bois De Tailles	19/07/1916	20/07/1916
War Diary	Grovetown	21/07/1916	21/07/1916
War Diary	Liongpre Porceville	21/07/1916	21/07/1916
War Diary	Longpree	22/07/1916	22/07/1916
War Diary	Arques	23/07/1916	23/07/1916
War Diary	Sercus	23/07/1916	26/07/1916
War Diary	Lynde	27/07/1916	28/07/1916
War Diary	Metern	29/07/1916	01/08/1916
Miscellaneous	Report On Attack Of 1st July 1916		
Miscellaneous	Report On Attack, July 1st, 1916	06/07/1916	06/07/1916
War Diary	Meteren	01/08/1916	05/08/1916
War Diary	Erquinghem	06/08/1916	07/08/1916
War Diary	B1 Sector Trenches	08/08/1916	11/08/1916
War Diary	B2 Sector Trenches	11/08/1916	13/08/1916
War Diary	B1 Sector Trenches	14/08/1916	14/08/1916
War Diary	Subsidiary Line B1 & B2 Sectors	15/08/1916	22/08/1916
War Diary	Erquinghem	23/08/1916	24/08/1916
War Diary	Bailleul	25/08/1916	25/08/1916
War Diary	St Pol	25/08/1916	25/08/1916
War Diary	Orlencourt	26/08/1916	05/09/1916
War Diary	Monchy Breton Training Area	27/08/1916	02/09/1916
War Diary	Orlencourt	03/09/1916	03/09/1916
War Diary	Monchy Breton Training Area	04/09/1916	05/09/1916
Heading	11th Bn Roy. Fusiliers September 1916 Also 1st to 9th October 1916		
War Diary	Orlencourt	06/09/1916	08/09/1916
War Diary	Maisnil St Pol	09/09/1916	09/09/1916
War Diary	Ivergny	10/09/1916	10/09/1916
War Diary	Raincheval	11/09/1916	23/09/1916
War Diary	Trenches	24/09/1916	27/09/1916
War Diary	Bois De Martinsart	28/09/1916	29/09/1916
War Diary	Mailly Mallet Wood	30/09/1916	03/10/1916
War Diary	Senlis	04/10/1916	05/10/1916
War Diary	Ribeaucourt And Domesmont	06/10/1916	09/10/1916
Miscellaneous	54th Infantry Brigade. Preliminary Instruction for Attack.	28/09/1916	28/09/1916
Miscellaneous	11th (S) Bn. Royal Fusiliers	02/10/1916	02/10/1916
Heading	For The Period 1st to 9th October sec September Diary.		
War Diary	Ribeaucourt	10/09/1916	15/11/1916
War Diary	Beauval	16/10/1916	16/10/1916
War Diary	Warloy Baillon	17/10/1916	17/10/1916
War Diary	Bouzincourt	18/10/1916	19/10/1916
War Diary	Albert	20/10/1916	23/10/1916
War Diary	Trenches	24/10/1916	25/10/1916
War Diary	Albert	26/10/1916	03/11/1916
War Diary	Trenches	04/11/1916	06/11/1916
War Diary	Albert	07/11/1916	13/11/1916
War Diary	Trenches	14/11/1916	17/11/1916

War Diary	Huts At Ovillers.	18/11/1916	21/11/1916
War Diary	Warloy Baillon	22/11/1916	22/11/1916
War Diary	Rubempre	23/11/1916	23/11/1916
War Diary	Doullens	24/11/1916	24/11/1916
War Diary	Berneuil	25/11/1916	25/11/1916
War Diary	Ribeaucourt	26/11/1916	26/11/1916
War Diary	St Riquer	27/11/1916	27/11/1916
War Diary	Drucat	28/11/1916	30/11/1916
Miscellaneous	D.A.G G H Q 3rd Echelon		
War Diary	Drucat	01/12/1916	14/12/1916
War Diary	Marcheville	15/12/1916	09/01/1917
Miscellaneous	Subject:- Duplicate War Diaries.	29/12/1916	29/12/1916
War Diary	Marcheville	10/01/1917	11/01/1917
War Diary	Maison-Rolland	12/01/1917	12/01/1917
War Diary	Berneuil	13/01/1917	14/01/1917
War Diary	La Vicogne	15/01/1917	16/01/1917
War Diary	Warwick Huts at R.F.A.	17/01/1917	17/01/1917
War Diary	Warwick Huts	17/01/1917	19/01/1917
War Diary	Trenches	20/01/1917	24/01/1917
War Diary	Warwick Huts	25/01/1917	27/01/1917
War Diary	Wellington Huts.	28/01/1917	08/02/1917
War Diary	Trenches	09/02/1917	09/02/1917
Heading	11th /R. Fus Feb 1917		
War Diary	Trenches	10/02/1917	11/02/1917
War Diary	Wellington Huts	12/02/1917	14/02/1917
War Diary	Trenches	15/02/1917	18/02/1917
War Diary	Monmouth Huts	19/02/1917	19/02/1917
War Diary	Senlis	20/02/1917	02/03/1917
War Diary	Tents Between Aijthuille And Thiepval	03/03/1917	09/03/1917
Operation(al) Order(s)	Operation Orders No. 60 by Lieut-Colonel. C.C. Carr. D.S.O. Commanding 11th Bn. Royal Fusiliers.	08/02/1917	08/02/1917
Miscellaneous	Relief Table.		
Operation(al) Order(s)	Operation Orders No 61 By Captain H.R. Mundey Commanding 11th Bn. Royal Fusiliers	10/02/1917	10/02/1917
Operation(al) Order(s)	Operation Orders No 62 By Captain H.R. Mundey Commanding 11th Bn. Royal Fusiliers	10/02/1917	10/02/1917
Operation(al) Order(s)	Preliminary Operation Orders No 64 By Lieut-Colonel C.C. Carr. D.S.O. Commanding 11th Bn. Royal Fusiliers	14/02/1917	14/02/1917
Miscellaneous	Operations Against S. Miraumont Trench On February 17th		
Operation(al) Order(s)	Operation Orders No 60 By Lieut Colonel C.C. Carr.D.S.O. Commanding 11th Bn. Royal Fusiliers	08/02/1917	08/02/1917
War Diary	In Tents Location Between Authville And Thiepval	10/03/1917	13/03/1917
War Diary	Battalion In Line	14/03/1917	14/03/1917
War Diary	In The Line	15/03/1917	20/03/1917
War Diary	Bihucourt	21/03/1917	21/03/1917
War Diary	Kitchener Huts	22/03/1917	22/03/1917
War Diary	Harponville	23/03/1917	23/03/1917
War Diary	Villers Bocage	24/03/1917	24/03/1917
War Diary	Dury	25/03/1917	26/03/1917
War Diary	On Train	27/03/1917	27/03/1917
War Diary	Thiennes	28/03/1917	28/03/1917
Operation(al) Order(s)	Preliminary Operation Orders No. 68. By Lieut Colonel C.C. Carr D.S.O. Commanding 11th Bn. Royal Fusiliers	21/03/1917	21/03/1917

Type	Description	Date From	Date To
Operation(al) Order(s)	Preliminary Operation Orders No. 69. By Lieut Colonel C.C. Carr D.S.O. Commanding 11th Bn. Royal Fusiliers	22/03/1917	22/03/1917
Miscellaneous	Warning Orders By Lieut Colonel C.C. Carr D.S.O. Commanding 11th Bn. Royal Fusiliers	23/03/1917	23/03/1917
Operation(al) Order(s)	Operation Orders No. 70 By Lieut Colonel C.C. Carr D.S.O. Commanding 11th Bn. Royal Fusiliers	24/03/1917	24/03/1917
War Diary	Thiennes	29/03/1917	09/04/1917
War Diary	Thiennes Map. Refce France Sheet 36A Edition 6 1/40000 I 15.16.21.22	09/04/1917	20/04/1917
War Diary	Moving by Road	20/04/1917	20/04/1917
War Diary	Le. Cornet Bourdois & La Miquellerie	20/04/1917	26/04/1917
War Diary	March by Road	26/04/1917	26/04/1917
War Diary	On Rail	27/04/1917	27/04/1917
War Diary	Neuville Vitasse	28/04/1917	28/04/1917
Operation(al) Order(s)	Operation Order No. 81	26/04/1917	26/04/1917
War Diary	In The Trenches	29/04/1917	02/05/1917
War Diary	Neuville Vitasse	02/05/1917	02/05/1917
War Diary	In The Trenches	03/05/1917	04/05/1917
War Diary	Neuville Vitasse	05/05/1917	12/05/1917
War Diary	Henin Sur Cojuel Map Refce France 51B S.W Edition 4A N31a TN 32 B	13/05/1917	01/06/1917
War Diary	Henin Sur Cojuel	13/05/1917	30/05/1917
War Diary	In The Line Map Refce Bullecourt Edition 2A 1/10000 Sheet 51B SW4	02/06/1917	04/06/1917
Miscellaneous	11th Bn. Royal Fusiliers Warning Order No.	02/06/1917	02/06/1917
Operation(al) Order(s)	Operation Order No. 33	12/05/1917	12/05/1917
Operation(al) Order(s)	Operation Order No. 82	12/06/1917	12/06/1917
War Diary	In The Line	04/06/1917	09/06/1917
War Diary	In The Line Near Heninel	10/06/1917	15/06/1917
War Diary	Reserve Bde Area Near Boyelles	16/06/1917	18/06/1917
War Diary	Gaudiempre	19/06/1917	03/07/1917
War Diary	Vicinity Of Beauvorde	05/07/1917	06/07/1917
War Diary	Dickebusch Camp	07/07/1917	09/07/1917
War Diary	In The Line	08/06/1917	09/06/1917
Miscellaneous	Administrative Orders		
War Diary	Dickebusch Area In Camp (Huts and Tents at H.20.c.9.2	10/07/1917	22/07/1917
War Diary	Dallington Camp	23/07/1917	24/07/1917
War Diary	Steenvoorde West	25/07/1917	29/07/1917
War Diary	Dickebusch Area Camp at H.20.c.9.2	30/07/1917	30/07/1917
War Diary	Chateau Segard Area No. 1	31/07/1917	31/07/1917
Operation(al) Order(s)	To Preliminary Operation Order No 6		
Operation(al) Order(s)	Preliminary Operation Order No. 6		
Miscellaneous	Appendix "A"		
Operation(al) Order(s)	Appendix "C" Issued Preliminary Operation Order No. 5		
Miscellaneous	Officer Commanding 7th Royal West Kent Regiment.	25/07/1917	25/07/1917
Miscellaneous	Administrative Order to Accompany Operation Orders No. 5		
Operation(al) Order(s)	Preliminary Operation Orders No.6		
Miscellaneous	Appendix D		
Operation(al) Order(s)	Operation Order No 8	21/07/1917	21/07/1917
Miscellaneous	After Order		
Operation(al) Order(s)	Operation Order No 6	21/07/1917	21/07/1917
Operation(al) Order(s)	Operation Order No 9	23/07/1917	23/07/1917

Type	Description	Date From	Date To
Miscellaneous	Officer Commanding	25/07/1917	25/07/1917
Operation(al) Order(s)	Operation Order No 7.	25/07/1917	25/07/1917
Operation(al) Order(s)	Operation Order No. 10	28/07/1917	28/07/1917
Operation(al) Order(s)	Operation Order No. 11	30/07/1917	30/07/1917
Operation(al) Order(s)	Operation Order No. 12	30/07/1917	30/07/1917
Miscellaneous	Addenda To Administrative Instructions Issued With Operation Order No. 5	30/07/1917	30/07/1917
War Diary	Ritz Area	01/08/1917	01/08/1917
War Diary	Dickebusch Area. Camp. at H.27.b. 2.6. (Huts)	02/08/1917	04/08/1917
War Diary	Chateau Segard Area No 1 Camp (Dugouts & Bivouacs)	04/08/1917	06/08/1917
War Diary	Battle Position	07/08/1917	09/08/1917
War Diary	Trenches	10/08/1917	10/08/1917
War Diary	Chateau Segard	11/08/1917	11/08/1917
War Diary	Dickebusch Huts	12/08/1917	12/08/1917
War Diary	Steenvoorde East Area	12/08/1917	15/08/1917
War Diary	Cost Houck Area	15/08/1917	03/09/1917
War Diary	Esquelbecq Area	03/09/1917	09/09/1917
Diagram etc			
Operation(al) Order(s)	Operation Orders No 13	04/08/1917	04/08/1917
Miscellaneous	54th Infantry Brigade Defence Scheme	06/08/1917	06/08/1917
Operation(al) Order(s)	Administrative Instructions to Accompany Operation Order No. 14	07/08/1917	07/08/1917
Operation(al) Order(s)	Operation Order No 15	07/08/1917	07/08/1917
Operation(al) Order(s)	Operation Order No. 14	07/08/1917	07/08/1917
Operation(al) Order(s)	Preliminary. Operation Order No. 15	07/08/1917	07/08/1917
Miscellaneous	11th Bn. Royal Fusiliers	09/10/1917	09/10/1917
Operation(al) Order(s)	Operation Order No. 16	12/08/1917	12/08/1917
Operation(al) Order(s)	Operation Order No. 17	14/08/1917	14/08/1917
War Diary	Esquelbecq	09/09/1917	23/09/1917
War Diary	St. Jan Ter Biezen	23/09/1917	09/10/1917
Operation(al) Order(s)	Operation Orders No. 18	03/09/1917	03/09/1917
Miscellaneous	Training Programme	09/09/1917	09/09/1917
Operation(al) Order(s)	Operation Orders No. 19		
Operation(al) Order(s)	Operation Orders No. 20		
Operation(al) Order(s)	Operation Orders No. 21	12/09/1917	12/09/1917
Diagram etc			
Miscellaneous		18/09/1917	18/09/1917
Diagram etc	Battalion Boundary		
Operation(al) Order(s)	Operation Order No 22	21/09/1917	21/09/1917
Miscellaneous	Programme Of Training		
Miscellaneous	Programme Of Training.	29/09/1917	29/09/1917
Diagram etc			
Miscellaneous	Programme Of Training	29/09/1917	29/09/1917
Map			
Miscellaneous			
War Diary	Tunnelling Camp	10/10/1917	14/10/1917
War Diary	Trenches	15/10/1917	18/10/1917
War Diary	Canal Dugouts	19/10/1917	21/10/1917
War Diary	Trenches	22/10/1917	24/10/1917
War Diary	Dirty Bucket Camp	25/10/1917	28/10/1917
War Diary	Proven Area	29/10/1917	31/10/1917
War Diary	Dirty Bucket Camp	25/10/1917	28/10/1917
War Diary	Proven Area	29/10/1917	31/10/1917
Miscellaneous	54th Brigade Memo No B.M.46 forwarded for information of Coy's		

Type	Description	Start	End
Operation(al) Order(s)	Operation Order No. 24	05/10/1917	05/10/1917
Operation(al) Order(s)	Operation Order No. 23	03/10/1917	03/10/1917
Operation(al) Order(s) Map	Operation Order No. 25	08/10/1917	08/10/1917
Operation(al) Order(s) Map	Operation Orders No. 26	11/10/1917	11/10/1917
Miscellaneous	Programme Of Training.	11/10/1917	11/10/1917
Operation(al) Order(s)	Operation Orders No. 27	24/10/1917	24/10/1917
Operation(al) Order(s)	Operation Orders No. 29	21/10/1917	21/10/1917
Operation(al) Order(s)	Operation Orders No. 30	28/10/1917	28/10/1917
War Diary	Picadilly Camp	01/11/1917	04/11/1917
War Diary	De Wippe Camp	05/11/1917	09/11/1917
War Diary	Trenches	10/11/1917	13/11/1917
War Diary	Baboon Camp	14/11/1917	16/11/1917
War Diary	De Wippe Camp	16/11/1917	21/11/1917
War Diary	Trenches	22/11/1917	25/11/1917
War Diary	Canal Bank Camp	26/11/1917	28/11/1917
War Diary	De Wippe Camp	28/11/1917	30/11/1917
Miscellaneous	Training Programme.		
Operation(al) Order(s)	Preliminary Operation Orders No 31		
Operation(al) Order(s)	Continuation Of Preliminary Operation Order No. 31	09/11/1917	09/11/1917
Operation(al) Order(s)	Special Operation Orders For Details. To go with Preliminary Operation Order No 31	09/11/1917	09/11/1917
Miscellaneous	Training Programme	18/11/1917	18/11/1917
Operation(al) Order(s)	Operation Orders No. 32	21/11/1917	21/11/1917
Miscellaneous	Special Operation Orders For Details.	21/11/1917	21/11/1917
War Diary	De Wippe Camp A. 11.b. 3.2. Sheet Map Belgium 28 N.W.	01/12/1917	04/12/1917
War Diary	Trenches	04/12/1917	07/12/1917
War Diary	H Camp A 10. a. o. 2 Sheet Belgium 28 N.W.	07/12/1917	10/12/1917
War Diary	H Camp	11/12/1917	14/12/1917
War Diary	Rousbrugge	16/12/1917	31/12/1917
Operation(al) Order(s)	Operation Orders No. 33	03/12/1917	03/12/1917
Operation(al) Order(s)	Trench Instructions To Accompany Operation Order No. 33	02/12/1917	02/12/1917
Miscellaneous	Special Operation Orders For Details.	03/12/1917	03/12/1917
Operation(al) Order(s)	Operation Orders No. 34	15/12/1917	15/12/1917
Miscellaneous	Programme Of Training	15/12/1917	15/12/1917
Miscellaneous	Training Programme	22/12/1917	22/12/1917
War Diary	Haringhe Area	01/01/1918	04/01/1918
War Diary	De Wippe	04/01/1918	10/01/1918
War Diary	Line	10/01/1918	14/01/1918
War Diary	Baboon Camp	14/01/1918	14/01/1918
War Diary	De Wippe	18/01/1918	18/01/1918
War Diary	Line	24/01/1918	26/01/1918
War Diary	Lower Baboon Camp	27/01/1918	28/01/1918
War Diary	Emile Camp	28/01/1918	30/01/1918
War Diary	Heidbek Camp	30/01/1918	30/01/1918
War Diary	Crombeke	31/01/1918	31/01/1918
Operation(al) Order(s)	Order No. 35	03/01/1918	03/01/1918
Operation(al) Order(s)	Operation Orders No. 37	09/01/1918	09/01/1918
Miscellaneous	Reference Dress for March tomorrow.		
Operation(al) Order(s)	Administrative Instructions To Accompany Orders No. 38		
Operation(al) Order(s)	Operation Order No. 38	23/01/1918	23/01/1918
Miscellaneous	Addenda To Operation Orders No. 38	23/01/1918	23/01/1918

Type	Description	Date From	Date To
Miscellaneous	Orders For Details Left Out Of Action.	23/01/1918	23/01/1918
Miscellaneous	Priority Of Work On Relief From The Line.	19/01/1918	19/01/1918
Operation(al) Order(s)	Order No 41	29/01/1918	29/01/1918
Miscellaneous	The Keynote of this series of training will be	31/01/1918	31/01/1918
War Diary	Heidebeek Camp Crombeke Area Belgium & France Sheet 19X20 Central	01/02/1918	01/02/1918
War Diary	Behericourt		
War Diary	Clastres	15/02/1918	26/02/1918
War Diary	Caillouel		
Miscellaneous	Programme Of Training.	07/02/1918	07/02/1918
Operation(al) Order(s)	Order No. 48	07/02/1918	07/02/1918
Operation(al) Order(s)	Order No. 43	19/02/1918	19/02/1918
Miscellaneous	Addenda To Order No. 43	19/02/1918	19/02/1918
Operation(al) Order(s)	Order No. 44		
Operation(al) Order(s)	Order No. 45		
Miscellaneous	Working Party For	16/02/1918	16/02/1918
Miscellaneous			
Miscellaneous	Working Party Table	17/02/1918	17/02/1918
Miscellaneous	Programme Of Training.	19/02/1918	19/02/1918
Miscellaneous	Working Party Table For 19/2/18	19/02/1918	19/02/1918
Miscellaneous	Working Party Table	20/02/1918	20/02/1918
Miscellaneous	Working Party Table	20/12/1918	20/12/1918
Miscellaneous	Working Party Table	22/02/1918	22/02/1918
Miscellaneous	Working Party Table	23/02/1918	23/02/1918
Miscellaneous	Working Party Table	24/02/1918	24/02/1918
Miscellaneous	11th Bn The Royal Fusiliers		
Miscellaneous			
Heading	11th Battn. The Royal Fusiliers. March 1918		
War Diary	Caillouel	01/03/1918	22/03/1918
War Diary	Near Jussy	22/03/1918	22/03/1918
War Diary	Jussy	22/03/1918	23/03/1918
War Diary	Caillouel	23/03/1918	25/03/1918
War Diary	Baboeuf	25/03/1918	26/03/1918
War Diary	Audignicourt	27/03/1918	30/03/1918
War Diary	Boves	30/03/1918	30/03/1918
War Diary	Gentelles	31/03/1918	31/03/1918
Operation(al) Order(s)	11th Bn. The Royal Fusiliers. Movement Order No. 1	09/04/1918	09/04/1918
Miscellaneous			
Miscellaneous	Action to be Taken in The Event of "Stand To" Order being Rec.		
Miscellaneous	Preliminary Orders.		
Heading	11th Battn. The Royal Fusiliers. April (1.4.18 to 1.5.18) 1918		
War Diary	Gentelles	01/04/1918	04/04/1918
War Diary	Bois De Hangard	05/04/1918	06/04/1918
War Diary	Boves	07/04/1918	09/04/1918
War Diary	Boutillerie	10/04/1918	18/04/1918
War Diary	St Acheul	19/04/1918	27/04/1918
War Diary	Belloy St Leonards	28/04/1918	24/05/1918
War Diary	Behencourt Wood	25/05/1918	02/06/1918
War Diary	Line	03/06/1918	08/06/1918
War Diary	Henencourt Wood	09/06/1918	14/06/1918
War Diary	Warloy	17/06/1918	19/06/1918
War Diary	Line	20/06/1918	02/07/1918
Operation(al) Order(s)	11th Bn. The Royal Fusiliers. Order No. 9	10/06/1918	10/06/1918
War Diary	Henencourt	03/07/1918	12/07/1918

War Diary	Guigne'ct	13/07/1918	31/07/1918
Heading	11th Battalion Royal Fusiliers August 1918		
Heading	11th Battn Royal Fusiliers War Diary for the period 1st to 21st August, 1918, Apparently Missing.		
War Diary	Railway Embkmt. S Of Albert	22/08/1918	22/08/1918
War Diary	Ancre	23/08/1918	31/08/1918
Miscellaneous	From O/C. "D" Coy	09/08/1918	09/08/1918
Miscellaneous	The Adjutant		
Miscellaneous	54th. Inf. Bde. Hqrs.	03/10/1918	03/10/1918
War Diary	Combles	01/09/1918	30/09/1918
Miscellaneous	Orders For The Presentation Of The "1914" Star.	03/09/1918	03/09/1918
Miscellaneous	Order	28/09/1918	28/09/1918
Miscellaneous	Narrative Of Operations carried out by 11th Bn. The Royal Fusiliers.		
Miscellaneous	A Form Messages And Signals.		
War Diary	Ronssoy	01/10/1918	21/10/1918
War Diary	Le Cateau	22/10/1918	24/10/1918
War Diary	Bousies.	25/10/1918	31/10/1918
War Diary	Robersart	01/11/1918	14/11/1918
War Diary	Serain	15/11/1918	30/11/1918
Miscellaneous	Report on Operations carried out by the 11th Bn. The Royal Fusiliers		
Operation(al) Order(s)	11th. Bn. The Royal Fusiliers. Order No. 19		
Miscellaneous	Report on Operations carried out by the 11th Bn. The Royal Fusiliers		
Operation(al) Order(s)	11th. Bn. The Royal Fusiliers. Order No. 19		
War Diary	Serain	01/12/1918	10/12/1918
War Diary	Walincourt	11/12/1918	31/01/1919
War Diary	Walincourt France	01/02/1919	28/02/1919
War Diary	Walincourt	01/03/1919	31/03/1919
War Diary		01/04/1919	30/04/1919

2045/1

11th Battalion

Royal Fusiliers

18TH DIVISION
54TH INFY BDE

11TH BN ROYAL FUS.
JULY 1915-APR 1919

MAPS/PLANS RECORDED

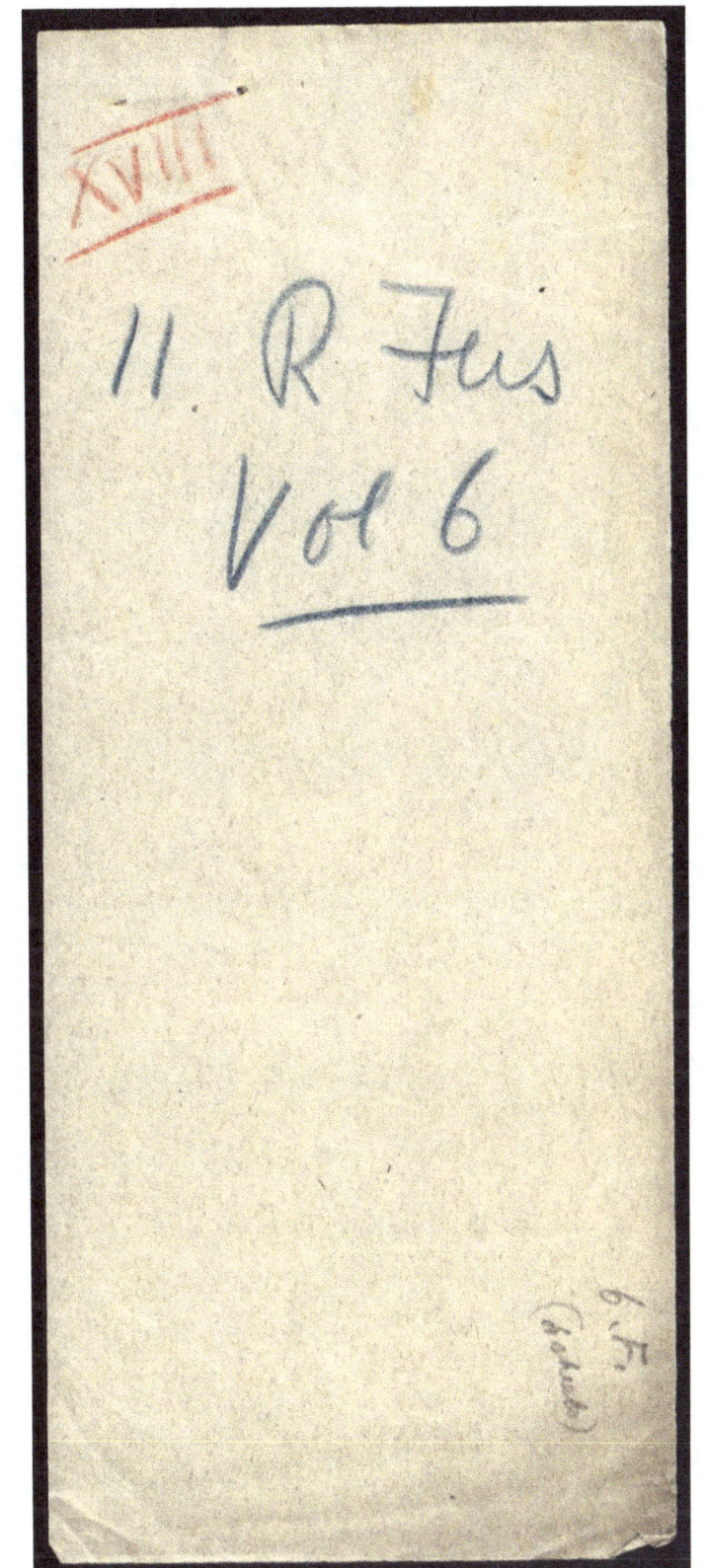

XVIII

11. R Fus
Vol 6

11th (S) Bn. Royal
Fusiliers

121/7432

I.F.
(11th ab)

54/18

18th Hussars

11th Royal Dusiliers
Vol: I
July to Oct 15

CONFIDENTIAL

WAR DIARY

OF

11TH (S) Bn. ROYAL FUSILIERS.

FROM 26TH JULY 1915. TO 31ST OCTOBER 1915.

(VOLUME I)

Army Form C. 2118

WAR DIARY
or
INTELLIGENCE SUMMARY
(Erase heading not required.)

Place	Date	Hour	Summary of Events and Information	Remarks and references to Appendices
CODFORD	26/7/15		Left CODFORD on 26.7.1915, half Bn left at 3.30pm and remainder at 4.45pm. Arrived at FOLKESTONE 10.30 PM 26.7.1915 and embarked on S.S. CERIOL proceeded	
FRANCE	27/7/15		to BOULOGNE arriving there at 1.30 AM, 27.4.1915. Marched to Rest Camp at AUSTROHOVE situate about 2 miles from landing stage. The Bn left	
	28/7/15		BOULOGNE at 8.30 PM on 28.7.1915 entrained, and arrived at FLESSELLES	
	29/7/15		at 4 AM on 29.7.1915, detrained and marched to TALMAS where the Battn was billeted.	
	4/8/15		Sergt G. Shriff was accidentally seriously wounded by a "PITCHER" bomb on 4.8.1915 being removed to Hospital the same day.	
	8/8/15		The Bn paraded at 4 PM on 8.8.1915 and marched to BONNAY arriving there about 9.30 P.M, went into billets until 13.8.1915 and left latter place	
	13/8/15		and marched to BRAY where Bn arrived about 9 PM. Bn paraded at	
	14/8/15		12 MN 14.8.1915 and marched to SUZANNE, where B and C Coys were billeted, A and D Coys proceeding to the trenches situated in "A" Sector, for instruction, the former under the 1st Bn Devon Regt and the latter under the 2nd Bn Manchester Regt. "A" and "D" Coys were	
	16/8/15		relieved by "B" and "C" on 16.8.1915. Major Hudson being slightly wounded on returning from the trenches. 2nd Lieut G.E. Cornaby carried out	

Army Form C. 2118

Instructions regarding War Diaries and Intelligence Summaries are contained in F. S. Regs., Part II. and the Staff Manual respectively. Title Pages will be prepared in manuscript.

WAR DIARY
or
INTELLIGENCE SUMMARY
(Erase heading not required.)

Place	Date	Hour	Summary of Events and Information	Remarks and references to Appendices
	22/8/15		successfully a bombing attack on the German trenches without sustaining any casualties. On the 22-8-1915 A and D Coys marched to MERICOURT	
	23/8/15		B and C Coys and 13th Hd Qrs proceeding on the 23rd. The Bn	
	24/8/15		marched to DERNANCOURT on the 24-8-1915. A B and D Coys going into billets. B Coy proceeding to BECORDEL BECOURT where 2 platoons were detailed to assist 148th Tunnelling Coy. R.E. The Bn moved from DERNANCOURT on the evening of the 4-9-1915	
	4/9/15		and proceeded for duty in the trenches, taking over sector D1. A Coy occupied left sector and B Coy the right sector of fire trenches. C and D Coys were in reserve.	
	8/9/15		On the morning of the 8th September 1915 C Coy relieved A and D Coy relieved B. On the night of the 4-9-1915 a successful operation was carried out, a mine being exploded near POINT 77 and the line of trench advanced to edge of crater formed. The Battn was specially complimented on this action by the	

WAR DIARY
or
INTELLIGENCE SUMMARY
(Erase heading not required.)

Army Form C. 2118

Place	Date	Hour	Summary of Events and Information	Remarks and references to Appendices
			G.O.C. 5th Bde. "My dear Baw, I wish you to let all ranks of the 11th (S) Bn Royal Fusiliers know how pleased I am with their demeanour and with the work they have done while in D1. The little operation of occupying the edge of the crater opposite 77 was well managed, and carried out with excellent spirit. I have told Genl Maxse and also Sir J Morland about it, and the latter has specially expressed his appreciation. I am so sorry you have suffered so many casualties, but the majority were pure bad luck, and not because proper arrangements were not made. You must be proud now, after a trying time, to find such an excellent spirit and tone in your Battn, and I congratulate you. Yours sincerely (Sd) W. Heneker Brig Genl Comdg 5th Bde.	

Army Form C. 2118

WAR DIARY
or
INTELLIGENCE SUMMARY
(Erase heading not required.)

Instructions regarding War Diaries and Intelligence Summaries are contained in F.S. Regs., Part II. and the Staff Manual respectively. Title Pages will be prepared in manuscript.

Place	Date	Hour	Summary of Events and Information	Remarks and references to Appendices
	9/9/15		On the night of 9.9.1915 the Battn was relieved by the 6th (S) Bn Northn Regt and formed the Brigade reserve. A Coy moving to BECORDEL BECOURT and B Coy to redoubt near POINT 107. Hed Qrs, C and D Coys proceeding to MEAULTE. Between the period 4.9.15 and 9.9.15 the following casualties occured:— Killed. 5 Wounded. 22 Gassed. 1 (through fumes of explosion)	
	14/9/15		On Sept 14th when on fatigue with his Company in parts of the trenches known as the TAMBOUR Cpl Fox shewed conspicuous gallantry in assisting to extricate some engineers who had been buried by a sap which had been blown in by a shell.	
	16/9/15		The Battn proceded to the trenches on 16.9.1915, taking over sector D1.	
	22/9/15		On 22.9.1915 the Artillery commenced bombarding the German trenches. On the 25th the Bn was relieved by the 6 Northants and proceded to billets at MORLANCOURT. During	
	25/9/15			

WAR DIARY
or
INTELLIGENCE SUMMARY
(Erase heading not required.)

Army Form C. 2118

Place	Date	Hour	Summary of Events and Information	Remarks and references to Appendices
	19/9/15		The period the Bn was in the trenches, the following casualties occurred. 6 Killed 6 Wounded.	
	3/10/15		A draft of 50 N.C.O's and men joined the Bn from Base Depot on 19th September 1915. On 3.10.1915 the Bn took over section D1 trenches. On night of	
	5/10/15		5th a German mine was exploded. Lieut H Sharp was killed when going out to see some bombers who he had posted to protect those repairing the parapet. L/Cpl Warner D Coy acted with conspicuous bravery and recovered Lieut Sharp's body from within 15 yards of the German trenches. On the night of the 6-10-1915 our miners	
	6/10/15		exploded a mine in the right sub section. On evening of 7 + 8th	
	7/10/15		and on the same evening another English mine was exploded	
	8/10/15		German camouflets was exploded. Considerable damage being done to German trenches also to our own, which were repaired. The Battn was relieved on the 11.10.1915 by the 6th (S) Bn Northampton Regt,	
	11/10/15		and returned to billets at MORLANCOURT. The following number of casualties occurred during tour of duty. 6 Killed 5 Wounded.	

WAR DIARY
or
INTELLIGENCE SUMMARY
(Erase heading not required.)

Army Form C. 2118

Place	Date	Hour	Summary of Events and Information	Remarks and references to Appendices
	19/10/15		On 19-10-1915, the Battalion took over Sector D1, relieving 6th Battn. Northants Regt. During tour of duty 3 German mines were exploded, but very little damage was done to our trenches.	
	25/10/15-26/10/15		On night of 25/26th Lieut G.F.G. Cumberlege, Corporal Bradly and Private Adams carried out a very arduous patrol and were complimented in Brigade Routine Orders for this work.	
	27/10/15		On morning of 27th a German deserter from 23rd Regiment, 6th Corps (Hanovian) came over at 10-30 a.m. On afternoon of 27th the Battalion was relieved by 6th Northants and proceeded into billets at MORLANCOURT. The following number of casualties occurred during tour of duty. 5 Killed. 13 Wounded.	

18th Division

12/
7631

G.F.
(3 sheets)

4th Royal Fusiliers
Vol 2

Nov. 15

11th (Service) Bn. Royal Fusiliers   11th (Service) Bn. Royal Fusiliers Army Form C. 2118

WAR DIARY

Instructions regarding War Diaries and Intelligence Summaries are contained in F. S. Regs., Part II. and the Staff Manual respectively. Title Pages will be prepared in manuscript.

INTELLIGENCE SUMMARY

(Erase heading not required.)

Place	Date	Hour	Summary of Events and Information	Remarks and references to Appendices
Morlancourt	28.10.15 to 2.11.15		Bn in rest billets.	
	2.11.15		Bn relieved 6th Northn R and took over D1 sector situated near BOIS FRANCAIS S of FRICOURT. Relief complete at 5 PM.	
	3.11.15		Morning very quiet, some shelling in the afternoon	
	4.11.15		A quiet day, enemy snipers active. Three or four cases of trench feet reported	
	5.11.15		Very quiet day.	
	6.11.15		Quiet day with the exception of a few "Aerial torpedoes"	
	7.11.15		Some shelling by enemy and a few "Aerial torpedoes" otherwise quiet.	
	8.11.15		Quiet day, nothing of importance occurred	
	9.11.15		Same do 8 th	
	10.11.15		The Bn was relieved by 6th Northn Regt and proceeded to billets in Morlancourt. The following casualties occurred during this tour in trenches. 2 Killed 11 Wounded	
MORLANCOURT	11.11.15 to 17.11.15		Battn in rest billets at MORLANCOURT.	
SECTOR D1	18.11.15		Battn relieved 6th Northants in sector D1 relief being complete by 5PM. German mine exploded at 5.55 PM - No casualties. Tw-	19 pairs of "trench feet"

1875 Wt. W593/826 1,000,000 4/15 J.B.C. & A. A.D.S.S./Forms/C. 2118.

Army Form C. 2118

WAR DIARY
INTELLIGENCE SUMMARY
(Erase heading not required.)

Instructions regarding War Diaries and Intelligence Summaries are contained in F.S. Regs., Part II. and the Staff Manual respectively. Title Pages will be prepared in manuscript.

Place	Date	Hour	Summary of Events and Information	Remarks and references to Appendices
SECTOR D1	19.11.15		About 30 yards of our parapet damaged.	
	20.11.15		Very quiet day. Trenches continually falling in owing to snow and rain.	
	21.11.15		Very quiet.	
	22.11.15		Quiet day, condition of trenches improved, 4 men wounded by "damage". Some shelling by enemy's trench mortar about 3.30 pm our artillery replying, otherwise quiet.	
	23.11.15		Enemy's snipers were active, also some damage was caused to trenches by enemy's trench mortars, no casualties.	
	24.11.15		Enemy's trench mortar again active in the afternoon, but soon silenced by our Artillery. Trench mortars and West Guns.	
	25.11.15		One man killed by German sniper, and trench mortars again active but were effectively silenced by our artillery.	
	26.11.15		This was a quiet day, the Bn being relieved by 6th Northn Regt and proceeding to rest billets in MORLANCOURT. Casualties during tour of duty 1 officer wounded 2 O.R. killed (2nd Lieut A.H. Barnard) 4 O.R. wounded	
MORLANCOURT	26.11.15 to 30.11.15		Bn in rest billets at MORLANCOURT.	
SECTOR D2	30.11.15		Bn relieved 12th Bn Middlesex Regt in sector D 2, N of D1 sector.	[illegible]

3. F.
(5 sheets)

11th Roy: Fus:
Vol: 3

7978/
121

545

18th R Fus

Army Form C. 2118

WAR DIARY
or
INTELLIGENCE SUMMARY
(Erase heading not required.)

Instructions regarding War Diaries and Intelligence Summaries are contained in F. S. Regs., Part II. and the Staff Manual respectively. Title Pages will be prepared in manuscript.

Place	Date	Hour	Summary of Events and Information	Remarks and references to Appendices
D 2	1.12.15		Very quiet all day, trenches in a very bad condition owing to incessant rain.	
D 2	2.12.15		Also very quiet, trenches still very bad. 16th (S) Bn Northumberland Fusiliers attached for instruction.	
D 2	3.12.15		Condition of trenches still very bad, nothing to report.	
D 2	4.12.15		Bn was relieved by 6th Bn Northamptonshire Regt, great difficulty being experienced in carrying out relief. Bn proceeded to billets in MORLANCOURT.	
MORLANCOURT	4.12.15 to 15.12.15		Bn in rest billets	
	15.12.15		Bn relieved 16th (S) Bn Northumberland Fusiliers and took over D 2 sector trenches.	[illegible]
D 2	16.12.15		Trenches in a bad condition, quiet day.	
	17.12.15		Germans shelled BECORDEL at 8.50am, we retaliated on FRICOURT FARM with our artillery.	

Army Form C. 2118

WAR DIARY
or
INTELLIGENCE SUMMARY
(Erase heading not required.)

Instructions regarding War Diaries and Intelligence Summaries are contained in F. S. Regs., Part II. and the Staff Manual respectively. Title Pages will be prepared in manuscript.

Place	Date	Hour	Summary of Events and Information	Remarks and references to Appendices
D2	18.12.15		Enemy were very active with rifle grenades and small trench mortars to which our Artillery replied.	
D2	19.12.15		Very quiet day.	
D2	20.12.15		Enemy active with trench mortars.	
D2	21.12.15		Enemy's artillery and trench mortars very active all day, our artillery replying.	
D2	22.12.15		Enemy's trench mortars again active.	
D2	23.12.15		Enemy's howitzer batteries and other artillery very active, also trench mortars causing some damage to our trenches. Our artillery retaliated.	
D2	24.12.15		Bn was relieved by 6th Northants and proceeded to Rest billets in MORLANCOURT.	
D2	25.12.15 to 1.1.16		Bn in rest-billets at MORLANCOURT.	

Army Form C. 2118

WAR DIARY
or
INTELLIGENCE SUMMARY

(Erase heading not required.)

Instructions regarding War Diaries and Intelligence Summaries are contained in F. S. Regs., Part II. and the Staff Manual respectively. Title Pages will be prepared in manuscript.

Place	Date	Hour	Summary of Events and Information	Remarks and references to Appendices
MORLANCOURT	28.12.15		Draft of 20 men joined Bn in MORLANCOURT.	
	29.12.15		Draft of 16 men joined Bn in MORLANCOURT.	
	30.12.15		Draft of 28 men joined Bn in MORLANCOURT.	
			Casualties during this tour of duty :-	
			Killed & Died from wounds 4	
			Wounded 7 OR and 1 Officer.	
			Evacuated with trench feet 1 (Lieut. W.H.E. Neild) approx.	

C. C. Carr M.Col.

11th (Service) Bn. Royal Fusiliers

APPENDIX "A". Distribution of 54th Infantry Brigade immediately before ZERO Hour.

UNIT	POSITION	BATTN. H.Q.	REMARKS
12th Middlesex Regt.: Also - 2 Sect: (2 guns) 54th M.G.Coy. 1 Sect: (2 mortars) 54th T.M.B. 1 Coy 11th R. Fusiliers (dug-out clearing party)	Forming-up trenches included in the Rectangle R.31.b.2.5 - a.6.6 - a.4.9 - c.6.9 - D.2.6 (less the actual trench running South of R.31.a.6.6 to R.31.c.4.6.	H.Q. 12th Middlesex Regt. In dug-outs immediately South of R.31.a.7.2.	
2 Companies 11th Royal Fusiliers: Also - 2 Sect: (2 guns) 54th M.G.Coy. 1 Sect: (2 mortars) 54th T.M.B.	In trench R.31.a.6.6 - d.4.0 & new communication trench from old British front line leading into old German front line N. of point R.31.a.5.5.		
11th Royal Fusiliers (less 2 Coys) .... Also - 1 Section 54th M.G. Coy.	In LEMBERG TRENCH AND QUARRY	H.Q. 11th R. Fusiliers in dugouts at R.31.d.6.9	
2 Sections 80th Field Coy. R.E.	In tunnel West of R.31.a.5.3		

6th Northamptonshire Regt. - 1 Company ....
                              1 Company ....
                              2 Companies ......
	In old German trench between X.1.b.1.8 - X.1.a.5.8 & old British front line South of that trench.
	In CAMPBELL AVENUE.
	In dug-outs SOUTH BLUFF.
		H.Q. 6th Northamptonshire Regt. In CAMPBELL POST Q.36.d.2.2.	

7th Bedfordshire Regt. - 2 Companies .... 2 Companies	In dug-outs NORTH BLUFF In PAISLEY AVENUE (THIEPVAL WOOD)	H.Q. 7th Bedfordshire Regt. In NORTH BLUFF.	
1 Section 80th Field Coy. R.E. 1 Section 54th M/Gun Company	In PAISLEY AVENUE (THIEPVAL WOOD)		
1 Section 54th Machine Gun Company	In position on HAMEL-MESNIL ridge (to bring direct overhead fire during the attack).		
Headquarters 54th Machine Gun Company 54th Trench Mortar Battery (less 1 section)	In NORTH BLUFF		

11th Roy: Fus:
Vol: 4

11th Royal Fusiliers
Jan 1916

Officer I/C
A G's Office
Base.

RF 76/15

Herewith War Diary
for month of January.

11.2.1916.

[signature] Lieut
for Major
Comdg 11 RF

Army Form C. 2118

WAR DIARY
or
INTELLIGENCE SUMMARY
(Erase heading not required.)

Instructions regarding War Diaries and Intelligence Summaries are contained in F.S. Regs., Part II. and the Staff Manual respectively. Title Pages will be prepared in manuscript.

Place	Date	Hour	Summary of Events and Information	Remarks and references to Appendices
D 2	3.1.16		Enemy's machine guns fairly active.	
"	4.1.16		Quiet day.	
"	5.1.16		Fairly quiet day, state of trenches improving	
"	6.1.16		Enemy less active with rifle and Machine Gun fire.	
"	7.1.16		Quiet day nothing unusual occurred.	
"	8.1.16		Our artillery fairly active.	
"	9.1.16		Enemy very active with rifle and Machine Gun fire. A small hostile bombing party approached our trenches and were driven off	
"	10.1.16		Quiet day nothing to report.	
"	11.1.16		Bn relieved by 6th Northants and went into Rest billets at MORLANCOURT	
MORLANCOURT	11.1.16 to 18.1.16		Bn in rest billets	
D 2	19.1.16		Bn relieved 6th Northants Regt in sector D 2. Machine Gun fire rather active on our right sub sector early in morning otherwise night was quiet.	

1875 Wt. W593/826 1,000,000 4/15 J.B.C. & A. A.D.S.S./Forms/C. 2118.

Army Form C. 2118

WAR DIARY
or
INTELLIGENCE SUMMARY
(Erase heading not required.)

Instructions regarding War Diaries and Intelligence Summaries are contained in F. S. Regs., Part II. and the Staff Manual respectively. Title Pages will be prepared in manuscript.

Place	Date	Hour	Summary of Events and Information	Remarks and references to Appendices
D 2	20.1.16		Quiet day. A patrol which went out from right out sector reported that our wire was in perfect condition. No German patrols were seen.	
	21.1.16 to 23.1.16		Very quiet during this period, nothing unusual occurring.	
	24.1.16		Machine Guns active during night otherwise nothing to report.	
	25.1.16		Machine Gun and rifle fire fairly active, number of former seems to have been increased.	
D 2	26.1.16		Bn relieved by 6th Northants Regt and proceeded to rest billets in MORLANCOURT. Casualties 2 killed. 1 Officer and 3 OR wounded.	[signature]
MORLANCOURT	31.1.16		Bn paraded at 8.30 am and marched to FRANVILLERS where Bn was in Divisional reserve.	
FRANVILLERS	31.1.16			

1875 Wt. W593/826 1,000,000 4/15 J.B.C. &A. A.D.S.S./Forms/C. 2118.

War Diaries.　　　　　　　　R.F. 140/16

The Officer i/c
A G's Office
Base.

Herewith War Diary
for the months of February
and April 1916.

　　　　　　　　G/Cumbeledge Lieut
　　　　　　　　　　Adjutant
　　　　　　　　　for
1.5.1916.　　　　Lieut Col
　　　　　　　Comdg 11 R.F.

WAR DIARY
INTELLIGENCE SUMMARY

11th (Service) Bn. Royal Fusiliers

Army Form C. 2118

Place	Date	Hour	Summary of Events and Information	Remarks and references to Appendices
to	29.2.16		While the Bn was in Divisional Reserve the time was spent in resting and getting rid of trench staleness. For training the Bn practised bombing, musketry, practice with gas helmets, attacks in the open and attacks from trenches. For recreation inter-Battn and platoon competitions were held of boxing, football, shooting etc.	

Army Form C. 2118

11th (Service) Bn Royal Fusiliers

5th/18

WAR DIARY
or
INTELLIGENCE SUMMARY

(Erase heading not required.)

Instructions regarding War Diaries and Intelligence Summaries are contained in F. S. Regs., Part II. and the Staff Manual respectively. Title Pages will be prepared in manuscript.

Place	Date	Hour	Summary of Events and Information	Remarks and references to Appendices
FRANVILLERS.	1.3.16		The Battalion paraded at 1.50pm and proceeded to CORBIE where it was billeted until the 5.3.1916.	
CORBIE.	6.3.16		The Battalion paraded at 3pm and marched to BRAY arriving about 8pm having stopped an hour on the way for tea.	
BRAY.	7.3.16		On 7.3.16 the Battn moved to BRONFAY FARM and BILLON WOOD, Bn Head Qrs and A Coy going to BRONFAY FARM and B, C and D Coys going to BILLON WOOD.	
BRONFAY FM 8.3.16 BILLON WD			The Bn relieved the 12th (S) Bn Middlesex Regt in sub-sector A1, which is situated NE of CARNOY, A Coy occupying the right sector, B Coy the centre and C Coy the left sector, D Coy being in reserve at Bn Head Qrs close to CARNOY. The trenches generally were in a very bad state of repair but after working hard on them they were put in good condition. Casualties :- 1 OR Killed. 3 OR Wounded.	

1875 Wt. W593/826 1,000,000 4/15 J.B.C. & A. A.D.S.S. [Forms/C. 2118.

11th (Service) Bn Royal Fusiliers
WAR DIARY
or
INTELLIGENCE SUMMARY
(Erase heading not required.)

Army Form C. 2118

Instructions regarding War Diaries and Intelligence Summaries are contained in F.S. Regs., Part II. and the Staff Manual respectively. Title Pages will be prepared in manuscript.

Place	Date	Hour	Summary of Events and Information	Remarks and references to Appendices
A.1. BRONFAY FARM BILLON WOOD	11.3.16		The Bn was relieved by 12th (S) Bn. Middlesex Regt and proceeded to BRONFAY FARM and BILLON WOOD, Hd Qrs and B Coy going to BRONFAY FARM, A, C and D Coys proceeding to BILLON WOOD. Owing to BRONFAY FARM being shelled 3 OR were wounded.	
A.1.	15.3.16		The Battn relieved the 12th (S) Bn Middlesex Regt in sub sector A.1., D Coy in right sector, B in the centre and C Coy in the left. A Coy being in reserve at Bn Hd Qrs close to CARNOY. Casualties :- 2 OR killed 1 OR wounded	
BRAY BRONFAY FM & BILLON WD	19.3.16		The Bn was relieved by the 12th (S) Bn Middlesex Regt and proceeded to rest billets in BRAY arriving about MN.	
A.1.	23.3.16		Bn relieved 12th Middx Regt in sub sector A.1. Coys being distributed as follows. D Coy in right sector, A Coy in the centre and C in the left sector, B Coy being in reserve at Bn Hd Qrs close to CARNOY. During the tours of duty when in the trenches, very	

Army Form C. 2118

11th (Service) Bn. Royal Fusiliers
WAR DIARY
or
INTELLIGENCE SUMMARY
(Erase heading not required.)

Instructions regarding War Diaries and Intelligence Summaries are contained in F.S. Regs., Part II. and the Staff Manual respectively. Title Pages will be prepared in manuscript.

Place	Date	Hour	Summary of Events and Information	Remarks and references to Appendices
BRONFAY FM AND BILLON WD	24.3.16		Little activity was shown by the enemy and all towns were generally speaking quiet. The Bn. was relieved by the 12th (S) Bn. Middlesex Regt., and proceeded to BRONFAY FARM and BILLON WOOD, Red Ors and C Coy going to the former and A, B and D Coys to the latter.	

Bluedupflint
for Lieut. Colonel
Comdt. 11th (Service) Bn. Royal Fusiliers

1875 Wt. W3931/826 1,000,000 4/15 J.B.C. & A. A.D.S.S./Forms/C. 2118.

WAR DIARY or INTELLIGENCE SUMMARY

11th (Service) Bn. Royal Fusiliers

Army Form C. 2118

(Erase heading not required.)

Place	Date	Hour	Summary of Events and Information	Remarks and references to Appendices
BILLON WOOD	1.4.16		Enemy shelled BILLON WOOD - Casualties 3 OR wounded.	
A.1.	2.4.16		Battalion relieved 12th (S) Bn Middlesex Regt, Coys being distributed as follows :- B Coy Left sub-sector, A Coy Centre sector, D Coy Right sub-sector, C Coy were in Reserve close to Bn Hd Qrs near CARNOY.	
A.1.	3.4.16	10 am	Enemy put about 12 shells between the PERONNE ROAD and TALUS BOISÉ - No damage was done.	
		8.30 pm	Enemy fired 15 red lights over MARICOURT WOOD which was followed by heavy shelling for about 10 minutes.	
A.1	4.4.16	—	During night of 3/4th hostile working party was detected in front of Centre Coy and was dispersed by our Machine Gun fire.	
		7 am	Enemy fired about 8 shells on our support line - no damage was done.	
		3 pm	Our Artillery bombarded enemy's craters in front of A2 sub sector on our left.	
		4.45 pm	Enemy put about 50 shells around our Hd Qrs near CARNOY in retaliation to our artillery bombardment of their craters - No damage or casualties occurred in our sub-sector.	

Army Form C. 2118

11th (Service) Bn Royal Fusiliers

WAR DIARY
or
INTELLIGENCE SUMMARY

(Erase heading not required.)

Instructions regarding War Diaries and Intelligence Summaries are contained in F. S. Regs., Part II. and the Staff Manual respectively. Title Pages will be prepared in manuscript.

Place	Date	Hour	Summary of Events and Information	Remarks and references to Appendices
A 1.	5.4.16	4/4.5am	In retaliation to our Machine Gun and rifle fire, which was concentrated during the night on portions of the enemy's front where wiring was being carried out; the enemy sent over about 25 10cm shells on our right Coy's front line, damaging the parapet, killing one man and wounding four. We retaliated with twenty 2" and 40 four inch Trench Mortar Bombs on enemy's front line. - results of our Trench Mortar Bombs were good.	
		11.30am	Enemy artillery was very active, they fired 150 rounds or so on our support trenches, also searching our front trenches for our Mortars.	
		12 noon	Enemy artillery fired in salvos afterwards slowing down their rate of fire. A large proportion of the enemy shells were "blind".	
	6.4.16		During the night of 5th/6th the enemy's machine guns and snipers were very active, being concentrated on spot where we were wiring – One OR was wounded.	
	7.4.16		Night of 6/7th enemy machine guns and snipers were again active	

Army Form C. 2118

11th (Service) Bn Royal Fusiliers
WAR DIARY
or
INTELLIGENCE SUMMARY
(Erase heading not required.)

Instructions regarding War Diaries and Intelligence Summaries are contained in F. S. Regs., Part II. and the Staff Manual respectively. Title Pages will be prepared in manuscript.

Place	Date	Hour	Summary of Events and Information	Remarks and references to Appendices
BRAY	8.4.16		against our wiring parties. - No casualties occurred. Total casualties during tour, 2nd to 9th: - 1 OR killed and 5 OR wounded. The Battalion was relieved by the 12th (S) Bn Middlesex Regt and proceeded to rest billets in BRAY arriving there about 11.45 p.m.	
BRAY	9.4.16 To 14.4.16		During this period the usual fatigues and training was carried out. The 12th Middlesex Regt in A1 Sub-Sector and the 6th Bn Northamptonshire Regt in A2 were heavily bombarded and raided by the Germans. Some prisoners were taken from the Middlesex Regt but the 6th Northants Regt in sub-sector A2, who were on the left of the 12th Middlesex, had no prisoners taken and inflicted more casualties on the Germans.	
A 1.	14.4.16		The Battn relieved the 12th (S) Bn Middlesex Regt in sub-sector A 1, NE of CARNOY, Coys being distributed as follows:- A Coy in centre sub-sector, B Coy in left sub-sector C Coy in right sub-sector and D Coy in reserve at Bn Hd Qrs near CARNOY	

Army Form C. 2118

11th (Service) Bn Royal Fusiliers

WAR DIARY
or
INTELLIGENCE SUMMARY
(Erase heading not required.)

Instructions regarding War Diaries and Intelligence Summaries are contained in F. S. Regs., Part II. and the Staff Manual respectively. Title Pages will be prepared in manuscript.

Place	Date	Hour	Summary of Events and Information	Remarks and references to Appendices
BRONFAY FARM BILLON WOOD	20.4.16		This tour of the trenches was uneventful. On the last night a very extremely heavy bombardment took place on the sector on our left, from which the effect of lachrymatory shells could be felt at our Bn Hd Qrs. This transpired to be another "cutting out" expedition by the enemy. Casualties during the tour were 1 OR killed 1 Died of wounds and 15 wounded. The Bn was relieved on the 20th by the 12th (S) Bn Middlesex Regt, Hd Qrs and "D" Coy proceeding to BRONFAY FARM "A", "B" and "C" Coys going to BILLON WOOD.	
	26.4.16		On the 26th the 1st (S) Bn Bedfordshire Regt occupying A 2 sub sector and the 12th (S) Bn Middlesex Regt made a joint "cutting out" expedition against the enemy in retaliation for the raid sustained by them on the night of the 12th April 1916. The one organised by the 1st Bedfordshire Regt was completely successful, they succeeded in entering the German trenches.	

1875 Wt. W593/826 1,000,000 4/15 J.B.C. & A. A.D.S.S./Forms/C. 2118.

Army Form C. 2118

11th (Service) Bn Royal Fusiliers

WAR DIARY
or
INTELLIGENCE SUMMARY
(Erase heading not required.)

Instructions regarding War Diaries and Intelligence Summaries are contained in F. S. Regs, Part II. and the Staff Manual respectively. Title Pages will be prepared in manuscript.

Place	Date	Hour	Summary of Events and Information	Remarks and references to Appendices
A.1.	27.4.16		killing about 40 of the enemy. The raid attempted by the 12th (S) Bn Middlesex Regt was not successful.	
			The Bn relieved the 12th (S) Bn Middlesex Regt in sub section A.1 on the night of the 27th April, and was distributed as follows:- "C" Coy in Left sub-section, "B" Coy in Centre sub section, "D" Coy in right sub section, Bn Hd Qrs near CARNOY and "A" Coy in reserve near Hd Qrs.	
	30.4.16		At 4.30 pm the Germans opened a heavy bombardment on our front line and on the 7th Bedfordshire Regt on our left. At 7.40 pm we ordered the "S.O.S" call which was immediately taken up by our Field Guns, 60 pounders, 4.2's, 6" and 8". At 7.55 pm the Artillery was ordered to slacken fire as the Germans made no attempt to attack, and their Artillery had by this time quietened down considerably. Casualties from 27-4-16 to 30-4-1916. 5 OR killed, 20 OR died of wounds and 7 OR wounded	[signature] Lieut Col 11 R.F.

Army Form C. 2118

XVIII 11 R. Sus
Vol 7

WAR DIARY
or
INTELLIGENCE SUMMARY
(Erase heading not required.)

Instructions regarding War Diaries and Intelligence Summaries are contained in F. S. Regs., Part II. and the Staff Manual respectively. Title Pages will be prepared in manuscript.

Place	Date	Hour	Summary of Events and Information	Remarks and references to Appendices
A. 1.	3.5.16		The Battn was relieved by the 2nd Bn Wiltshire Regt and marched to the BOIS CELESTINES, CHIPILLY, where the Bn arrived at 4 am on May 4th and went into tents.	
CHIPILLY	4.5.16 to 31.5.16		The Battalion was employed during the month by the C.E. 13th Corps, on hut building, road making and quarrying.	A Newbridge Lieut Aft M.C.?

1875 Wt. W 593/826 1,000,000 4/15 J.B.C. & A. A.D.S.S./Forms/C. 2118.

Army Form C. 2118

XVIII 11th (Service) Bn. Royal Fusiliers

WAR DIARY
or
INTELLIGENCE SUMMARY

(Erase heading not required.)

Instructions regarding War Diaries and Intelligence Summaries are contained in F.S. Regs., Part II. and the Staff Manual respectively. Title Pages will be prepared in manuscript.

Vol 8

Place	Date	Hour	Summary of Events and Information	Remarks and references to Appendices
BOIS CELESTINE –CHIPILLY–	1/6/16 to 3/6/16		The Battalion was employed on R.E. fatigues – unloading Barges, Road making etc, at CHIPILLY.	
	3/6/16	12·15 pm	The Battalion was formed up and marched to MERICOURT where it entrained and proceeded to AILLY-SUR-SOMME, arriving there about 5pm. Tea was taken just outside the village, after which the Bn. marched to SAISSEVAL, arriving there at 12 midnight.	
BRIQUEMESNIL	4/6/16	10 am	The Battalion marched to BRIQUEMESNIL. Day was spent cleaning up etc.	
"	5/6/16			
"	6/6/16 to 10/6/16		The Battalion was employed on Digging Practice Trenches near AILLY-SUR-SOMME	
"	11/6/16		The Battalion proceeded to the Digging area in full marching order and at about 6·30 pm marched into PICQUIGNY.	
PICQUIGNY	11/6/16 to 22/6/16		During this period the Battalion carried out Practising the Attack on the training area near AILLY-SUR-SOMME. Dinners were usually had out on the training area at ST. CHRISTS farm. Teas were had in Billets on return about 7pm.	
	23/6/16	4·15 am	The Battalion Paraded and marched to AILLY-SUR-SOMME where it entrained and proceeded to MEILLY, arriving there about noon; detrained and marched to BRAY, making a halt on the BRAY-CORBIE Road for dinner	S.F. (behate)
		7 pm	arrived at BRAY.	

Army Form C. 2118

WAR DIARY
or
INTELLIGENCE SUMMARY
(Erase heading not required.)

11th (Service) Bn Royal Fusiliers

Place	Date	Hour	Summary of Events and Information	Remarks and references to Appendices
BRAY.	24/6/16		Day was spent cleaning up generally.	
CARNOY.	25/6/16	7pm	'A' and 'B' Coys proceeded to CARNOY, accompanied by Bn Hd Qr Details.	
"	26/6/16	7pm	'C' and 'D' Coys proceeded to join remainder of Battalion at CARNOY.	
"	27/6/16		In Reserve at CARNOY.	
"	28/6/16		In Reserve at CARNOY.	
"	29/6/16		In Reserve at CARNOY.	
"	30/6/16		In Reserve at CARNOY.	
			During the whole of the Reserve period at CARNOY our Artillery carried out a continuous bombardment. The German Artillery retaliation caused the following casualties during period 25th to 30th.	
			8 Killed	
			6 Died of Wounds	
			46 Wounded (6 of whom returned to duty)	
			3 Shell Shock.	
	30/6/16	11pm	Battalion relieved 12th Middlesex Regt, taking over 1st Line trenches at about 11pm.	

54th Inf.Bde.
18th Div.

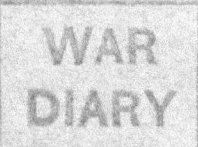

11th BATTN. THE ROYAL FUSILIERS.

J U L Y

1 9 1 6

Attached:

Report on Attack
of 1st July.

WAR DIARY.

Army Form C. 2118.

WAR DIARY
or
INTELLIGENCE SUMMARY.   11/Royal Fusiliers.

(Erase heading not required.)

July 1916

Place	Date	Hour	Summary of Events and Information	Remarks and references to Appendices
	1/7/16	7-30 a.m.	Attack on the German 1st Line Trenches was carried out. (See special Report attached.) Casualties in the attack were as follows:— 4 Officers Killed. 6 Died of Wounds. 148 Wounded. 17 missing. 4 Shell Shock.	
	2/7/16	11 p.m.	Battalion was relieved by 12th Middlesex Regt. and proceed to CARNOY.	

Army Form C. 2118

WAR DIARY
or
INTELLIGENCE SUMMARY

(Erase heading not required.)

Place	Date	Hour	Summary of Events and Information	Remarks and references to Appendices
CARNOY.	3/7/16 to 6/7/16		In Reserve at CARNOY.	
	7/7/16 8/7/16		B and D. Coys supported 7th Bedford Regt in the trenches on night of 7/8th and were relieved by 12th West York Regt. The remaining Coys (A & C) and Hd. Qr. Details at CARNOY were relieved by the 4th Royal Fusiliers	
		8-30 pm	The Battalion proceeded - by companies - to BOIS DES TAILLES, arriving there just after midnight.	
BOIS DES TAILLES.	9/7/16 to 12/7/16		During this period Battalion was refitted, bathed, and drill parades were carried out.	4th (Service) Bn: Royal Fusiliers

Army Form C. 2118

WAR DIARY or INTELLIGENCE SUMMARY
(Erase heading not required.)

11th (Service) Bn Royal Fusiliers

Place	Date	Hour	Summary of Events and Information	Remarks and references to Appendices
BOIS DES TAILLES	13/7/16	6·30 AM	Battalion paraded and marched to TRIGGER VALLEY forming part of supporting Brigade.	
TRIGGER VALLEY	14/7/16	2·0 AM	Sudden alarm — Battalion 100 ordered out to support Bde attacking TRONES WOOD. Battalion moved up in fighting order and took up position in German front line trenches	
MARICOURT TRENCHES		4·0 AM 9·0 AM	'C' and 'D' Coys taking up forward position, 'A' & 'B' Coys in rear as support ie. C & D SUNKEN ROAD / A & B DUBLIN TRENCH. Headquarters being in rear of DUBLIN TRENCH viz CASEMENT TRENCH During the attack on TRONES WOOD our Batton of D Coy went up and reinforced the 12th Middlesex Regt. The Germans were completely driven out of TRONES WOOD during the morning, and remainder of day, but a very heavy barrage on TRONES WOOD and the approaches to it	
			Our casualties for the day being 2nd Lieut A Wey wounded. One OR Killed 14 OR Wounded 2 OR Shell Shock	
	15/7/16		Battalion still remained in supporting positions and found carrying and working parties. Artillery on both sides was very active. Germans sent over a large quantity of Lachrymatory Shells on Battn near Headquarters. Anti Gas Goggles had to be worn.	
		12 noon	Enemy Shelled CASEMENT TRENCH with 77 MM and 10 CM Shells, apparently	

Army Form C. 2118

WAR DIARY
or
INTELLIGENCE SUMMARY
(Erase heading not required.)

11th (Service) Bn Royal Fusiliers

Place	Date	Hour	Summary of Events and Information	Remarks and references to Appendices
MARICOURT TRENCHES	16/9/16	—	Searching for our Battn: the parapet of trench near Headquarters was knocked in otherwise no damage was done and there were no casualties. Trench mortars on to the Battery in the vicinity. Our casualties for the day were 1 wounded/killed/shell shock. Artillery very active all through the night but quietened down at dawn. During the late morning and afternoon artillery again became very active — our guns being employed in cutting the wire in front of GUILLEMONT trenches, the enemy's putting heavy barrages in and around TRONES WOOD.	
		8.0 pm	Enemy again used Lachrymatory shells in large quantities and antigas goggles had to be worn. Our casualties for the day were 4 wounded.	
	17/9/16		Artillery very active throughout night. At intervals throughout the day enemy's artillery searched TRONES WOOD and trenches in rear with high explosive shrapnel and S.9 howitzers. Our casualties for the day were one wounded.	
	18/9/16		Slight lull in artillery activity during the night, but during the morning was again very active. Enemy concentration artillery fire on "C" Coy in SUNKEN ROAD, many H.E. Shrapnel and S.9 Howitzers. "C" Coy had to be moved in a hail of shell fire, and it was at the final Captain to P.G. Hoare and two of his Sergeants showed conspicuous bravery in digging out a 2d Scout who had been buried alive by a shell. One of the Sergeants who was assisting in digging out was wounded but Capt Hoare and the remaining Sergeant was succeeded in saving the buried sergeant life	
		9.0 pm	The Battalion was relieved by and proceeded	

Army Form C. 2118

WAR DIARY
or
INTELLIGENCE SUMMARY
(Erase heading not required.)

11th (Service) Bn Royal Fusiliers

Instructions regarding War Diaries and Intelligence Summaries are contained in F.S. Regs., Part II. and the Staff Manual respectively. Title Pages will be prepared in manuscript.

Place	Date	Hour	Summary of Events and Information	Remarks and references to Appendices
BOIS DE TAILLES	19/7/16		to BOIS DES TAILLES arriving there about 2-30 am. Our Casualties for the day were: 3 Killed 6 Wounded 1 missing 2 Shell Shock	
	20/7/16		Battalion cleaned up, Bathed &c. Drills were carried out and preparations made for move.	
GROVETOWN	21/7/16	8-0 AM	Battalion paraded and marched to GROVETOWN where it entrained at 9-30 AM for proceeding to LONGPREE. The Journey took almost all day, as the Battalion did not reach LONGPREE till 9-30 pm.	
LONGPRE FORCEVILLE		8-30 pm	Battalion entrained - on branch line - at LONGPREE and proceeded to FORCEVILLE arriving there about 9-15 pm. and marched into billets in the Village.	
LONGPREE	22/7/16		morning spent in cleaning up &c.	
		4.30 pm	Orders received for move at 9 pm.	
		9-0 pm	Battalion moved off on a march to LONGPREE (about 12 miles) arriving there at 4-30 am. on 23/7/16.	
ARQUES	23/7/16	4.30 am	Battalion entrained and proceeded to ARQUES arriving there about 11-30 am. Breakfast was taken and Battalion moved off on a march to SERCUS, arriving at the village at 6-30 and proceeded to Billets	
SERCUS		2-30 pm		

Army Form C. 2118

WAR DIARY
or
INTELLIGENCE SUMMARY
(Erase heading not required.)

11th (Service) Bn Royal Fusiliers

Instructions regarding War Diaries and Intelligence Summaries are contained in F.S. Regs, Part II. and the Staff Manual respectively. Title Pages will be prepared in manuscript.

Place	Date	Hour	Summary of Events and Information	Remarks and references to Appendices
SERCUS	24/7/16		Battalion cleaned up generally.	
"	25/7/16		Organized Bombing, Signalling, Lewis Gunners &c and arranged classes.	
"	26/7/16	11-45am	Major General Nixon C.V.O. C.B. D.S.O. inspected Battalion (see Lomston)	
		2-30 pm	Battalion paraded and moved off to LYNDE arriving in billets at 4-30 pm	
LYNDE	27/7/16		Battalion refitted, and organized classes got to work – signalling, Bombing, Machine Gunners &c.	
	28/7/16	5-30 AM	Battalion paraded and marched off to WALLON CAPPEL where remainder of Brigade was met, and at 9 am Bn moved off with Brigade to BAILLEUL area; the Battalion proceeding to billets at METEREN arriving there at 2-0 pm.	
METEREN	29/7/16 to 4/8/16		Battalion carried out training as per programme drawn up including training of Specialists ie Signallers, Bombers, Machine Gunners.	

11th (Service) Bn. Royal Fusiliers

REPORT ON ATTACK OF 1ST JULY 1916.

REPORT ON ATTACK, JULY 1ST., 1916.

11th. Bn. Royal Fusiliers.

The Battalion formed the left assaulting Battalion of the 54th. Brigade, the 7th. Bedfordshires being on the right. The Manchesters of the 91st. Brigade were on our left.

By 2.0a.m. the Battalion was ready in the forming-up trenches, in the following order:-

```
"A" Coy. |                    |                    | "B" Coy.
         |                    |                    |
              "C" Coy.
         |                                         |
              "D" Coy.
         |                                         |
```

At 7.30a.m. (Zero hour) "A" and "B" Coys. led off, advancing in four waves in extended order, the Supporting and Reserve Coys. following up in artillery formation. The intervals between the advancing waves from 100 to 150 yards. In comparison with the hurricane bombardment which had been opened by our concentrated artillery, 2" and Stokes Mortars, the enemy's reply was feeble, so that the casualties which we suffered in crossing no-man's-land were few. Some machine guns, however, opened on the flanks, and these knocked out a few, but in no way held up the steady advance. One of these guns was rushed and captured with great dash by L/Cpl. Payne of "B" Coy. The enemy's front lines offered no opposition, and EMDEN TRENCH was reached bang up to time. In BUND TRENCH a few Bosch were encountered, but were easily dealt with. At this point it was possible to look round and see how things stood. The 7th. Bedfordshires on our right had kept touch perfectly with us; on the left the Manchesters seemed to be rather hung up. It was, therefore, imperative to watch the left flank, and this fell to Major Hudson, in command of "A" Coy., who was most careful on this point, and was kept well backed up by Capt. Hoare, in command of "C" Company.

It was on the advance from BUND to POMMIERS TRENCH that 2/Lt. Parr Dudley dealt so effectively with a party of 30 Germans who were attempting to counter-attack from the direction of MAMETZ. He wheeled his platoon half-left and charged them, using rifles, bayonets and bombs. Not one of the enemy escaped, but unfortunately Parr Dudley was killed - the only one of the party.

The POMMIERS TRENCH was manned to some extent by riflemen, and a machine gun in a bedded emplacement kept up a steady fire even after the first two waves had got into the trench, but the man behind the gun was soon dealt with and his gun captured.

As, according to scheduled time, there was a 20 minutes' wait in this trench, some hand-to-hand fighting took place, as the dug-outs contained a lot of Bosch. Many were bombed effectively before they had time to make a bolt into the trench.

The REDOUBT and MAPLE TRENCH line was a tougher nut to crack, and, as the first waves of the Bedfordshires and our men got out of POMMIERS, rifles and machine guns opened fire from the REDOUBT and mowed them down.

On the East face of the REDOUBT the wire was much damaged, but on the West it was in sufficiently good repair to enable the enemy to hold us. Several times the men reached the wire only to be shot. As the frontal attack on the REDOUBT was not progressing, Capt. Johnston, commanding "B" Coy., decided to take his men up BLACK ALLEY with the intention of bombing up MAPLE TRENCH and so into the REDOUBT, but the last 60 yards of this trench is straight and a machine gun held him up. He then decided he would attack the REDOUBT in the rear over the open, but was bothered by German snipers who were established in BEETLE ALLEY, so he asked 2/Lt. Savage, who was with "A" Coy, on the left, to rush them out of the trench. He carried out this operation so thoroughly and quickly

(contd.)

that Capt. Johnston was able to get his men up to the REDOUBT without a casualty. The Germans were very thick in the REDOUBT, and were firing head and shoulders over the parapet. Capt. Johnston put his Lewis guns at the end of BLACK ALLEY so as to enfilade the front of the REDOUBT, and they successfully wiped out all the Germans who were in the trench, which enabled the Bedfordshires and ourselves to dash in and finish the rest. This is practically the story of the Right Company.

The Left Company were unfortunate in losing Lt. Nield, who was killed near the German front line. The POMMIERS line was reached easily, and the dug-outs in BLACK ALLEY received many bombs. At the junction of POMMIERS and BLACK ALLEY there was some hand-to-hand fighting, a German officer suddenly appearing from a dug-out followed by some men - they were all killed. This Company's task was difficult and dangerous, as the Battalion on our left had not secured DANTZIG ALLEY, and the left was consequently in the air. 2/Lt. Savage was helping "B" Coy. by clearing BEETLE ALLEY of snipers, and it was then that he was killed by a sniper while trying to see how things were going on the left. He had been hit in the foot from the very start at 7.30a.m. but had stuck on and led his men gallantly the whole time. Some good work was done by the Lewis Guns with this Coy., who got their guns into position to command the approach from FRITZ ALLEY, which was full of Bosche, and it was entirely due to the way in which the machine guns and Savage's platoon dealt with the situation that our left remained secure. Capt. Hooke, with his Stokes mortars, rendered great assistance by pounding FRITZ TRENCH and causing the Germans to bolt, presenting a splendid target to our Lewis guns, who bowled them over in the open.

The Support and Reserve Coys. supported closely and did excellent work in repelling small counter-attacks which had been launched from the flanks. The programme was that they should pass through the assaulting Coys. at BEETLE TRENCH and secure the final objective at WHITE TRENCH, but, on consultation between the Commanding Officers, it was decided that it would be a dangerous undertaking while the Brigades on the left and right were so hung up.

The Battalion set to making its strong points and making fire steps, and parties from the Dumps soon came up with wire, stakes, bombs, ammunition and water. The men were all in the best of spirits and seemed delighted with the fight. Later on in the afternoon a reconnaisance was made to WHITE TRENCH, which was found to be unoccupied - so a small garrison was put here.

Communication:- It was very seldom that the telephone worked satisfactorily, but admirable work was done by our Signallers, who, by means of shutter and flag, succeeded in getting our messages through. One of the finest things witnessed was the performance of Pte. Hughes, who, knowing his message to be important, selected the white signalling flag, &mounted to the top of the parados in spite of shot and shell which were all round him. He did not give in till a shell dealt him a terrible injury.

It is difficult to pick out any one incident of gallantry and devotion to duty when every man behaved with such dash, but such episodes as the following give an idea of individual pluck:-

(1) Pte. H.R.Wheeler found himself alone in EMDEN TRENCH, in which were 7 Germans. Three of these he managed to shoot before his bolt got jammed by the sock breech cover. He retired behind a traverse and jumped on to the top of the trench, shooting the remaining four with a revolver he had found.

(2) Sgt. Brisby was called upon for assistance by a bombing section who had run into some German bombers in BLACK ALLEY. He went over from his position in the open on the left of BLACK ALLEY, and shot one of the Germans who had thrown bombs at him from the fire step. He then jumped into the trench and bayoneted the remaining three.

(Contd.)

Mention must be made of the fine way in which the dug-out clearing parties of the 6th. Northamptonshires behaved. They did not scruple to enter dug-outs whether they contained live Germans or not, and in this way secured many prisoners.

At the end of the day the Battalion was disposed as follows:-

- 1 Coy. in MAPLE TRENCH and garrisoning No. 5 Strong Point.
- 3 Coys. in BEETLE TRENCH and 1 platoon pushed out as an outpost to the WHITE TRENCH.

On the night of July 2nd. the Battalion was relieved by the 12th. Middlesex Regt.

P. P. Carr
Lieut.Col.
Commanding 11th. Royal Fusiliers

6th. July, 1916

Army Form C. 2118

WAR DIARY
or
INTELLIGENCE SUMMARY
(Erase heading not required.)

11th (Service) Bn Royal Fusiliers

Place	Date	Hour	Summary of Events and Information	Remarks and references to Appendices
METEREN	1/8/16 to 4/8/16		Battalion carried out training as per programme arranged	
"	5/8/16	6 pm	Battalion paraded in full marching order and proceeded to march up the line being billeted at a large convent laundry between ERQUINGHEM and ARMENTIERES.	
ERQUINGHEM	6/8/16		Battalion bathed and awaiting orders. Enemy aircraft active. One man was wounded by an enemy aircraft bomb.	
	7/8/16	9 pm	Battalion proceeded to trenches by Company. This Battalion was right Battalion of Brigade in the Bois GRENIER Sector relieved by Battalion turning known as "B1" Battalion of Coys were as follows:—	
			D Rt Subsector	One man was wounded during relief.
			B Right "	
			C Right Support line	
			A Left "	
B1 SECTOR TRENCHES	8/8/16	4-15 AM	Enemy machine guns fairly active. 3 searchlights swept our parapet at intervals throughout the night.	
		11-30 AM	Situation Normal	
		3-45 pm	Situation quiet, practically no artillery firing on either side. During the day Coys were working in building up Bays and revetting and building up parapets and started building bomb stores.	
	9/8/16	4 am	Enemy machine guns active throughout night, and two searchlights swept the line at intervals	
"		11-30 am	Situation quiet	

Army Form C. 2118

WAR DIARY
or
INTELLIGENCE SUMMARY
(Erase heading not required.)

11th (Service) Bn Royal Fusiliers

Instructions regarding War Diaries and Intelligence Summaries are contained in F.S. Regs., Part II and the Staff Manual respectively. Title Pages will be prepared in manuscript.

Place	Date	Hour	Summary of Events and Information	Remarks and references to Appendices
B I SECTOR. TRENCHES	9/8/16	3-30 am	Situation quiet, artillery of enemy and artillery quiet. During the day, boys were employed on resetting bays man RE supervision. Parapets were built up and back walks cleaned and drained.	
"	10/8/16	4 AM	Enemy machine guns and searchlights active about midnight. Enemy threw two of their bombs from their trench to no apparent reason — on the explosion of these bombs enemy used the searchlights and put up a number of Very lights. Our patrols did nothing.	
		9-30 am	Situation quiet, no shelling — artillery on both sides inactive.	
		3-20 am	Situation quiet. One man was wounded by a piece of Trench mortar Bomb. Boys continued work on support line and traverses of firing line	
"	11/8/16	4 am	Enemy machine guns active, searchlight nearly used, wire on our front thoroughly examined and found to be an effective obstacle everywhere. About 1.10am Enemy rang two blue rockets and shouted Very lights were put up in large numbers and he opened out with all his machine guns. He seems very nervous.	
		9-30 am	Situation quiet.	
		3-15 pm	Situation quiet. During the day Boys worked on repairing and strengthening the line and built new front stairs.	

Army Form C. 2118

Instructions regarding War Diaries and Intelligence Summaries are contained in F.S. Regs., Part II. and the Staff Manual respectively. Title Pages will be prepared in manuscript.

WAR DIARY
or
INTELLIGENCE SUMMARY
(Erase heading not required.)

11th (Service) Bn Royal Fusiliers

Place	Date	Hour	Summary of Events and Information	Remarks and references to Appendices
B2 SECTOR TRENCHES	11/8/16	6 pm	Throughout day artillery was very quiet. Battalion carried out an inter-Coy relief, dispositions after relief were as follows:-	
			"A" Coy Right Subsector	
			"B" " " Support	
			"C" " Left Subsector	
			"D" " " Support.	
	12/8/16		Relief was satisfactorily carried out - no casualties.	
		4-0 AM	Enemy again employed his searchlights which seemed to be quite near his front line. One machine gun fired several times at Right line without apparent effect. Normal amount of rifle and machine gun fire throughout night	
		9-50 am	Situation quiet.	
		3-20 pm	Situation quiet. Artillery on both sides inactive. Continued work on Boys under RE supervision. Generally repaired and swept up. Duck walks taken up and cleaned.	
	13/8/16	4 AM	Very quiet night. Enemy machine guns not so active as usual - probably due to relief having taken place.	
		9-45 am	Situation quiet.	
		3-30 pm	Our artillery registered on their front line R. which brought retaliation from enemy with small trench mortar bombs.	

WAR DIARY
or
INTELLIGENCE SUMMARY

Army Form C. 2118

11th (Service) Bn Royal Fusiliers

Place	Date	Hour	Summary of Events and Information	Remarks and references to Appendices
B1 SECTOR TRENCHES	17/8/16	4·0 AM	Wire caused damage to our front line, but we supplied no casualties. Patrol work was carried out much as previous and wire Balls were made. During the evening our artillery cut enemy wire. Artillery on both sides more active than usual. Our Casualties were 1 OR wounded.	
		9·30 am	Quiet night. Enemy's machine guns active at stand-to but quietened down about 11 am. Patrol examined enemy's wire which had been shelled with our artillery and found that gaps had been successfully cut. Situation quiet.	
		3·30 pm	Artillery active on both sides. Enemy retaliating on our trenches.	
		7 pm	5th Bde Trench mortars replied on enemy line to which he replied with 77mm shells on our support and front line. An artillery shoot on Dummy road had been organised. Zero hour being 7 pm. See special report attached.	
	18/8/16		Our total casualties during Dummy Road were one officer wounded - other Rks 5 OR killed, 9 OR wounded.	
		9·30 am	Quiet night - about 1·30 am Enemy sounded a gas alarm him but no gas was not sent over by the Enemy or ourselves. Situation quiet.	
		2·30 pm	Battalion was relieved by the 12th Middlesex Regt and took over subsidiary line previously held by them.	

Army Form C. 2118

WAR DIARY
or
INTELLIGENCE SUMMARY
(Erase heading not required.)

11th (Service) Bn Royal Fusiliers

Place	Date	Hour	Summary of Events and Information	Remarks and references to Appendices
SUBSIDIARY LINE B1 & B2	15/8/16	5.0 pm	During the relief we had one man wounded. Relief complete and Battalion held Subsidiary Line.	
SECTORS.	16/8/16 to 22/8/16		Battalion Bathed, working parties for R.E. supplied, Physical drill carried out, Snipers were practiced. The new Lewis Gunners were taken in hand for further instruction. Smoke Helmet drill "Alert position" practiced.	
	23/8/16	10.0 pm about	Battalion was relieved by the 21st Bn Northumberland Fusiliers (2nd Tyneside Scottish) and moved into billets at ERQUINGHEM.	
ERQUINGHEM.	23/8/16		Battalion Bathed, and generally cleaned up.	
	24/8/16	11.30 am	Battalion marched out of ERQUINGHEM to BAILLEUL arriving there at 3.30 am on 25/8/16.	
BAILLEUL	25/8/16	4.30 am	Battalion and transport proceeded by Rail to ST POL arriving there at 8.30 am same day.	
ST POL	25/8/16	8.30 am	Battalion marched from ST POL station to a field just outside the town where Breakfasts was supplied from the Cookers. — Transport moved on independently to the Billeting area.	
"		11.45 am	Battalion marched to ORLENCOURT. and moved into billets	

Army Form C. 2118

WAR DIARY
or
INTELLIGENCE SUMMARY
(Erase heading not required.)

Instructions regarding War Diaries and Intelligence Summaries are contained in F. S. Regs., Part II. and the Staff Manual respectively. Title Pages will be prepared in manuscript.

11th (Service) Bn Royal Fusiliers

Place	Date	Hour	Summary of Events and Information	Remarks and references to Appendices
ORLENCOURT	26/8/16 to 5/9/16	=	Training as follows:-	
MONCHY BRETON TRAINING AREA.	27/8/16	1-30pm to 6pm	Two Coy. Lewis Gunners and employed on Range for half the afternoon while the remainder took practise in rapid loading, bayonet fighting, & extension and day drill and extension order, then the boys changed over.	
"	28/8/16	8am to 1pm	Battalion carried out practise in Wood fighting and manoevring on Compass trainings.	
"	29/8/16	1-30pm to 6pm	Close Order and extended order drill - musketry - bayonet fighting and bombing was practised by Battalion.	
"	30/8/16	8am to 1pm	Bn Practised 29th inst. but trenches were used to illustrate consolidation. Attacking from and attacking entrenched position, also bombing in trench was carried out. Battn was reinforced by draft of 40 O.R's	
"	31/8/16		Bn was engaged on Brigade Training. Battalion was reinforced by draft of 80 Other Ranks.	
"	1/9/16	1-30pm to 6pm	Battalion practised musketry - bombing - bayonet fighting and extended order drill.	
"	2/9/16	8am to 1pm	Battalion carried out Wood fighting practise.	

Army Form C. 2118

WAR DIARY
or
INTELLIGENCE SUMMARY

11th (Service) Bn Royal Fusiliers

(Erase heading not required.)

Instructions regarding War Diaries and Intelligence Summaries are contained in F.S. Regs., Part II. and the Staff Manual respectively. Title Pages will be prepared in manuscript.

Place	Date	Hour	Summary of Events and Information	Remarks and references to Appendices
ORLENCOURT	3/9/16	10 am	Church Parade. At intervals throughout the day Coys and Hd Qrs Bathed at MICHEL-SUR-TERNOISE. Battalion was reinforced by draft of 55 other Ranks.	
MONCHY BRETON TRAINING AREA	4/9/16		Battalion was engaged on Brigade Training	
	5/9/16		Coys practised the attack and consolidating the position taken — marching on compass bearings. During this period of training Signallers, Lewis Gunners, Bombers and one or two of the n.c.o. classes were further instructed under their respective officers. New Rummers were put under training. Every available man was taken out with the Battalion on the Training Area. At times when Battn was not on Training Area "Spotting" was carried out.	

N. B. Weakley 2nd Lieut
A/Adjutant,
11th (Service) Bn. Royal Fusiliers

11th Bn Roy. Fusiliers

September 1916

Also
1st to 9th October 1916

WAR DIARY / INTELLIGENCE SUMMARY

Army Form C. 2118

11th (Service) Bn Royal Fusiliers Vol II

Place	Date	Hour	Summary of Events and Information	Remarks and references to Appendices
ORLENCOURT	6/9/16	8-30 AM	Battalion paraded and marched to training area, work carried out:- following up of barrage to Practise attack	
		2 pm	Bn returned to Billets for Dinners	
"	7/9/16	2-45 AM	Battalion marched out to training area and practised the attack by night.	
		1-30 PM	Battalion paraded and marched out to training area and following up of Barrage	
"	8/9/16	9-30	The Battalion, complete with Transport, paraded in full marching order and moved off on a two days march at LA BELLE EPINE the Battalion joined the Brigade from LA BELLE EPINE the Brigade marched to TERNOIS. At this place the Battalion left Brigade column and marched off to the night marching through FOUFFLIN-RICAMETZ & MAISNIL ST POL. arriving at the latter village at 12-15 pm and proceeded to Billets.	
MAISNIL ST POL	9/9/16	10 AM	The Battalion complete with transport, paraded in full marching order, passing through BURIEVILLE then to MONCHEUX where it met the remainder of Brigade. The Brigade proceeded on the march passing through HOUVIN, HOUVIGNEUL, WAMIN, OPPY at the last named village the Battalion left Brigade and proceeded to IVERGNY arriving there at 2-30 pm and took over billets	
IVERGNY	10/9/16	7-45 AM	33 Bugles were allotted the Battalion N. proceeding to HALLOY. The Battalion entrained at 4-45 am. & Transport was Brigaded and proceeded independently at HALLOY the Battalion left	

Army Form C. 2118

WAR DIARY
INTELLIGENCE SUMMARY
(Erase heading not required.)

11th (Service) Bn. Royal Fusiliers

Place	Date	Hour	Summary of Events and Information	Remarks and references to Appendices
RAINCHEVAL	11/9/16	9-0 AM to 1 PM	Bn. ϟϟ and marched through THIEVRES, MARIEUX to RAINCHEVAL where the Battalion proceeded to Billets. Time of arrival at RAINCHEVAL 3pm. During the two days march the total number of men who fell out was five.	
"	12/9/16	9-6 7-30 AM	Coys paraded under Coy arrangements. Bombers, Signallers, Snipers and Lewis Gunners under their respective officers.	
		9-30 to 1pm	Coys carried out Running and Physical Exercises. Bn. found Town mayors fatigue, Sanitary police &c.	
			Bn. moved to Training Area. Training of Specialists was carried out and Coys practised extended clapping under supervision of RE.	
"	13/9/16	7AM to 8AM	Running Parade & Physical Exercises carried out. East Coy detailed on Fatigue under specialists. Bn. moved to Training Area and prepared a Rifle Range.	
		9-30 AM to 1 pm	Coys marched out to Training area and practised bombing Musketry Physical drill etc. Training of specialists also carried out. A party of 24 men under 2/Lt Connolly dug bombing trenches on Training Ground.	
"	14/9/16	9-30	Coys marched out to Training area where bombing, musketry, Physical Drill etc were carried out. Specialists paraded under their respective Officers. Town mayors fatigue was carried out. 20 men under Sgt Bowley were engaged in making Bomb buckets.	

1875 Wt. W593/826 1,000,000 4/15 J.B.C. & A. A.D.S.S./Forms/C. 2118.

WAR DIARY
INTELLIGENCE SUMMARY
(Erase heading not required.)

Army Form C. 2118

11th (Service) Bn. Royal Fusiliers

Instructions regarding War Diaries and Intelligence Summaries are contained in F.S. Regs., Part II. and the Staff Manual respectively. Title Pages will be prepared in manuscript.

Place	Date	Hour	Summary of Events and Information	Remarks and references to Appendices
RAINCHEVAL	15/9/16	9.30 am	Coys paraded marched to Training Area where usual practice was carried out.	
		2-0 pm	Battalion paraded for Outpost Scheme.	
"	16/9/16	7 am	Running & Physical Drill carried out	
		9.30	Coys marched to training area where Bombing, musketry, digging etc was practised. Som major fatigues were filled by the Bn. Draft of 2 NCOs reinforced the Bn.	
"	17/9/16	10.0 am	Battalion paraded for Church Parade.	
		2.30 pm	Stokes Battery gave a Demonstration	
"	18/9/16	9 am	Coys on the training area practising intensified digging and note Dugout frames under RE superintendence. Physical Drill Section demonstration, attack formation re Specialist Classes continued as usual.	
		4.30		
"	19/9/16	9 am	Training carried out as yesterday. Town major fatigues performed by the Bn. The following Awards were published in Battalion Orders today: CSM J. Hunt awarded DSO, Sgt Ashton DCM, Pte Hughes DCM	
		4.30		
"	20/9/16	9 am	Bn Bathed at Bertl adjoining Training area. Training carried out as on 18th-19th.	
		4.30		

Army Form C. 2118

WAR DIARY
or
INTELLIGENCE SUMMARY
(Erase heading not required.)

11th (Service) Bn. Royal Fusiliers

Place	Date	Hour	Summary of Events and Information	Remarks and references to Appendices
RAINCHEVAL	21/9/16	9 am & 4-30	Training carried out as yesterday	
	22/9/16	9 am	Scheme of attack carried out with Bomps &c &c by the Battalion Coys on training area, bombing, musketry, &c &c.	
		2-0 pm	During period Bn was at Raincheval, rifling was carried out by the Coys. All deficiencies in was certain equipment & living made up. Jerries choletras kelch were sewn on all haversacks and Steeled with the letter of Coy & Headquarters. Smoke helmets inspected and deficiencies made up, and Iron Rations completed. CO 2nd in Command and Coy officers were taken in turn to view heights at THIEPVAL. Battalion complete with transport & reached no full marching order and marched off to HEDAUVILLE passing through ARQUEVES, LEALVILLERS, ACHEUX, FORCEVILLE. The Bn halted outside HEDAUVILLE and had dinner, and at 3-30 proceeded into the TRUG. The Battalion was reinforced with a draft of 'Y' ORs.	
TRENCHES	23/9/16	10-0 am		
	24/9/16	10-0 am	Battalion moved up to trenches relieving 5th West Riding Regt in Support trenches in the LEIPZIG SECTOR	
	25/9/16		Bn in Reserve trenches.	
	26/9/16	9-0 am	C & D Coys moved up for the attack on THIEPVAL with a TO following as support	
		12-35 pm	- Zero hour 12 Pindolliere was detailed to attacking Bn. Burfort Coys (C & D Coys) went right in with them and seized the Objective with the assistance of our supporting Coys (A & B Coys) THIEPVAL village was captured and held. See Special Report of Battle attached.	

1875 Wt. W5931826 1,000,000 4/15 J.B.C. & A. A.D.S.S./Forms/C. 2118.

Army Form C. 2118

WAR DIARY
INTELLIGENCE SUMMARY
(Erase heading not required.)

11th (Service) Bn Royal Fusiliers

Instructions regarding War Diaries and Intelligence Summaries are contained in F. S. Regs., Part II. and the Staff Manual respectively. Title Pages will be prepared in manuscript.

Place	Date	Hour	Summary of Events and Information	Remarks and references to Appendices
TRENCHES	27/9/16		Battalion was relieved at 9-0 am by 7/4 Bedfordshire Regt and proceeded to BOIS DE MARTINSART being billeted in huts.	
BOIS DE MARTINSART	28/9/16		Battalion rested and cleaned up and met as possible. Draft of 19 ORs reinforced the Battalion.	
"	29/9/16 4.0 pm		Battalion moved off to MAILLY MAILLET WOOD being billeted in huts and matin canvas	
MAILLY MAILLET WOOD	30/9/16		Time spent cleaning & smartening up	
"	1/10/16		Battalion Bath workshops were established for refitting Boot and equipment repairing &c.	
"	2/10/16		Parades carried out by section - no long parades being possible owing to lack of accommodation.	
"	3/10/16	2.0 pm	Battalion moved off to SENLIS. Draft of 4 ORs reinforced the Battalion.	
SENLIS	4/10/16		Battalion cleaned up and time spent by resting.	
"	5/10/16	11-30 AM	Enemy at Senior 24/9/16 to 5/10/16 Transport and Quartermaster Store were stationed in a field just outside the village of HEDAUVILLE. Battalion (less transport) paraded in full marching order and proceeded to ACHEUX where it entrained and moved off at 4 pm - arriving at CANDAS at 7.30 pm. detrained and marched off that same evening thence towards FIENVILLERS & BERNAVILLE where A and B Coys proceeded to billets at DOMESMONT, JH among at BERNAVILLE of Brandon Band D Coys and Headquarters moved to K'SEAUCOURT.	

Army Form C. 2118

WAR DIARY
or
INTELLIGENCE SUMMARY
(Erase heading not required.)

Instructions regarding War Diaries and Intelligence Summaries are contained in F. S. Regs., Part II. and the Staff Manual respectively. Title Pages will be prepared in manuscript.

Place	Date	Hour	Summary of Events and Information	Remarks and references to Appendices
RIBEAUCOURT and DOMESMONT	6/10/16		arriving there and taking over huts at about 10 p.m. Time spent cleaning up &c.	
	7/10/16		Battalion carried out parades by Coys, practising musketry drill, Physical Drill &c.	
	8/10/16		Coys did parades as yesterday.	
	9/10/16		Battalion was inoculated	

A B Mitchell
A Adjt
11th (Service) Bn. Royal Fusiliers

ORDERLY ROOM
9 OCT 1916
11th (Service) Bn. Royal Fusiliers

SECRET. 　　　　　　　　　　　　　　　　　　　Order No. 3

54TH INFANTRY BRIGADE.

Preliminary Instructions for Attack.

Reference Map
Sheet 57.d.N.W. 1/20,000.
Special Map attached.

September 25th 1916.

(1) The Reserve Army is about to make a general attack on the ridge which runs from North West of COURCELETTE to the SCHWABEN Redoubt.

The 18th Division is the left Division in the attack, with the 11th Division on its right.

The dividing line between formations is shown on the special map thus

The objectives of the 18th Division are marked on the special map :-
  First Objective .... Blue line.
  Second Objective .... Green line.
  Final Objective .... Red line.

The main line to be consolidated in rear of the final objective is shown on the special map thus

The 18th Division will attack with the 53rd Brigade on the right and the 54th Brigade on the left. The 55th Infantry Brigade will be in Divisional Reserve.

The 140th Infantry Brigade (47th Division) will continue to hold its present line.

(2) Task of the 54th Infantry Brigade.

The task of the 54th Infantry Brigade is to capture and hold the final objective and take every opportunity of exploiting success by pushing forward patrols and Lewis guns to inflict casualties on retiring enemy.

(3) Distribution of Brigade at Zero Hour.

See Appendix "A" attached.

(4) Role of Battalions.

12th Middlesex Regt. Will act as the assaulting battalion and fight its way through to the final objective. It will first consolidate the line shown on the special map.

11th Royal Fusiliers. The special task of the 11th Royal Fusiliers is to capture the Bosch front line trench from R.31.a.6.9 to R.25.a.9.1, and clear all dug-outs South of the trench running from R.25.b.7.3 to R.25.b.3.4. To ensure that the 12th Middlesex Regt. is neither attacked in flank from the Bosch front line trench named or from the rear by any enemy that may come out of dug-outs after the assaulting battalion has passed.

Battalion will be distributed as follows :-
  1 Company detailed for the special task of clearing the present Bosch front line from R.31.a.6.9 to R.25.a.9.1. At the latter point it will establish a block.
  1 Company attached to 12th Middlesex Regt. as dug-out clearing parties. This Company will be responsible for clearing all dug-outs South of enemy trench running from R.25.b.7.3 to R.25.b.3.4, and will not proceed beyond the trench named. It will be allotted definite objectives for dug-out clearing by the O.C. 12th Middlesex.
  1 Company for attachment to the 12th Middlesex for dug-out clearing and other special purposes during the advance from the second to the final objective. This Company will reach the first objective in

sufficient time to take part in the advance of the
12th Middlesex on its final objective.

1 Company Battalion Reserve for use in support of the
remaining Companies of the Battalion.

6th Northamptonshire Regt. Will act as support to the 12th
Middlesex Regt. and will be prepared to support that
battalion in its advance from the second to the final
objective. It will also find two platoons for carrying
from the Dump referred to in para. 9.

7th Bedfordshire Regt. In Brigade Reserve.

(5) Strong Points. Strong Points will be established at the
points shown on the special map. Those in the final
objective will be made and garrisoned by the 12th Middlesex
Regt. That in the Second Objective by the 11th Royal
Fusiliers. The 80th Field Coy. R.E. will assist in the
supervision and construction of these Strong Points. Strong
Points will be capable of accommodating and garrisoning one
platoon, and will be provided with Vickers Guns and Stokes
Mortars as stated in paras. 7 and 8.

(6) Barrages. Details regarding barrages have not yet been
received, but it is understood that the form of barrage to
be adopted will be a "creeping" one, and it is essential
that assaulting waves should follow it as closely as possible
throughout the attack.

(7) 54th Machine Gun Company. Distribution of this Company will
be as follows :-

    2 guns each to 11th Royal Fusiliers and 12th
    Middlesex Regt. respectively.

    1 gun from LEIPZIG QUARRY to be detailed to
    proceed to Strong Point R.25.b.3.3.

    Remaining guns in LEIPZIG QUARRY in Brigade
    Reserve.

    1 Section from THIEPVAL WOOD to proceed to final
objective as soon as it is consolidated. 2 guns of this
Section to be earmarked for Strong Points R.20.d.1.5 and
R.19.d.5.4.

    1 Section covering fire from high ground just South
of BAMEL.

(8) 54th Trench Mortar Battery. Distribution of this Battery
will be as follows :-

    2 mortars each to accompany 11th Royal Fusiliers
    and 12th Middlesex Regt. in the attack.

    Remainder of Battery in Brigade Reserve.

    2 mortars to be earmarked for Strong Points
    R.20.d.1.5 and R.19.d.5.4.

(3)

(9) **Dumps.** All Dumps will be under the control of the Brigade Bombing Officer.
Forward Dumps will be established at R.31.a.4.5 and in PAISLEY AVENUE (THIEPVAL WOOD). Carrying parties will be provided as follows :-
For that in THIEPVAL WOOD .. special parties detailed from all battalions.
For that at R.31.a.4.5 ..... by two platoons of the 6th Northamptonshire Regt.

(10) **"Tanks".** Two "Tanks" are to be allotted to the 54th Brigade. Instructions regarding their use have not yet been issued from Divisional Hd. Qrs. but all ranks should be informed that they will take part in the attack.

(11) **Special Communications.** As soon as the second objective is occupied a special communication trench will be constructed from our present front line trench R.25.b.5.4 to R.25.b.7.4.

(12) **Tools and S.A.A.** Will be carried on the scale laid down for the attack on July 1st. Those required in excess of those already in possession will be drawn from LANCASHIRE DUMP.

(13) **Medical Arrangements.** Will be in accordance with 18th Div. Q.R.10 of 23rd instant.

(14) **Prisoners of War.** Prisoners of war will be dealt with in accordance with 18th Div. Q.R.11 of 23rd September. All prisoners will, as far as possible, be handed over to the 11th Royal Fusiliers. Where this is not possible, Battalions capturing prisoners will conduct them to Divisional Cage. A written receipt should be obtained for all prisoners handed in at the Divisional Cage. These receipts should be forwarded to Brigade Hd. Qrs.

(15) **Stragglers.** Police Posts for the collection of stragglers will be established under Brigade arrangements at BLACK HORSE BRIDGE, W. end of CAMPBELL AVENUE, AUTHUILLE BRIDGE, SOUTH CAUSEWAY.

(16) **Pack Dumps.** Will be selected by Battalions as follows :-

11th Royal Fusiliers ..... in neighbourhood of QUARRY R.31.c.3.4.
7th Bedfordshire Regt ... N. BLUFF.
6th Northamptonshire Regt S. BLUFF.
12th Middlesex Regt ...... under Battalion arrangements.

Battalions will leave two men in charge of their Pack Dumps.

(17) **Rations.** Arrangements will be in accordance with 18th Div. Q.R.12 of 23rd inst. except that para. 2(b) is altered as follows :-
"First Line Transport will deliver rations at
"LANCASHIRE DUMP Q.35.d.3.8 by day as early as
"possible. Rations will then be transferred
"to tram line and conveyed to AUTHUILLE whence
"they will be carried by hand under battalion
"arrangements."

(18) **Grenades.** Instructions regarding number of grenades to be carried have been issued in S.C.692 of the 24th instant.

(4)

(19) **Communications.**

Telephone. Every effort will be made to keep lines going to Battn. H. Qrs. through the Brigade Exchanges at CAMPBELLS POST and NORTH BLUFF. These exchanges will be always kept open.

Visual. Battn. H. Qrs. will take forward Trench signalling lamps as well as ordinary visual kit.
Divisional Reading Station is at Q.23.c.8.5 - call AU - and is in full view from West side of THIEPVAL ridge.
D.D. messages repeated three times to be sent to this Station.

Runners. Runners returning from front should come via CAMPBELLS POST or NORTH BLUFF or PAISLEY DUMP, at all of which places messages can be wired on to the Brigade.
Brigade Runner Posts will be at CAMPBELLS POST and the BLUFF.

(20) **Liaison Officers.** Will be detailed as under :-

11th Division	Maj. MILLS,	7th Bedfordshire Regt.
18th Division	Capt. MORTON,	11th Royal Fusiliers.
53rd Bde. H.Q.	Maj. MEYRICKS,	11th Royal Fusiliers.
54th Bde. H.Q.	Maj. CHARRINGTON,	6th Northamptonshire Regt.

54th Bde. Observation Posts :-
Lieut. KEMP, 7th Bedfordshire Regt.
Lieut. ASHMOLE, 11th Royal Fusiliers.

The hour at which these Officers should report at their respective posts will be notified later.

(signed)
Captain,
Brigade Major,
54th Inf. Bde.

11TH (S) BN. ROYAL FUSILIERS

REPORT ON THE THIEPVAL OPERATIONS ON SEPTEMBER 26th/27th 1916

At 12-35.pm on September 26th 1916 (Zero hour) the Battalion was formed up as follows;-
"D" Company (Captain.R.K.V.Thompson) in waves on left of Middlesex Regt.
"C" Company (Lieut.A.E.Sulman) mixed in with the assulting Coy's of the Middlesex Regt in the forming up trenches.
"B" Company (Captain W.H.H.Johnston) in two columns each of two platoons - one in old Bosch front line, the other in PRINCE STREET. The head of each column was level with the Middlesex 4th Company.
"A" Company (Major.A.C.Hudon) in reserve about the QUARRY.

"D" and "C" Coys went forward with the Middlesex at "Zero Hour", "B" and "A" Coys following as soon as the Middlesex were clear, in the order named. The latter two Coys suffered heavily from the German barrage.

"D" Company found a strong point at point R.31.a.6.7. and part of BRAWN TRENCH was held. This held up the Coy and also the left flank of the Middlesex, but the rest of the attack went on. Captain Thompson sent part of his company over the top to help the Middlesex in BRAWN TRENCH, and assulted the strong point with the rest of his men in the same way. It was while leading his men in this attack that Captain Thompson was Killed, and in the hand-to-hand fighting that followed Lieut.R.A.Miall-Smith was killed and Lieut.G.E.Cornaby wounded. Numbers of Bosches were killed in this fight and 25 men taken prisoners and sent across "No mans land" "D" Coy then continued along the Bosch front line fighting every yard. They found the Bosches waiting for them in the trench the whole way. The Lewis Guns were pushed up and did useful work shooting along the trench, but the teams suffered a number of casualties including Sgt.Casson the "D" Coy Lewis Gun Sergeant who was killed. "D" Coy found point R.25.c.7.2. strongly held and there was a great fight round this corner. In the meantime the Middlesex had been checked on the right by an intense fire from the CHATEAU but the timely arrival of a TANK enabled them to get on, and also relieved the pressure on point 7.2.

The position therefore about 1.pm was roughly;"D" Coy going forward with the Middlesex in the region og the CHATEAU; "B" Coy in the trench round R.25.c.8.1. and "A" Coy on their right - Major Hudson seeing that the Middlesex were in difficulties at the CHATEAU immediately threw in his Coy ("A") to assist them and went forward with them. "B" Coy had suffered considerably getting through the barrage and from Machine Gun Fire,and on reorganising it was found that 2nd.Lieut.Goddard had been killed, 2nd.Lieut.Walker wounded, all the full rank N.C.O's except 1 Sergeant and 2 Corporals were gone,and nearly half the rank and file. The Middlesex now seemed to be getting on well on the right, but the left still made slow progress,as in addition to holding his front line strongly the Bosch had a lot of men in the trenches running from point R.25.c.7.2. to c.9.4. Captain Johnston noticing this and also that the Middlesex who were going on were swing too much to the right, feared that there would be a large gap in the attack and put in his Company ("B") on the line R.25.c.7.2. to d.1.2. and attacked North. Lieut. Sulman who had gone forward with the right part of the attack noticed the same thing and dropped two platoons between the CHATEAU and R.25.b. 4.0. to clean dugouts and form a flank guard. "D" and "B" Coy's with part of "A" and some Middlesex made slow but steady progress. Practically every inch of the ground had to be covered as in addition to the organised defence there were snipers in every other shell hole - At point 9.4. L/Cpl. Tovey of "B" Coy captured a Machine Gun single handed, bayoneting both the men who were working it. Another Machine Gun was accounted for near point R.25.d.1.7. In this way we finally reached the line R.25.d.0.8. - D.38 meeting with a stubborn resistance all the way. "D" Coy cleared altogether 25 Dugouts in the front line and in many of them the Germans showed fight. In one of them particular there was a large number of the enemy with two Machine Guns and as they could not be got out peaceably the place was set on fire. Several are believed to have perished in the flames and 11 men were killed as they came out; an additional 14 who were only wounded were sent to the rear. In addition to the prisoners mentioned above another 40 men were captured and sent back.

The advance of this force on the left made a lot of Germans bolt North, but owing to the broken nature of the ground they were as difficult to hit as snipe, and a large percentage got away. Further on, however, "C" Coy guns, posted on the defensive flank, infiladed them as they ran and Lieut Sulman estimates that they bagged at least 50.

While the left was advancing on to the line R.25.d.0.8. - 3.8. the remained of "A" Coy and two platoons of "C" went on to the second objective which they hit somewhere about R.25.b.7.3. The Middlesex were on their right, which shows how much the attack had been deflected.

They immediately began bombing left until they reached (approximately) R.25.b.6.3. capturing two Officers and 45 other ranks which were sent to the rear. They were unable to go further as their bombs ran out, so made a block on their left and consolidated their position. It was while advancing on to the second objective that Major Hudson was hit. "C" Coy was meanwhile doing good work clearing dugouts, capturing a few men here and there. One specially meritorious bit of work may be mentioned - about half an hour before "Zero" Lieut Sulman was given a copy of a German map which showed the position of the telephone headquarters: He showed it to his men and told them to do their best to find the place and put the operators out of commission. L/Cpl. Ruddy and four men nosed about until they found the dugout - quite a palatial place, with a magnificent installation. They captured over 20 men inside and cut all the wires.

The above represents the position as it really was at 3.pm on September 26th, but not as we knew it at the time. Then it seemed something like this. The Fusiliers held the line R.25.d.0.8. to 3.8. but were not in touch with "C" Coy on the right. It was impossible to get any further owing to the cross fire from German strong Points at R.25.d.0.8. and R.25.b.2.1. (approximately). Another Machine Gun firing from somewhere about R.25.b.4.3. and a Heavy Trench Mortar from about R.25.b.3.5. were also very trouble

"C" Coy's flanking party had both flanks in the air and Lieut Sulman was asking the O.C.Middlesex for reinforcements. 50 men were sent but only 6 reached him. "A" Coy and two platoons of "C" and the bulk of the Middlesex were somewhere in the northern end of the village but it was impossible to locate them owing to the contradictory nature of the messages received. Most of the messages came from N.C.O's (the officers having become casualties) and as some of them had not marked maps, great accuracy was not be be expected.

The first TANK had broken down about 150 yards North of the CHATEAU, and the second got stuck just South of the village and did not come into action at all. Lieut-Colonel Carr and the Adjutant - Lieut G.F.J.Cumberlege - of the Royal Fusiliers had been wounded about half an hour after the start and Captain Johnston was in Command of the Fusiliers. The enemy had a barrage on the Southern edge of the village and beyond, and was displaying great bombing activity on our left flank - there was a pronounced shortage of bombs and S.A.A.

By 4-30.pm the position was cleared up to a large extent, "D" "B" and a part of "A" Coy and some Middlesex were still holding the line R.25.d.0.8. to 3.8.. There was a gap of about 100 yards between the latter point and "C" Coy's flanking platoons which were disposed diagonally across the village approximately on the line R.25.d.3.9. to R.25.b.4.1. This part of the line was dangerously weak. "A" Coy and two platoons of "C" were on the second objective on the line about R.25.b.6.5. to 7.3. with the Middlesex on the right and mixed in with them to some extent, and they were in touch with the Percy on their right.

The Fusiliers had not a bomb left and were dangerously short of S.A.A. One Lewis Gun had only 188 rounds left.

The enemy activity on the extreme left continued unabated. Once they rushed point R25 d.0.8. but were driven back again. Several attempts had been made by our men to rush the strong point on the left but they were beaten back each time by intense cross Machine Gun fire and bombs. It was not unusual to see from 12 to 20 German stick bombs in the air at the same time, and the whole area looked like a firework display owing to the number of egg bombs the enemy showered on us

Captain Johnston reported the situation to Colonel Maxwell who was in chief command and he gave him a company of Northants which had just come up to make another attempt on the strong point and to strengthen his line to the right of R.25.d.3.8. The Northants were put in at 4-45.pm. Two platoons attacked from East to West on a line approximately R.25.d.3.8. to R.25.b.4.0. while the other two pushed through out line R.25.d.0.8. to 3.8., the idea being to rush the strong point simultaneously from two sides. It was a failure - the troops could not form up properly owing to the constant Machine Gun and shell fire, the Officers became casualties, and the men owing to the fearfully broken state of the ground, the galling cross Machine Gun fire and the impossibility of exercising effective control, lost direction or took refuge in shell holes. Capt Johnston reported the position to Col Maxwell at 5-45.pm and was instructed to dig in on his present line, hemming in the strong points as much as possible and to connect up with the troops on the second objective. Captain Johnston therefore collected all the Fusiliers, Middlesex and Northants available and formed them into a front line and support line with about 30 to 50 yards distance between the two. The front line consisted of posts of six men each constituting a double sentry post at intervals of 12 to 15 yards. These men dug towards each other to form a continuous line if possible. The support line was not continuous as there was not sufficient men, so the men were put in groups with a single sentry over each. The left flank of the support line was slightly drawn back to protect the CHATEAU, as the German activity round R.25.d.0.8. continued. For the same reason double sentry posts were placed at 15 yards intervals from point 0.8. to R.25.c.8.6 and beyond. A strong point was made round the standed TANK at R.26.d.3.8. consisting of the Machine Guns taken out of the TANK and about 20 additional men.

The line finally ran from point R.25.d.0.8. to d.3.8., thence north for about 100 yards, then diagonally towards approximately R.25.b.6.3. and along the northern end of the village.

From the time we reached the point R.25.d.0.8. to about 11.pm. there was continual bomb fighting there, and men were replaced as they became casualties. Altogether 35 men were sent to this block, of whom 28 became casualties. Bombing Sergeant Etwell was killed there. The German also made bombing raids from the Trench running South through R.25.d.1.9. but were each time unsuccessful. Fearing that the Germans might counter attack from this side and getting behind us, Captain Johnston asked for a barrage on the Bosch front and support trenches North of our line. This was gradually brought down until it was only about 50 to 75 yards in front of our line. By 11.pm the enemy had had enough of it and retired from the bombing contest and vacated his strong point about R.25.d.0.9. judging by his Very Lights. From this time till dawn the enemy kept a heavy barrage on out line from R.25.d.0.8. to 3.8.

At 4.am the Bedfords arrived and Captain Johnston and Lieut Sulman were instructed by Colonel Maxwell to place them in attack formation in front of our line. This was done and at dawn they carried the N.W. corner of the village in a dashing assault. The Fusiliers then went out of the line.

All through, owing to the very fine fight put up by the 180th Regiment, the Fusiliers had to take a not inconsiderable part in the assault of the village, in addition they fulfilled their original role and all through the attack not a single man on our side was shot in the back.

All the Map references in this report are taken from THIEPVAL, Edition 4 Scale 1/5,000.

The above report was written by Captain W.H.H.Johnston who I instructed to do so, as he was in a much better position to describe the operations; embodied in it are extracts from the accounts of other officers of the Battalion. Captain Johnston was in actual command of the Battalion from the time Colonel Carr was hit (about 1.pm) till I arrived about 6.pm and noone could have done better.

The success of the Battalion is in a very great degree due to his energy and resource and also to the assistance rendered to him by Lieut A.E.Sulman.

R.J.F. Macquaker
MAJOR.
COMMANDING 11TH ROYAL FUSILIERS.

2/10/1916

For the period
1st to 9th October,
see
September Diary

WAR DIARY
or
INTELLIGENCE SUMMARY
(Erase heading not required.)

Army Form C. 2118

11th (Service) Bn Royal Fusiliers

Place	Date	Hour	Summary of Events and Information	Remarks and references to Appendices
RIBEAUCOURT	10/9/16		Right wing A - Lectures. Squad Drill without rifles. Passing of messages - carried out by Boys owing to the 'Battalion' being inoculated.	
"	11/9/16		20 ORs joined the Battalion.	
"	"		C.S. Major Ponnee - Gymnastic Instructor - gave demonstration to Officers and N.C.O's of Bn. Right work only carried out owing to inoculation.	
"			The Commander in Chief visited the Battalion and expressed himself as very pleased with, and extremely grateful to the Battalion for the fine work it had recently performed.	
"	12/9/16	morning and afternoon	Battalion carried out shooting on the Range and intensive digging. Elementary musketry in the 'Attack', extended order drill, artillery formation and barrage was practised.	
"	13/9/16	7 am morning and afternoon	Running Drill. Firing on Range and intensive digging carried out. Extended order drill, artillery formation and 'attack' was practised. Back wd allotted to the battalion. Draft of 15th other Ranks joined the Battalion. Lewis Gunners fired the war of Range.	
"	14/9/16	7 am	Running Drill. Practised rifle exercises, saluting drill and Coy. Drill. Lewis Gunners had war of Butts during the morning. Draft of 57 other Ranks joined the Battalion.	
"	15/9/16	9-50	The Battalion moved off to BEAUVAL. Headquarters "C" Coy. Drums, and "D" Coy. left RIBEAUCOURT at 9-50 am: meeting "A" and "B" Coys at the CHURCH BERNAVILLE at 11 am. The Battalion then marched as such passing through CANDAS enroute and arriving at BEAUVAL about 2 pm. Lorries were placed at	12 F (extract)

1875 Wt. W593/826 1,000,000 4/15 J.B.C. & A. A.D.S.S/Forms/C. 2118.

Army Form C. 2118

WAR DIARY
or
INTELLIGENCE SUMMARY
(Erase heading not required.)

11th (Service) Bn Royal Fusiliers

Place	Date	Hour	Summary of Events and Information	Remarks and references to Appendices
			the disposal of Battalion for carrying Blankets and extra Kits.	
BEAUVAL	16/10/16	6.45 AM	The Battalion paraded and marched off to S area, passing through BEAUQUESNE, PUCHEVILLERS, TOUTENCOURT, VADENCOURT thence to WARLOY-BAILLON, arriving at later place at about 3-30 p.m. Battalion was billeted just outside the village main canvas Bivouacs were erected just on the march so that on arrival of Battn everything was ready for the troops. Motor Transport accompanied the Battalion for line transport Bivouacs being available as before for cartage of Blankets and extra baggage.	
WARLOY-BAILLON	17/10/16	9.30 AM	The Battalion formed up and moved off at 9-30 a.m. A distance being kept between Coys. Leon of Hostile aircraft observation arrived in billets at BOUZINCOURT about 10 a.m. Transport and baggage moved independently.	
BOUZINCOURT	18/10/16	9-30 AM	Coys paraded for training under Coy arrangements. Specialists under their respective Officers Stretcher bearers being taken in hand by the Medical Officer.	
"	19/10/16	7-30 AM	The Battalion paraded and marched to ALBERT arriving their at about 10-30 a.m. Transport moved independently and took up lines at the Brickfields just outside the town. Five officers of the 12th Middlesex Regt joined Battalion for attachment.	
ALBERT	20/10/16	9-30	Coys were at the disposal of their Coy Commanders for training and marched Platoon Barrage etc 6 other Ranks - draft - joined the Battalion.	
"	21/10/16	9-30	The Battalion paraded for training. Barrage to being practised Stretcher bearers being taken out to training area	

1875 Wt. W593/826 1,000,000 4/15 J.B.C. & A. A.D.S.S./Forms/C. 2118.

Army Form C. 2118.

WAR DIARY
or
INTELLIGENCE SUMMARY

(Erase heading not required.)

11th (Service) Bn. Royal Fusiliers

Instructions regarding War Diaries and Intelligence Summaries are contained in F.S. Regs., Part II. and the Staff Manual respectively. Title Pages will be prepared in manuscript.

Place	Date	Hour	Summary of Events and Information	Remarks and references to Appendices
ALBERT	22/10/16	9.30 AM and 2 pm	Jnr training area the Medical Officer and 26 Other Ranks joined the Battalion. The Battalion proceeded to training area and were formed up as at "Zero hour"; barrage and attack being practiced.	
"	23/10/16		The Battalion relieved the 8th Norfolks in sector of trenches occupying R.23. Coys moving out of ALBERT by Platoons (not party starting at 1.15 pm. A and B Coys held front line, C and D Coys being in support.	
TRENCHES	24/10/16		Weather bad and rain made trenches in a very wet and muddy state. Artillery very active on both sides otherwise nothing to report.	
"	25/10/16		Very bad weather still prevailed. Rain being almost continuous. The men got very wet. The Battalion was relieved by 12th Middlesex Regt and men arrived in billets at ALBERT in rather an exhausted condition owing to the heavy going. The total casualties for the tour being Captain W.J.G. Hoare D.S.O. Killed, 23 Wounded, 1 OR other ranks, 2 ORs missing 12 ORs killed 1 OR missing believed killed	

2449 Wt. W14957/M90 750,000 1/16 J.B.C. & A. Forms/C.2118/12.

Army Form C. 2118.

WAR DIARY
or
INTELLIGENCE SUMMARY

(Erase heading not required.)

11th (Service) Bn. Royal Fusiliers

Place	Date	Hour	Summary of Events and Information	Remarks and references to Appendices
ALBERT.	26/10/16		All day was spent in cleaning up and drying clothes &c.	
"	27/10/16	9.30 AM	Bn. were at the disposal of their Coy Commanders for training &c.	
"	28/10/16	9.30 AM	Coys paraded independently and proceeded to training area. Practising following Barrage, 'attack' &c. Draft of 10 Other Ranks joined the Battalion.	
"	29/10/16	9.30 AM	Coys practised Coy Drill, Barrage 'attack' etc on training area. Signalling, Bombers, Lewis Gunners &c being trained under their respective Officers.	
"	30/10/16	9.30 AM	Training carried out as on the 30th inst	
"	31/10/16	9.30 AM	Training carried out as on the 30th inst	
"	1/11/16	9.30 AM 3.p.m.	Training carried out as on the 30th inst. Major General Maxse C.V.O. C.B. D.S.O. pinned decorations on men of the Battalion who had been awarded them since July 1st. The Battalion formed up in Square, ALBERT, for this purpose.	
"	2/11/16	9.30 2 p.m.	Training carried out under Coy arrangements. Battalion took over fresh Billet in ALBERT.	

Army Form C. 2118.

WAR DIARY
or
INTELLIGENCE SUMMARY

11th (Service) Bn. Royal Fusiliers

(Erase heading not required.)

Instructions regarding War Diaries and Intelligence Summaries are contained in F.S. Regs., Part II. and the Staff Manual respectively. Title Pages will be prepared in manuscript.

Place	Date	Hour	Summary of Events and Information	Remarks and references to Appendices
ALBERT	3/11/16		The Battalion relieved the 8th Royal Fusiliers in sector of trenches R.23. Relief was carried out in two parts. 'A' and 'B' Coys. being Comm. Attack and 'Reserve'. 'A' and 'B' Coys. relieved in daylight and left Billets approximately at 'C' and 'D' Coys went right front line and relieved at night. Coys reported and relieved at night leaving Billets approximately at. 2nd Lieuts G.A. Blake and H.R. Cray joined the Battalion for duty. Draft of 2 ORs joined the Bn. from Base Depot.	
TRENCHES	4/11/16		Weather very bad. Artillery very active on both sides.	
"	5/11/16		Intermittent rain and muddy trenches made the routine heavy. Going Artillery very active on both sides. Into Coy. near look place without casualties. Draft of 14 ORs joined the Bn.	
"	6/11/16		The Battalion was relieved by 12th Middlesex Regt. Reserve Coys coming out by day and front line Coys by night. 3rd out was provided regimentally in the troops at RED CROSS CORNER. from there Busses conveyed men to their Billets in ALBERT. Total casualties for tour: 15 ORs wounded, 4 ORs killed 1 OR missing, 1 OR Shell Shock, 1 OR Injured Back.	
ALBERT	7/11/16		Day was spent in cleaning up. Baths were available also clean clothes, and all men who came out of trenches attended the Bathing Parade.	
"	8/11/16		Coys were at the disposal of their Commander for training. A working party of two platoons was found by the Bn. for	

2449 Wt. W14957/M90 750,000 1/16 J.B.C. & A. Forms/C.2118/12.

Army Form C. 2118.

WAR DIARY
or
INTELLIGENCE SUMMARY

(Erase heading not required.)

11th (Service) Bn Royal Fusiliers

Instructions regarding War Diaries and Intelligence Summaries are contained in F. S. Regs., Part II. and the Staff Manual respectively. Title Pages will be prepared in manuscript.

Place	Date	Hour	Summary of Events and Information	Remarks and references to Appendices
ALBERT.	9/11/16		work in trenches.	
			The Battalion was employed on work in Trenches. Two Coys starting at 4 a.m. One Coy at 3-30 p.m, and one Coy at 7-30 p.m.	

A. B. Mukein
Lieut
a/adj. 11th R.Fus.

9.XI.16

11th (Service) Bn. Royal Fusiliers

Army Form C. 2118.

13 F.
(8 sheets)

WAR DIARY
or
INTELLIGENCE SUMMARY

11th Bn. Royal Fusiliers

(Erase heading not required.)

Instructions regarding War Diaries and Intelligence Summaries are contained in F.S. Regs., Part II. and the Staff Manual respectively. Title Pages will be prepared in manuscript.

Place	Date	Hour	Summary of Events and Information	Remarks and references to Appendices
ALBERT	10/11/16		The Battalion found large parties for working on trenches.	
"	11/11/16		Coys were at the disposal of their Company Commanders for training. Parading at 6.30am. Draft of 3 men joined the Battn.	
"	12/11/16	9-30am	Coys were at the disposal of their Commanding Officers. Parading at 9-30am. Men training to be given the opportunity to do so. One Platoon of D Coy was employed on Kindle making under R.E. at AVELUY WOOD	
"	13/11/16	11am	The Battalion proceeded to Huts at OVILLERS, moving by Coy at 5 minute intervals with order "C", "B", "A" and "D". Reaving Battalion Cooks at 11am. Battalion had dinner at OVILLERS Huts, proceeding in same order and relieved the 8th Norfolk Regt in the trenches as follows:- leading Platoon of "C" Company reaching CENTRE WAY IN 8's end at 4pm, D Coy at 4-50pm, A Coy at 5-30pm and B Coy at 6-10pm. 5 minute intervals between each platoon. Battalion Headquarters in Conjunction with HQ was at R.29 Central. Attack orders. Instns. received up in Walloppoy Street.	
Trenches	14/11/16		"A" and "B" Coys were in REGINA TRENCH. Am right B on left "C" was Counter attack Coy in VANCOUVER TRENCH. D Coy was in Reserve in TABECK TRENCH. D Coy and HQnrs Details found all carrying parties. Situation Normal.	
"	15/11/16		Trenches were in very bad condition. Situation normal. A considerable amount of work was done in the trenches. Some artillery activity on your right.	

Army Form C. 2118.

WAR DIARY
or
INTELLIGENCE SUMMARY

(Erase heading not required.)

11th Bn Royal Fusiliers

Place	Date	Hour	Summary of Events and Information	Remarks and references to Appendices
TRENCHES	16/1/16		Battalion quiet. Artillery active on both sides.	
	17/1/16		An inter-company relief was carried out. 'B' Coy relieved 'A' Coy and 'D' Coy relieved 'B' Coy. The relief was delayed by a considerable bombardment with Phosgene and Lachrymatory gas shells. Two men were gassed, one severely the other slightly.	
		midnight	The Battalion was relieved by the 87th Canadian Regt and proceeded to Huts at OVILLERS. The following casualties occurred during the tour in the trenches. 10 ORs killed – 24 ORs wounded – 2 ORs gassed.	
HUTS AT OVILLERS.	18/1/16		Battalion rested and cleaned up as much as was possible.	
	19/1/16		Battalion stood by ready to move at an hour's notice. A proportion of Service Dress was fitted. Draft of 3 men joined the 13 Battalion.	
	20/1/16		Battalion was employed in working in trenches two Coys working a morning shift and remainder the afternoon shift. Medical Orders paraded with their Coys in the future. Draft of 5 men joined the Bn	
	21/1/16		Battalion left Huts, OVILLERS at 11 am and started on a seven days march. The Battalion passed through BOUZINCOURT and SENLIS. thence to WARLOY arriving there at 3.15 pm when billets were taken over. The Transport and Quartermaster Store however had crossed midnight from ALBERT to WARLOY motor Lorries were available for Conveyor of Blankets and (2nd Lt 139 Longmore joined Bn for duty.)	

2449 Wt. W14957/M90 750,000 1/16 J.B.C. & A. Forms/C.2118/12.

Army Form C. 2118.

11th Bn. Royal Fusiliers

WAR DIARY
or
INTELLIGENCE SUMMARY

(Erase heading not required.)

Instructions regarding War Diaries and Intelligence
Summaries are contained in F. S. Regs., Part II.
and the Staff Manual respectively. Title Pages
will be prepared in manuscript.

Place	Date	Hour	Summary of Events and Information	Remarks and references to Appendices
WARLOY BAILLON	22/11/16		extra baggage. B, C and D - Coys took over tents just on outskirts of village. A was billeted in the village	
RUBEMPRÉ	23/11/16		Battalion paraded at 9am and marched through VADENCOURT, CONTAY, HERISSART thence to RUBEMPRÉ arriving there at 12-10 pm and took over billets. Transport proceeded with the Battalion and Lorries were available for cartage of Blankets and extra baggage.	
DOULLENS	24/11/16		Battalion paraded at 8-30 am and proceeded DOULLENS through BEAUVAL and arriving at DOULLENS at 1-40 pm and took over billets. Transport accompanied the Battalion on the march. Lorries were available for cartage of Blankets etc. Draft of 3 men joined the Battalion.	
BERNEUIL	25/11/16		The Battalion paraded at 8-30 am and proceeded to BERNEUIL passing through CANDAS, FIENVILLERS. BERNEUIL arriving there at 1 pm. Transport accompanied the Battalion on the march. Lorries were available for cartage of Blankets and extra baggage.	
			The Battalion paraded at 10-50 am and proceeded to RIBEAUCOURT arriving there at 12-10 pm. There was considerable rain during the march. Transport accompanied the Battalion. Lorries were available for cartage of Blankets etc.	

2449 Wt. W14957/M90 750,000 1/16 J.B.C. & A. Forms/C.2118/12.

Army Form C. 2118.

11th Bn. Royal Fusiliers

WAR DIARY
or
INTELLIGENCE SUMMARY
(Erase heading not required.)

Place	Date	Hour	Summary of Events and Information	Remarks and references to Appendices
RIBEAUCOURT	26/11/16		The Battalion paraded at 9-50am and marched to ST. RIQUIER, having passed through TRANSY and BOMQUEUR, three to ST. RIQUIER arriving at 12-35pm. Transport proceeded with Battalion. Limbers were available for kitbags, Blankets and extra baggage. Drafts of 5 Ranks joined Battalion - 2nd Lieut A v.S. Malcolm joined the Battalion for duty.	
St RIQUIER	27/11/16.		The Battalion paraded at 9.55am and proceeded to DRUCAT having passed through MILENCOURT thence to DRUCAT. Major General F.G. Moore, the Divisional Commander saw the Battalion march past at the Cross roads ½ mile N. of MILENCOURT. He expressed his appreciation of the smart appearance of the Battalion and the fine way in which they marched. He said "I have never seen them look better". 1 man Draft joined the Battalion.	
DRUCAT	28/11/16		The Battalion spent the day in making huts as comfortable as was possible.	
	29/11/16		Coys marched out to the training area, and during the morning practised physical drill, musketry, squad drill etc. The afternoon was devoted to sports ie. football, Boxing. A & B Coys bathed.	
	30/11/16.		Training on Nov. 29th. A B & C Coys bathed.	

D.a.G.
G.H.Q.
3rd Echelon.

Reference attached.
  It is not quite
understood, as we are
already in possession
of the Duplicate, and
the Diary for period
10-11-16 — 9-12-16 returned
herewith is the Original.
  Can you explain
please.

[stamp: ORDERLY ROOM / Reg. No M.5.a.a / 0 JAN 1917 / 11th (Service) Bn. Royal Fusiliers]

1/1/17

[signature]
Capt
Adjutant
for Lt.Col.
Commanding
11th Bn Royal Fusiliers

Army Form C. 2118.

WAR DIARY
or
INTELLIGENCE SUMMARY

(Erase heading not required.)

11th Bn Royal Fusiliers

Place	Date	Hour	Summary of Events and Information	Remarks and references to Appendices
DRUCAT	1/12/16		Battalion practiced Battalion digging. Practice trenches representing the attack on MIRAUMONT.	
"	2/12/16		Practiced intensive digging on or 1st Dec.	
"	3/12/16		Church parade – remainder of day allotted for rest and football.	2nd Rev. R.E. Evans
"	4/12/16		Battalion practiced intensive digging joined the Battalion for duty	
"	5/12/16		Battalion scheme of attack practiced.	
"	6/12/16		Coys marched out to training area independently and practiced Squad Drill, Musketry, Coy drill & Physical Drill &c.	
"	7/12/16		Battalion practiced an Attack Scheme on the training area. Draft of 2 men joined the Battalion.	
"	8/12/16		Coys marched out to training area independently and practiced Physical Drill, Rifle Exercises, Advancing in screens &c.	

Army Form C. 2118.

WAR DIARY
or
INTELLIGENCE SUMMARY
(Erase heading not required.)

Instructions regarding War Diaries and Intelligence Summaries are contained in F. S. Regs., Part II and the Staff Manual respectively. Title Pages will be prepared in manuscript.

Place	Date	Hour	Summary of Events and Information	Remarks and references to Appendices
DRUCAT	9/1/16		Battalion took part in a Brigade Scheme on training area. 2nd part of 2 men joined 2nd Lieut. B.P. Wedelin and attached joined Battalion for duty. During the period 27/11/16 to 9/1/16. Relieving of Battalion was done. Drovers were engaged in making the billets comfortable and putting up huts for the men, and extension, for training. hid 2 refs anyone were entertained & some old training pits cleaned.	

M. Mitchell Lieut
a/adjt
11th Bn Royal Inniskilling

Army Form C. 2118.

Vol 5/4

WAR DIARY or INTELLIGENCE SUMMARY

(Erase heading not required.)

11th (Service) Bn. Royal Fusiliers

Place	Date	Hour	Summary of Events and Information	Remarks and references to Appendices
DRUCAT	10/12/16 to 13/12/16		Battalion carried out training on the St Riquier training area. Organisation schemes were carried out. Barrage and attack schemes were practised. Coys practised Signal drill, Extended order drill and Coy drill. Specialists were trained under their respective officers. A draft of 192 Other ranks arrived on the 11th Dec.	
	14/12/16		Battalion moved to MARCHEVILLE. A & B Coys paraded and moved off at 9-40 am independently as they were detailed to dig trenches for the Brigade Bomb School at MARCHEVILLE. The Battalion less above mentioned Coys moved out of DRUCAT at 8-50 and arrived at MARCHEVILLE at 1-30 pm and took over billets.	
MARCHEVILLE	15/12/16 to 9/1/17		During the period of training the following was carried out. On 15th Dec. the Commanding Officer inspected all Coys in their respective parade grounds. Musketry on local range, close order drill, Lectures and demonstration in Trench discipline, Platoon drill, Bayonet drill, Saluting drill, Guard duties, Tactical exercises for young officers and NCOs, forming up in assembly trenches, Smoke helmet drill and inspections, Live bomb throwing, forming up in the dark, wiring and sandbag meeting.	
			Christmas day was devoted to holiday - A & B Coys had dinner at 5 pm - C & D at 12-30 pm.	
			On 27th December the Battalion paraded at 9 am for a Brigade attack scheme and marched to the St Riquier training area, arriving there at about 9-30 am. The Battalion acted as left assaulting Battalion. After carrying out the scheme the Battalion moved off, arriving at MARCHEVILLE about 5-45 pm. Bookers were taken out and not sent was served to the men on the training ground	

Army Form C. 2118.

WAR DIARY
or
INTELLIGENCE SUMMARY
(Erase heading not required.)

14th (Service) Bn. Royal Fusiliers

Instructions regarding War Diaries and Intelligence Summaries are contained in F.S. Regs., Part II. and the Staff Manual respectively. Title Pages will be prepared in manuscript.

Place	Date	Hour	Summary of Events and Information	Remarks and references to Appendices
MORCHEVILLE	29/12/16	10-30 am	"D" Coy paraded and moved off to 18th Divisional School situated at ABBEY near BUGNY, where they acted as Demonstration Coy for period 29/12/16 – 9/1/17. They were rationed and billeted by the Divisional School during that period.	
			CSM Longmuir, Gymnastic Instructor, was attached to the battalion for the week ending 29th December for instructing NCOs in Bayonet fighting, physical drill etc. The medical officer gave lectures to the Battalion.	
	15/12/16 to 9/1/17		Lewis Gun teams all paraded under the Lewis Gun Officer for training. The Signalling Officer and all Signallers of the Battalion were at the 54th Brigade Signal School for training/under the Brigade Signal Officer. The Battalion sent two officers and ten men each week to the 54th to 53rd Trench Mortar Battery School for training. 8 NCOs were sent each week to the 54th Brigade Bomb School for qualifying as efficient instructors – 4 officers attended the school during period of training. On January 3rd Battalion paraded at 8-30 am for a Route march and arrived back in billets at about 2pm. Baths at CRECHY were allotted to Battalion on Monday of each week and all coys regularly Bathed. Afternoon hours of parade were 9am to 12-30pm and 2pm to 3-30pm.	

WAR DIARY or INTELLIGENCE SUMMARY

Army Form C. 2118

11th (Service) Bn Royal Fusiliers

Place	Date	Hour	Summary of Events and Information	Remarks and references to Appendices
MARCHEVILLE	21/12/16 to 9/1/17		Draft of 1 NCO and 10 men joined Battalion Battalion was fitted with the new Box Respirators and was put through the Gas Chamber. On the 5th January a regrettable Bomb accident occurred whilst 'C' Coy were practicing Bombing. 2NCO's and 4 men were wounded of these 1 NCO and 2 men returned to duty after being medicated and dressed at the Field Ambulance. The New Gun identity discs were stamped and issued to all officers and men of the Battalion. Rifles, Arms & equipment and kit was carried out throughout the Battalion. Concerts were given by the Sgt Sgts Pierrot Troupe and were patronised by all ranks. Sundays were set aside as a day of rest. Sports were arranged for the men, these included Inter Divisional Inter Battalion Football matches, Battalion Boxing Tournaments, Inter Battalion Runs, and Battalion runs.	

CONFIDENTIAL

Subject:- Duplicate War Diaries.

To:- OC

11 Royal Ins

A.G.'s OFFICE AT THE BASE.
War Diaries & Records.
DATE 29-12-16
C.R. No. 8700/651

The enclosed Duplicate War Diary is returned to you please, as "Duplicates" are not required in this Office, vide:- General Routine Order, No.1125. 1598

To Home Records

General Headquarters,
3rd Echelon,
/ /1916.

Staff-Captain,
for D.A.G.

Army Form C. 2118.

WAR DIARY
or
INTELLIGENCE SUMMARY

(Erase heading not required.)

11th (Service) Bn. Royal Fusiliers

WO/95

15 F.
(2 sheet)

Place	Date	Hour	Summary of Events and Information	Remarks and references to Appendices
MARCHEVILLE	10/1/17		Battalion spent day in preparing for move. All Officers and men at schools and courses returned Battalion for duty.	
	11/1/17	10.20 a.m.	Battalion, accompanied by Transport, moved off at 10.20 a.m. Coy. Hqrs. and Transport proceeded to the Cross Roads ½ mile S.E. of MARCHEVILLE Church, when they formed up and moved off to MAISON-ROLLAND, arriving there at 2.40 p.m. and took over billets. Weather very bad for marching – wet and cold.	
MAISON-ROLLAND	12/1/17	10.55 a.m.	Battalion accompanied by Transport moved off to BERNEUIL. Coys. Hd Qrs. and transport moved off independently of the shopping point – Cross Roads LE PLOUY arriving there at 10.55 a.m. and proceeding on the march. Battalion arrived at BERNEUIL at 2 p.m. and took over billets. Bad weather prevailed. Sleet falling continuously.	
BERNEUIL	13/1/17		Battalion remained in billets. Time was spent in cleaning men's clothing & rifles. 2 nd Lieut Will Rae joined Battalion for duty.	
BERNEUIL	14/1/17	10.45 a.m. 10.45 p.m.	The Battalion, accompanied by Transport, formed up and moved off at 10.45 a.m. to LA VICOGNE via CANAPLES – HAVERNAS and NADURS. arriving at LA VICOGNE at about 3.30 pm. Arrived then fell Haversed & before the Battalion moved off, the weather throughout the march was poor.	

2449 Wt. W14957/M90 750,000 1/16 J.B.C. & A. Forms/C.2118/12.

WAR DIARY
INTELLIGENCE SUMMARY

Army Form C. 2118.

11th (Service) Bn. Royal Fusiliers

Place	Date	Hour	Summary of Events and Information	Remarks and references to Appendices
BERNEUIL	14/1/17		But the roads were heavy owing to lack of accommodation in billets "B" Coy had to march to TALMAS, where they arrived in billets.	
LA VICOGNE	15/1/17		Battalion remained in Billets.	
	16/1/17	11.30 am	Battalion moved off in twos, at 11.30 am and proceeded to AVELUY where they dis-embussed and marched by Coys to WARWICK HUTS at R/a sheet 57½D S.E. Relieving the 2/f of Warwickshire Territorials who were right Battalion infront. Relief was complete at 9 p.m. Owing to the new Battalion infront. Binney enterior to signed to the men before an the Trench. Throughout the journey cups from hot tea and oxo was available. Throughout the march indulgently by men. Got ten thousand The transport arrived undulgently by men. A Coy proceeded to F.D.B.1.C.K. to the men on arrival at the huts. A Coy proceeded to F.D.B.1.C.K. TRENCH where they acted as attached working party to 6/Northampton Line Regiment. The Battalion (less A Coy) remained in huts. The following farewell order was received from Lieut-General Sir Ivor Maxse KCB,CVO, D.S.O. "I cannot relinquish the command of the 18th Division without expressing to every Officer, N.C.O and man my admiration for the indomitable spirit and my confidence in their ability to beat the enemy having seen the Division grow from infancy	
WARWICK HUTS at R.1.a	16/1/17			

Army Form C. 2118.

WAR DIARY
or
INTELLIGENCE SUMMARY

(Erase heading not required.)

11th (Service) Bn. Royal Fusiliers

Instructions regarding War Diaries and Intelligence Summaries are contained in F.S. Regs., Part II. and the Staff Manual respectively. Title Pages will be prepared in manuscript.

Place	Date	Hour	Summary of Events and Information	Remarks and references to Appendices
WARWICK HUTS	17/1/17		Civilians in October 1914, into silence in January 1917. I speak with them with supreme regret.	
			(Sd) Ivor Maxse, Lieut. General Commanding 18th Division	
WARWICK HUTS.	18/1/17		The Battalion (less A Coy) remained in WARWICK HUTS.	
WARWICK HUTS.	19/1/17	4 pm	The Battalion proceeded to the line and relieved the 6th Northamptonshire Regt. Relief was carried out without a casualty and all two Compys. at 9.30 pm. One A Coy was relieved by a Company of the 6th Northamptonshire Regt. who remained in dug-outs in the vicinity of Battalion Headquarters and were attached to the Battalion for carrying rations &c.	
TRENCHES	20/1/17	4 am	Situation was quiet, nothing unusual occurred. Enemy's artillery was very active. The Huns Boards from REGINA TRENCH to forward sap were shelled and standing fire was directed in neighbourhood of FABECK TRENCH to our Batteries. Weather very cold — hard frost all day.	
"	21/1/17	4 am 4 pm	Artillery on either side normal — nothing unusual occurred. Situation quiet. Never artillery activity. No casualties occurred and no damage was done to trenches. Weather very cold — hard frost all day.	
			2/Lieuts L.G. Ambridge, D.C. Beeching, A.V. Payne, M.R. Turner Joined Battalion for duty.	

Army Form C. 2118.

WAR DIARY
or
INTELLIGENCE SUMMARY
(Erase heading not required.)

11th (Service) Bn. Royal Fusiliers

Place	Date	Hour	Summary of Events and Information	Remarks and references to Appendices
TRENCHES	22/1/17	4 a.m.	Situation Quiet. Some artillery activity. No casualties occured and no damage was done to trenches.	
		4 p.m.	Situation normal - nothing unusual occured.	
	23/1/17	4 a.m.	Enemy artillery was too active. New were was put out by enemy about R.1 S.1.S. for length of 100 yds or so. Situation generally normal.	
		4 p.m.	Enemy's artillery activity normal. Great aerial activity. One enemy machine was brought down behind our lines. A camera and a Maxim Gun was thrown out by the German aviator before descending. The machine gun was picked up by Corpnal Bentley of this Battalion and the camera was claimed by an officer of the attached by of 6th Northamptonshire Regt. Weather very bad - visibility bad that - freezing hard.	
	24/1/17	4 a.m.	Situation Quiet. Enemy artillery was rather above normal. Enemy's artillery was fairly active several times sent over WIGAN, HESSIAN and REGINA TRENCHES. Our artillery was more active than usual.	
		4 p.m.	Battalion was relieved in the line by 6th Northamptonshire Regt. Relief all completed and carried out without casualties before midnight. Battalion proceed to WARWICK HUTS. "A" Coy remains in the line, acting as carrying party.	
WARWICK HUTS	25/1/17		Battalion rested no night working Battalion.	
	26/1/17			

Army Form C. 2118

WAR DIARY
INTELLIGENCE SUMMARY
(Erase heading not required.)

11th (Service) Bn. Royal Fusiliers

Place	Date	Hour	Summary of Events and Information	Remarks and references to Appendices
WARWICK HUTS.	29/1/17	2 p.m.	Battalion moved out of WARWICK HUTS into WELLINGTON HUTS situated at W 12. c.	
WELLINGTON HUTS.	29/1/17 to 8/2/17		During this period Battalion was employed on fatigues, with 3rd Royal Sussex (Pioneers) and 80th Field Coy R.E. 4 men were wounded whilst on these fatigues. Splitting, packing Equipment and Kit repairing was carried out, when not on fatigue. Coy aid Physical and Bayonet Drill and Practised the attack. Owing to shortage of fuel parties were sent daily to AUTHUILLE WOOD to collect wood. Severe weather prevailed during this period - frost being continuous. Aerial activity was above normal, and each night the Bosch aeroplanes came over, and dropped bombs on AVELUY also firing his machine gun at traffic on the roads in the vicinity of the huts. The Officer Commanding 3rd Royal Sussex Pioneers wishes especially to congratulate the Battalion on their good work digging SOBURY TRENCH which now connects up the front line - DESIRE TRENCH with FABECK TRENCH. C.C. Carr D.S.O. Lieut-Colonel. C.C. Carr D.S.O. joined the Battalion on the 3rd February and took over command, being away from the	

WAR DIARY or INTELLIGENCE SUMMARY

Army Form C. 2118

11th (Service) Bn. Royal Fusiliers

Place	Date	Hour	Summary of Events and Information	Remarks and references to Appendices
WELLINGTON HUTS.			Battalion since 26 September, 1916 when it was wounded in Headquarters and Capture of THIEPVAL. Lieut-Colonel R.I.V. Meyrick left Battalion on 3rd February 1917 and took command of the 6th Northamptonshire Regt.	
"	8/2/17		Battalion left WELLINGTON HUTS and proceeded to the trenches relieving the 8th Bn. The Norfolk Regiment. Relief was complete at 8.30 p.m. No casualties occurred.	
TRENCHES	9/2/17	4 a.m.	Situation quiet. Enemy artillery, rifle and machine gun fire also Trench Mortars unusually quiet.	

A. Churchill
Captain
11th Bn. Royal Fusiliers

C. Churchill
Captain
11th Bn. Royal Fusiliers

11th/ R. Fus.

Feb 1917

WAR DIARY or INTELLIGENCE SUMMARY

Army Form C. 2118.
11th (Service) Bn. Royal Fusiliers
Feb 1917

Vol 10

(12 sheets)

Place	Date	Hour	Summary of Events and Information	Remarks and references to Appendices
Trenches	10/2/17		"A" Company made an attack on a German "Strong Point". There was no artillery bombardment, only a few rounds being fired on the point from the Stokes Guns at 9.20pm the attack was launched. 2nd Lieut. B.G. Synson and B.P. Webster being the Officers in command of the assaulting platoons. The Strong point was rushed and captured. The enemy then evacuated a Heavy Machine Gun and Rifle Grenade fire on them but Lieut. Synson and a large number of casualties amongst our two platoons. Both Officers were hit and almost all the N.C.O.s went down also. The remains of the Company was sent out but they also suffered casualties. The enemy then counter attacked under the cover of a Heavy Rifle Grenade and Machine Gun fire which made it impossible for the few remaining men to occupy the trenches and they were forced to retire. Our total casualties were 1 officer Killed 1 Officer wounded 5 O.R. Killed, O.R. wounded 17 OR Missing 6. 3 of the wounded returned to duty a/n being Knocked out.	
Trenches	11/2/17	7 am	Artillery on both sides was very active, otherwise nothing of importance occurred. At about 7pm the Battalion was relieved by the 8th East Surrey Regt. & Batt was carried out without casualties. The Battalion proceeded to Wellington Huts about 1000 yards NW of Aveluy.	

Army Form C. 2118.

WAR DIARY
INTELLIGENCE SUMMARY
(Erase heading not required.)

11th (Service) Bn. Royal Fusiliers

Place	Date	Hour	Summary of Events and Information	Remarks and references to Appendices
Wellington Huts	12/2/17 to 14/2/17		Battalion cleaned up. Parties were sent to Authuille Wood daily for fuel for the Battalion. and large working parties were found by the Coy digging trenches working parties unloading ammunition etc on the 14th not half were attached to the Battalion.	
Trenches	15/2/17		Battalion less "A" Coy proceeded to the Line. Disitribution of Coys was as follows:- A. Coy. Wellington Huts B. Coy. Battn Front Line C. Coy. Mouquet Farm D. Coy. Yatrick and Nisorar Trenches Headquarters. Snelling Trench.	
Trenches	16/2/17		Preparations were made for an attack on enemy's trenches on the 17th inst	
Trenches	17/2/17		Attacked German trenches - all official account attached Casualties :- 2 Officers Killed 1 Officer Died of Wounds 11 Officers wounded 1 Officer Shell Shock 36 OR Killed in action 6 OR Died of wounds 162 OR wounded 69 OR missing On the night of 17th. the Battalion was relieved by 12th Middlesex Regt. and occupied dugouts at Mouquet Farm. Headquarters being at Dugout in Snelling Trench.	

WAR DIARY

INTELLIGENCE SUMMARY

11th (Service) Bn. Royal Fusiliers

Army Form C. 2118

Place	Date	Hour	Summary of Events and Information	Remarks and references to Appendices
Junction (Acheux)	18/2/17		Battalion was relieved and marched to Monmouth Huts near AVELUY.	
MONMOUTH HUTS	19/2/17		Battalion accompanied by transport marched from Monmouth Huts to SENLIS.	
SENLIS	20/2/17		Battalion cleaned up and was allotted Baths and clean clothing.	
"	21/2/17 to 1/3/17		Party of 25 men were found each day for Town Sanitary Fatigue. One platoon was daily employed on unloading ammunition at Acheville Dump. Rifles of Battalion was carried out, Kit and equipment Inspected, replaced and retained. Companies did training according to programme laid down. C.S.M. O'Brien Army Gymnastic Staff was attached to the Battalion and 1st Giving instruction to Coys in physical drill and Bayonet fighting. The Commanding Officer Inspected the Battalion in full marching order. Shoots were put in for training in Signalling, Lewis Gunners. Sir Claud Jacob K.C.B. Gen. Commanding 2nd Corps Inspected the Battalion on the 25th February 1917 and highly complimented the Battalion on the fine fight on the morning of the 17th February. Draft of 61 other ranks joined the Battalion on 28th inst.	

WAR DIARY
INTELLIGENCE SUMMARY

(Erase heading not required.)

11th (Service) Bn. Royal Fusiliers

Army Form C. 2118

Place	Date	Hour	Summary of Events and Information	Remarks and references to Appendices
SENLIS	2/3/17		Battalion marched out of SENLIS and occupied tents between AUTHUILLE and THIEPVAL	
TENTS BETWEEN AUTHUILLE AND THIEPVAL	3/3/17 to 7/3/17		The Battalion remained at Camp during the period finding large fatigue parties, road making etc. A Company was attached from the Battalion on the 4th March and proceeded to meet where they did fatigues under the 1st ANZACs and remained this the evening of March 9th. Training was carried out in the neighbourhood of Camp by Coys who were not finding working parties. New Lewis Gunners were trained also Signallers Coys and Lewis Gunners did firing on range in the vicinity of Camp. Draft of Seven officers arrived on the 5th March. Draft of three officers and eleven other ranks joined Battalion on the 8th March. Major Beal joined Battalion on the 5th March.	

J.H. Pemberton
Captain
Adjutant
11th Bn Royal Fusiliers

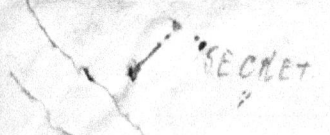

"OPERATION ORDERS"
BY
LIEUT-COLONEL C.C.CARR.D.S.O.
COMMANDING 11TH BN. ROYAL FUSILIERS.
8TH FEBRUARY, 1917.

NO. 60

1. The Battalion will relieve the 8th Norfolks in the line this afternoon.

2. Reliefs will be carried out in accordance with attached table.

3. Box Respirators will be worn at the Alert Position during relief.

4. Completion of all reliefs will be reported to Battalion Headquarters by Code "O.K.--- p.m.

5. Platoons will move at 100 yards interval.

6. Lists of Trench Stores taken over will be handed XXXXX to Orderly Room by Runner Post on the morning of the 9th.

7. G.S.Wagons will be sent to Wellington Huts at 2pm to take down Blankets, Kits &c. All blankets will be rolled, tied, labelled, and dumped in front of the Orderly Room nearest the road by 1-30 pm. All Officers Kits, Mess Stores ect. will be ready stacked on the same dump by 4 pm. The Pioneers will furnish the loading parties.

8. Coys and Hd. Qrs. Details will be responsible that their lines and huts are left absolutely clean and that no camp furniture is removed.

9. Guides will be at MOUQUET FARM on the scale of one per platoon and one for Bn. Hqrs. Beyond REGINA TRENCH the Duck Boards to the Right Coy only will be used. Those to the left Coy are out of bounds. All traffic to the Left Coy must be via Right Coy Hqrs.

10. Officers Commanding will ensure that every mans' feet are rubbed with whale oil before starting for the Trenches. While in the Trenches whale oil will be suppliedd daily. Puttees will not be worn by men in the front trenches, but their socks will be pulled up over their trousers and boots will be fastened loosely. Sentries will be provided with Sandbags filed with straw for putting their legs in. - Vide B.O.No.3 of 6th inst.

11. "D" Coy will find all ration carrying parties in the trenches. Parties of over 20 will be under an officer. Rations will go via Wigan Lane as far as REGINA TRENCH.

12. Half the Snipers will be accommodated with front Coys and half with Battalion Hqrs. Lieut. Ashmole will take command of the Snipers for the tour in Trenches.

13. Lewis Gunners will take in their own drums and will relieve with their Coys.

14. The question of dress is left to discretion of Coy Commanders but men of the same Coy must be uniform.

15. Small Advance Parties may be sent after dinners by "C" & "D" Coys.

16. Dinners to-day will be at 12 noon and teas at 3-15 pm.

17. All water bottles will be filled before moving off.

CONTINUED.

8.

18. "Stand To" The hour of Stand To will be notified on arrival.

19. Coys & Hqrs will eich send a servant to take charge of their Kits going forward. They will report at Orderly Room to R.S.M. at 4 p.m.

(SIGNED) G.F.J.CUMBERLGE, CAPTAIN.

ADJUTANT 11TH BN. ROYAL FUSILIERS.

re

RELIEF TABLE.

COY	FROM	TO	ROUTE	TIME LEAVING WELLINGTON HUTS	PASSING NAB JUNCTION AT
B.H.Q	Wellington Huts	B.H.Q. Fabick Trench	Nab Junction - Mouquet Farm	3-50.pm	4-40.pm
"A"	"	Left Front Line	"	3-55.pm	4-45.pm
"B"	"	Right Front Line	"	4-5.pm	4-50.pm 4-55 pm
"C"	"	2 Platoons & C.Hd.Qrs - Hessian 2 Platoons Zollern.	"	4-15.pm	5-0.pm 5-5 pm
"D"	"	2 Platoons & C.Hd.Qrs Zollern 2 Platoons at B.Hd.Qrs.	"	4-25.pm	5-10.pm 5-15 pm

8/2/17.

(Sd) G.F.J.Cumberlege Capt.
Adjt.11th R.Fus.

"OPERATION ORDERS"   No.61.
BY
CAPTAIN H.R.MUNDEY
COMMANDING 11TH BN.ROYAL FUSILIERS
10TH FEBRUARY 1917

(1) Your Company ("A") will at an hour to be notified later attack and hold point R.16.b.8.5., the garrison of this post are to be killed or captured.

(2) The 12th Middlesex Regt. on your left will at the same hour seize all the ground where GRANDCOURT TRENCH runs E. & W. of SIXTEEN ROAD. i.e. Points R.16.a.8.7. R.16.a.9.8. They will then push down GRANDCOURT TRENCH IN an E. & W. direction on either side of SIXTEEN ROAD. On completion of this operation you will get in touch with Midd'x and take over frontage as far as SIXTEEN ROAD, readjusting posts as necessary.

(3) During operations an Officer will be at your Hd.Qrs at telephone.

(4) Artillery will be firing along GRANDCOURT TRENCH in R.11.c.

(5) After point 85 has been captured and consolidated every effort must be made to locate enemy and ascertain his dispositions and Strength.

(6) Higher Command think it possible that GRANDCOURT TRENCH W. of RAVINE may be unoccupied.

CONTINUED.

(2)

(7) Supporting platoon from REGINA should be made use of as required. B.H.Q. will be informed if they are moved forward from REGINA.

                                Capt.
                                Adjutant.
           11th Bn. Royal Fusiliers.

Addressed to "A" Company. and
    repeated to;- "B" Coy,
                 "C" Coy,
                 "D" Coy,
                 12th Middlesex Regt
    for information.

AFTER ORDERS

(8) ZERO hour will be 8-5.pm.

(9) No papers of importance are to be carried by the raiding party.

<u>SECRET</u> "OPERATION ORDERS" No. 62.
BY
CAPTAIN H.R.MUNDEY
COMMANDING 11TH BN. ROYAL FUSILIERS
10TH FEBRUARY 1917

(1) Battalion will be relieved by 8th East Surrey Regiment tomorrow evening 11th February 1917.

(2) On completion of relief Coys. and Hd.Qrs. will march independently to WELLINGTON HUTS, occupying the same huts and tents as Coys. were accommodated in before.

(3) "B", "C" and "D" Coys. will each send five reliable men who have thoroughly reconnoitred the way to act as Guides to incoming Unit. The Guides for the Left Coy. ("A") will be found by Bn. H.Q. Runners. All Guides will report to the ADJUTANT at Battalion Headquarters at 3-30.pm sharp. The incoming Battalion will have Coys. so arranged so that they arrive in the order in which they are required for posts. On reaching Coy.Hd.Qrs, O.C. "A" and "B" Coys. will have competent Guide ready to lead off sentries to each post.

(4) Lewis Gunners will carry their Guns and Drums to MAP JUNCTION - here two limbered wagons will meet them. The wagons will be at this point at 7-30.pm.

(5) Kits and Baggage in Trenches will be sent to HESSIAN Railhead by 6-30.pm by "A", "B", and "C" Coys. "D" Coys. and Battalion Headquarters Kit will be sent to RIFLE DUMP by 7.pm. The R.S.M. will be in charge at RIFLE DUMP and will see to the safe despatch to KAY DUMP of all kits. Wagons will be at KAY DUMP at 8.pm and will not leave till arrival of R.S.M. Each Coy. and Hd.Qrs will send an Officers Servant to be responsible for their respective kits and stores.

CONTINUED

(2)

(6) Quartermaster will arrange for all blankets, kits, Mess Stores etc., to be at WELLINGTON HUTS before 7.pm, dumped in the Huts by Coys. and Details.

(7) C.Q.M.Sgts., will meet Coys. at the Huts as usual and arrange for hot tea or soup to be issued.

(8) Transport Officer will arrange for a Water Cart to be at Huts as before.   The Limbers which are being sent to KAY DUMP for taking back to Huts kits and stores, will bring up 100 tins of water for the use of the incoming Unit.

(9) The 8th East Surrey Regt will arrange to relieve the KAY DUMP Tramway party during the afternoon, 11th inst with an Officer and a platoon of not less than 24 men.   They should report to 2nd Lieut R.B.Sayer 11th R.Fus at KAY DUMP and take over all duties from him.

(10) Order of relief - Battn.Hd.Qrs, Left Front Coy, Right Front Coy, Counter Attack Coy, Reserve Coy. The first Coy. East Surrey's will arrive approximately at 6-30.pm.

(11) Coys. and Hd.Qrs will forward to Orderly Room by 5-30.pm lists of Stores to be handed over. Proformas attached.   "A" Coy. will despatch a runner with lists as soon as it is dark.

(12) Completion of Relief to be reported to Battn.Hd. Qrs. by code word "SATISFACTORY" - pm.

ACKNOWLEDGE.

Capt.
Adjutant
11th Bn.Royal Fusiliers.

SECRET   "PRELIMINARY OPERATION ORDERS" No.
BY
LIEUT-COLONEL C.C.CARR. D.S.O.
COMMANDING 11TH BN.ROYAL FUSILIERS
14TH FEBRUARY 1917

The Battalion will relieve the 8th East Surrey's
in the line tomorrow and will, on completion, be
holding the Battle frontage.
Dispositions probably:
  "B" Coy.holding the line with one platoon
      in REGINA.
  "D" Coy.two platoons in HESSIAN, two platoons
      in FABECK.
  "A" Coy.MOUQUET FARM.
  "C" Coy.FABECK TRENCH, including the old Battn
      Hd.Qrs Dugout.
Headquarters will be in dugout No.8., the large
Chalk Mound about 400 yards up SUDBURY TRENCH.
The relief will take place about normal time and
Coys will be moving off about 4.pm.
All blankets will be labelled and dumped in the
normal way, on the usual dump by 10.am.
Kits and other stores to be on the dump by 4.pm.
Dress:- Full marching order (including Packs)
Leather Jerkins to be rolled inside the waterproof
sheet and carried on top of the packs.   The
next evening the men will change into battle order,
wearing leather jerkins.   The Packs will be
dumped with Great Coats and all washing and
cleaning kits inside them at some suitable point
before marching up.

                          (Sd.) G.F.J.Cumberlege Capt
                                Adjt.11th Bn.R.Fus.

OPERATIONS AGAINST S.MIRAUMONT TRENCH ON FEBRUARY 17TH 1917 AND THE PART PLAYED BY THE IITH BATTN. ROYAL FUSILIERS

To appreciate the difficulties of communication and passing of orders and messages from Battalion Headquarters to Coys. previous to the attack, the location of Coys. 12 hours before "ZERO" must be considered.

"A" Coy. who were to form the left assaulting Coy were at WELLINGTON HUTS.
"B" Coy. (4th Coy.) were holding the Battle Front.
"C" Coy. (Right assaulting Coy.) were at MOUQUET FARM.
"D" Coy. (3rd Coy.) in HESSIAN and FABECK trenches.

Intercommunication by telephone was practically impossible owing to the congested state of the lines and communication by Runner to the front Coy. was difficult by daylight. Consequently programmes of Barrage - Maps, Aeroplane Photos and the hundred and one orders which necessarily pour in during the last 24 hours, could not be circulated as quickly as we would have liked, and we could hardly ask Company Commanders if every man knew everything there was to know about the attack. Here one must remark that it would be everything if in future operations the line could be held by another unit, probably a Coy. of the 4th Battalion right up till the time when the assaulting Battalion has taken over the line in its Battle positions. The advantages are, I think, obvious.

(1) the troops holding the line cannot be really fresh when the hour for the attack comes.
(2) the difficulties of communication, seeing the Coy Commander and issuing him final instructions, and for the Coy Commander himself his difficulty of getting hold of his Officers and N.C.O's when they are in advanced posts.
(3) The extra labour imposed on a third Coy. carrying dinners, water, rations, stores etc., to the Coy. in the line.

Forming up

The move forward to the forming up positions had to be started very early - the Coy. from WELLINGTON HUTS leaving at 9-45.pm.
Every man had a large hot dinner before starting and carried in his mess tin a bully beef sandwich and a hard boiled egg.
There was very serious congestion at RIFLE DUMP, where the Police control was inadequate and a single line of duck boards insufficient. Consequently there was a block composed of Coy's. moving forward to form up - Coy's. coming back from fatigues,- R.E's - and these of all Brigades of the Division. "C" Coy. narrowly missed being late on account of this. It must be remembered that the night was pitch dark and the duck boards and trenches were getting greasy and slippery. By 5-30.am all Coy's. were reported formed up and ready, but not before they had sustained heavy casualties, especially in the case of the right assaulting Coy. who had three shells land amongst the platoons killing one Officer and a lot of N.C.O's and men. The enemy had quite obviously spotted the attack, for from 4-30.am onwards he kept up a steady bombardment of our forming up lines, and it was especially severe along the GULLY and at OXFORD CIRCUS. Considering these things it was wonderful in what good order the men were formed up. A little before "ZERO HOUR" the enemy's barrage slackened a bit. At "ZERO HOUR" (5-45.am) our barrage opened and the men moved forward - they had been formed up in waves with two sections of the dugout clearing party of the 12th Middlesex Regt., which consisted in all of one Coy. formed up behind each of our waves. The sniping and machine gun fire must have been very heavy if only from the fact that not one of our Coy. officers got further than the wire of GRANDCOURT TRENCH, and of all those that started at "ZERO HOUR" not one was killed or wounded by shells. Throughout the operations it was remarkable the high percentage of men that were hit through the head, shewing beyond a doubt that these Germans who had to meet us were no mean marksmen.
The wire in front of GRANDCOURT TRENCH was found, on the right especially

to be

to be still fairly strong - the wire cutting operations could not have been as effective as had been thought.   The delay in getting through this wire was accountable for a number of casualties, and as already pointed out there were no officers to lead the men beyond this point.   Thenceforward Coy's. were commanded by N.C.O's. "A" Coy by a Corporal, "B" Coy by C.S.M.Fitterer of whose conduct one cannot speak too highly - he took command of the assaulting wave of all the Coy's.from GRANDCOURT TRENCH up to the final objective. "C" Coy. was commanded by Sergeant Berry and "D" Coy by Sergeant Hazell both these N.C.O's did valuable work in reorganising their Coys. By the time BOOM RAVINE was reached the Battalion had diminished very considerably and men of all units were mixed together - 53rd and 54th Brigades and 2nd Division.   C.S.M.Fitterer made efforts to organise a line consisting of men of these various units to make an advance on the final objective.   The line pushed forward sustaining a few casualties from machine gun fire from a N.E.direction.   On reaching S.MIRAUMONT TRENCH the wire was found to be so little cut that it was thought inadvisable to attempt to push through to the trench, so a line of shell holes was occupied.   This must have been at about 8.am and the barrage was of course right away on the approaches from MIRAUMONT.   After this position had been occupied for about half an hour an enemy counter attack from the direction of P.5.central led by an officer was seen to develop and the troops on the right and left began to retire.   C.S.M.Fitterer seeing that he and his men were being left in the air deemed it advisable to withdraw his men.   The right Division continued to retire and were for taking up a line on the N. bank of BOOM RAVINE and along the W.MIRAUMONT ROAD, but a few were rallied and were brought up to the crest about 300 yards N. of BOOM RAVINE.   This was about 9-30.am The Battalion took up a line along the bank in R.10.d. just North of and running parallel to BOOM RAVINE. joining the Suffolks.   Here a position was dug and wire was put out.   This constituted the main line of defence, for the remainder of the day but posts were pushed forward as far as 350 yards ahead of BOOM RAVINE.   The enemy must then have had snipers out in shell holes in front of S.MIRAUMONT TRENCH as in laying out a strong point Lieut Inman R.E. and others of 90th Field Coy were hit from close quarters.   Towards the evening the enemy started to shell BOOM RAVINE, up till then he had kept up a steady fire on the GULLY and the RAVINE and had not shortened his barrage at all.

The reason for the failure to reach the final objective and the lessons to be learnt have been fully dealt with by courts of enquiry and there need therefore be no further remarks added in this account.

An advance on which so many men displayed the greatest gallantry and devotion to duty, it is hard to select particular cases but the following certainly deserve mention in any true account of the fighting C.S.M.Fitterer mentioned frequently in this account is a shining example of a man who takes the lead without question when Officers have become casualties, who reasons coolly and acts promptly whatever the circumstances, and who is looked up to and obeyed promptly by all - he was followed and supported throughout the day by Pte.Winter & Pte Taylor, two gallant Runners.   He had command of the leading waves from GRANDCOURT TRENCH up to the final objective.
C.S.M.Hazell and Sgt.Berry who were commanding Coys.shewed the same qualities and rendered C.S.M. Fitterer the greatest assistance.
Corporal Franklin, a Lewis Gunner, behaved with the greatest coolness throughout the day; and although his guns were firing hard all day he never failed to keep up an ample supply of ammunition. He handled his guns boldly, choosing positions in a way which shewed great skill.
L.Cpl.Morgan, a signaller, when three Runners had been knocked out in the effort to deliver an important message he volunteered and delivered it safely to the Company Commander in spite of the fact that he was blown over by a shell.   Later he was invaluable in helping to rally men of the 2nd Division, he cheered them on and got them into positions under heavy Machine Gun and Rifle fire.   He was then twice hit.
L.Cpl.Butler, a Lewis Gunner, shewed most conspicuous gallantry. He advanced his guns to a very forward position and accounted for a large percentage of the enemy who were endeavouring to counter attack.

"OPERATION ORDERS"
of
LIEUT. COLONEL C.C. CARR. D.S.O.
COMMANDING 11TH BN. ROYAL FUSILIERS.
8TH FEBRUARY, 1917.

No. 60A

1. The Battalion will relieve the 8th Norfolks in the line this afternoon.

2. Reliefs will be carried out in accordance with attached schedule.

3. Box Respirators will be worn at the Alert Position during relief.

4. Completion of all Reliefs will be reported to Battalion Headquarters by Code "O.K." p.m.

5. Platoons will move at 100 yards interval.

6. Lists of Trench Stores taken over will be handed IN to Orderly Room by Runner Post on the morning of the 9th.

7. G.S. Wagons will be sent to Wellington Huts at 2pm to take down Blankets Kits &c. All Blankets will be rolled, tied, labelled, and dumped in front of the Orderly Room nearest the road by 1-30 pm. All Officers Kits, Mess Stores etc. will be ready stacked on the same dump by 2 pm. The Pioneers will furnish the loading parties.

8. Coys and Hd.Qrs. Details will be responsible that their tents and huts are left absolutely clean and that no camp furniture is removed.

9. Guides will be at MOUQUET FARM on the scale of one per Platoon and one for Bn. Hqrs. Beyond REGINA TRENCH the Duck Boards to the Right Coy only will be used. These is the Left Company out of bounds. All traffic to the Left Coy must be via Right Coy Hqrs.

10. Officers Commanding will ensure that every man's feet are rubbed with whale oil before starting for the Trenches. While in the Trenches whale oil will be supplied daily. Putees will not be worn by men in the front trenches, but their socks will be pulled up over their trousers and boots will be fastened loosely. Sentries will be provided with Sandbags filled with straw for putting their legs in. Vide B.O.No.3 of 6th inst.

11. "D" Coy will find all ration carrying parties in the trenches. Parties of over 20 will be under an officer. Rations will go via Wigan Lane as far as REGINA TRENCH.

12. Half the Snipers will be accommodated with front Coys and half with Battalion Hqrs. Lieut. Ashmole will take command of the Snipers for the tour in Trenches.

13. Lewis Gunners will take in their own drums and will relieve with their Coys.

14. The question of dress is left to discretion of Coy Commanders but men of the same Coy must be uniform.

15. Small Advance Parties may be sent after dinners by "O" &.

16. Dinners to-day will be at 12 noon and teas at 3-15 p.m.

17. All water bottles will be filled before moving off.

CONTINUED

WAR DIARY / INTELLIGENCE SUMMARY

Army Form C. 2118

11th Suffolks

Nov 17 [struck through, "March 1917" in red]

17.F (Peake)

Place	Date	Hour	Summary of Events and Information	Remarks and references to Appendices
In tents location between AUTHUILLE and THIEPVAL	10/3/17		Battalion had n.e. of Baths at CRUCIFIX CORNER near AVELUY. Usual training was carried out. D Coy being employed on fatigue. Captain J.A. Hare – Bowers B.S.O. (Brown) commander of A Company.	
"	11/3/17		Battalion carried out training as per programme. C.S.M. O'Brien was at the disposal of Bn. C/S to Coy. receiving instruction in Physical drill & Bayonet fighting. D Coy was employed on fatigues.	
"	12/3/17		Battalion carried out training and each man drew off his pack conforming or blanket at the Quartermasters Stores on account of Bn. going into the line.	
"	13/3/17	7 p.m.	From 7 p.m. onwards Coys moved off at intervals into the line. B Coy took over vats in front hill from 8th Norfolks – A C & D Coys and Battalion Headquarters stationed at MIRAUMONT QUARRY.	
BATTALION IN LINE	14/3/17		Enemy evacuated the LOUPART LINE in front of our section. B Coy. supported by C Coy on their left shoved forward and occupied the LOUPART LINE. D Coy. was pushed forward to RESURRECTION TRENCH (touching Railway). Advanced Bn. Hd Qrs was in Dugouts in RESURRECTION TRENCH. 2nd Lieut H.W. Brookling joined Bn. for duty.	

WAR DIARY
or
INTELLIGENCE SUMMARY

(Erase heading not required.)

Army Form C. 2118

Place	Date	Hour	Summary of Events and Information	Remarks and references to Appendices
IN THE LINE	15/3/17		Battalion remained in position evacuated by the enemy.	
"	16/3/17		Battalion still occupied the LOUPART LINE. The whole time the Bn was in the LOUPART LINE it was very heavily shelled by the enemy.	
"	17/3/17		Battalion held LOUPART LINE and when it was found the enemy had evacuated the BIHUCOURT LINE, Bn moved on and occupied this line.	
"	18/3/17		Enemy still retreating. The Battalion moved on and bivouaced at a point about 1000 yards West of BEHAGNIES and SAPIGNIES.	
"	19/3/17		At midday the Battalion moved on and relieved 1st Kings Regt (2nd Division) taking over posts just in front of MORY. Battalion Hd Qrs was in the ruined village of MORY. A & B Coys were in support at ABBEY C & D Coys held the posts.	
"	20/3/17		Battalion was relieved by 2nd Gordons (Yth Division) and moved out of MORY in small parties at about 3 pm and marched to BIHUCOURT where the Battalion was billeted. During this turn in the line the following casualties occurred:— 2nd Lieut N R Neale — wounded Capt R Batt — killed during R Batt — killed 2nd Lieut Y G Dale — wounded. Y Other Ranks Killed 8 Other Ranks wounded	
BIHUCOURT	21/3/17	10 am	Battalion moved out of BIHUCOURT and marched to KITCHENER HUTS arriving there at about 4.30 pm packs containing one Blanket were picked up at Quayhymartin Stores — AUTHUILLE. Major F C Beal left Bn for 11th SP 2nd Lieut H A Day joined the Battalion.	

WAR DIARY or INTELLIGENCE SUMMARY

Army Form C. 2118

Place	Date	Hour	Summary of Events and Information	Remarks and references to Appendices
KITCHENER HUTS	22/3/17	9am	Battalion, accompanied by Transport moved out of HUTS and marched to HARPONVILLE, arriving there at 3-10 pm. and took over billets. Capt N R Neate rejoined Bn from wounded.	
HARPONVILLE	23/3/17	9.30 am	Battalion marched to VILLERS BOCAGE, accompanied by Transport arriving at 1-45 pm and took over billets.	
VILLERS BOCAGE	24/3/17	1-30 pm	Battalion was due to move by Bus to DURY at 8-30 am but Busses did not arrive till about 1-15 pm. Bn debused just outside DURY at about 3-30 pm. Transport marched independently.	
DURY.	25/3/17		Day spent at DURY.	
DURY.	26/3/17	2am	At 2am Battalion paraded and marched to railhead — BACOUEL. Transport proceeded to railhead independently and moved out of DURY at 1am. Battalion arrived at railhead about 4am and men were served out with hot tea. Owing to late arrival of train Battalion remained around railhead about 16 hours. At 8.30 pm transport and troops were entrained and moved out of BACOUEL at 12 midnight. A Coy moved off by early train in advance of Battalion hasty to get billets fixed up for Remainder of Battalion	

11th R Fus
March 1917

Army Form C. 2118

WAR DIARY
or
INTELLIGENCE SUMMARY
(Erase heading not required.)

Place	Date	Hour	Summary of Events and Information	Remarks and references to Appendices
ON TRAIN.	27/3/17		6.00 A Coy Battalion & transport arrived at BURGUETTE and detrained. Hot tea & a coke was given each man from the Y.M.C.A. canteen. The Battalion accompanied by transport moved off. to THIENNES arriving there at about 11 hrs. and took up Billets.	
THIENNES	28/3/17		Day was spent in cleaning up and making billets comfortable.	

SECRET
URGENT.
PRELIMINARY
"OPERATION ORDERS"
BY
LIEUT-COLONEL G.G.CARR D.S.O.
COMMANDING 11TH BN.ROYAL FUSILIERS
21ST MARCH 1917.

No. 68.

INTENTION. The Battalion will move tomorrow to HARPONVILLE. - probable time of start 8.am. Order of march;- Hd.Qrs, "A", "B", "C", "D" Coy's.

DRESS. Full marching order, - Caps. Steel Helmets to be carried on the pack - Jerkins rolled in mackintosh sheet on top of pack.

BLANKETS. Blankets will be rolled in bundles of ten and labelled in the usual way. They will be dumped in front of the huts nearest the road together with all kits and mess stores and Hd.Qr. Cooking equipment at 7-30.am. The Hd.Qr. Cooking equipment and Hd.Qr.Officers Kits will go on the especially detailed Limber.

SANITATION. Before leaving Camp the Sanitary Corporal will see that all Latrines are clean and in a fit condition to hand over. All huts and lines must be left scrupulously clean and an Officer from each Coy will report his lines clean or otherwise to the Adjutant before his Coy moves off. Immediately on arrival at destination Latrines must be reconnoitred and dug where they are deficient. All ranks must be warned where they are situated. This is a standing order for all moves.

DETAIL. Details in Battalion Orders of tonight is cancelled and the following substituted:- Reveille 5-45.am Breakfast 6-30.am Sick Parade 6-45.am. Dinners will be eaten on arrival. Haversack Ration will be carried.

TRANSPORT. One Limber, Maltese Cart, Mess Cart, Horses for Cookers will be at Camp by 7-15.am.

Starting Point and exact times for passing it will be notified as soon as received.- also particulars of advance party. The Advance party will be under 2nd Lieut G.S.Pearcy and will consist of 4 C.Q.M.Sgts and Cpl.Farley and a representative of the transport.

ACKNOWLEDGE.

(SIGNED) G.F.J.CUMBERLEGE CAPT.
ADJUTANT 11TH BN.ROYAL FUSILIERS.

COPIES TO:- All Coy Commanders
Medical Officer
Quartermaster
Transport Officer
Adjutant.
R.S.M.
O.C.Hd.Qr.Details.
Spare.
War Diary.

"PRELIMINARY OPERATION ORDERS" No. 59
BY
LIEUT COLONEL G.C. CARR D.S.O.
COMMANDING 11TH BN. ROYAL FUSILIERS
22ND MARCH, 1917

ATTENTION. The Battalion will move tomorrow to VILLERS BOCAGE via TOUTENCOURT, HERISSART, RUBEMPRE. (distance about 9 miles). Hour of start will be at 9-30.am

ADVANCED PARTY. The usual advanced party consisting of 4 C.Q.M.Sgts, Cpl. Farley and representative of Transport under 2nd Lieut. G.S. Pearcy will report to Town Major at VILLERS BOCAGE at 9.am. for particulars of billets allotted to Battalion. This party will parade at Orderly Room at 7 am.

ORDER OF MARCH. Headquarters, "B" Coy, Drums, "C" Coy, "D" Coy, "A" Coy, Police, 1st Line Transport. To be formed up ready to march off by 9-15.am. Head of column at the W. end of the village by the Church facing W. towards TOUTENCOURT.

DRESS As for today. Coy's must be most carefully inspected before moving off to see that all men are properly dressed and clean and that no extra gear is being carried.

COACH. Blankets, Stores etc. to be at Q.M.Stores by 8.am Transport Officer will arrange for a Limber to take Hd.Qrs and "B" Coy's cooking utensils and Hd.Qr.Officers kits. The Mess Cart and Maltese Cart will report to Q.Qr.Mess and Medical Inspection Room respectively at 8-30.am. Officers Chargers will be round at 9.am.

SANITATION. Vide Standing Orders" in last nights Operation Orders. Coy on duty will leave behind a party consisting of 1 Cpl and 6 men who will be responsible that no billets are left dirty. This does not absolve Coy's of the responsibility that their billets are left scrupulously clean.

ADVANCED DETACHMENT. Coy Commanders and O.C.Hd.Qr.Details will instruct all men who fell out on the line of march today to report to the Orderly Officer at Battalion Headquarters at 6-15.am. The Orderly Officer will march this party at this hour to VILLERS BOCAGE.

DETAIL Reveille:- 6-15.am Breakfast:- 7.am Sick Parade:- 7-30.am The Medical Officer will arrange to see first those men who are proceeding with the advanced detachment

FALLING OUT STATE. Coy's will send a list to Orderly Room directly the Battalion has arrived by march in a new Billeting Area, of men who have fallen out, stating whether they fell out with or without permission.

(SIGNED) G.F.J. CUMBERLEGE CAPT.
ADJUTANT 11TH BN. ROYAL FUSILIERS.

"WARNING ORDER"
BY
LIEUT-COLONEL C.C.CARR D.S.O.
COMMANDING 11TH BN. ROYAL FUSILIERS
23RD MARCH 1917.

INTENTION.   The Battalion will embuss tomorrow at about 11.a.m and
                proceed to an area South of AMIENS.   1st Line Transport
                will probably leave at 10.a.m.   Coys. will send to
                Orderly Room not later than 7.p.m this evening a state
                showing numbers to be taken on Busses.

DRESS.   Full marching order.   Jerkins to be worn, one blanket
                to be carried folded under the arm, the other to be folded
                flat and carried under the pack straps.   All Blankets
                surplus to the two per man will be rolled and sent to
                Q.M.Stores together with Mess Stores and Kit before 9.a.m.

TRANSPORT.   Maltese Cart, and Mess Cart will report to Medical Inspection
                Room and Hd.Qr. Mess respectively at 9.a.m.   The usual
                Limber will be detailed to carry cooking equipment of "B"
                Coy and Hd.Qrs and will report at the same hour.

RATIONS   All tomorrows Rations will be issued under Coy arrangements
                before embussing.   Tomorrow's rations will consist
                wholly of preserved meat and biscuits.   Dinners will be
                eaten on Busses.

WATER   All waterbottles must be filled before leaving.
BOTTLES.

                            (SIGNED)   C.W.J.NUMBERLSON   CAPT.
                            ADJUTANT 11TH BN. ROYAL FUSILIERS.

"OPERATION ORDERS" No. ...

LIEUT-COLONEL C.L. CAMP D.S.O.
COMMANDING 11TH R. ROYAL FUSILIERS
24TH MARCH 1917.

The Battalion will move today by Busses to DURY
Coy's will be formed up in the order:-
            Headquarters & Drums.
                "C" Coy
                "D" Coy
                "A" Coy
                "B" Coy
on the E. side of the AMIENS-TALMAS Road facing S. - Head
of the column being just W. of the MONTONVILLERS-VILLERS
BOCAGE Road.
Each Coy will detail 1 Officer and 4 N.C.O's (1 per platoon)
to report to Staff Captain 54th Bde at Cross Roads at ... and
VILLERS BOCAGE at 11-30.am. These parties will take
over their allotment of Busses and guide their platoons
to them.   Hd.Qrs will detail 1 Sgt and 5 O.R's and will
be grouped in parties of 25 prior to embussment.
Busses will hold 25 men and converted lorries 20 men.
On reaching position before embussment the men will be
fallen out clear of the road till road till their guides
arrive.

DRESS.   Packs must be worn slung so that men can remove them easily
             when in the Busses.   Great Coats XXXXX and Jerkins will
             be worn - One Blanket carried in Pack and one carried
             folded over the arm.

BAGGAGE.   Owing to Transport starting earlier than previously arranged
             Kits and Stores will be sent to Quartermaster Stores by 8-30
             All Blankets surplus to the 2 per man carried will be at
             Stores by 8-30.am.

SICK   Motor Ambulance for conveyance of nursing sick will report
             at Bn.Hd.Qrs at 11.am.

RATIONS
REFILLING   Refilling will take place at 8-30.am at same place as
POINT.   yesterday.

TRANSPORT   Transport will march at 9-15.am starting point ... Junction of
             BERTANGLES - VILLERS BOCAGE and TALMAS-AMIENS Roads Route
             BERTANGLES thence to FLESSELLES - AMIENS Road - Road ...
             ... of CITADELLE through Western outskirts of AMIENS.

ADVANCED   Advanced Party consisting of Lieut.D.H.Faller, 4 C.Q.M.S.
PARTY.   and Cpl.Farley will report to 2nd.Lieut.Waddy at the Church
             DURY at 10-30.am.   This party must proceed on bicycles
             as the roads are 1st class.   They will report to XXX
             D.A.A. ... at Orders Room at 7-30.am.

                              (SIGNED) G.F.J.CHAMBERLAIN, CAPT.
                              ADJUTANT 11TH ROYAL FUSILIERS

WAR DIARY
or
INTELLIGENCE SUMMARY.

Army Form C. 2118.

11th Royal Fusiliers
April 1917.

Place	Date	Hour	Summary of Events and Information	Remarks and references to Appendices
THIENNES	29/3/17 to 9/4/17		This period was devoted to refitting men, Bathing, Equipment repairing, &c. Training was carried out according to programme laid down, which constituted Coy drill, Platoon drill, Bayonet fighting, Extended Order drill, Inspections, Lectures, early morning Physical & Running drill. Parade hours 7-15am – 3-15pm. Sports were organised – Football, Boxing, Running. Bde Transport show and Divisional Transport Show. D. Coy cooker took 1st prize in Bde Show and 2nd prize in Divisional show. Capt. G. Davison-Brown and 2nd Lieut W Thomas joined Bn 1/4/17. 2nd Lieuts A M Gray and Blakemore Dawson joined Bn on duty 5/4/17. 2nd Lieuts GS Beagley and EAN Rogers joined Bn on duty 28/3/17. Major A E Sulman assumed 2nd in Command. Br. Genl. Clonel Jacob, KCB, Commanding, Inspected the Battalion on Church Parade	

[signatures]
Capt.
a/Lt. Col.
11th Bn Royal Fusiliers

WAR DIARY
INTELLIGENCE SUMMARY

11th (Service) Bn Royal Fusiliers — Army Form C. 2118

18. F.
(1 sheet)

Place	Date	Hour	Summary of Events and Information	Remarks and references to Appendices
THIENNES MAP. REFCE FRANCE Sheet 36A Edition 6. 1/40000 T 15, 16, 21, 22.	1917 April 9th to 20th		The Battalion during this period was in reserve to the L. of C. under the administrative instructions of the 1st Army. The period was devoted to General Training which included:- Early morning running and Physical training; Section, Platoon & Company Drill; Extended order drill; Gas Helmet drill; Bombing; Musketry and firing on the range; Route marches; Attack in open formation; Simple Tactical schemes and in outposts, Advanced Guards, attacks on strong points were carried out. Lectures were frequently given by Platoon and Company Officers. On April 12th 1917 the Platoons of the Battalion were organized in accordance with the requirements of "Instructions for Training Platoons for Offensive Action 1917." When this new organization was completed Brigadier General C. Coolidge Owen; C.B. inspected the Battalion paraded in this new formation. The Lewis Gun Sections were inspected by drills and instructed in the use and handling of the Lewis gun and on April 13/1917 the O.C. 54th Machine Gun Coy tested the teams and pronounced the A. Coy teams to be the best. Officers, N.C.O's and men were sent to various schools for instruction in General Musketry; Bombing; Lewis gun; Anti Gas &c.	

WAR DIARY or INTELLIGENCE SUMMARY

Army Form C. 2118

11th (Service) Bn Royal Fusiliers

(Erase heading not required.)

Instructions regarding War Diaries and Intelligence Summaries are contained in F.S. Regs., Part II. and the Staff Manual respectively. Title Pages will be prepared in manuscript.

Place	Date	Hour	Summary of Events and Information	Remarks and references to Appendices
THIENNES Map Ref^{ce} FRANCE. Sheet 36 A Edition b 1/40000. I.15.16 21.22.	1917 Sept 9th to 20th.		The Battalion bathed on various dates, at the Divisional Baths at AIRE. Church Parades; Concerts; Boxing Competitions and Inter Company Football matches were arranged. A canteen was also established. The Battalion ran an unsuccessful team of 20 men in a 10 mile cross country relay race organized by the Division. A riding class for Junior Officers was instituted. At the Divisional Sports held at AIRE for the "Bois Leven out Competition" the Battalion was awarded 2nd prize for a Pack Animal. Between these dates the weather varied from cold winds and snow to mild warm sunny days — rain falling mainly on some days. The inhabitants were accidentally kind to the battalion doing all they could to make the troops as comfortable and happy as possible. Some Officers availed themselves of the privilege of leave to Paris during this period a scheme for the issuing and recovery of waste fat from the cookhouses was initiated. The fat, thus collected being sent to D.A.D.D.S. 18th Division; and is used for munition making. On April 11th a Court of Enquiry sat to enquire into the death of No 15401 Pte F. LONG who was shot during the practice of Rapid Loading. Pte F.LONG was buried in AIRE churchyard with military Honours April 11th 1917.	

1875 Wt. W593/826 1,000,000 4/15 J.B.C. & A. A.D.S.S./Forms/C. 2118.

WAR DIARY
or
INTELLIGENCE SUMMARY

(Erase heading not required.)

Army Form C. 2118

11th (Service) Bn. Royal Fusiliers

Place	Date	Hour	Summary of Events and Information	Remarks and references to Appendices
THIENNES 1917 MAPREFCE FRANCE Sheet 36A Edition 6 48000 I.15.16. 21.22.	Apl 9	1	Promotions:- Captain D.A. HARE-BOWERS, D.S.O. to be MAJOR. 2nd/Lieut H.M. GRAY. to be LIEUTENANT.	
	Apl 12		110R Reinforcements (authority 18th Division N° 8/188 "A" d/9-4-17) arrived	
	Apl 15		Lieutenant B. ASHMOLE to be CAPTAIN. 2nd/Lieut G. DEKIN " " LIEUTENANT. 9 O.Rs Reinforcement joined Battalion	
	Apl 13		AWARDS & DECORATIONS. The MILITARY MEDAL awarded to:- N° 9701. Cpl. W. WHARE. B. Coy. 7801. L/Cpl. E. CARROL. C. Coy. 7248. L/Cpl. T. WATSON. D. Coy.	
	Apl 19		The MILITARY CROSS awarded to:- Captain N.R. NEATE. B. Coy 2nd Lieut E.L. JONES. C. Coy	
	Apl 16		Captain G.A FRANKS joined for duty and was posted to D. Coy.	
	Apl 18		8 O.Rs Reinforcements joined Battalion	

WAR DIARY
or
INTELLIGENCE SUMMARY

11th (Service) Bn Royal Fusiliers

Army Form C. 2118

(Erase heading not required.)

Place	Date	Hour	Summary of Events and Information	Remarks and references to Appendices
MOVING by ROAD	1917 Apr 20		The battalion moved from THIENNES to LE CORNET BOURDOIS and LA MIQUELLERIE (MAP REF C.E. Sheet. FRANCE. 36A. Edin 4 40000.) O 28. 29. 30. 34. 35. 36. March route via GUARBECQUE.	
LE. CORNET BOURDOIS to LA MIQUELLERIE	from Apr 20 To Apr 26.		The Battalion (less B, C & D Coys) billeted in LA MIQUELLERIE and B, C & D Coys in LE CORNET BOURDOIS. During this period General Training was carried out. 22 O.R. Reinforcement arrived on 22nd April 1917. , 25th , 15 O.R.	
MARCH by ROAD	Apr 26		The Battalion marched from LE CORNET BOURDOIS and LA MIQUELLERIE to the PERNES AREA. The route was via LILLERS and PERNES to MAREST where the battalion less A & B Coy billeted for the night. A Coy being at NOYELLES and B Coy at GRICOURT.	
on rail	Apr 27		The Battalion marched to PERNES station to entrain but on arrival it was found that an engine was derailed. It was decided for the battn to march via BOURS and VALHUON to BRYAS STATION	

WAR DIARY
or
INTELLIGENCE SUMMARY.

Army Form C. 2118.

11th (Service) Bn. Royal Fusiliers

Place	Date	Hour	Summary of Events and Information	Remarks and references to Appendices
On rail	1917 Apr 27	—	entraining therefor ARRAS which was reached about 5:30 pm. Here they were ordered to march to NEUVILLE VITASSE (Mapref. France Sheet 51B. S.W. Edition 4A. ½000) N 20 A. Here the battalion bivouacked in the trenches of the HINDENBURG LINE for the night. The transport proceeded from MAREST to between BEAURAINS and NEUVILLE VITASSE (about same map ref.) M 18 central by road.	
NEUVILLE VITASSE	Apr 28		This day was spent in inspection of equipment & parades. During the night 29/30 April the Battalion proceeded to the trenches taking over from the Manchester Regt. The battalion (less two Coys. viz C & D) occupied trenches (Mapref. France Sheet 51B S.W. Edition 4A. ½000) N 29 D – headquarters being N 29 D 3.4. C & D Coys occupied trenches in N 30 C (about) 452-157. The Battalion was in support to the 62 NORTHANTS who held the front line.	

OPERATION ORDER NO. 81.

1. In continuation of telephone conversation &c. 54th Brigade will move to FERNES area to-day, entraining to-morrow.

2. Coys should arrange for dinners to be not later than 12 noon.

3. Lewis Gun limbers will be sent one for "A" & "B" Coys, one for "C" & "D" Coys at Zero - 1½ hours, reporting at their respective Hd.Qrs. These will be packed under the supervision of Sgts. Franklin and Diamond respectively. The handcarts will be taken exactly as on the march to this area from THIENNES. The pack cobs will be sent by the Transport Officer to Coy's Hd.Qrs. at Zero - 1 hour after being loaded with S.A.A. at Q.M.Stores. Distribution of handcarts "A" Coy 1, "B" Coy 2, "C" Coy 2, "D" Coy 1.

4. Dress. Full marching order, steel helmets will be worn, caps carried peaks uppermost on back of packs. Waterproof sheets will be folded under the flap of the pack in the way they used to be carried.

5. Baggage will be collected by G.S. wagons. Coys will make dumps beside the road by their Coy Hd.Qrs. so as to facilitate loading. Baggage to be ready by Zero - 1 hour.

6. The following will report at Q.M.Stores at 1 p.m. to-day :-

   "A" Coy.
   No.1909 Pte.Covell T.

   "B" Coy.
   No.51801 Pte.Baker

   "C" Coy.
   No.60380 Pte.Oliver F.

   "D" Coy.
   No.5464 Pte.Ward H.C.
   51852 Pte.Brown J.S.

   They will be used as loading party.

7. Time and starting point will be notified as soon as possible.

8. An Officer of each Coy will be kept near the phone.

26-4-17.

(SIGNED) G.F.J.CUMBERLEGE CAPTAIN.
ADJUTANT 11TH BN. ROYAL FUSILIERS.

11th (S) Bn
Royal Fusiliers.

May 1917.

WAR DIARY
or
INTELLIGENCE SUMMARY.

Army Form C. 2118.

Place	Date	Hour	Summary of Events and Information	Remarks and references to Appendices
In the TRENCHES	Apl 29 to May 1.		The battalion occupied the trenches mentioned above. Trenches were deepened and "cubby-holes" made. Parties were made detailed to bury bodies lying about. The Lewis Gunners in shellholes spots carried on with practice and instruction. During this period although subjected to shelling only one (wounded) casualty was suffered.	
	May 1/2nd	PM 8+ onwards	The battalion was relieved by the BEDFORD and MIDDLESEX Regts and proceed to bivouac at NEUVILLE VITASSE (same map refer. as above)	
NEUVILLE VITASSE	2nd		Day spent in explaining to the Battalion details re. the attack planned for the early morning of May 3rd 1917.	

Army Form C. 2118.

11th (Service) Bn. Royal Fusiliers

WAR DIARY
or
INTELLIGENCE SUMMARY

(Erase heading not required.)

Instructions regarding War Diaries and Intelligence Summaries are contained in F.S. Regs., Part II. and the Staff Manual respectively. Title pages will be prepared in manuscript.

Place	Date	Hour	Summary of Events and Information	Remarks and references to Appendices
In the Trenches	1917 May 3	A.M. 3.45	The object being to capture the village of CHERISY (O.26.+O.32) and establish itself on the open to the East of that village. The objectives of the Brigade were:— 1st objective:— a line running from U.3.a.2.5. to O.33.d.O.5.90½ known as the Blue Line 2nd objective:— a line running from U.4.c.30.25. to O.34.c. 50. 20. known as the Red Line. The advance was to be made from a line running from O.31.a.95.25. to O.25.c.9.3. which was known as the Brown Line. The dividing line between the 73rd Brigade [?] the 12th Middlesex was a straight line drawn from O.31.d.50.75. to U.4.a.00.50. The dividing line between the 54th Bde and the 5/5th Lond (which was on [?] left [?]) was a line drawn from O.25.d.9.5.30.———————— to O.34.c.5.2. and between the 54th Bde and the 110 Bde on the right was a line drawn from O.31.A.95.2.0. to U.4.C.4.2. The role of the 11th Royal Fusiliers.— Two Coys to move forward and occupy original British front line as soon as the Blue line has been captured by the two assaulting Battalions. The whole battalion plus the Carrying Company (A) will eventually concentrate approximately on the line of the railway which runs North and South through O.32.d.81 until held stage, or ready to support the assaulting battalions is required. The 11th R.F. will detail parties for Provost, Rescue, and two regimental aid posts to be on duty at the Brigade assembly posts for prisoners at N.29.6.8.0. Parties in to form prisoners into batches of 20 and forward them under escort to Advanced Division Cage at N.24.5.7.4. —————— At 3.45 AM (it was dark and a mist overhang the ground) which was Zero Hour the barrage opened and the [crossed out] assaulting troops moved forward. Owing to the darkness division was lost, the Bn began swerving	

A 534   Wt. W4973 M637 750,000 8/16 D. D. & L. Ltd. Forms/C.2118/13.

WAR DIARY or INTELLIGENCE SUMMARY.

Army Form C. 2118.

11th (Service) Bn Royal Fusiliers

Place	Date	Hour	Summary of Events and Information	Remarks and references to Appendices
In the TRENCHES.	1917 May 2nd	9 p.m. onwards	The Battalion proceeded to the trenches preparatory to carrying out its battle role. The journey up was uneventful except that in the valley S.20.c (german sheet) there was gas which necessitated the putting on of gas helmets for a short distance. Major A.C. Sulivan MC acted as Liason Officer between Bde and 11th R.F. Dispositions of the Battalion:— (M.P Officer: Sheet ETERPIGNY. Edition 5F. Zurdo. Special Sheet Pont y Ognes 5. NW. NE and SW, SE)	
	MAY 3rd	A.M. 3.45	At Brig. on N.30.d.04. A. Coy = Carrying party detailed to R.E. for moving forward Brigade dump as much the bulk of the 52nd Brigade bombing material. B. Coy = This company was attached to and under the command of O.C. 12th Middlesex Regt to be used by them as dig out cleaning parties. C. Coy was distributed in trenches at about N.30.c and other available trenches close to, but in front of these. D. Coy (less two platoons) distributed as "C" Coy. The two platoons of D Coy (Nos 13. & 15.) were attached to and under the command ? The O.C. 7th Bedfort R.F. to be used for him as dig out cleaning parties. The 7th Bedfords line Regt occupied the right sector of the Brigade front from O.31.a.95.20 to O.31.6.45.70. The 12th Middlesex occupied the left sector from O.31.6.45.70 to O.25.c.d.95.30. The 11th Royal Fusiliers (less B Coy and the two platoons of D Coy and A Coy) was in support to the Bedford & Middlesex Regts. The 6th Normands being in reserve. C. Coy being on the night D Coy on the night	

WAR DIARY
or
INTELLIGENCE SUMMARY.

(Erase heading not required.)

11th (Service) Bn Royal Fusiliers Army Form C. 2118.

Instructions regarding War Diaries and Intelligence Summaries are contained in F.S. Regs. Part II. and the Staff Manual respectively. Title pages will be prepared in manuscript.

Place	Date	Hour	Summary of Events and Information	Remarks and references to Appendices
In the TRENCHES	1917 May 3	AM 3.45 to 12 mid- night	to the right and the middle, 2 to the left. The two platoons of D. Coy & one of B. Coy formed the Bedfords and when they were held up by machine guns and snipers took refuge in shell holes where they lay the whole day and returned to BATTn. Hdqrs when it was dark at night. B. Coy followed the 11th Cheshires and parties of those were reported as being seen on the Eastside of CHERISY. Parties of B. Coy & those returned after dark to Battn Hd Qrs. The attack of the 54th Brigade was held up chiefly owing to FONTAINE TRENCH (which runs in O.32.A & b.) not being taken. At 9.A.M. Lt. Col Carr D.S.O. (who had been placed in command of the 11th R.F. to that advance and the 6th Northants) decided to send forward O Coy of the 11th R.F. to make an advance in open formation on FONTAINE TRENCH. The Coy advanced but was held up by heavy machine gun fire after proceeding about 200 yards and had to retire after losing several men. A general retirement along the whole line took place about 10 A.M. but this was checked and the original British front line between our original front-line and the enemy trenches it was decided to reoccupy by our troops. As there was a great number of our troops lying out between our original front-line and the enemy trenches it was decided to make an attack at 6.15 pm on FONTAINE TRENCH as that the men lying out might be relieved. The C & D Coy's were detailed to carry out this operation and they relieved the C & D Coy (less 2 platoons) of the 11th R.F. Those two Coys formed Strongpoints (in O.31.a) on the night of the 6th Northants. During the day A. Coy were used to carry Ammunition rations to Battn Hdqrs. During the night 3/4th May 1917 several parties from 13 & 10 Corps returned to Battn Hdqrs.	
	4th	6 to 10pm	Held same positions as yesterday. Rehoboam quiet with intermittent shelling. 11th R.F. evacuated their positions under Brigade orders and returned to their Rendezvous at NEUVILLE VITASSE	

Army Form C. 2118.

WAR DIARY
or
INTELLIGENCE SUMMARY.
(Erase heading not required)

11th (Service) Bn Royal Fusiliers

Instructions regarding War Diaries and Intelligence Summaries are contained in F. S. Regs., Part II. and the Staff Manual respectively. Title pages will be prepared in manuscript.

Place	Date	Hour	Summary of Events and Information	Remarks and references to Appendices
NEUVILLE VITASSE	1917 May 5 to May 9		The total casualties suffered during the last three days (May 2, 3rd & 4th) were:- Killed Officers 2. Other ranks 10. (B.Coy & advance/when officers shot at point-Missing " 3. " 32. blank range) Wounded " 2. " 74. (in the main attack) Many of these killed:- 2nd/Lt C. Corder 2nd/Lt F.C. Randon " " Missing - Capt W.N.R. Nealer M.C. 2nd/Lt W.F. Are 2nd/Lt H Paris " " Wounded Capt H.R. Munday. 2nd/Lt- W M many ogr.	
Do	May 5 May 5th		During this period detachment of several having arrived the Company recognised the Battalion. The Batt. bathed at the divisional Baths in NEUVILLE VITASSE.	
	May 6		A Coy beginning was tied to engineers extending men of the B. who were taken to the front lines tunnel at the Transport lines.	
	May 7th night 6/7		The Bn was engaged in digging a communication trench from HENIN to the front line whilst doing this Capt N.B. MITCHELL was wounded.	
	May 8		Lieut D.M. FULLER Transferred from C Coy to command B. Coy. " " " " B " " " D. Coy " " " " A " " " C. Coy	
Do	May 8/9 night		Battalion provided fatigue and carrying parties to the Royal Engineer Pioneers	

Army Form C. 2118.

1st Bn Scots Guards

WAR DIARY
or
INTELLIGENCE SUMMARY.

(Erase heading not required.)

May 1917

Place	Date	Hour	Summary of Events and Information	Remarks and references to Appendices
NEUVILLE VITASSE	1917 May 10th to 12th		The battalion during these three days provided working parties at night and rested during the morning, carrying on with general training during the afternoon.	
HENIN-SUR-COJUEL (Map Ref. FRANCE 51B SW Edition 4A N31d & N32c)	May 13th to June 1		The battalion moved during the day to new quarters at HENIN-SUR-COJUEL. The greater part of the day was spent in making "bivvies" for men as here quarters consisted only of the old German line running thro' N31d & 32b.

Between these dates (May 13 + June 1 – inclusive) the Brigade was the Brigade in support. On alternate nights working and fatigue parties were found for digging – carrying stores & RE material in the front line. During the day similar training to that carried on at NEUVILLE VITASSE, took place. Brigade Schemes, including attack defence of position) were engaged in. Competitions in WIRING, between coy parties, carried out in the dark resulted in B + D coys being equal. – Shooting on the | |

Army Form C. 2118.

WAR DIARY
or
INTELLIGENCE SUMMARY.
(Erase heading not required.)

Place	Date	Hour	Summary of Events and Information	Remarks and references to Appendices
HENIN SUR COJUEL	1917 May 13 to June 1		Range near the camp. Patrol work at night — wire above fences. The training — Rifle bombing shooting was also carried out. On various days reconnaissances of the front line took place.	
	May 18		A.F.G.C.M. was held in the camp to try certain men of the [Brigade] who left the front line on May 3rd/1917 and reported to the various battalion transport lines.	
	19		A Boche aeroplane flew over the camp lines, at a very low altitude — our Lewis guns and rifles were fired at it as it passed down the camp.	
	24		This day Battalion Sports were held — races of a humorous nature predominated and provided much merriment.	
June 1			General training and aerial reconnaissance of the line prior to taking it over.	

Army Form C. 2118.

WAR DIARY
or
INTELLIGENCE SUMMARY.
(Erase heading not required.)

Instructions regarding War Diaries and Intelligence Summaries are contained in F. S. Regs. Part II. and the Staff Manual respectively. Title pages will be prepared in manuscript.

Place	Date	Hour	Summary of Events and Information	Remarks and references to Appendices
HENIN SUR COJEUL	1917 May 18		The Military Cross was awarded to Lieut. D.M. FULLER.	
	29		Lieut. O.C. Whitman rejoined the Battalion from the Brigade and on May 20/1917 undertook the duties of Adjutant to the Battalion. Lieut E.H. Cliffe (wounded 26.3/1917 at BOOM RAVINE) rejoined the Battalion from England and Lts:- E.W. Ede (To A Coy) V. Haddon (to B Coy) J. Long (To C Coy) H.J. Sanson & W.A. Smith (to D Coy) joined the Battalion.	
	30		Lieut G. Sefton and Lieut H.M. Gray were authorised to wear the badges & rank of Temporary Captains.	
In the line	June 2		The Battalion relieved the EAST SURREY (8th Bn) in the line during the afternoon and evening. Companies took up the following dispositions:— Battalion Headquarters. In the HINDENBURG (SUPPORT) LINE. T.5.6.37. A. Coy. BROWN TRENCH — posts in TANK TRENCH & BUSH TRENCH. B. Coy PUG LANE with posts = farthest point being at - U.16.b.3.5. C.) Coy HINDENBURGH } from PUG LANE to U.16.d.5.60. D. } (SUPPORT) LINE } (T.6.b.10.2.5.) All the 4 Coys (A.B.C. + D.) held their areas by posts garrisoned by Lewis Guns.	
MAP REFCE BULLECOURT Edn No. 2 A 1/10000 Sheet-51B SWA	June 3	A.M. 4.30	Posts in BROWN TRENCH were heavily shelled. PUG LANE + BUSH trenches were lightly shelled. Snipping active against our posts. Communication with flank battalions established.	
-do-	4		Shelling continued general throughout the day with very light intervals, over all our snipping with rifle machine guns on our line by enemy during the day. line	

A5834. Wt. W.4473 M687 750,000 8/16 D.D. & L. Ltd. Forms/C.2118/13.

11TH BN. ROYAL FUSILIERS

Ref. Map
Sh. 1. N.W.
Edit. 4a.
STEENWERCK.
Edit. 5m.
(Specially marked)

WARNING ORDERS   No.

1. The Battalion will move this evening to its Battle position in support.
    "C" and "D" Coy's will be distributed in trenches at about N.30.d. and other available trenches close to, but in front of these trenches. Battalion Headquarters at N.30.d.O.4. - in small copse not marked on map.
    "B" Coy - 2 platoons attached to and under the Command of O.C.12th Midd'x. Regt.
          2   "   "   "   "   "   "   O.C. 7th Bed'f. Regt.
    "A" Coy Will be used for moving forward Brigade Dumps under the orders of 54th Brigade Bombing Officer – orders for them will be issued later.

2. Coy's and Hd.Qrs will move forward this evening in "Battle Order" with waterproof sheets rolled on belts. Greatcoats will not be taken. Coy's will be in possession of all extra bandoliers, Grenades, Tools, Sandbags, Very Pistols and other equipment for battle.

3. Rations for tomorrow will be distributed before moving off and will be carried in the Mess Tin. All waterbottles will be filled. The Qr.Mr. will arrange for 5 IMPL petrol tins full of water per Coy and Hd.Qrs to be dumped by the Cookhouse at N.29.Central. These will be picked up by Coy's etc., on their way up to the line tonight, and will be used for refilling waterbottles before "Zero" hour.

4. All Blankets and Packs will be dumped by the road as early as possible this afternoon. The Blankets will be tied into bundles of ten and labelled. Men should be warned to put into their packs all articles of special value.

5. Lewis Guns and 20 Drums per Gun will be loaded on to one Limbered Wagon under the supervision of Sgt Franklin. Approximate hour of arrival 7.30.pm. The Wagon will be off loaded at the Cookhouse at N.29.Central and Guns and Drums will be carried forward from this point by Coy's. "A" Coy's will be taken to Battalion Headquarters at N.30.d.O.4. and left there under the charge of their Nos.1. N. 2 of each Gun team.

6. Two Wagons for Cooking Utensils, Mess Stores etc will arrive at about 8.30.pm. They must be loaded as soon as they arrive.

7. The following will not go into action:-

	"A" Coy.	"B" Coy	"C" Coy	"D" Coy	Hd.Qrs	Total
N.C.O's	5	5	5	5	-	20
Signallers	6	4	4	4	4	22
Lewis Gunners	1	1	1	1	-	4
Pioneers					5	5
Orderly Room					2	2

The N.C.O's to be left out will be one understudy C.S.M. and one understudy Platoon Sgt per Coy.

8. Box Respirators will be worn in the "ALERT" position.

9. "C" and "D" Coy's will report to Battalion Hd.Qrs (N.30.d.O.4.) as soon as they are in position.

Issued at   PM.   2/6/1917.   (Sd.) G.F.J. Cumberlege   Capt.
                                            Adjutant 11th Bn. Royal Fusiliers.

XXX/7.   OPERATION ORDER NO. 83.

1. The Battalion will move to-morrow to BOIRY BECQUERELLE area. Coys will hold themselves in readiness to move at any time during the morning.

2. The Coy on duty will detail a fatigue of 10 men to report to L/Cpl.Bishop (Pioneer Cpl) at 7 a.m.

3. All buildings shelters &c.,must be taken down by 9 a.m.

4. Men must be once urged to carry any posts whether iron or wood,also any spare canvas sheeting &c.,in fact anything that will assist them in making shelters at the new area.   There will be no shelters at the other end and all ranks will have to make their own protection against weather &c.   If men who have stakes that will be of use in erecting shelters cannot carry them when moving,they will be allowed to fetch them later in the day.   Coy Commanders will see that all tables,benches,chairs &c. are dumped by the Cemetery at 10 a.m.

5. Transport.
       (A) A limber will be at the cross-roads at the Cemetery at 9 a.m.,for the Lewis Guns.   Cpl.Franklin will superintend and be responsible for the loading and re-issue the guns to Coys on arrival at the other end.   Guns must be dumped by 8.45 a.m.
       (B) The Mess Cart will be at the Cemetery at 9 a.m.   Coys will have their Mess Boxes &c ready for loading at that hour on their cook waggons.
       (C) 4 limbered waggons will be at the cemetery for moving tents,orderly room,bath-room,tables,benches,chairs &c. and also officers' kits.   All officers' kits &c must be at the dump by the Cemetery by 10 a.m.
       (D) Horses will report to move Coy Cookers at 9 a.m.

6. DRESS:- Full marching order,steel helmets to be worn,caps carried on the pack, each man will carry his own blanket which must be neatly folded round the pack.

7. If the move is ordered for / the morning dinners will be eaten at the other end.

12-5-17.

ISSUED AT 3.10 p.m.   (SIGNED) G.F.J.CUTHBERIDGE CAPT.
                                                        ADJUTANT 17TH BN. ROYAL FUSILIERS.

CONTINUATION OF OPERATION ORDER No.22.

(1) The Battalion will move to the new Area tomorrow.
 Coy's will move off as under:-

 Headquarters ....10.0. a.m.
 "A" Company........10.15.a.m.
 "B" Company........10.30.a.m.
 "C" Company........10.45.a.m.
 "D" Company........10.45.a.m.

(2) March Route.   Coy's will proceed along the main MESVILLE-VIGNACOURT -
 .... COISUL road until they are met by the Adjutant.
 Map Ref for road:- Map FRANCE 51.D.S.W. Edit.4.A. road running through
 N.12., N.25., and N.22.

(3) All latrines and refuse pits are to be properly filled in before
 Coy's move.

(4) All Coy lines will be left scrupulously clean. Each Coy will
 detail an Officer to inspect the Coy lines and report whether clean
 or otherwise to the Orderly Room before Coy's move off.

(5) Dinners will be eaten on arrival at new Camp.

(6) Sick Parade will be at 6.am.

             (sd)   C.P.J.Cumberlegs Capt.
                    Adjutant 11th Bn.Royal Fusiliers.
12/8/1917.
Issued at 10.30.p.

WAR DIARY
or
INTELLIGENCE SUMMARY

(Erase heading not required.)

Army Form C. 2118.

Place	Date	Hour	Summary of Events and Information	Remarks and references to Appendices
HEBUTERNE IN THE LINE	1917 June 4		General shelling continued all day and night, also snipers with pipe machine gun fire. Great aerial activity. Lachrymatory shells thrown in to our line in Shelp-Trench. A Patrol from "B" Coy under 2nd Lt. ZIMM went out at 10.30pm and 8 units took out the points (from the 6" howitzers) in ROTTEN ROW — The patrol reported that BUSH Trench from U10.89 to U16.45 was not dug. 2nd Lt. J. Sarvis proceeded to YORK SAP to discover enemy movements — but no sign of the enemy was seen.	
	5		Great aerial activity — shelling continued throughout the day. Chiefly from the direction of Vis en Artois & Kyplin Wood. Some small parties of the enemy were observed moving opposite town position. One enemy plane put out two bombs between shaft trench and Fritz Lane — another into our position. Another enemy plane dropped bombs on the same position.	
		AM 5.45		
	6		Aerial activity moderate. Shelling general all day — nightfall Battn HQrs HdQrs shelled. Have never seen any enemy in his back area observed.	
	7		Enemy artillery not so intense as previously. Every machine gun active. A patrol under 2nd Lt. W.A. Smith from "B" Coy proceeded to YORK SAP HEAD — worked down the sap and then N.E. along YORK Trench. The patrol went out with the	

A5834 Wt.W4973 M687 750,000 8/16 D.D.&L.Ltd. Forms/C.2118/13.

WAR DIARY
or
INTELLIGENCE SUMMARY

Army Form C. 2118.

Place	Date	Hour	Summary of Events and Information	Remarks and references to Appendices
Hebuterne	June 7th 92		Intention of capturing a prisoner but no enemy were encountered. Intermittent shelling during the day - nothing special happening. During the period the Battalion has been in the line Carriage work and general improvement and strengthening of the trenches has been carried out. The Casualties suffered have been slightly heavy - one killed - four wounded and two wounded returned to duty.	
"	8/9 "	about midnight 12	The evening had been hot and oppressive and as the afternoon wore on it became darker and darker. Although the moon was up heavy black clouds hung low over the land. The wind was blowing from the North West. It was a night suitable for seeing movement. Every thing was quiet in front. There was no sign of enemy activity. In front on our wire working parties were digging and in their tracks when about midnight and away on our right (in the next division front) a heavy bombardment of the enemy line took place. So thick the enemy replied by putting up this "S.O.S" and gradually this moved up the line until at CHERISY, it was opposite to us. The enemy in reply to this S.O.A. Heavily shelled York Branch - York Sap, and the whole of our front, including our post in BUSH LANE. PUG LANE was subjected to very heavy shelling and also to bombardment by light and heavy trench mortarshells, rifle grenades and incidentally amount of rifle and machine gun fire - all of which came from the direction of FONTAINE WOOD and FONTAINE TRENCH. No battalion headquarters except those on duty, at the PUG LANE first laid down when the signalling commenced reported that the projectiles were being heavily admitted with trench mortar bombs.	

Prepared West Newman & Co., Ltd.
3,584 WT W4973 M687 750,000 8/16 D/D & L Ltd. Forms/C.2118/15.

11th Regt Fusiliers   Army Form C. 2118.

Vol 20

20 F
(past B)

WAR DIARY
or
INTELLIGENCE SUMMARY.
(Erase heading not required.)

Place	Date	Hour	Summary of Events and Information	Remarks and references to Appendices
IN THE LINE Near HENINEL	10/6/17 to 15/6/17		Battalion remained in Brigade Reserve. Headquarters, 'A' and 'B' Coys being in SHAFT TRENCH. 'B' Coy in GREY STREET and 'D' Coy in EPARS COURT, all situated about N.34.d. - Sheet 51.B. S.W. of the village of HENINEL.) No normal artillery activity was kept up of both sides during the whole of this period. Coys found nightly working parties who were occupied in digging a new front line trench.	
RESERVE BDE AREA near BOYELLES	16/6/17		The Battalion was relieved by the 4th Yorkshire Regt (150th Bde 50th Division) and proceeded to the Reserve Brigade Area at S.14. - Sheet 51.B. S.W. - that East of BOYELLES and took over camp previously occupied by 4th Yorks.	
	17/6/17		The day was spent cleaning up ready in the morning. Battalion had the rest of the afternoon swimming Baths at BOIRY-BECQUERELLE.	
	18/6/17	4.45 am	The Battalion accompanied by 1st Line Transport moved to VII Corps Rest Area. At 4.50am the column moved off passing through BOIRY and ADINFER. The Battalion and transport halted on the outskirts of ADINFER WOOD about 9.30 am. Billeting party was sent to MONCHY-AU-BOIS to take over billets for Battalion. The accommodation was found inconvenient and it was decided to march on to the next destination (GAUDIEMPRE) in the evening.	
		5-30 pm	At 5:30pm the Battalion moved off accompanied by transport and passed through MONCHY-AU-BOIS, BIENVILLERS-AU-BOIS, POMMIER. HUMBERCAMP to GAUDIEMPRE arriving at the latter village at about 9-15 pm. Battalion then took over billets which consisted of huts.	
GAUDIEMPRE	19/6/17 to 24/6/17		During the period the Battalion carried out training for warfare. Battalion training was not possible owing to back ground not being available. Coys practice mobility, crossing war of range. Close and open Order Drill, Bayonet fighting, wiring, running and	

WAR DIARY
INTELLIGENCE SUMMARY

Army Form C. 2118.

Place	Date	Hour	Summary of Events and Information	Remarks and references to Appendices
GAUDIEMPRE	19th June 1917 & 2nd July 1917		Physical drill, Platoon drill etc etc. The following Drafts of Officers and Other Ranks joined the Battalion during this period as reinforcements:- 2nd Lieut A acey joined the Battalion on the 19th June 2nd Lieut B G Willet " " " " " " 2nd Lieut P D Bircham " " " " " " 98 Other Ranks joined Battalion on 19th June 1 " " " " " 23rd June 126 " " " " " 1st July The Battalion had three of W.O class of subalterns Both subalterns wore the clothes of Battalion Bath, and clean clothes were provided each & equipment was issued. On the 20th June Lieut-General Sir J.A.O Snow KCB, KCMG commanding VII Corps presented military medal Ribbons & etc unmentioned recipients:- No 8242 Sgt Taylor M "D" Coy No 12225 Sgt Martin S "B" Coy 11453 Sgt Scotton E "B" Coy 9701 Cpl Clare B "B" Coy 7810 Cpl Eanes E "C" Coy 4248 L/C Eaton J "D" Coy 8043 Pte Brown S "D" Coy 4673 Pte Miles J "D" Coy On the 26th June 2nd Lieut Richardson RE gave special instruction in angle wire RE's option laying out and digging Etabs. All Coys had instruction. Classes for NCO's under the R.S.M for instruction in Guard mounting and Guard duties were held daily. On the 23rd June the following officers were appointed 2nd in-Command of Coys 2nd Lieut W Brookling "A" Coy 2nd Lieut J J A Horton "B" Coy 2nd Lieut A acey "B" Coy 2nd Lieut W R Ewing "D" Coy	

Army Form C. 2118.

WAR DIARY
or
INTELLIGENCE SUMMARY.
(Erase heading not required.)

Instructions regarding War Diaries and Intelligence Summaries are contained in F. S. Regs., Part II. and the Staff Manual respectively. Title pages will be prepared in manuscript.

Place	Date	Hour	Summary of Events and Information	Remarks and references to Appendices
GAUDIEMPRE	19/6/17 to 2/7/17		The Medical Officer lectured all Coys and Headquarters on Hygiene. On the 27th June the Battalion was put under a Gas test and Box Respirators were refitted. On the 29th June 2nd Lieut G.H. Stoves was accidentally wounded during bombing practice. A Court of Inquiry was held. 99 a Horton. - Capt H.M. Gray. Members:- 2nd Lt a dly + 2nd Lieut. The neat of the officer who was wounded. Finding of Court was "Lack of precaution on part of the wounded." The following parties and officers were sent on leave during the period:—	
			Lieut-Col. G.G. Barr on 20th June 18 Other Ranks " 20th June 3 " " 27th June 3 " " 28th June 7 " " 2nd July 2nd Lieut E.P. Jones " 27th June Lieut + Q.M. W.S. Minchin " 28th June Major D.A. Hair Bowers " 2nd July 2nd Lieut J.H.R. Creevy " 3rd July	
		6 p.m.	On 2nd July B Company complete with cookers proceeded by march route to DOULLENS North Station and performed the duties of loading party to the 54th Brigade. This Coy moved independently and entrained at DOULLENS at 10 a.m. on the 4th July for GODEWAERSVELDE	
GAUDIEMPRE	3/7/17	7·30 p.m.	The Battalion (less B Coy) and Transport moved out of GAUDIEMPRE and proceeded by march route to DOULLENS via HALTE to DOULLENS- ARRAS Road, POMMIER to DOULLENS' North Station. The Transport went ahead of Column going to having to be at Station three hours before departure of train. The Battalion (less B Coy) arrived at DOULLENS about 11 p.m. The tea	

Army Form C. 2118.

WAR DIARY
or
INTELLIGENCE SUMMARY.
(Erase heading not required.)

Instructions regarding War Diaries and Intelligence Summaries are contained in F. S. Regs., Part II. and the Staff Manual respectively. Title pages will be prepared in manuscript.

Place	Date	Hour	Summary of Events and Information	Remarks and references to Appendices
VICINITY OF BEAUVORDE	5/7/17		Moved to the Battalion in a field near the North Station immediately on its arrival. When tea was finished the Battalion (less B Coy) entrained and moved out of DOULLENS at 2-19am on the 4th July 1917 arriving at GODEWAERSVELD at about 10am on 4th July. The Battalion (less B Coy) marched out of GODEWAERSVELD station and had breakfast on the road side. The Battalion (less B Coy) then marched to billets in the vicinity of BEAUVORDE between STENVOORDE and ABEELE. "B" Coy arrived at GODEWAERSVELD and joined Battalion in the evening of the 4th July 1917.	
BEAUVORDE			Battalion cleaned up and coys were at the disposal of their commanders for training	
"	6/7/17	6-20 pm	At 6-20pm the Battalion accompanied by transport moved by march route to DICKEBUSCH CAMP at M.20.c.9.1. Guides met the 28 Belgium and Inagres where the Battalion were taken over from the 8th East Surrey Regt.	
DICKEBUSCH CAMP	7/7/17		Battalion carried out training or for on wire repairs	
"	8/7/17		A, B & D Coy and two platoons of C Coy were employed on cable burying. Nos 14 platoons left camp at 9.30 - 7.10pm and worked until 2am	
"	9/7/17		Battalion carried out training in the vicinity of Camp.	

Geo. H. Stevens Lieut.
A/Adjt
1/6 Bn Royal Irish Regt

Army Form C. 2118.

WAR DIARY
or
INTELLIGENCE SUMMARY.
(Erase heading not required.)

Place	Date 1917	Hour	Summary of Events and Information	Remarks and references to Appendices
IN THE LINE	June 8/9	About Midnight 12	At the same time that this message was received the sentry at Butts Hot Qrs reported very heavy shelling on the left of our line. With this information the officer on duty woke the Comdg Offr who immediately telephoned to B Coy HQ Post (North Pug Lane). B Company then became the enemy intimated trying to cut out their post at the far end of PUG LANE, and, that, at that moment they were pushing up the L.O.D. In taking this the C.O. on taking this gave orders for the L.O.D. to be sent up. At the same time he (the CO) ordered the Lewis gunners to telephone to Brigade orders to post on the L.O.S. fire. As the red very lights flamed in the enemy darkness of the night warned the artillery gunners open fire; and all around the sky became alight with the blaze of guns firing; and the precious very lights alone with the shells [?] to their objective. Over and above the roar of the guns the rattle of machine guns and rifles heard. Down in the dug out companies were being communicated with by telephone and touch with the situation in front maintained; above the dug out keen watch was kept for any signals. As the barrage opened so were the working parties in no mans land taken back into the trenches and there they manned. ap[?] about 10 minutes barrage the ground post in PUG-LANE reported that enemy activity in their neighbourhood was less. On leaving this the artillery were advised that they could ease down their fire and again resume their normal pace. The working parties did not proceed to their work again but returned to their various quarters. The Royal Indies [?] 'slopt to' the whole night after this affair which ended with only two men being slightly wounded and the forward portion of the Front being blown in: an.	
		9th	Shelling generally below normal. In the afternoon and evening the battalion was relieved by the 12/5 Middlesex Regt. The Battalion went into Brigade Reserve. Bn Hd Qrs A + C Coys being in SHAFT TRENCH. B Coy in GREY STREET. D Coy in EARLS COURT. All arrivals about N.34.d	

[signatures]

ADMINISTRATIVE ORDERS

2ND MAY 1917

1. DUMPS.
   Attached is table shewing contents of Dumps of which there are two
   (a) Brigade Dump. N.29.c.8.2.
   (b) Forward Brigade Dump N.33.b.Central.
   Coy's in need of any of the stores on these Dumps must arrange to send for them themselves.
   After "ZERO" hour these dumps will be moved forward to O.32.c.9.7, in Sunken road and later to O.33.c.8.5.
   Water will be moved forward as soon as possible to O.32.c.9.7.

2. RATIONS
   Each Coy will arrange to send one Guide to Battalion Hd.Qrs at 3.pm to proceed to Brigade Hd.Qrs and guide rations forward to where their Coys and Hd.Qrs are situated.
   The Transport Officer and Quartermaster will report to Staff Captain at Brigade Hd.Qrs at N.33.b.Central after 6.pm to obtain latest information as regards the situation and pick up the guides. The Qr.Mr. must arrange to provide a carrying party from those men he has at the Stores at his disposal.

3. MEDICAL.
   All Stretcher Bearers will be at Battalion Hd.Qrs under the Orders of the Medical Officer. Walking wounded will report to him at Battalion Hd.Qrs, N.30.d.0.4. where the Regimental Aid Post will be situated. Medical Officer will issue necessary instructions to walking wounded the route to be taken.

4. CASUALTY REPORTS.
   These will be reported as usual under two headings (1) Estimated Casualties of Officers and other ranks this return will be accumulative i.e. each report will include the totals of the previous reports until orders are received to begin a new phase. It should if possible give the names of Officers. (2) Accurate Daily Casualty return to be despatched so as to reach Battalion Headquarters at 4.pm. This will give names of Officers and accurate number of men stating whether Killed, Wounded or Missing.

5. BURIAL
   Coy's are responsible for burying all dead in their area as soon as they can possibly do it. Effects to be collected & forwarded to Battalion Headquarters.
   All Ranks are to be warned that any N.C.O. or Man found in unlawful possession of any article taken from Killed or Wounded Comrade will be tried by Field General Court Martial.

(Sd) G.F.J.Cumberlege Capt,
Adjutant 11th Bn.Royal Fusiliers.

WAR DIARY or INTELLIGENCE SUMMARY

Army Form C. 2118.

11th Bn. Royal Fusiliers.

(Erase heading not required.)

Vol 21

Place	Date	Hour	Summary of Events and Information	Remarks and references to Appendices
DICKEBUSCH AREA in Camp (Huts and Tents at H.20.c.9.2.	Period 10th July 17 to 21st July 17		During this period the Battalion was called upon to furnish large working parties, consisting of about 14 platoons - the only nights on which the Battalion did not find these working parties were the 10th, 13th and 19th July 1917. The work done was carrying cable, digging trenches for cable, carrying forward ammunition, Stores &c to forward areas. All these working parties did their tasks at night, consequently very little training was possible. On days when training could be done, Musketry was practiced, Drill Inspections and Organisation was carried out by all Coy's. Owing to clear weather, and the camp being under observation from enemy's balloons, Battalion could not do training on a large scale. Aerial activity was above normal between these dates, and the Lewis Guns, manned by Bn.Lewis Gunners, and posted around the camp, were, on several occasions called upon to deal with enemy planes. The Baths (Hot Shower) at RENINGHELST were used by the Battalion on the 11th and 18th of July 1917, clean clothing i.e. Shirt, pants and Socks, being issued to the men on each occasion. The following reinforcements joined the Battalion for duty during this period:- 80 Other Ranks on the 12th July 1917. and the undermentioned Officers, W.O's, N.C.O's and men were granted Leave;- Lieut.C.E.Wilkin. and 15 Other Ranks. The Divisional Gas Officer inspected all Box Respirators of the Battalion on the 12th July 1917. On the 15th July 1917 the Battalion paraded for Divine Service in the vicinity of the camp. The following casualties occurred during the period Battalion found working parties;- 1 Other Rank - Killed 10 Other Ranks - Wounded. During this period Operation Orders and Administrative Orders were prepared for the forthcoming attack on the enemy's positions. Copies of these orders are attached and are headed "PRELIMINARY OPERATION ORDERS No.5, with Appendices "A" & "C" attached""ADDENDA TO ADMINISTRATIVE ORDERS ISSUED WITH OPERATION ORDERS No.5. ""INSTRUCTIONS FOR "MOPPING UP"BATTALION i.e 7TH ROYAL WEST KENT REGIMENT" "ADMINISTRATIVE ORDERS TO TRANSPORT OFFICER" "PRELIMINARY ORDERS No.6." OPERATION ORDERS No.7."	All Map references can be traced on SHEET 28 BELGIUM & FRANCE Edition 3. Scale 1/40,000
"	22/7/17	9.a.m	Battalion accompanied by Transport moved by march route to WIPPENHOEK AREA (see OPERATION ORDERS No.6 attached) and arrived at DALLINGTON CAMP at about 11-30.a.m.	Map Reference SHEET 27 BELGIUM & FRANCE Ed.2. 1/40,000

Army Form C. 2118.

WAR DIARY 11th Bn. Royal Fusiliers.

INTELLIGENCE SUMMARY.

(Erase heading not required.)

Instructions regarding War Diaries and Intelligence Summaries are contained in F. S. Regs., Part II. and the Staff Manual respectively. Title pages will be prepared in manuscript.

Place	Date	Hour	Summary of Events and Information	Remarks and references to Appendices
DALLINGTON CAMP	23/7/17		Battalion cleaned up and remained at DALLINGTON CAMP.	MAP REF. SHEET 27 BELGIUM & FRANCE Ed.2. 1/40,000
"	24/7/17	7-30.am	The Battalion accompanied by 1st line Transport moved by route march to STEENVOORDE AREA (see Operation Orders No.9 attached) arriving in camp at about 10.am.	
STEENVOORDE WEST.	25/7/17 to 28/7/17		The Battalion complete remained at Camp in STEENVOORDE AREA during this period. Training was carried out consisting of "Following Barrages" Practicing the attack "Coy Drill" "Inspections" Etc. On the 27th the undermentioned Officers were granted authority to wear badges of higher rank as stated, pending confirmation of higher authority:- Lieutenant O.C.Whiteman........Captain. 2nd.Lieut. A.Aley...........Lieutenant. 2nd.Lieut. H.R.Cressy........Lieutenant.	do
ditto	29/7/17	6.am	The Battalion and 1st line Transport moved by route march to DICKEBUSCH AREA (see Operation Orders No.10 attached) and arrived in Camp at H.29.c.9.2 at 10-50.pm.	Sheet 28 BELGIUM & FRANCE Ed.3. 1/40,000
DICKEBUSCH AREA Camp at H.20.c.9.2.	30/7/17	10..pm	Day was spent in drawing Battle Stores and making final preparations for the attack as outlined in Operation Orders No.5. At 10.pm the Battalion, less 1st Line Transport and Specialists, moved up the line to CHATEAU SEGARD AREA (see operation orders No.11 attached)	
CHATEAU SEGARD AREA No.1.	31/7/17	6.am	At 6.am the Battalion moved from CHATEAU SEGARD AREA to RITZ AREA (see operation Orders No.12. attached) The 30th Division were held up in front of the BLACK LINE and it was decided that the Battalion (11th Royal Fusiliers) should carry out their part of the attack after the 30th Division had launched a fresh attack on the BLACK LINE on the 1st August 1917, but owing to very wet weather setting in all operations had to be cancelled. The Battalion casualties were as follows:- 1 Officer(2nd.Lt.Savours) Wounded -(Gas-Shell) 29 Other Ranks Wounded (Gas-Shell) 1 Officer(Lt.A.Aley) Wounded 7 Other Ranks Wounded.	do do

Army Form C. 2118.

WAR DIARY
11th Bn. Royal Fusiliers

INTELLIGENCE SUMMARY.

(Erase heading not required.)

Place	Date	Hour	Summary of Events and Information	Remarks and references to Appendices
			During the period 22/7/17 to 9/8/1917 the undermentioned were granted leave. Lt(A/Capt) G.Dekin and 39 Other Ranks. During the period 10/7/1917 to 9/8/17 Service dress (unserviceable) was replaced with New, and the Workshops i.e. Shoemakers, Tailors & Armourers, were engaged in overhauling Arms and equipment. The Regimental Band played selections during the evening whenever possible. When circumstances permitted the afternoons were devoted to Games & sports.	

[signature]
Lt-Col.
Commanding 11th Bn. Royal Fusiliers

ADDENDUM TO PRELIMINARY OPERATION ORDER NO.6.

Throughout Preliminary Operation Orders No.5 and appendix "D", for "2nd Royal West Kent Regiment" read "1/4th Middlesex Regiment" and vice versa.

SECRET.

Reference Map. Sheet 20 S.W.
                Regional Paper. 1/10,000.
Special Map attached.

PRELIMINARY OPERATION ORDER NO.

1. GENERAL PLAN. as explained in 54th Bde. Preliminary Operation Order No.35, already sent to Coy Commanders for information.

2. TASK OF 54TH BRIGADE.(& attached Troops)
The following additional troops will be placed under the orders of the G.O.C. 54th Infantry Brigade for these operations:-
            7th Queens Regiment (55th Inf. Bde.)
            7th Royal West Kent Regiment (55th Inf. Bde).
            80th Field Coy R.E.
About 1½ hours after Zero the 54th Infantry Brigade, with attached troops will commence to move forward from the CHATEAU SEGARD area to the RITZ Area (just E. of ZILLEBEKE).
The time table of these moves is shown in appendix "D".
~~The 54th Infantry Brigade will move forward from the assembly trenches~~
The 54th Infantry Brigade will not move forward from the assembly trenches in the RITZ Area without orders from Divisional Hd.Qrs. but will be prepared to adopt either of the following courses:-

(a). After ZERO plus 2 hours 40 minutes, to send forward the 11th Royal Fusiliers to form a right flank, and the 7th Queens & 7th Royal West Kent Regiments to garrison certain strong points(vide appendix "C" attached) in support of the 53rd Inf. Bde. if the lines mentioned in sub-paras (ii) or (iii) of para 1 (b). above are reached by that Brigade.

In the event of the situation developing so favourably as to admit of troops of the 53rd Infantry Brigade gaining the RED LINE, the remainder of the 54th Infantry Brigade will be moved forward to relieve the assaulting Battalions of the 53rd Inf. Bde. and to continue the consolidation of the ground gained.

In the event of the enemy being found to be holding the line E. of MOLENAARELSTHOEK and E. of ZONNEBEKE (or some other line in this vicinity) it is not intended to attack this line on "Z" day or before sufficient artillery support is available, the 53rd Infantry Brigade in such an eventuality, is to establish itself in a line within assaulting distance of the enemy.

(b). To pass through the 53rd Infantry Brigade and attack the RED LINE on "Z" plus one day.

Should the 54th Infantry Brigade be required to attack on "Z" plus one day, the RED LINE from the GREEN LINE or from any line between the GREEN & RED LINES which may have been reached by the 53rd Inf.Bde., the action to be taken by it will be as follows:-

The three assaulting Battalions will be ordered to move forward N of the RITZ AREA to the Western edge of POLYGONE WOOD in the following order:-

                                        11th Royal Fusiliers (Right Attack). leading.
            followed by   6th Northamptonshire Regt(Centre attack)
            followed by   7th Bedfordshire Regt (Left Attack).

They will each be accompanied by such other troops as are allotted to them for the attack vide paragraph 4 & 5.

The route to be followed by these Battalions from the RITZ AREA to POLYGONE WOOD will be the Divisional Track marked in BROWN on the attached special map.

2.

On arrival at the Western edge of POLYGON WOOD, they will deploy into attack formation between the boundaries allotted to them (in Yellow) on the attached special map.

When all three Battalions have deployed into attack formation, they will move forward simultaneously until they arrive at the line which has been reached by the 53rd Inf. Bde., where they will halt until ZERO HOUR, notified for the 54th Bde. attack.

The roles of the assaulting Battalions will then be as laid down in para 4. The 12th Middlesex (Supporting Battalion) less 2½ Coys, will, at the same time, be ordered forward by Bde. Hd.Qrs. to a position in rear of the three assaulting Battalions referred to above. The exact position will be dependent on circumstances. The 12th Middlesex Regiment will move forward to this position which will be notified to them later, in rear of the 7th Bedfordshire Regt, using the Divisional Track referred to above.

As the attack progresses, the garrison platoons of the 7th Queens' and 7th Royal West Kent Regiments, Sections of the 80th Field Coy R.E., and Machine Gun Detachments of the 54th Machine Gun Coy (vide appendix "C") will be ordered forward by Bde.Hqrs. to construct and garrison their respective points as soon as the ground on which they are situated has been captured.

3. Distribution of 54th Brigade & Attached Troops on Z/Z Night, at ZERO HOUR and time table of movements after ZERO - see Appendix "B" to be issued later.

4. ROLE OF BATTALION.

The 11th Royal Fusiliers will form the right assaulting Battalion of the 54th Infantry Bde. attack and will be responsible for the protection of the right flank of the attack on the RED LINE, whether it be carried out by the 53rd Inf. Bde. on Z Day or by the 54th Inf. Bde on "Z" plus I day.

1. In the event of the attack on the RED LINE being made by the 53rd Inf. Bde.

Special instructions will be issued to this Battalion by the G.O.C. 53rd Inf. Bde. but it is understood that the frontage which will be allotted to it in the RED LINE will be the same as mentioned in (1) above.

For this operation also, two platoons 12th Middlesex Regt will be attached for "mopping up" purposes.

2.

In the event of the attack on the RED LINE being made by the 54th Inf. Bde.

This Battalion will be responsible for the capture of the RED LINE between its junction with the GREEN LINE at J.9.d.3.0. and the Strong Point No.26 at J.5.c.1.5. (exclusive), including the high ground on which Strong Points 20, 21 & 22 are situated.

Two platoons, 12th Middlesex Regt will be attached to this Battalion to act as "mopping up" parties.

& ATTACHED TROOPS

ROLE OF COMPANIES. On arrival at the Western edge of POLYGON WOOD the Battalion will deploy into attack formation on a two Company front, in four waves (8 lines) each Coy on a 2 Platoon front. See diagram.

```
        D Coy.                              B Coy.
   ▲▲▲▲   ▲▲▲▲                    ▲▲▲▲   ▲▲▲▲   ] 1st WAVE
   ▲▲▲▲   ▲▲▲▲                    ▲▲▲▲   ▲▲▲▲   ] MOPPERS UP
                                                 ] 2nd WAVE

   ─────────────                    ─────────────  ] 3rd WAVE
        A Coy                            C Coy     ] 4th WAVE
```

The "Mopping up" parties of the 12th Middlesex will be formed up behind the Second Line of the first wave and will be responsible for clearing all dug-outs, trenches and buildings within the objective of the Battalion. The "mopping up" platoon behind "D" Coy will also be responsible for the dug-outs on the RACE COURSE in POLYGON WOOD. The "mopping up" platoon behind "B" Coy will not have finished its task until the trench in J.10.b.2.6 within the Battalion boundary has been cleared.

The Battalion & Attached Platoons will move forward in accordance with para 2.b. In forming up, the right of "B" Coy will rest about point J.9.c.8.0. and be in touch with the Battalion of the 30th Division on its right. The left of "D" Coy will be in touch with the right assaulting Coy of the 6th Northamptonshire Regt. about J.9.c.7.4.

The frontage of the leading Coys will be about 100 Yards each as shown on special map.

At ZERO Hour the Battalion will fight its way through to the
RED LINE. As each Company arrives opposite its position on the
shown on map it will face South East.
Each Coy will occupy the following frontage:-

"C" Company. From junction with 30th Division at J.9.d.30. to J.10.c.1.5.
(Strong Point 13 exclusive)

~~"A" Company. From J.10.~~

"A" Company. From J.10.c.1.5.(Strong Point 13 inclusive)to J.10.a.75.20.
(Strong Point 16 exclusive).

"B" Company. From J.10.a.75.20 (Strong Point 16 inclusive) to J.4.d.45.00
(Strong Point 22 exclusive)

"D" Company. From J.4.d.45.00(Strong Point 22 inclusive) to J.5.c.1.5.-
(Strong Point exclusive - in touch with 8th Northant's Regt)

When the Battalion is in this position Coys will immediately
push out patrols to their front and eventually occupy a line at least 200 Yards in
front of the Strong Points,pending the arrival of the Garrisons.
Each Coy Commander must have a small reserve at his disposal.
The 11th Royal Fusiliers will protect the garrisons of these Strong Points during
construction.

When the Strong Points have been constructed and garrisoned,
Coy Commanders will then be free to exploit success by means of patrols.
Further particulars concerning objectives of these patrols will be issued later.

The 11th Royal Fusiliers,if driven back by very heavy enemy
attack,will fall back to the line of Strong Points,consolidate the ground,and
fight on the line between these strong Points.

The Divisional Commander has ordered this line to be held at all costs.

Lateral communication must be constantly maintained,not only between
the battalions on the flanks of "C" & "D" Coys,but also between all Companies of
the Battalion.

The mopping up parties on completion of their task will return to their
Battalion,probably in square J.4.c.
The 2 Sections Machine Gun Coy will remain in reserve at Battalion
Headquarters.

Battalion Headquarters during the forming up will be at J.9.a.3.4.to the
right of the Divisional track going up and to left of the Divisional Track
coming down. It will be marked with a notice board.
After the objective has been taken,Battalion Headquarters will be moved
to Strong Point 7 about J.9 central.

ROLE OF OTHER UNITS OF BRIGADE.

1. 8th Northamptonshire Regiment,and 1 Company of 12th Middlesex Regiment will
attack on the left of the 11th Royal Fusiliers between the yellow line on map
from J.9.c.8.4. to J.9.c.6.8. and be responsible for the capture of the ground
from J.5.c.1.5. Strong Point (inclusive) to J.5.b.2.8.,Strong Point 33 (inclusive)

2. 7th Bedfordshire Regiment will attack on the left of the 8th Northamptons between
the the yellow lines on map from J.9.c.6.8. to J.9.a.35.30 and be responsible for
the capture of MOLENAARSTHOEK and between J.5.b.2.8.,Strong Point 33 (exclusive)
and D.29.a.25.10.,Strong Point 36 (Inclusive) and the sites of Strong Points 38 & 40.

ON NO ACCOUNT WILL THE ASSAULTING BATTALION COMMANDERS ISSUE ORDERS FOR ANY
OF THE GARRISONS OF THE STRONG POINTS REFERRED TO IN APPENDIX XXX "C"
TO MOVE THEIR POSITIONS ONCE THEY HAVE ESTABLISHED THEMSELVES ON THE SITE
ALLOCATED TO THEM.

3. 12th Middlesex Regiment.(less 2 Coys providing "mopping up" parties vide
para 5) will be in close support to the three assaulting Battalions,and will
be moved forward by the Brigade Commander to a position from which it can
easily support any one of the three assaulting Battalions.
The exact position will be dependent on circumstances,but will probably
be in Square J.4.c.
As soon as the "mopping up" parties have completed their task,the whole
Battalion will be concentrated in the above position.

a.4. 7th Queens' Regiment will provide garrisons of an officer and 1 Platoon each for Strong Points "E" and Nos.18 to 27 (inclusive),vide Appendix "C".

a.5. 7th Royal West Kent Regiment (consisting of 12 platoons) will provide garrisons of an officer and 1 Platoon each for the Strong Points F,G & H and Nos.28 to 38 (inclusive).

a.6. 54th Machine Gun Coy will be distributed as follows :-

1½ Sections attached to the Three Assaulting Battalions.
(2 Machine Gun Detachments to each).
1 Section to be held in readiness to go forward to Strong Points E, F, G & H, vide appendix "C".
1½ Sections in Brigade reserve, to move forward in rear of 12.th Middlesex Regt. as far as the GREEN LINE.

NOTE. In the event of the 33rd Infantry Brigade attacking the RED LINE on "Z" Day, the G.O.C.33rd Infantry Brigade will have a call on a portion of the 54th Machine Gun Coy.

a.7. 54th Trench Mortar Battery.
1 Section with 4 Mortars, with all personnel, in Brigade Reserve, to move forward in rear of the 12th Middlesex Regiment, as far as the GREEN LINE.

NOTE. Two of these mortars, with 80 rounds each, will be ready to move forward to assist the assaulting infantry if necessary.
The four mortars of the other section will not be taken into action.

a.8. 80th Field Coy.R.E.

4 Sections, with their affiliated Infantry Platoons, will be held in readiness to go forward to construct and occupy Strong Points E, F, G & H, (one Section to each), vide appendix "C".

ORDERS FOR
5. "MOPPING UP" PARTIES.
The 12th Middlesex Regt., will detail "mopping up" parties to be attached to the assaulting Battalions as follows:-

1 Company attached to 7th Bedfordshire Regt.
1 Company attached to 6th Northamptonshire Regt.
2 Platoons attached to 11th Royal Fusiliers.

These parties will join the Battalions to whom they are attached after the arrival of the Brigade in the RITZ Area.
In the attack they will not proceed East of the Line of the road which runs from J.4.d.9.5. to J.4.b.1.5.
As soon as they have completed the task of "mopping up"

allotted to them, they will rejoin their Battalion in square J.4.c.(vide para 4(a.3)) or in such other position as it may be at the time.

6. ARTILLERY & BARRAGE ARRANGEMENTS.
later
Artillery and barrage arrangements will be notified to all concerned.

7. TOOLS.
Assaulting Battalions will not carry large tools.

8. S.A.A. GRENADES &c., &c.,   See appendix "A".

9. Signal Communications. See appendix "D" (To be issued later).

10. ADMINISTRATIVE ARRANGEMENTS. will be issued later.

11. "Z" Day, ZERO HOUR & Hours for synchronisation of watches will be notified later.

12. Men equipped with wire cutters or wire breakers will wear a piece of white tape tied to the right shoulder strap.
The usual distinguishing arm-bands for runners, signallers etc., will be worn round the left fore-arm.

APPENDIX "A".

AMMUNITION TO BE CARRIED ON THE MAN.

S.A.A.   Every man will carry an extra bandolier except Bombers, Lewis Gunners, Signallers, Runners & Scouts.

Mills No.5.   Every man with exception of above will carry 2 bombs.
    Bombing Section: Each man will carry 5 Mills No.23 with rods and cartridges (or No.5 if insufficient No.23 available).

Rifle Grenades.   Five for each man in Rifle Bombers Section.

Very Pistol Ammunition 1" White.   24 per Coy & 12 per Battalion Hd.Qrs.

S.O.S.   8 per Coy & 16 per Battalion Hd.Qrs.

Flares. 120 BY per Coy.

Lethal Bombs.   4 per Coy.

SANDBAGS.   2 per man.

Pistol Ammunition.   About 20 rounds per Coy available at Dump at H.23.c.9.2.

The above will be drawn from Dump at H.23.c.9.2. on arrival in CHATEAU SEGARD Area, at times to be notified later and carried on the man on "Z" Day.

APPENDIX "C" issued with Preliminary Operation Order No.5.

INSTRUCTIONS FOR THE GARRISONS OF STRONG POINTS.

Sites for 45 Strong Points have been selected by Divisional Headquarters and are shown on the special Map, Appendix "A".

    8 of these are marked by letters A – H.

    36 " " " " " numbers 1 – 36 (excluding No.6).

The garrison of each of the lettered
    Strong Points will be   1 Infantry Platoon.
                                             (Including 1 L.G.Section).
                                           1 R.E.Section.
                                           (With its affiliated Inf.Platoon)
                                           1 Machine Gun Detachment.

The garrison of each of the Numbered
    Strong Points will be   1 Infantry Platoon.
                                             (Including 1 L.G.Section).

In the case of the lettered Strong Points, the senior officer present, whether he be R.E., Infantry or Machine Gun Company, will be in command of the garrison of the Strong Point.

Garrisons for the above Strong Points will be detailed as under:-

Strong Points lettered "A" "B" "C" and "D")
   "   " numbered 1, 2, 3, 4, 5, 7, 8, 9)   By the 53rd
                10, 11 and 12.   )   Infantry Brigade.

Strong Points Nos. 13,14,15,16.....1st Coy 7th Queens Regt. (1 Platoon).
   "   "   17,18,19,20.....2nd Coy   -do-   -do-
   "   "   Letter "E" & Nos.21
                   22,25...........3rd Coy   -do-   -do-
   "   "   Nos. 23,24,26,27.....4th Coy   -do-   -do-
   "   "   Letters "F" "G" &
                Nos.28,29......1st Coy 7th R.W.Kent Regt.   -do-
   "   "   Nos.30,31,32,33.....2nd Coy   -do-   -do-
   "   "   Letter "H" & Nos.34,
                35 & 36..3rd Coy.   -do-   -do-

NOTE. In addition to the above, the garrison of Strong Points "E" "F" "G" "H" will also each include 1 Section 90th Field Coy R.E. (with affiliated Infantry Platoon) and 1 Machine Gun Detachment 54th Machine Gun Coy.

After the arrival of the 54th Brigade in the RITZ Area, the troops detailed to garrison Strong Points will remain, in the above Company groups, in the positions allotted to them (vide Appendix "B") until they receive orders from 54th Bde Hqrs to move forward.

On receipt of such orders they will be moved up, via the Divisional track, to positions a short distance in rear of the attacking Battalions in order to be ready to go forward to construct and occupy the Strong Points allotted to them the moment the site has been captured by the attacking Battalions of either 53rd or 54th Infantry Brigades (vide para 2(a).

These garrisons will move forward equipped with sufficient S.A.A., Grenades, rations and water, to remain on garrison duty for 48 hours.

THEY WILL UNDER NO CIRCUMSTANCES LEAVE THEIR POSTS UNTIL RELIEVED. ORDERS FOR THEIR RELIEF WILL BE ISSUED BY DIVISIONAL HEADQUARTERS ONLY.

SECRET.

To:) Officer Commanding
     7th Royal West Kent Regiment.

The following orders for "Mopping up" parties effecting your Battalion are sent you for information.

EXTRACT FROM BATTALION OPERATION ORDERS NO.5.

"In the event of the attack by 54th Brigade on RED LINE"

This Battalion (11th Bn. Royal Fusiliers) will be responsible for the capture of the RED LINE between the junction with the GREEN LINE J.9.d.3.0. and the Strong Point No.26 at J.5.c.1.5. (exclusive) including the high ground on which Strong Points 20, 21 & 22 are situated.

2 Platoons 7th Royal West Kent Regiment will be attached to this Battalion to act as mopping up parties.

ROLE OF COMPANIES & ATTACHED TROOPS.

On arrival at the Western edge of POLYGON WOOD the Battalion will deploy into attack formation on a 2 Company front, in four waves (8 Lines) each Coy on a 2 Platoon front. (See diagram).

```
      D Coy                              B Coy
   ▭▭▭▭▭▭▭▭▭              ▭▭▭▭▭▭▭▭▭    1st wave
   △△△△  △△△△              △△△△  △△△△   } moppers
   △△△△  △△△△              △△△△  △△△△   }  up
   ▭▭▭▭▭▭▭▭▭              ▭▭▭▭▭▭▭▭▭    2nd wave
   ▭▭▭▭▭▭▭▭▭              ▭▭▭▭▭▭▭▭▭    3rd wave
      A Coy                              C Coy
   ▭▭▭▭▭▭▭▭▭              ▭▭▭▭▭▭▭▭▭    4th wave
```

The "Mopping Up" parties of the 7th Royal West Kents will be formed up behind the 2nd Line of the First Wave and will be responsible for clearing all dug outs, trenches and buildings within the objective of the Battalion. The "mopping up" platoon behind "B" Coy will also be responsible for the dug outs on the RACECOURSE in POLYGONE WOOD. The mopping up" platoon behind "B" Coy will not have finished its task until the trench in J.10.b.2.6. within the Battn. boundary has been cleared.

In forming up the right of "B" Coy will rest about point J.9.c.8.0. and be in touch with Battalion of the 30th Division on its right. The left of "D" Coy will be in touch with the right assaulting Coy of the 6th Northamptonshire Regt about J.9.c.7.6.

The frontage of the leading Coys will be about 100 Yards each.
The "mopping up" parties on completion of their task will return to their Battalion probably in square J.4.c.

25th July, 1917

(Sd) O.b.Whiteman
                            Lieutenant.
                            A/Adjutant.
                         for Lieut-Col.
                    Commanding 11th Bn. Royal Fusiliers.

SECRET.

To:- Transport Officer.

ADMINISTRATIVE ORDERS TO ACCOMPANY OPERATION ORDERS NO.5.

1. **Ammunition.**

    The following dumps have been formed:-

    (a) Divisional Bomb Store.   H.23.c.9.1.
    (b) Brigade Bomb Store.   I.22.d.8.9.
    (b) Battalion Dump   H.23.c.9.1.

2. **Method of Supply.**

    A pack train of 60 animals will be formed by the Divisional Ammunition Column.

    This train will move up to the vicinity of H.23.c.9.1. on the afternoon of "Z" Day.

3. **Control.** Guides for the pack animal train and Guards for advancing dumps will be detailed by O.C. Carrying Party.

4. **Transport Of Supplies for "Z" plus 2 days.**
    1. Rations etc will be delivered by Train Waggons to ZILLEBEKE. From thence they will be taken forward by Pack Transport.
    2. As it is impossible to foresee how many Units may have to be supplied by Pack Transport, it has been decided to form a Divisional Pack Train under the Command of the Officer Commanding the 18th Divisional Train.
    3. The animals for the Divisional Pack train will be found as follows:-

UNIT.	For Rations & Fuel.	For Water.	Spare.	Total.
Each Battalion.	10.	12.	2.	24.
54th M.G.Coy.	3.	3.	1.	7.

    4. A leader for each animal and 3 leaders per Battalion will be detailed, also a N.C.O. at the rate of 1 N.C.O. for every 12 mules.
    5. Animals and personnel to report to O.C. 18th Divisional Train at G.22.d.1.1. by 9 a.m. "Y" Day.
    6. Transport Officers will be under the orders of the O.C. 18th Divisional Train.
    7. Supplies will be carried on the ordinary riding saddles, in the same way as during the advance on the ANCRE. Pack saddles will only be required for Water and spare animals.
    8. Personnel and animals to be rationed up to and including "Z" Day. Necessary spare men to act as cooks must be sent, with sufficient Camp Kettles etc to prepare meals. Picketing gear, nosebags etc must accompany animals.
    9. Animals which are to be detailed for the pack train and which have not been used for for carrying pack loads must be constantly practised in this form of Transport.
    10. Transport Officers will demand on Officer Commanding Pack Train for the Transport required. They will be responsible for leading and taking supplies up to their units, and on completion will return the pack animals to O.C. Pack Train.

    PETROL TINS. The supply of petrol tins is very limited: if petrol tins are not returned on the day following that of issue, there will be a shortage of water; All troops must be warned of this shortage. Tins must in no case be punctured in order to make water run more freely. Screw plugs must be attached to the tins by wire or stout string.

VETINARY ARRANGEMENTS.

1. (a) On "Z" Day the Mobile Vetinary Section will be located at L.24.c.3.9.

   (b). An advanced Section of the Mobile Vetinary Section will be located at H.33a.6.3.

2. (a). On the capture of the final objective the Mobile Vetinary Section will move forward to H.33.a.6.3.

   (b). An advanced Section will be located at approximately I.22.b.6.3.
   (The D.A.D.V.S. will arrange to have sign boards at suitable points directing to this advanced Section).

3. Units sending horses to the Advanced Section must be prepared to provide conducting parties to take the animals back to the Mobile Vetinary Section after they have received first aid at the Advanced Post.

PRISONERS OF WAR. Returning escorts will be sent to report to their Regimental Transport Officer with the supply Pack Train at MOATED GRANGE, who will arrange for their return to their Units.

SALVAGE. Units must make every endeavour to salve as much material as possible, especially rifles and equipment.

Dumps will be formed on the side of the mule track, which will run from ZILLEBEKE to POLYGON WOOD.

Transport Officers must see that their pack animals are loaded up with all articles of salvage that it is possible to carry back.

The main Divisional Salvage Dump will be formed in the vicinity of I.22b.8.4.

WATER SUPPLY. Pack
Water for the supply and grenade Section of the Divisional Train will be arranged by the C.R.E. by troughs and pumps from MOATED GRANGE. 16 Extra Water Carts will be available at Headquarter Coy of the Divisional Train. - These are for issue to units in case of emergency, horses will not be available, but will have to be supplied by the Units demanding the Water Carts.

FIRST LINE TRANSPORT. First Line Transport will be Brigaded on "Y/Z" Night at CANAL RESERVE CAMP H.27.b.2.6.

Areas will be allotted to Units by Brigade Transport Officer.

SURPLUS KIT & PACKS. All packs and surplus kit will be dumped at Brigade Dump in CANAL RESERVE CAMP at H.27.b.2.6. on or before "Y" day.

No other dumps will be formed.

Regimental Baggage Waggons will be loaded ready for moving "Y/Z" Night.

PRELIMINARY OPERATION ORDERS NO.6.

Reference Operation Orders No.5.

RECONAISSANCE.

Before leaving CHATEAU SEGARD AREA, each Company will send forward a party to allot accommodation to their platoons in WELLINGTON STREET.

As soon as the situation allows after arrival in RITZ AREA Coys will arrange for 1 officer and 1 N.C.O. per Coy to go forward and reconnoitre the route to the front. Subsequently they will send forward other officers, N.C.O's and men, so that the route will be known to as many as possible.

As soon as the line which the 54th Brigade will have to take over or on which it will have to form up for an attack on Z plus 1 day, becomes known, Coys will send forward sufficient Officers & N.C.O's to ensure that the operation of forming up will be successful.

R.E. Tape will be issued to Coys for marking out forming up lines.

MAPS.

Following maps will be carried by Officers and senior N.C.O's as far as distribution admits:-

1. Belgium Sheet 28 N.E. 1/20,000.
2. C.16 - K.33 or C.10.-P.12
   or
A composite map formed from ZONNEBEKE, GHELUVELT and ZILLEBEKE, 1/10,000 Sheet.

No maps shewing positions of any kind are to be made on maps which are going forward of Brigade Headquarters.

BRIGADE FORWARD OBSERVATION POST
will be established at J.14.c.3.9.

30TH DIVISION - DRESS OF OFFICERS.

All officers of the 30th Division taking part in the operations will be dressed and armed exactly the same as the men; they will wear a piece of Red Tape 2" x 9" through the right shoulder strap as a distinguishing mark. *This is to be made known to all ranks.*

AMMUNITION.   The following dumps have been formed:-

(a) Divisional Bomb Store H.23.c.9.1.

(b) Brigade Bomb Store   I.22.d.8.9.

(c) Battalion Dump.   H.23.c.9.1.

Map co-ordinates of dumps formed by Units in the first phase of the attack will be wired to All Coys as soon as available.

As soon as circumstances permit, the Brigade Dump will be moved forward along the line of the Divisional Pack Animal Track.

Brigade Dump will be established in trenches crossing Track at J.9.a.5.5. and an Advanced Brigade Dump at J.14.b.7.0.

For Scale of Ammunition to be carried on the man see Appendix "D" attached.

RATIONS & WATER.

Water Bottles must be full at ZERO Plus 6 Hours.

All Water drunk in RITZ AREA must be drawn from petrol tins which will be dumped in camps occupied by Coys on Y/Z night. These tins must be carried by Coys on "Z" Day.

All troops will move up carrying unconsumed rations for "Z" day, rations for "Z" plus 1 day, and Iron Rations.

Coys will have breakfasts before leaving CHATEAU SEGARD AREA and teas before leaving RITZ AREA.

PETROL TINS.

The supply of petrol tins is very limited; if petrol tins are not returned on the day following that of issue, there will be a shortage of water. All troops must be warned of this shortage.

Tins must in no case be punctured in order to make water run more freely. Screw plugs must be attached to the tins by wire or stout string.

MEDICAL ARRANGEMENTS.

A mule track will be formed as soon as possible which will follow approximately the line ZILLEBEKE – DORMY HOUSE – MAPLE LODGE – I.18.d.central Junction IGNORANCE LANE & IGNORANCE ROW – J.13.central – SURBITON VILLA – Junction JARGON SWITCH & JARGON TRENCH – Northern end of NONNE BOSSCHEN WOOD – POLYGONEVELD – J.4.central. Walking wounded will follow this track when it is completed. Pending completion of same, walking wounded will come back on the line of their advance as far as the YPRES MENIN ROAD where the A.D.M.S. will arrange to have them met. Cases which cannot walk any further will be diverted to the Advanced Dressing Station in J.13.a, the remaining will be directed to the Walking Wounded Collecting Post at I.22.b.8.3. where it is hoped that the Corps will assist by providing lorries to carry the worst cases. From MENIN YPRES ROAD the track mentioned above will be flagged and furnished with direction boards, showing the way to the Walking Wounded Collecting Post at I.22.b.8.3.

PRISONERS OF WAR.

An advanced Prisoners of War cage will be established at I.22.b.7.5.

Returning escorts will be sent to report to their Regimental Transport Officers with the supply pack train at MOATED GRANGE, who will arrange for their return to their Units.

R.E. STORES

An advanced R.E. Dump will be formed in ZILLEBEKE at I.22.b.8.4.

SURPLUS KIT & PACKS.

All packs and surplus kits will be stored at Brigade Dump in CANAL RESERVE CAMP at H.27.b.2.6. on or before "Y" Day.

No other dumps will be formed.

CAPTURED GUNS &C.

Position of captured Field Guns must be reported to Battn. Hq. with a statement showing whether the guns are capable of being moved or not, and whether it is possible to get horse teams up to them, by day or by night.

Captured Machine Guns and small Mortars will be collected under Coy arrangements and eventually sent to Battalion Hq. when opportunity affords.

Position of captured heavy trench mortars and ammunition dumps will be reported to Battalion Headquarters.

CASUALTIES.

Estimated casualties should be wired at least every 2 hours and should be sent priority and include previous estimates. Officers casualties should be reported by name.

(SIGNED) O.S.WHITEMAN, LIEUTENANT,
A/ADJUTANT 11TH BN. ROYAL FUSILIERS.

Appendix D.

SCALE OF DISTRIBUTION OF AMMUNITION TO BE CARRIED ON THE MAN.

(Cancelling Appendix "A", issued with Operation Orders No.5).

SECTIONS.	S.A.A. Rounds.	Mills No.5.	Rifle Grenades.	Flares.	S.O.S. Signals.	V.P.A. 1"	Sand bags.	Remarks.
Rifleman.	170.	2.	–	1.	8 per Coy.	24 per Coy.	2.	
Rifle Grenadiers	170.	–	6.	1.	10 B.H.Q.	Balance to B.H.Q. (24)	2.	
Bombers.	170.	5.	–	1.			2.	
Lewis Gunners.	50.	–	–	1.			2.	

As Bombers are only carrying 5 bombs they will carry the 50 rounds additional S.A.A.

SECRET.   OPERATION ORDER No 8.

Ref.Maps.Belgium &
France Sheets 27 & 28.
    1/40,000.

Intention.	The 54th Brigade will move to WIPPENHOEK AREA to-morrow. The Battalion will proceed to DALLINGTON CAMP L.36.b.15 (Sheet 27 not in possession of Coys). The Batt
Parade.	The Battalion, less working parties and attached R.E.Platoon, will parade on Coy parade grounds, ready to move off at 9 a.m. in the following order:- Hd.Qrs.,Drums,"B","C","D","A".
Interval.	An interval of 200 Yards will be maintained between Coys east of Cross Road in G.32.d.
Route.	GOED MEOT MILL - OUDERDOM - CROSS ROADS G.29 b.Central - CROSS ROADS L.36 d.2.3.
Advance Party.	Advance Party on the scale of 1 Per Coy,Hqrs., & Transport will report with bicycles to 2nd.Lieut.E.L.Jones,M.C.,at Orderly Room at 8-45 a.m.
First Line Transport.	First Line Transport will accompany the Battalion.
Baggage.	Officers' Kits and baggage will be dumped by Coys at the Q.M.Stores by 8 a.m. Mess & Maltese Carts will be at Medical Inspection Room and Hd.Qrs.Mess by 8 a.m.
Working Parties.	Special instructions for the parties detailed in the working programme of 21/22nd will be issued later.
Dress.	Full Marching Order. Steel Helmets will be carried under the pack straps.
Water Bottles.	Water Carts and water bottles will be filled before leaving present area.
Sanitation.	All huts must be swept and tent curtains rolled up, and the camp left in a scrupulously clean condition.

21st July, 1917.

(Signed) O.C.Whiteman, Lieutenant.
A/Adjutant 11th Bn. Royal Fusiliers.

After Order.

Two G.S.Waggons only will be available for the move to and from the back area. A dump for surplus stores is being formed under a Guard in the present area access to which will be possible on the return of the Battalion (probably to the same Camp).

Surplus kits of Officers, Mess Stores, Orderly Room Boxes, Workshop material, Q.M.Stores &c., not actually required for the march, will be dumped outside the Q.M.Stores by 2 p.m. to-morrow.

As men should march as lightly as possible, all property other than the regulation kit must be left behind and bagged under Coy arrangements.

All packages dumped must be clearly marked with the owners name & Coy.

(Sd) O.C.Whiteman, Lieutenant.
A/Adjutant 11th Bn. Royal Fusiliers.

SECRET.   OPERATION ORDER NO.6.

Ref.Maps.Belgium &
France Sheets 27 & 28.
      1/40,000.

Intention.	The 54th Brigade will move to WIPPENHOEK AREA to-morrow. The Battalion will proceed to DALLINGTON CAMP L.35.b.15 (Sheet 27 not in possession of Coys). The Batt
Parade.	The Battalion, less working parties and attached R.E.Platoon, will parade on Coy parade grounds, ready to move off at 9 a.m. in the following order:- Hd.Qrs,Drums,"B","C","D","A".
Interval.	An interval of 200 Yards will be maintained between Coys east of Cross Road in G.32.d.
Route.	GODEWAERSVELDE - OUDERDOM - CROSS ROADS G.29 b.Central - CROSS ROADS L.35 d.2.5.
Advance Party.	Advance Party on the scale of 1 Per Coy,Hqrs., & Transport will report with bicycles to 2nd.Lieut.H.L.Jones,M.C.,at Orderly Room at 8-45 a.m.
First Line Transport.	First Line Transport will accompany the Battalion.
Baggage.	Officers' Kits and baggage will be dumped by Coys at the Q.M.Stores by 8 a.m. Mess & Maltese Carts will be at Medical Inspection Room and Hd.Qrs.Mess by 8 a.m.
Working Parties.	Special instructions for the parties detailed in the working programme of 21/22nd will be issued later.
Dress.	Full Marching Order. Steel Helmets will be carried under the pack straps.
Water Bottles.	Water Carts and water bottles will be filled before leaving present area.
Sanitation.	All huts must be swept and tent curtains rolled up, and the camp left in a scrupulously clean condition.

21st July. 1917.

(Signed) O.C.Whiteman, Lieutenant.
A/Adjutant 11th Bn. Royal Fusiliers.

SECRET   OPERATION ORDERS NO. 9.   23rd July 1917.

INTENTION   The 54th. Infantry Brigade will move tomorrow to STEENVOORDE WEST.

DETAIL   Orderly Officer tomorrow:-   2nd.Lieut.H.W.Brookling.
             Coy. on duty tomorrow:-   "D" Coy.
             Reveille:- 5-30 a.m.   Breakfast:- 6a.m.
             Sick Parade:- & C.O's Orders:- On arrival at new area.

PARADE.   The Battalion will parade on Coy. parade grounds ready to move off at 7-30
             a.m. in the following order:- Hqrs.,"D" Coy.,"A" Coy., Drums, "B" & "C" Coys.

TRANSPORT.   First LIne TRansport will move with the Battalion.

ROUTE.   ABEELE- STEENVOORDE.

ADVANCED   Advanced Party on the scale of 1 per Coy. Hqrs. & Transport will report
PARTY.   to Lieut E.H.Cliff at 7 a.m. and proceed on bicycles to STEENVOORDE AREA.

BAGGAGE.   All Officers' kits and baggage will be dumped at Q.M.Stores by Coys. by
             7 a.m. Coys.will detail a N.C.O. who will be responsible for Coy. baggage,
             to report to the Quartermaster at 6-45. Mess kits must be packed on cookers
             by 7 a.m. Mess cart & Maltese cart will be at Hqrs. Mess & Medical
             Inspection Room respectively by & 7a.m.

DRESS.   Full marching order. Steel helmets will be worn between pack straps.

SANITATION. O.C.Coys. will see that the present is left in a scrupulously clean condition.

HANDING   2nd. Lieut H.W.Brookling will remain behind and hand over camp to Officer
OVER.   of 89th. Infantry Brigade.

                                            (SIGNED) O.C.WHITEMAN, LIEUTENANT.
                                            A/ADJUTANT 11TH. BATTALION
                                                       ROYAL FUSILIERS.

SECRET.

To:) Officer Commanding
7th Royal West Kent Regiment.

The following orders for "Mopping up" parties effecting your Battalion are sent you for information.

EXTRACT FROM BATTALION OPERATION ORDERS NO.5.

"In the event of the attack by 54th Brigade on RED LINE"

This Battalion (11th Bn. Royal Fusiliers) will be responsible for the capture of the RED LINE between the junction with the GREEN LINE J.9.d.3.0. and the Strong Point No.26 at J.5.c.1.5. (exclusive) including the high ground on which Strong Points 20,21 & 22 are situated.

2 Platoons 7th Royal West Kent Regiment will be attached to this Battalion to act as mopping up parties.

ROLE OF COMPANIES & ATTACHED TROOPS.

On arrival at the Western edge of POLYGON WOOD the Battalion will deploy into attack formation on a 2 Company front, in four waves (8 Lines) each Coy on a 2 Platoon front. (See diagram).

The "Mopping Up" parties of the 7th Royal West Kents will be formed up behind the 2nd Line of the First Wave and will be responsible for clearing all dug outs, trenches and buildings within the objective of the Battalion. The "mopping up" platoon behind "B" Coy will also be responsible for the dug outs on the RACECOURSE in POLYGONE WOOD. The mopping up" platoon behind "B" Coy will not have finished its task until the trench in J.10.b.2.6. within the Battn. boundary has been cleared.

In forming up the right of "B" Coy will rest about point J.9.c.8.0. and be in touch with Battalion of the 30th Division on its right. The left of "D" Coy will be in touch with the right assaulting Coy of the 6th Northamptonshire Regt about J.9.c.7.4.

The frontage of the leading Coys will be about 100 Yards each.
The "mopping up" parties on completion of their task will return to their Battalion probably in square J.4.c.

25th July, 1917

Lieutenant.
A/Adjutant.
for Lieut-Col.
Commanding 11th Bn. Royal Fusiliers.

SECRET.   OPERATION ORDERS NO. 7.

In continuation of Operation Order No.6.

Para 4.1. In the event of the attack on the RED LINE being made by the 53rd Inf. Bde.

"C" & "A" Coys, 11th Royal Fusiliers will form up behind the right flank of the 8th Suffolk Regiment, with "C" Coy on the right and "A" Coy on the left of of "C" Coy. They will conform to the operations of the 8th Suffolk Regiment. At Zero plus 8-40 they will be in a position to push forward their patrols to make good the ground after which "C" Coy will move forward and take up its battle position. On the FURTHER of the 8th Suffolk Regt. "A" Coy will adopt a similar course, continuing the flank between the left of "C" Coy and the right of the 8th Suffolks. "C" & "A" Coys and M.G.Section (one gun with each Coy.) will take up a position about 200 Yards in front of garrison Posts and will treat it as an Outpost Position, digging trenches in on the picquet line with the entrenching tool. On the construction of the strong points being completed, O/s C. "C" & "A" Coys will be free to exploit further success.

No.14 Strong Point should be the right flank of "A" Coy and included in that Coy's frontage.

INFORMATION. Every effort must be made to get early information of points reached and enemy seen, back to the 8th Suffolks Regt at S.P.3 or Forward Bde.Signal Officer at J.9.a.5.6. on Divisional Track.

COMMUNICATION. Constant communication must be maintained with troops on either flank.

LOCATION. At ZERO plus 5-45, "C" & "A" Coys will be formed up in I.15.c. N. of STANLEY STREET and will cross STANLEY STREET at 5.50.

MOVE. These Coys will leave certain lines approximately at the hours shown below;

        BLUE LINE   ZERO plus 6-50.
        BLACK LINE   ZERO plus 7-10.
                    and should arrive at the S.W. corner of POLYGONE WOOD
at ZERO plus 7-46.   The Battalion and Machine Gun Coy attached will be in
CHATEAU SEGARD area on Y/Z night.

RECONNAISSANCE. O.C. "C" Coy will send forward one Officer and escort to reconnoitre track and get in touch with 8th Suffolk Regiment, prior to the arrival of these Coys at POLYGONE WOOD.

                                    (SIGNED) O.C. WITTEMAN, LIEUTENANT.
                                    A/ADJUTANT 11TH BN. ROYAL FUSILIERS.
25th July, 1917.

SECRET.   OPERATION ORDERS NO. 10   28th July, 1917.

1. **Intention.** The 54th Infantry Brigade will move to DICKEBUSCH AREA to-morrow, halting during the day in the WIPPENHOEK AREA in the same camps as occupied by Battalions on the 25rd. The Battalion will arrive at DALLINGTON CAMP, will remain there for dinners and teas, continuing the march at a time to be notified later.

2. **Detail.** Company on duty to-morrow :- "A" Company.
   Reveille :- 3-50 a.m.   Breakfast :- 4 a.m.
   Sick Parade: Time to be notified later.

3. **Parade.** The Battalion will parade in column of route and move by the nearest routes to the starting point K.31.d.2.2. ready to move off at 5 a.m. The Battalion will move forward from the starting point in the following order :- Headquarters, "A", "B" Drums, "C", "D".
   "D" Coy will not pass Cross Roads at K.31.c.7.2. before "C" Coy. has passed.

4. **Transport.** First Line Transport will accompany the Battalion.

5. **Route.** ARNEKE - STEENVOORDE - DALLINGTON CAMP - RENINGHELST - Cross Roads G.29.b.central - OUDERDOM. An interval of 200 Yards between Coys will be maintained E. of Cross Roads G.32.d.

6. **Advanced Party.** Advanced Party on the scale of 1 N.C.O. per Coy, Hd.Qrs & Transport will report to Lieut. Cliff at B.H.Q. at DALLINGTON CAMP at 5 p.m. and proceed to the DICKEBUSCH AREA, on bicycles.

7. **Baggage.** Officers Kits and baggage will be dumped outside their Coy HQ. ready for collection by 4-45 a.m. Mess Kits must be packed on cookers by 5 a.m. Cookers will join the Transport at starting Point. Mess & Maltese Carts will be at B.H.Q. and Medical Inspection Room respectively by 5 a.m.

8. **Packs.** Lorries on the scale of 1 per 2 Coys will be available for the carriage of packs and steel helmets. Packs and steel Helmets must be dumped at Coy HQ. ready for collection at 6-30 a.m. Two bad marchers per Coy will be detailed as loaders and will accompany the lorries to DICKEBUSCH AREA. These men must carry their day's rations.
   1 Guide per Coy will be at B.H.Q. at 6-15 a.m. to conduct the lorries to Coy Hqrs.

9. **Area Stores.** All tents and bivouac shelters will be dumped with the packs and collected by the lorries, and will be delivered to the Area Commandant's Office STEENVOORDE and a receipt obtained.

10. **Dress.** Battle Order.

11. **Water.** Water Carts and Water Bottles will be filled before 8-30 p.m. this evening.

12. **Sanitation.** Officers Commanding Companies will see that present area is left in a scrupulously clean condition.

13. **Map References.** Map Sheet 27 Ed.2. can be seen at Orderly Room to-day.

28th July, 1917.   (SIGNED) O.C. WHITEMAN, LIEUTENANT.
                                    CAPTAIN A/ADJUTANT IITH BN. ROYAL FUSILIERS.

SECRET.

OPERATION ORDERS NO. 50.

30 / July, 1917.

INTENTION.	The Battalion will move to the CHATEAU SEGARD AREA No.4,H.30.a.8.8.to-night. The Battalion will parade on Coy Parade Grounds ready to move off at 10 p.m. Coys will move off by platoons in the following order:- Hd.Qrs., "C", "A", "B", "D". An interval of 200 Yards between platoons will be maintained.
ROUTE.	Main Road DICKEBUSCH - CAFE BELGE - H.30.a.8.8. Platoons will be conducted by Platoon Guides.
TEAS.	Teas will be issued at 6 p.m. to-night.
BREAKFASTS.	Breakfasts will be issued at 2 a.m. to-morrow morning 31st inst.
OFFICERS KITS & BAGGAGE.	Officers Kits, baggage and Mess-kit not required for operations will be dumped by Coys at Q.M.Stores by 8 p.m.
PACKS & CAPS.	Packs and Caps will be dumped by Coys at Q.M.Stores by 8 p.m. Cap will be marked.
COOKERS & WATER CARTS.	Cookers and Water Carts will accompany the Battalion in the CHATEAU SEGARD AREA. Breakfast ration for to-morrow will be carried on Cookers.
WATER.	Water for teas in the RITZ AREA will be carried by mules, one mule carrying 8 tins, will accompany each Coy & Battalion Hd.Qrs. Transport Officer will arrange for these animals to report to Coy HQ. at 9-45 p.m. this evening. Rations for the animal and men must be carried. On completion of task animals will return to First Line Transport with the empty tins.
REPORTS.	Coys will report arrival in the CHATEAU SEGARD AREA to Battalion Hq.
RATIONS.	Rations for the 31st July & 1st August will be issued this afternoon.
AMMUNITION BOMBS, SANDBAGS, VERY LIGHTS & S.O.S.	will be issued this afternoon.
INSPECTION.	Coy Commanders will inspect their Coys at 7 p.m. in "Battle Order", fully equipped with rations as above, bombs &c., and report complete equipment to Orderly Room by 8-30 p.m.
WATER BOTTLES.	Water Bottles must be filled not later than 3 p.m. and on no account is this water to be drunk until after the Coys have left the RITZ AREA.
BOX RESPIRATORS	will be worn in the alert position.
MEN LEFT OUT OF ACTION.	Nominal rolls of all men left out of action, and instructions regarding their accommodation will be issued later. 2nd.Lieut.E.P.Chaffey will be in charge of this detachment.

(SIGNED) O.C.WHITEMAN, LIEUTENANT.
A/ADJUTANT 11TH BN. ROYAL FUSILIERS.

SECRET.

OPERATION ORDER. NO. 12.

30th July, 1917.

1. The Battalion will move from CHATEAU SEGARD AREA to WELLINGTON CRESCENT tomorrow, July 31st in the following order:- "C", "A", "B", "D" Hqrs. Coys will move at one minute interval between platoons. Leading Platoon will pass the starting point at ZERO plus 1-30. Starting Point - Junction of Road & Divisional Track at H.30.a.9.7.

2. ROUTE. Divisional Track.

3. GUIDES. O.C.Coys will send on 1 Officer and 1 Guide per Platoon to arrange accommodation in WELLINGTON CRESCENT.
"A" Coy should be on the left of Divisional Track and "C" Coy on right of track going East, where track crosses WELLINGTON CRESCENT.
"B" Coy will be on the left of "A" & "D" Coy on the left of "B" Coy.

4. TEAS. Teas will be made on Tommy's Cookers on arrival in WELLINGTON CRESCENT and the eme ration consumed.

5. WATER. Water for Teas will be carried by mules vide Operation Order No.18.

6. WATER BOTTLES. On no account will any water be taken from water bottles in the RITZ AREA. All ranks are to be reminded that no further water will be available till nightfall tomorrow.

7. MOVE FROM RITZ AREA. Coys will leave WELLINGTON CRESCENT in the following order "C", "A", "B", "D" & Hqrs. "C" & "A" Coys will move by platoons at one minute intervals - leading platoon "C" Coy leaving WELLINGTON CRESCENT at ZERO plus 6 to cross STANLEY STREET at ZERO plus 6-30. "B", "D" & Hqrs. will move in the same manner leading platoon of "B" Coy leaving WELLINGTON CRESCENT at ZERO plus 6-30 to cross STANLEY STREET at ZERO plus 7.
Coys are reminded of the difficulty of getting out of WELLINGTON CRESCENT which is deep and narrow and plenty of time must be allowed.
Lieut. Cliff will meet Coys on Divisional Track near Suffolks Headquarters J.10.a.8.5 and will give Coys further instructions. If Lieut. Cliff is not met on the Track O.C. "C" Coy will send forward an Officer to Suffolk's Headquarters at Strong Point A, for further instructions. Unless stopped Coys will proceed to GREEN LINE as per instructions, getting into touch with 8th Suffolks Regt., on the GREEN LINE. Battalion Headquarters will probably be at J.9.a.8.8. and on capture of RED LINE be moved to J.9.Central. Coys will be informed of any change in these positions.

8. Gun Teams of 34th Machine Gun Coy will accompany "A" & "C" Coys throughout all moves.

ZERO hour will be notified later.

30th July, 1917.

(Sd) G.C.Whitsun, Capt.,
A/Adjutant 11th Bn. Royal Fusiliers.

SECRET.

ADDENDA TO ADMINISTRATIVE INSTRUCTIONS
ISSUED WITH OPERATION ORDER NO. 5.

FLARES. The definite hours for shewing white flares will be as follows:-

        Zero plus 1 Hour.
        Zero plus 2 hours 30 Minutes.
        Zero plus 5 hours.
        Zero plus 9 hours.

and at any other time on demand being made by the contact aeroplanes sounding a Klaxon Horn or dropping a white light.

RATIONS & WATER. Coys must arrange to find their own ration carrying parties. Location of ration dump will be notified later.

ADVANCED REPORT CENTRES. Advanced Report Centres will be established approximately as follows:-

    53rd Brigade J.14.a.5.9.

    8th Suffolks   ) J.9.c.3.5.
    6th Royal Berks)

    10th Essex.   ) J.14.a.3.2.
    1 Coy 8th Norfolks.)

    8th Norfolk Regt. RITZ AREA.

DUMPS. 1. The following are the dumps of the 30th Division:-

    <u>Right Brigade Battalion Dumps.</u>

        I.24.d.5.1.
        I.24.d.40.75.
        I.24.b.23.60.

    <u>Left Brigade Battalion Dump.</u>

        I.24.b.1.5.
        I.24.b.40.55.

    <u>Right Brigade Dump.</u>

        I.24.a.25.40.

    <u>Left Brigade Dump.</u>

        I.23.b.9.3.

  2. <u>After the Advance.</u> Advanced Brigade Dumps will be formed at
        J.13.b.2.4. and J.16.d.5.9. (FITZCLARENCE FARM).

  3. 53rd INFANTRY BRIGADE DUMPS.

    Brigade Dump, Church, ZILLEBEKE, I.22.d.6.9.

    <u>After the Advance</u> Advanced Brigade Dumps J.8.c.2.2.
                                          J.3.b.7.0.
                                          J.9.c.0.4.

In the event of an easy advance by the 53rd Infantry Brigade to the RED LINE, a more advanced Brigade Dump will be formed about J.9.b.4.9.

MEDICAL. The following instructions apply during the march forward to the GREEN LINE:-

  1. No Regimental Stretcher Bearers are to be sent back with wounded during the march to the GREEN LINE.
  2. Men wounded during the march are to be left lying to where they fall. They will be cleared by the Field Ambulance.

2.

WATER. The well in DONKY COPSE has been found to be absolutely impure, and will NOT under no circumstances be used.

STRAGGLERS POSTS. Posts consisting of 2 Regimental Police will be established as under:-

Location.	Area.	Found by.
J.9.a.Central	To patrol along mule track from J.9.a.central to J.7.d.9.0.	11th R.F.
J.7.d.9.0.	To patrol along mule track from J.7.d.9.0. to our old front line.	7th Bedfordshire Rt.

Their duties will be to take the numbers, names and units of all stragglers; send those who are fit back to their Units, and pass the remainder to the rear via the Divisional KHAKI Mule Track.
To direct wounded to the nearest Advanced Dressing Station.
To marshal all prisoners and direct escorts to I.22.b.7.3.

NOTE: ANY MAN FOUND LOOTING THE DEAD OR WOUNDED WILL BE SHOT ON THE SPOT.
THIS ORDER MUST BE READ OUT TO ALL RANKS.

DRESS.
Fighting Order.
Haversack on Back.
Box Respirator at the Alert.
Officers will be dressed exactly as the men.
Sticks are not to be carried.

CONSOLIDATION. It must be impressed on all ranks, especially the garrisons of Strong Points, the importance of consolidation of objectives immediately they are captured.

The objectives laid down are only naturally approximate and the commander on the spot must decide the exact points to be consolidated in addition to Strong Points laid down.

Instructions regarding Artillery Barrage, Machine Gun Barrage, co-operation with Contact Aeroplanes, and action of tanks, have been issued under separate appendices but it must be impressed on all ranks that on no account are troops to wait for the tanks.
IF THE LATTER DO NOT ARRIVE UP TO TIME THE OPERATION WILL BE CARRIED OUT WITHOUT THEM.
Troops must on no account follow tanks as there is great danger of their losing direction by doing so.

ENEMY AIRCRAFT. All Ranks are to be warned that in the event of enemy aircraft flying over the MINE AREA or, when the 54th Brigade has begun to operate over newly captured positions all movement must be kept down to a minimum and men must be forbidden to look up at the enemy aeroplane. If these precautions are not observed heavy hostile shelling will be the result.

30th July, 1917.

Issued at 6 p.m.

(SIGNED) O.C. WHITEMAN, CAPTAIN.
A/ADJUTANT 11TH BN. ROYAL FUSILIERS.

WAR DIARY 11th Bn. Royal Fusiliers Army Form C. 2118.

or

INTELLIGENCE SUMMARY.

(Erase heading not required.)

Place	Date	Hour	Summary of Events and Information	Remarks and references to Appendices
RITZ AREA	1/8/17		the Wounded -(Gas-Shell) cases were caused by the Germans using "Mustard Oil"	MAP REF. SHEET 28 BELGIUM & FRANCE Ed.3. 1/40,000
			The Battalion remained in RITZ AREA. The following casualties occurred:- 9 Other Ranks Wounded -(Gas-Shell) 2 Other Ranks Wounded. again the Gassed cases were caused by the Germans using "Mustard Oil" This Gas burned the mens flesh and caused their eyes to become bad.	
		6.pm	At about 6.pm the Battalion left the RITZ AREA and proceeded to DICKEBUSCH AREA occupying Huts at H.27.b.2.6.	
DICKEBUSCH AREA. Camp at H.27.b.2.6. (Huts)	2/8/17 & 3/8/17		Remained in Huts at H.27.b.2.6. "A" Coy only had the use of the Baths near OUDERDOM on the 3rd August, but a clean dry change of underclothing was issued to the whole of the Battalion.	
	4/8/17		Draft of IXEM 18 Other Ranks joined the Battalion on the 3rd August 1917 The Battalion less 1st Line Transport and Specialists moved by route march to CHATEAU SEGARD AREA (see Operation Order No.13. attached) and arrived at No.1. Camp at about 7.pm. 2nd Lieuts. G.G.Gore, R.R.Porter and B.H.Barnett joined the Bn. for duty and were posted to "C" "D" Coy's respectively.	
CHATEAU SEGARD AREA. No.1. Camp.(Dugouts. & Bivouacs.)	4/8/17 to 6/8/17		The Battalion remained at No.1. Camp (CHATEAU SEGARD AREA) Orders for "Defence" were issued to all concerned (see copy attached) Operation Orders No.14 and Administrative Orders (copies of both attached) were prepared and issued to all concerned. Enemy Artillery shelled vicinity of camp continuously, apparently in search of numerous batteries aground - no shells did any damage to camp and no casualties occurred.	
BATTLE POSITION	7/8/17		The Battalion less Transport and Specialists moved by route march to Battle positions (see Operation Orders No.15. attached)	
do	8/8/17		Coy's and Headquarters remained in their Battle Positions.	
do	9/8/17		Coy's and Headquarters remained in their Battle Positions.	

Army Form C. 2118.

WAR DIARY
or
INTELLIGENCE SUMMARY.
(Erase heading not required.)

11th (Service) Bn. Royal Fusiliers

Place	Date	Hour	Summary of Events and Information	Remarks and references to Appendices
			party of men to the Sea-side. These were accepted and men who came out of the Battle of 10th August were sent.	
			Captain O.C. Whiteman and one Other Rank proceeded on Leave.	
			O.C., 80th Field Coy, R.E. gave special instruction in Consolidation and Wiring. All available Officers and N.C.O's. attended.	
			The Divisional Gas Officer have a Lecture at the Schoolroom, ARNEKE. 1 Officer and 2 N.C.O's. per Company attended. "A" and "B" Companies sent an additional Officer.	
			The Commanding Officer, Major A.E. Sulman, M.C. inspected Reinforcements which joined the Battalion on the 17th September, at 2.30 p.m. RSM Taylor and one Other Rank proceeded on Leave.	
			On the 21st September 1917, instruction in Wiring was given by O.C., 80th Field Coy, R.E. 20 men per Company equal 80, actually did the Wiring. 1 Officer per Company and as many N.C.O's. as could be spared attended.	
			6 Pairs of Field Glasses were issued to the Battalion Observers. 4 Pocket Magnetic Compasses per Company equals 16, were issued to Platoon Sergeants and an additional 6 for Observers.	
			The Field Marshal Commander-in-Chief under authority delegated by His Majesty THE KING awarded the DISTINGUISHED CONDUCT MEDAL to the following N.C.O's. and men for gallantry and devotion to duty in the	

WAR DIARY
INTELLIGENCE SUMMARY
(Erase heading not required.)

Army Form C. 2118.

XI Battalion The Royal Fusiliers

Place	Date	Hour	Summary of Events and Information	Remarks and references to Appendices
TRENCHES	10/8/17		The 11th Bn. Battalion attacked the HOOK OPERATION according to operation orders No.1. (att.)	
			A. & B. Companies (Major J.G.) Pritchard	
			C. & D. Companies Captain H.M Fuller. "M" Company - 2nd Lieut. Wyatt and "C" Coy - Died	
			/Capt. H.V. Gay. The Battalion was Commanded by Major F. Coulson, M.C. The Battalion went	
			on going into action was 27 Officers, 821 Other ranks. Strength on coming out of action 20 officers	
			567 Other ranks. Below is a list of the Battle. The following are listed as Casualties	
			during this battle.	
			Capt. D.V. Fuller. Killed. Lieut. A/Capt. H.A. Coy. Wounded. Lt.W.P. Cass. Missing	
			2nd.Lt. A/Capt. T. M. Moore. Killed. 2nd. Lt. H.M. Dew Killed. A.C. Miller. Missing	
			2nd.Lt. G. T. Storeld. Missing 2nd.Lt. V.J.A. Horton. Wounded 2nd. Lieut. W. Haddon Missing	
			2nd.Lt. H. P. Charity. Killed. 2nd.Lt. R.T. Hatt. Missing 2nd.Lt. D.E. Battye Died of Wds.	
			2nd.Lt. A.G.Calthrop. Missing 2.Lt. G.J.Lang. Wounded 2nd.Lt G.G. Cane. Missing	
			2nd.Lt. G.W.H. Rogers. Missing 2nd.Lt. R.H. Barnett. Missing	
			Other Rank casualties. 528.	
		2.am	The Battalion was relieved by the 8th Norfolk Regiment and proceeded to CHATEAU SEGARD area No.1.	
			near KRUISSTRAATHOEK	

Army Form C. 2118.

WAR DIARY
INTELLIGENCE SUMMARY.
(Erase heading not required.)

Instructions regarding War Diaries and Intelligence Summaries are contained in F. S. Regs., Part II. and the Staff Manual respectively. Title pages will be prepared in manuscript.

2nd BATTALION
THE
ROYAL FUSILIERS

Place	Date	Hour	Summary of Events and Information	Remarks and references to Appendices
CHATEAU SEGARD	11/8/17		The Battalion moved out of CHATEAU SEGARD Area No.1. and proceeded to DICKEBUSCH HUTS - H.20.c.9.2. (Map Sheet.27 28.N.W. BELGIUM & FRANCE) Hot Tea was waiting for the men on arrival at Huts.	
DICKEBUSCH HUTS	12/8/17		The Battalion proceeded by march route to BUSSEBOOM where it embussed at 11.a.m (See copy of Operation Orders attached No.16.) The Battalion then proceeded to STEENVOORDE EAST Area and after half an hours march after debussing arrived in billets at 3.p.m. The 1st line Transport moved independently from Dickebusch huts by road under arrangements of 54th Inf. Bde.	
STEENVOORDE EAST AREA	12/8/17 14/8/17		The Battalion rested, cleaned up and were refitted as much as was possible.	
-do-	15/8/17		The Battalion (less Transport - which proceeded by road under Brigade arrangements) proceeded by march route to ABEELE (see Operation Orders No.17 attached). On arrival at ABEELE Station the Battalion entrained - arrived and detrained at ARNEKE. The Battalion then marched to OOST HOUCK and took over billets in the vicinity of the village.	
OOST HOUCK AREA	15/8/17 to 3/9/17.		During this period the Battalion carried out training according to programmes laid down Musketry, Close order drill, Platoon Drill, Platoon attack, Coy Organisation, Physical drill Rapid Wiring and Bayonet fighting were constantly practised. The Rifle Range at EPERLECQUES was allotted to and used by the Battalion on the 22nd August 28th August and 1st September . The Lewis Gunners were allotted special targets on each occasion.	

Army Form C. 2118.

WAR DIARY
INTELLIGENCE SUMMARY.
(Erase heading not required.)

11TH BATTALION.
THE
ROYAL FUSILIERS.

Place	Date	Hour	Summary of Events and Information	Remarks and references to Appendices
COST HOUCK AREA	16/8/17 to 3/9/17.		Motor Lorries were placed at the disposal of the Battalion to convey the men to the Range. On the first occasion the lorries made a halt at ST OMER in the evening to enable the men to have a look round the town. On the other two occasions no halt was made owing to the heavy work placed on the lorries.	
			All Signallers, recruit and trained men, were billeted at Battalion Headquarters to enable the Signalling Sergeant to take them in hand for instruction daily.	
			Trained and Recruit Lewis Gunners were under the Lewis Gun Officer and Lewis Gun N.C.O's for instruction daily. Staff Sgt. Instructor Newton - G.H.Q.Lewis Gun School - gave practical instruction to the Lewis Gunners on the 17th, 18th, 19th and 20th August.	
			All equipment, Battle Stores, were overhauled, deficiencies made good and repairs carried out. Steel Helmets were all painted and flashed. Particular attention was paid to the completeness of Ammunition, Field Dressings, P.H.Helmets, Box Respirators, Identity Discs and Rifles. Latrine Seats, Buckets and Ablution buckets were obtained and issued to all coy's and Bn,Qrs. for use in the areas occupied by them.	
			Church Parades were held on the 19th, and 26th August and 2nd September in the Field adjoining Battalion Headquarters.	

Army Form C. 2118.

WAR DIARY
INTELLIGENCE SUMMARY.
(Erase heading not required.)

11TH BATTALION
THE
ROYAL FUSILIERS.

Place	Date	Hour	Summary of Events and Information	Remarks and references to Appendices
OOST HOUCK AREA	16/8/17 to 2/9/17		On the 20th and 21st August all the Rifles of the Battalion were inspected by the Brigade Armourer.	
			The Commanding Officer inspected Coy Organisation on the 21st August at 9-30.am	
			The G.O.C.54th Inf.Bde.inspected Battalion Organisation at 2-15.pm on the 21st August.	
			On the 19th August authority was given, pending confirmation by higher authority, for the following officers to wear badges of higher rank:-	
			Lieut.A/Capt.G.Dakin......Captain. 2nd.Lieut.G.S.Pearey......Lieutenant.	
			2nd.Lieut.E.L.Jones......Lieutenant.	
			On the 23rd August Sgt.Instructor Bumpstead gave instruction to all Companies N.C.O's in Bayonet Fighting.	
			On the 25th August the Battalion was fitted with Box Respirators under the direction of the 54th Brigade Anti-Gas N.C.O.	
			The Brigade Rifle Range at FOREST d'HAM was used by D and C Coy's on the 26th August.	
			The Medical Officer inoculated all Officers and Men who had not been inoculated since March 1916. 2 Officers and 8 men were done.	
			Battalion had baths and clean clothing on the 23rd August and 31st August.	
			On the 30th August the Brigade Rifle Range at FOREST d'HAM was used by A and B Coy's.	

Army Form C. 2118.

WAR DIARY
INTELLIGENCE SUMMARY.
(Erase heading not required.)

11TH BATTALION.
THE
ROYAL FUSILIERS.

Instructions regarding War Diaries and Intelligence Summaries are contained in F. S. Regs., Part II. and the Staff Manual respectively. Title pages will be prepared in manuscript.

Place	Date	Hour	Summary of Events and Information	Remarks and references to Appendices
OOST HOUCK AREA	16/8/17 to 3/9/17		On the 30th August Lieut.E.H.Cliff and Lieut.G.S.Pearcy were authorised to wear badges of Captain whilst Commanding Companies. Sports and Games were organised whenever possible. Battalion Boxing Tournaments and Football competitions were held. The following Officers and Other ranks reinforced the Battalion during this period. Captain A.D Welstead) Lieut. E.R.Weaker) Joined the Battalion 2nd.Lt. W. Taylor.) on 14th August. 2nd.Lt. J.Puxton.) 2nd.Lt.E.H.Beckett. Joined Battalion 16-8-17 2nd.Lt.C.C.S.Stockwell ditto 18-8-17 2nd.Lt. G.S.Knott. ditto 18-8-17 Lieut.A.Aley. ditto 20-8-17 2nd.Lt.F.Hankin. ditto 2-9-17. 18 Other ranks joined the Battalion 16-8-17. 2 ditto 23-8-17. 57 ditto 24-8-17. 90 ditto 26-8-17. 8 ditto 28-8-17. 64 ditto 1-9-17. 9 ditto 2-9-17. Total 249.	

Army Form C. 2118.

11th BATTALION,
THE
ROYAL FUSILIERS.

WAR DIARY

INTELLIGENCE SUMMARY.

(Erase heading not required.)

Instructions regarding War Diaries and Intelligence Summaries are contained in F. S. Regs., Part II. and the Staff Manual respectively. Title pages will be prepared in manuscript.

Place	Date	Hour	Summary of Events and Information	Remarks and references to Appendices
OOST HOUCK AREA	2/9/17		The Battalion accompanied by 1st Line Transport moved off at 12-45.pm to ESQUELBECQ Area see operation Orders No. 18 attached) The battalion arrived in Tents and billets at 3-30.pm.	
ESQUELBECQ AREA	3/9/17 to 9/9/17		"A" Coy occupying Billets, "B" Company occupying billets, Hd.Qrs. "C" and "D" Coy's occupying tents. During this period training was carried out by Companies on same lines as for the OOST HOUCK Area. but special attention was paid to a new formation attack, and Day and night patrolling was practised by all Coy's. Signallers and Lewis Gunners continued training under their respective officers. On the 3rd September Lieut F.R.Meaker and Lieut.A.Aley were authorised to wear the badges of Captain being the two Officers allotted for the new "Additional" acting Captaincy as laid down in Army Council instructions. The Brigade Rifle meeting was held on the 6th September at FOREST d'HAM. Open Competition:- C.S.M.Bailey No.16816 was awarded 3rd Prize. Inter Battalion Officers Competition:- 1st Prize 11th Battalion Royal Fusiliers. Individual Prize, Captain.G.S.Pearcy and Lieut.W.S.Minchin tied for 1st Prize. The Battalion carried out an Attack Scheme on the 7th September (see Operation Orders No.19 attached) On the 8th September the Battalion marched to I.T.A. Sheet 27 Belgium and France and were put through a Gas Cloud.	

A6945 Wt. W1442/M1160 350,000 12/16 D.D. & L. Forms/C/2118/14.

Army Form C. 2118.

WAR DIARY
INTELLIGENCE SUMMARY.
(Erase heading not required.)

Place	Date	Hour	Summary of Events and Information	Remarks and references to Appendices
ESQUELBECQ AREA	3/9/17 to 9/9/17		On the 9th September the Baths at WORMHOUDT were allotted to the battalion - clean clothing was issued to each man. Voluntary services for all denominations were held. During this period the undermentioned reinforced the Battalion:- 2nd.Lt. F.A.Leatherland. 2nd.Lt.S.W.Collings. 2nd.Lt.W.H.Stanley. 2nd.Lt. J.J.Lawrence. 2nd.Lt.R.G.Simmons. 2nd.Lt.T.Hordfeck. 2nd.Lt. E.G.Hanwell. 2nd.Lt.H.J.H.Saunders. 2nd.Lt.E.James. 2nd.Lt. H.L.Smedley. 2nd.Lt.F.F.Atterbury. 2nd.Lt.R.W.Gale. 2nd.Lt. R.Tantram.) All these Officers joined Battalion for duty on 6th September 1917. During the period 10th August to 9th September 30 Other ranks proceeded on leave, also Major A.J.Sulman, 2nd.Lt.H.W.Brookling and 2nd.Lt. W.Thomas.	

R.S. Greig Captain
Adjutant
17th Bn Royal Fusiliers

17TH BATTALION
THE
ROYAL FUSILIERS.

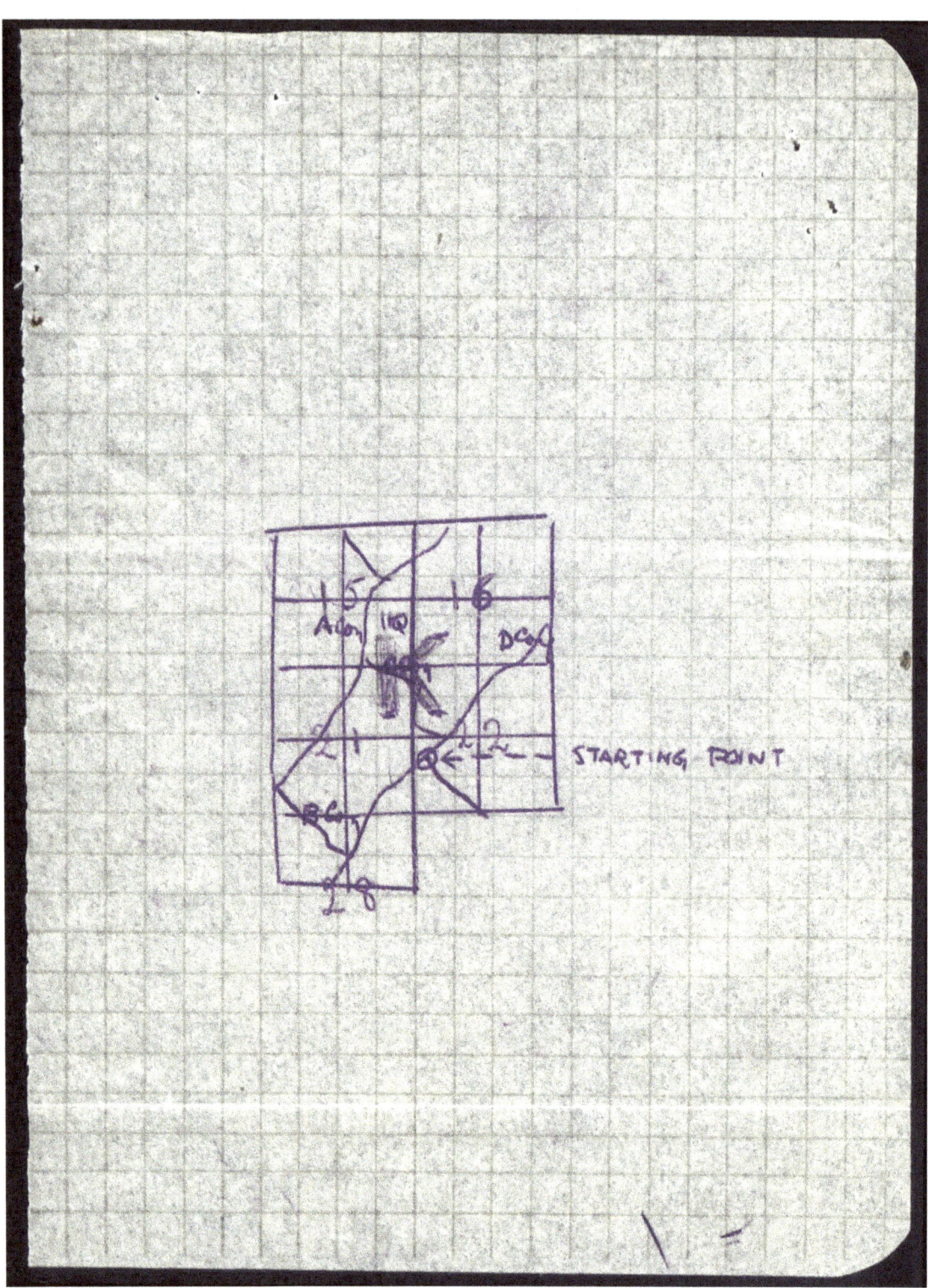

S E C R E T

"OPERATION ORDERS"
No.13.

1. The Battalion, less Details and 1st Line Transport will move to the
CHATEAU SEGARD AREA No.1. this evening.
The Battalion will parade on Coy Parade Grounds and move off at 6.pm
in the following order;- Hd.Qrs, "A", "B", "C" "D" Coys.
Coy's will move by platoons with an interval of 100 yards between platoons.
Route;- DICKEBUSCH - CAFE BELGE - CHATEAU SEGARD.

2. Baggage. Officers Mess Kits and baggage required for new area, must be
loaded on Wagon near "A" Coy's Office at 5.pm. This Wagon will accompany
the Battalion.
All Baggage not required for the new area will be dumped separately
on wagon near "A" Coy Office by 5 p.m. for storage with First Line Transport.
Officers Green Mess Box will be carried on the Cookers.

3. Teas will be ready at 4-30 p.m. Later tea will be provided on arrival.

4. Water Bottles will be filled before leaving.

5. Water Carts and Cookers will proceed in advance to new area at 5 p.m.

6. Bombs, S.A.A., & S.O.S. Rockets. All Battle Stores will be taken to the new area,
and arrangements for collection will be notified later.

7. DRESS:- Full Marching Order, - Steel Helmets will be worn. Caps will be
sacked by Coys and dumped with other baggage on the waggon with the spare kit.

8. Mess Cart, Maltese Cart & Limbers for Lewis Guns and Headquarters Limber
will be at "A" Coy's Office at 5 p.m.

9. Coys & Headquarters will be clear of their billets by 5-30 p.m.
The Camp will then be cleaned up by a small party per Coy & Hqrs. before
Battalion moves off. Coys will report when their lines and huts are clean.

4th AUGUST, 1917.
(Sd) O.C.Whiteman, Captain.
A/Adjutant 11th Bn. Royal Fusiliers.

SECRET   B.M.X/11.

54TH INFANTRY BRIGADE

DEFENCE SCHEME

1. **GENERAL PRINCIPLE.**

    The present front line running from Cross Roads at J.7.d.90.15 (exclusive) to YPRES - MENIN Road, J.14.c.0.7.(inclusive) will be the main line of defence and must be held at all costs.

    The second line of defence will be the trench line IGNORANCE CRESCENT - JACKDAW SUPPORT(J.13.a.5.0. - J.13.c.6.0.).

2. **ACTION IN CASE OF HOSTILE ATTACK.**

    (a) <u>Battalion holding front line.</u>

    The two companies in front line will hold this line at all costs.
    The company in the Tunnel under the YPRES - MENIN Road will be detailed as a counter-attack company and will immediately counter-attack any part of the front line in which the enemy may have gained a footing.
    The company in JACKDAW SUPPORT will garrison the second line of defence.

    (b) <u>Battalion in Support.</u>

    The two forward companies will be detailed as counter-attack companies and in the event of the front line falling will immediately counter-attack under orders of O.C.Support Battalion,if possible after communication with O.C.Front Line Battalion.
    The company in ZOUAVE WOOD will move up and reinforce the second line of defence, i.e. the IGNORANCE CRESCENT - JACKDAW SUPPORT LINE.
    The company in WELLINGTON CRESCENT will move up to ZOUAVE WOOD under orders from Brigade Headquarters where it will remain in Battalion Reserve.

    (c) Battalion in RAILWAY DUGOUTS, will move up to BIT. AREA under orders from Brigade Headquarters and will send an Officer to report at 54th Brigade Headquarters in RIDGE STREET, I.17.c.95.15.

    (d) Battalion in CH.SEGARD AREA.   )
        54TH MACHINE GUN COY.(RESERVE GUNS)) will move up to RAILWAY DUGOUTS under Brigade Orders and will each send a mounted Officer forward to report at 54th Brigade Headquarters.

    (e) 54th Trench Mortar Battery, will move forward as quickly as possible with available guns to BIT AREA and will send an Officer to report at 54th Brigade Headquarters.

3. All Officers and N.C.O's must reconnoitre routes and be thoroughly acquainted with the ground over which they have to move in case of a hostile attack.

                                            (Sd) G.F.J.Cumberlege Capt.
                                                        Brigade Major.
    6th August 1917.   54th Inf.Bde.

    All Coy's
        Signalling Officer.

                    Forwarded for information.

                                            Sd. O.C.Whiteman. Capt.
    6th August 1917.   A/Adjt.11th Bn.Royal Fusiliers.

SECRET.

ADMINISTRATIVE INSTRUCTIONS
to accompany
OPERATION ORDER No.14.

I. AMMUNITION.

1. Dumps. The following dumps have been established:-

(a). Brigade Bomb Store..............ZILLEBEKE CHURCH I.22.d.8.8.
(b). Advanced Brigade Dump...........TUNNEL J.13.a.9.3.

After the assault an advanced dump will be formed in JARGON TRENCH J.14.a.8.4.

2. Carrying Party.
One Company 8th Northamptonshire Regiment has been detailed as a carrying party.

3. Control.
The Dump at J.13.a.9.3.and J.14.a.8.4.will be controlled by the Officer Commanding the carrying party.

II. RATIONS & WATER.

1. Every man will carry a complete days rations and iron rations.

2. All water bottles must be filled at ZERO.

3. A small Brigade Reserve of water will be dumped in petrol tins at J.13.a.9.3.

4. Rations for "Z" plus 1 day will be brought up on pack animals on the evening of "Z" Day as far as Battalion Headquarters.

III. MEDICAL. Line of evacuation - along the YPRES - MENIN ROAD.

IV. PRISONERS OF WAR.

(a) Divisional Cage............I.22.b.7.5.

(b) Brigade Collecting Post...J.13.a.9.3.

V. STRAGGLERS POSTS. Posts consisting of 2 Regimental Police will be established at Battalion Hq. J.13.a.9.3.
Their duties will be :-

i. To direct wounded to the nearest Dressing Station.
ii. To take the numbers,names and units of all stragglers and to send all those that are fit back to their units.

7th August,1917.

(Signed) C.C.Whiteman,Captain.
A/Adjutant 11th Bn: Royal Fusiliers.

SECRET

"OPERATION ORDERS" No.15.   7TH AUGUST 1917.
----

1. THE Battalion will move to the forward area and take over the
    Battle Frontage in the following order relieving the 12th Middlesex
    Regt;-
            "A" "C" Hd.Qrs, "B" "D" Coy's.
    "A" "C" Coy's and Hd.Qrs will move by platoons at 2 minutes interval.

2. Parade.   "A" Coy will move with its right platoon leading and leave
    CHATEAU SEGARD Area at 7-30.pm. followed by "C" Coy and Hd.Wrs with
    intervals as mentioned above.
            "B" & "D" Coy's will leave CHATEAU SEGARD Area at 4.am 8th
    August with two minute intervals between platoons.
            The junction of A.T.N. Track and ZELLEBEKE - YPRES Road
    will be passed at the following times;-
            "A" Coy........9-30.pm
            "C" " 9-45.pm
            H.Q. 10.0.pm
            "B" " 6-0.am
            "D" " 6-15.am

3. Guides.   Guides for "A" and "C" Coy's from 12th Middlesex Regt will
    be at Junction of A.T.N. Track and old British Front Line at 10-30.pm
            Guides for remainder of Bn. will not be provided.
                                                        JACKDAW SUPPORT.
4. Location.   "C" Coy will be located about J.13.c.4.8./   Bn.Hq. at
    J.13.a.9.3.   "B" & "D" Coy's in RITZ TRENCHES.

5. Advanced Party, should be sent on under Coy arrangements.

6. Route;-   A.T.N.Track.

7. Teas. for "B" & "D" Coy's will be ready at 3.am before leaving CHATEAU SEGARD
    Area.

8. Reports.   Coy's will report completion of relief by "SAMMY.....pm.
                                                                  am.

                                    (Sd) O.C.Whiteman. Capt.
                                        A/Adjutant 11th Bn.Royal Fusiliers.

SECRET.

OPERATION ORDERS NO. 14.

1. The II Corps will capture at an early date INVERNESS COPSE, GLENCORSE WOOD and the Southern end of the WESTHOEK RIDGE.

2. The 18th Division will attack with 55th Bde. on the right and the 54th Bde. on the left. The 7th Bde. (25th Division) will attack on the left of the 54th Bde.

3. The 54th Bde. will attack with the 11th Royal Fusiliers on the right and the 7th Bedfordshire Regt on the left. One Coy of 6th Northamptonshire Regt will be attached to each of the assaulting Battalions for "mopping up". One Coy will be detailed for carrying and 1 Coy for consolidation and garrisoning Strong Points as shown in Appendix "A". Boundaries between Battalions are marked in black on Appendix "A".

4. The 11th Royal Fusiliers, forming the right assaulting Battalion, will form up on the general line J.14.c.15.55 - J.14.a.0.0. - J.13.b.9.5. They will fight their way through to the final objective and will consolidate and hold it.
The task of the 7th Bedfordshire Regt will be similar. They will form up along the line J.13.b.9.5. - J.7.d.95.15. road exclusive.
The approximate boundary line between these two Battalions is J.13.b.9.5.- J.14.a. 90.55 - J.14.b.65.85; between the 11th Royal Fusiliers and 55th Bde, J.14.c.15.55 - J.14.c.6.6. - J.14.d.5.7.

5. **Role of Companies.**
    The Battalion will be formed up as per diagram already in possession of Coys with "D" Coy on the right and "B" Coy on the left.
    The right of "D" Coy will be approximately J.14.c.16 in touch with the 7th Queens, the left approximately at J.14.c.1.9. and in touch with "B" Coy.
    The right of "B" Coy will be at J.14.c.1.9. in touch with "D" Coy and the left will be at J.14.a.1.3. and in touch with the 7th Bedfordshire Regt.
    "C" Company in support.
    "A" Company in reserve.

6. OBJECTIVES. "D" & "B" Coys will fight their way through to the final objectives as marked on Appendix "A".
    "C" Coy in support will finally occupy the unnamed trench running parallel to JARGON TRENCH.
    All objectives must be consolidated.

7. LINE OF EXPLOITATION. When "D" & "B" Coys arrive on their final objective patrols will be immediately pushed out to line of exploitation marked on Appendix "A"

8. ARTILLERY ARRANGEMENTS & BARRAGE MAP. See Appendix "C".

9. SIGNAL FOR ADVANCE. The signal for advance will be the opening of the shrapnel barrage, when bayonets will be fixed.

10. FLANK COMPANIES. "A" Coy, 7th Queens (Captain Hoskins) will be on the right of "D" Coy
    "C" Coy, 7th Bedfordshire Regt (Capt. Kingdon) will be on the left of "B" Coy.

11. COMMUNICATION. Constant communication to flanks as well as to rear must be maintained by all lines during operations. When final objective has been reached Battalion Headquarters must be informed of the situation.

12. STRONG POINTS. Location see Appendix "A".

13. BATTALION HEADQUARTERS. will be situated at J.13.a.9.3. and this location must be made known to all ranks.

14. SIGNALS. The Signal Officer will establish communication with Coys either by telephone or by visual as soon as possible.

15. COUNTER ATTACK. On final objective being reached Coys must make immediate provision for repelling counter attacks. Rifles must be kept clean.

16. The O.C. 54th Machine Gun Coy will detail 1 Gun for each of the Strong Points 1, 2, 3, & 6, and these guns will move forward with the strong point garrisons. Strong Points 4, 5 & 7 will, after the attack, be filled by the Vickers Guns sent forward with the assaulting Battalions; Strong Points 4 & 5 by the 11th Royal Fusiliers' Guns and Strong Point 7 by one of the Guns with the 7th Bedfordshire Regt.

17. The 54th Trench Mortar Battery will provide 1 Gun to go forward with each assaulting Battalion, complete with 80 rounds. 1 Gun will occupy Strong Point No. 1 and One Gun Strong Point No. 2.

18. EQUIPMENT S.A.A., GRENADES & TOOLS. The men will go over as light as possible. Assaulting Battalions will carry :-

        Riflemen.....................170 Rounds S.A.A.
        Bombers......................5 No.5's,120 Rounds S.A.A.
        Rifle Bombers................5 No.24's,.120 Rounds S.A.A.
        "Moppers Up".................5 No.24's or No.5's,120 Rounds S.A.A.
                                        usual

Signallers, Runners, &c., will carry their/complements.
Men must carry rations for 1 day plus 1 iron ration.
Steel helmets must be covered or mudded so as to ensure that they do not shine in the moonlight.

APPENDICES "A" & "C" CAN BE SEEN AT HEADQUARTERS AT CHATEAU SEGARD, these appendices should be seen at once as the final objective and line of exploitation has been moved further east.

7th AUGUST, 1917.

                                                  (Sd) O.C.Whiteman, Captain.
                                            A/Adjutant 11th Bn. Royal Fusiliers.

SECRET.

PRELIMINARY.

OPERATION ORDER NO. 15.

1. The Battalion will be prepared to move at 6-30 p.m. this evening to forward area. Officers kits and stores not wanted for forward area will be dumped at B.H.Q. by 5 p.m. Packs will be dumped by Coys at Battalion Headquarters by same time. Officers green mess boxes will be returned to Transport Lines on the Cookers. Water Bottles will be filled before leaving and a certificate will be sent to Orderly Room at once stating that Coys are complete with all Battle Stores.

2. Lewis Guns will be carried forward on pack mules - One mule per Coy.

3. One mule per Coy & HQ. will each carry forward 8 petrol tins of water and will report at Coy Hqrs by 6 p.m.

4. Order of march, advanced parties &c., will be notified later.

5. To-morrow's rations (issued) will be carried on the man.

Each Coy will detail one man to look after the kits and to supervise their loading.

(SIGNED) O.C.WHITEMAN CAPTAIN.
A/ADJUTANT IITH BN. ROYAL FUSILIERS.

7-8-17.

MAP REFERENCE
Trench Map
ZILLEBEKE
Sheets 28 N.W. 4
& N.E. 3 (parts
of) Ed-5.A. 1/10,000

11TH BN. ROYAL FUSILIERS

REPORT ON OPERATIONS OF 9TH/10TH AUGUST 1917

FORMING UP FOR THE ATTACK.

Tapes were laid in "no mans land" for the troops to form up on. The 11th Royal Fusiliers boundaries were from J.13.b.8.3. on left to J.13.d.9.6 on the right.

ZERO. The kick off at "Zero" was good with touch on left flank. On the right the 7th Queens Regt were late in starting and were 100 yards behind the line of 11th Royal Fusiliers first wave.

The companies were in position in good time.

FORMATION.

"B" and "D" Companies in front in two waves, "Moppers up" behind first wave.
"C" Company in Support along Battalion frontage.
"A" Company in Reserve behind "C" Company.

OBJECTIVES.

The two attacking Companies and the support Company reached the JARGON SUPPORT LINE from J.14.b.0.5. to about J.14.b.3.0. just north of FITZCLARENCE FARM.
The right attacking Company with its supports lost direction to a certain extent and did not occupy about 150 yards of trench on the right of the Battalion frontage.
A Party of the 7th Queens Regt moved on the right flank of the 11th Royal Fusiliers, but were not seen on the objective.
The objective was reached in good order and close behind the barrage, but came under destructive frontal machine gun fire. Time about 5.5.am.
The Lewis Gunners of the 11th Royal Fusiliers and the 8th Northamptonshire Regt. clearing party came into action here in the attempt to counter the enemy's Machine Guns and snipers.
The position remained the same until about 6.am by which time all the Officers and many of the N.C.O's were casualties. The enemy then developed a well planned counter attack from INVERNESS COPSE Supported by strong Machine Gun fire. The attack took the form of bombing up trenches from the Southern flank and also took our right company in rear. The effect was the uncovered flank of the Battalion was rolled up and driven back to the crest line of the strong point in J.14.a. which was consolidated and held until the battalion was relieved by the 8th Norfolk Regt.
The reserve Company in the attack reached its objective on the Right railway line running by the farm in J.14.b. This turned out to be a very exposed position on the forward slope and became untenable when the Germans counter attacked from the Copse. This company commander (NIGEL TWIEHOARE) withdrew to the crest line mentioned and reorganised the Battalion until he was killed.
The main cause of the Battalion being unable to remain on its objective was the enemy being in possession of our right flank. This extended for 700 yards and the Germans had that space to manoeuvre in against our flank and rear.
All the Officers and senior N.C.O's becoming casualties just before the critical moment a very dangerous situation remained uncounteracted for want of leaders.
There was a remarkable amount of rifle ammunition used in this battle and the Lewis Guns that survived used all their drums before returning.

Major.
11th Bn. Royal Fusiliers.

SECRET

MAP REF.
SHEETS 27 & 28   "OPERATION ORDERS"   No.15.
BELGIUM & FRANCE
SCALE 1/40,000

1. Move.   The Battalion will move today by Bus to the STEENVOORDE EAST Area
    from HOOGRAAF. C.14.d.9.5.   Route:- OUDERDOM - BUSSEBOOM.O.13.c.b.1.6.

2. PARADE.   The Battalion will parade ready to move off at 7-45.am in the
    following order:-   Bn.Qrs - Drums - "A" - "B" - "C" - "D" Coy's.
    Parade Ground - Site of old Quartermasters Stores.

3. DETAIL.   Reveille:- 5.am   Breakfast - 5-45.am
               Sick:- 6-30.am - Urgent cases only.

4. BAGGAGE.   Officers Kits, Mens Packs, &c will be dumped by Coy's and Hd.Qrs
    on the site of the old Qr.Mr.Stores, ready for loading by 7-15.am. Two bad
    marchers per Coy will be detailed as loaders and will report to Qr.Mr. at
    7.am at the spot where Baggage is dumped.   Officers Green Mess Boxes
    will be carried on the Cookers and be loaded by 7-30.am.

5. LORRIES.   Two Lorries will be placed at the disposal of the Battalion,
    for carrying Packs & surplus kit.   The Quartermaster will arrange to
    send a man to Bde.Hd.Qrs at 8.am to act as guide for lorries and will conduct
    them to loading point.

6. TRANSPORT. Mess Cart and Maltese Cart will be at Hd.Qr.Mess and Medical Inspection
    Room respectively at 7-15.am.
               The 1st Line Transport and attached G.S.Wagons will move
    independently under orders of the Transport Officer in accordance with special
    instructions issued to him.
               Limbers for Lewis Guns will be at Pack Dump Site of old Qr.Mr.
    Stores - at 7-15.am.   Guns etc should be on the Dump by 7.am.

7. RATIONS.   The unexpended portion of todays rations will be carried on the
    Cookers.   Rations for the 13th inst will be carried on the Supply Wagons.

8. DRESS.   Battle Order.

9. SICK.   Sick will be seen on arrival in new area.

10. ADVANCED PARTY.   The Advanced Party consisting of 2nd.Lieut.N.W.Brookling,
    2 men per Coy, 1 man Bd.Qrs., and one Cycle Orderly will parade at Bn.Hd.Qrs
    at 7-30.am under 2nd.Lieut.N.W.Brookling.   This party will report to
    Staff Captain at 54th Bde.Hd.Qrs at 8.am.   They will be conveyed to the
    forward area in lorries.   The Cycle Orderly will take Cycle.

11. WATER BOTTLES.   All waterbottles must be filled before starting.

12. SANITATION.   Coy's and Hd.Qrs will detail the usual cleaning up party
    and Coy's will report to the Adjutant on parade that their Huts and Lines
    are clean or otherwise.

                                        (Sd) O.C.Whiteman. Capt.
                                        A/Adjutant 11th Bn.Royal Fusiliers.
12th August 1917.

    Issued at:- 6.am to all concerned.

MAP REF.
SHEET 27
BELGIUM &
FRANCE
1/40,000
(not in possession
of Coy's)

"OPERATION ORDERS" No.17.   Copy No..... 3

S E C R E T

1. The 54th Bde will move to the BUYSSCHEURE AREA tomorrow August 15th by train from ABEELE.

2. The Battalion will parade with the head of the column on the starting point ready to move off at 5-30.AM. in column of route.
Order of march:- Hd.Qrs. "D" "B" "Drums" "C" "A" Coy's.
Starting point K.22.c.2.8. as marked on attached diagram.

3. 1st Line Transport will proceed by road in accordance with instructions issued to Transport Officer.

4. Motor Lorries on the scale of one per Battalion will report to Battalion Headquarters at 8-30.am.   The Quartermaster will detail a Guide to report to 54th Bde Headquarters - STEENVOORDE at 7-45.am to conduct this Lorry to the Qr.Mr.Stores.

5. Officers Kits and Baggage must be dumped at Company Headquarters at 5-30.AM under a guard of one man (bad marcher) ready for collection.   The Transport Officer will arrange to collect these Kits and convey them to the Qr.Mr. Stores.   Officers Green Mess Boxes will be carried on the Cookers.
Mess Cart & Maltese Cart will report at same hour.

6. Reveille:- 4.AM Breakfast:- 4-30.AM.   Haversack Ration must be carried on the man.

7. Waterbottles must be filled before leaving.

8. Billeting Returns for this Area must be handed to the Adjutant before entraining.

9. An entraining State shewing exact numbers going on train Officers and Other Ranks will be sent to the Orderly Room before moving off from Billets.
All Coy's , Hd.Qrs & Quartermaster will render this return.

10. Route:- BELGIUM FRONTIER - ABEELE .   Detraining Station:- NOORDPEENE.
Final Destination:- H.32.d.0.5.

11. Dress:- Full marching Order, Steel Helmets will be carried under the Pack straps.

12. Lewis Guns:- Limbers for Lewis Guns will report to Coy Hd.Qrs at 5.am. and after loading will rejoin and move with the 1st Line Transport.

13. All Billets will be left scrupulously clean.

14. Coy's will report arrival in new area, giving map location if possible.

15. Officers Chargers will accompany the Battalion to ABEELE Station when they th will proceed by road to the new area.

(Sd) O.C.Whiteman Capt.
A/Adjutant 11th Bn.Royal Fusiliers.

14th August 1917
Issued at 1.am August 15th 1917.

COPIES TO:-   1 Adjutant   10 R.S.M.
               2 War Diary   11 Cook Sgt.
               3 War Diary   12 Officers Mess
               4 Spare   13 Transport Officer
               5 Hd.Qrs.   14 Quartermaster
               6 O.C. "A" Coy   15 Lewis Gun Sgt
               7 O.C. "B" Coy
               8 O.C. "C" Coy
               9 O.C. "D" Coy.

Army Form C. 2118.

WAR DIARY
or
INTELLIGENCE SUMMARY.
(Erase heading not required.)

11th (Service) Bn. Royal Fusiliers

Place	Date	Hour	Summary of Events and Information	Remarks and references to Appendices
ESQUELBECQ.	1917 9th Sept. to 23rd Sept		During this period Training was carried out as per Programme laid down, which included Attack Schemes, Mopping-up Parties, Physical Drill, Bayonet Fighting, New Attack Formation, Platoon Attack, Musketry, Rifle Bombing, Close Order Drill, Rapid Wiring, etc. (See Programme attached) Re-fitting, Repairs to Equipment, Boots and Service Dress, were executed throughout the Battalion. Companies were thoroughly organized. Sports and Games were carried out whenever possible. Stretcher Bearers were given special instruction under the Medical Officer. On the 10th inst., C.R.A. 18th Division, gave a Lecture at School House, LEDRINGHEM, at 4 p.m. All Company Officers below the rank of Lieutenants, and Platoon Sergeants attended. The "Pung" of the Battalion played each evening in the Place, ESQUELBECQ from 5 - 6 p.m. The 12th Middlesex Pierrots gave a show in the Bandstand, ESQUELBECQ. On the 11th inst., Lorries were placed at the disposal of the Battalion, for taking men who came out of the Battle on the 10th August, to the Seaside. This trip was carried out without incident. Lieut. A. Aley was in charge of the party. On the 12th September, Lieut-Colonel C.C. Carr, D.S.O., relinquished command of the Battalion, and Proceeded to England for reporting to the War Office. Spawning open Operation Orders (N°20 Copy attached) was carried out Captain A.P. Welsted proceeded to 18th Divisional Headquarters for employment with D.H.	23.F. (attd)

Army Form C. 2118.

WAR DIARY
or
INTELLIGENCE SUMMARY. 11th (Service) Bn Royal Fusiliers

(Erase heading not required.)

Instructions regarding War Diaries and Intelligence
Summaries are contained in F. S. Regs., Part II.
and the Staff Manual respectively. Title pages
will be prepared in manuscript.

Place	Date	Hour	Summary of Events and Information	Remarks and references to Appendices
			On the 13th September, the Battalion carried out an Attack Scheme on the Training Area.	
			2nd Lieut. F.G. Maxwell and 8 Other Ranks were sent to Fifth Army Musketry School for instruction.	
			On the 14th September, an Officer of the 80th Field Coy. R.E., gave a demonstration on Consolidation of Shell Holes.	
			Captain R.W. Mosler was detailed as Observing Officer, and proceeded to take Observation Section in hand for training.	
			5 Other Ranks proceeded to Fifth Army Summer Rest Camp.	
			84 Other Ranks joined the Battalion as Reinforcements. Strength of Battalion :- 39 Officers, 804 O.R's.	
			On the 15th September, 3 Sergeants and 3 Corporals joined the Battalion for duty. 3 Other Ranks proceeded on Leave.	
			Credit for Francs 42.35 was received for Dripping despatched for Munition purposes.	
			On the 16th September (Sunday) Church Parade was held at 9.30 a.m.	
			No. 8120, Pte Fletcher, E., was awarded the MILITARY MEDAL for gallantry and devotion to duty during the operations against WESTHOEK RIDGE on 10th August 1917.	
			The following were recipients of "Parchments" issued by Divisional Commander, in recognition of bravery and devotion to duty during operations against WESTHOEK RIDGE on August 10th 1917 :-	

Army Form C. 2118.

WAR DIARY
or
INTELLIGENCE SUMMARY. 11th (Service) Bn. Royal Fusiliers

(Erase heading not required.)

Place	Date	Hour	Summary of Events and Information	Remarks and references to Appendices
			"A" COMPANY. "B" COMPANY. "C" COMPANY. "D" COMPANY.	
			No. 15560 Pte Adams, T. No. 35742 Pte Higgs, A. No.47353 Pte Bougourd,A. No. 8120 Pte Fletcher, S.	
			54822 " Glenwood,G. 7595 Cpl Hallett, H. 8265 Sgt Berry, H. 35149 " Howard, P.	
			7322 " Hilton, F. 7631 Pte Leverett,A. 7291 Cpl Emerson, F. 66997 " Jakes, A.	
			50578 L/c Maguire, J. 3560 L/c Rickards,W. 9949 L/c Sibley, W. 21878 L/c Jones, P.	
			50388 " Pitcher, H. 1224 Sgt Whittington,G. 1696 Sgt Wilson, E. 36733 Cpl Pike, G.	
			7674 Pte Rake, F. 29957 Pte Winter, W. 7255 Cpl Butterworth,F. 5007 Pte Wright, T.	
			60326 " Scriven, A. 7767 CSM Birch, W.	
			4756 L/c Wright, T. 44001 L/c Eveniss, E.	
			703 Pte Watkins, A. 7912 Sgt Norton, G.	
			7977 Pte Tomkins, A.	
			2nd Lieutenant H.L. Smedley took over training of Battalion Observers from Captain E.R. Meaker.	
			On the 17th September 1917, the Corps Commander awarded the MILITARY MEDAL to the following N.C.O's.	
			and men for gallantry and devotion to duty during the operations against WESTHOEK RIDGE on the 10th	
			August 1917 :-	

Army Form C. 2118.

WAR DIARY
or
INTELLIGENCE SUMMARY.   11th (Service) Bn. Royal Fusiliers

(Erase heading not required.)

Instructions regarding War Diaries and Intelligence Summaries are contained in F.S. Regs., Part II. and the Staff Manual respectively. Title pages will be prepared in manuscript.

Place	Date	Hour	Summary of Events and Information	Remarks and references to Appendices
			"A" COMPANY.	
			No. 703 Pte Watkins, A. No. 7631 Pte Leverett, A.	
			7322 " Hilton, F. 29937 L/c Winter, H.	
			50578 L/c Maguire, J. 12247 Sgt Whittington, G.	
			50388 " Pitcher, H. 3560 Cpl Rickards, W.	
			60326 Pte Bake, F. 35742 Pte Higgs, A.	
			54922 " Glenwood, A.	
			"B" COMPANY.	
			No. 7255 L/c Butterworth,F. No66997 Pte Jakes, A.	
			9949 Cpl Sibley, H. 35732 A/Sgt Pike, G.	
			47363 Pte Bougourd, A. 35149 Pte Howard, P.	
			7977 Pte Tomkins, A. 5007 " Wright, T.	
			44001 L/c Eveniss, E. 21878 L/c Jones, F.	
			"D" COMPANY.	
			2nd Lieutenant F.A. Leatherland and 9 Other Ranks proceeded to Fifth Army Musketry School on a Course.	
			69 Other Ranks reinforced Battalion. 2 Other Ranks proceeded on Leave.	
			On the 18th September 1917, the Corps Commander awarded the Bar to the MILITARY MEDAL to:-	
			No. 7291 Cpl. Emerson, F. 7912 Sgt Norton, G.	
			Training as per Divation Orders No 2. (see copy attached) was carried out	
			Two Other Ranks proceeded on Leave. Captain E.H. Cliff proceeded on Leave.	
			On the 19th September 1917, the Battalion carried out an Attack Scheme on Training Area.	
			The O.C., 80th Field Coy. R.E. gave a demonstration in four methods of wiring. All Company Officers	
			and Platoon Sergeants attended.	
			On the 20th September 1917, Lorries were again placed at the disposal of the Battalion, for taking a	

Army Form C. 2118.

WAR DIARY
or
INTELLIGENCE SUMMARY.
(Erase heading not required.)

11th (Service) Bn. Royal Fusiliers

Place	Date	Hour	Summary of Events and Information	Remarks and references to Appendices
			In the Battle of WESTHOEK RIDGE on August 10th 1917.	
			No. 7767 Sgt (A/CSM) Birch, W.J. No. 7695 Cpl Hallett, H.	
			8263 Sgt Berry, H. 7456 L/c Wright, T.	
			1696 Sgt Wilson, E. 15560 Pte Adams, T.	
			2nd Lieut. G.S. Pearcy, M.C. - BAR TO THE MILITARY CROSS.	
			10 Other Ranks were sent to the Fifth Army Musketry Camp for instruction.	
			Warning Orders were issued that the Battalion would move to the ST. JAN TER BIEZEN Area on the 23rd inst.	
			2nd Lieut. E.W. Ede proceeded on Leave.	
			Strength of Battalion :- 38 Officers and 963 Other Ranks.	
			On the 22nd September, the Battalion moved to the ST JAN TER BIEZEN Area by rail, in accordance with	
			Operation Orders No. 22 (copy attached). Transport was Brigaded and moved independently.	
			The Battalion detrained at POPERINGHE siding near POPERINGHE, and marched to Tunnelling Camp (F.27 a. central	
			Map Sheet 27 BELGIUM and FRANCE), and arrived in Camp at 7.45 p.m. "A" Company occupying Huts, "B"	
			Company Huts, "C" Company Huts, and "D" Company and Headquarters, Tents. 3/ Other Ranks proceeded on	
			Leave.	

Army Form C. 2118.

WAR DIARY
or
INTELLIGENCE SUMMARY.

11th (Service) Bn. Royal Fusiliers

(Erase heading not required.)

Instructions regarding War Diaries and Intelligence Summaries are contained in F. S. Regs., Part II. and the Staff Manual respectively. Title pages will be prepared in manuscript.

Place	Date	Hour	Summary of Events and Information	Remarks and references to Appendices
ST. JAN TER BIEZEN	23rd Sept. to 9th Oct.		Training. See Programme attached. During this period was continued as for period 9th - 23rd September. Working Parties were found for erection of Baths in vicinity of Camp, consisting of 1 N.C.O. and 10 men. Also every other day two men were employed on pumping water into Tank for Ablution purposes. Enemy Aircraft was abnormally active during the brilliant moonlight nights, and bombs were nightly dropped in vicinity of Camp. No casualties occurred in this Battalion. On the 23rd September 1917, (Sunday) Church Parade was held at 10.30 a.m. on ground adjoining Camp. On the 24th September 1917, 2 Other Ranks proceeded on Leave. Company Officers were sent to Special Course of Lectures at XVIII Corps School. On the 25th September 1917, 2 Other Ranks proceeded on Leave. On the 26th September 1917, 6 Other Ranks proceeded to Fifth Army Summer Rest Camp. 2 Other Ranks proceeded on Leave. On the 27th September 1917, the following Officers joined the Battalion for duty, and were posted to Companies as stated :- "A" COMPANY. "B" COMPANY. "C" COMPANY. "D" COMPANY. 2nd Lieut. R.E. Killingback. 2nd Lieut. J.P. Turnbull. 2nd Lieut. G. Normen. 2nd Lt. I.P.Cruikshank. 2nd Lieut. W.A.Spence. 2nd Lt.W.F. Roper. On the 28th September 1917, 2 Other Ranks proceeded on Leave.	

Army Form C. 2118.

WAR DIARY
or
INTELLIGENCE SUMMARY. 11th (Service) Bn. Royal Fusiliers

(Erase heading not required.)

Place	Date	Hour	Summary of Events and Information	Remarks and references to Appendices
			Strength of Battalion :- 44 Officers and 983 Other Ranks.	
			On the 29th September 1917, usual Training carried out. Nothing to report.	
			On the 30th September 1917, (Sunday) Church Parade was held at 10 a.m. on ground adjoining Camp. A special Platoon for work under the Royal Engineers were sent 80th Field Coy. R.E., under the command of 2nd Lieut. W.A. Smith.	
			2nd Lieuts. R.E. Killingbeck and J.P. Turnbull proceeded to Divisional Gas School for Course.	
			2nd Lieut. J.J. Lawrence and No. 60337, Sgt Whiffin, W., proceeded to 4th Army Infantry School for a five weeks Course.	
			Credit for Francs 80.50 was received for Dripping despatched for Munition purposes.	
			Captain J.C. Sale, M.C. (R.A.M.C.) the Medical Officer attached to the Battalion, proceeded on Leave.	
			On the 1st October 1917, authority for 2nd Lieut. B.P. Webster to wear badges of Lieutenant was received.	
			The Battalion entered a Shooting Competition against the 12th Middlesex Regiment, and beat them. Scores :- 462 - 425.	
			On the 2nd October 1917, 2nd Lieut. R.W. Gale and 2nd Lieut. J.P. Cruikshank proceeded to Divisional Gas School for Course. Training was carried out in accordance with Operation Order No 33. (Copy attached)	
			Captain O.C. Whiteman was confirmed in appointment as Adjutant of the Battalion under date 17.7.17.	

Army Form C. 2118.

WAR DIARY
or
INTELLIGENCE SUMMARY. 11th (Service) Bn Royal Fusiliers

(Erase heading not required.)

Instructions regarding War Diaries and Intelligence Summaries are contained in F. S. Regs., Part II. and the Staff Manual respectively. Title pages will be prepared in manuscript.

Place	Date	Hour	Summary of Events and Information	Remarks and references to Appendices
			Three Other Ranks proceeded on Leave.	
			On the 3rd October 1917, No. 50290, Cpl. A. Price, was sent to England as Candidate for a Commission.	
			"D" Company was temporarily detached from Battalion and proceeded to forward Area (BRAKE CAMP - G.6.b., Sheet 28 N.W.) where they were employed on carrying ammunition for Siege Battery.	
			On the 4th October 1917, 2nd Lieut. R.F. Killingback and 27 Other Ranks proceeded to Fifth Army Musketry Camp.	
			On the 5th October 1917, a Court of Inquiry was held under the Presidency of Captain G. Dekin and Membership of Lieut. E.L. Jones, M.C. and 2nd Lieut. C. Tentram, to enquire into and report on the wounding of No. 1844, L/c Proudlove, J. Training was carried out as per Order Order No 24 (copy attached)	
			Two Busses were placed at the disposal of the Battalion to convey Officers and N.C.O's. to see Model Battle Area near POPERINGHE.	
			The Brigade Rifle Range in the vicinity of Camp was placed at the disposal of the Battalion and was allotted to Companies from 9 a.m. to 4.15 p.m.	
			Captain R.N. Ford, M.C. joined the Battalion for duty. Strength of Battalion :- 44 Officers, 996 O.R's.	
			On the 5th October 1917, Major A.E. Sulman, M.C. was authorised to wear badges of Lieutenant-Colonel while commanding the Battalion.	

Army Form C. 2118.

WAR DIARY
or
INTELLIGENCE SUMMARY.
(Erase heading not required.)

11th (Service) Bn. Royal Fusiliers

Place	Date	Hour	Summary of Events and Information	Remarks and references to Appendices
			On night of 6/7th October 1917, Summer time ceased. Watches were at 1 a.m. put back to 12 midnight.	
			Conduct Sheets were checked by Captain R.H. Ford, M.C.	
			2nd Lieuts. C.C.M. Stockwell and E.G. Henwell proceeded to XVIII Corps School for a Platoon Commanders Course. "D" Company rejoined Battalion from ammunition	
			carrying, the casualties were 1 Other Rank wounded and 2 Other Ranks shell shock	
			On the 7th October 1917, Sgt. Hallet, H. No. 7595, "B" Company, proceeded to XVIII Corps School for Lewis Gun Course. Church Parade was held on ground adjoining Camp at 10 a.m.	
			On the 8th October 1917, 8 Other Ranks proceeded to Fifth Army Summer Rest Camp. *(having was cured out in accordance with Operation Order No.25 (copy attached)*	
			20 Other Ranks proceeded to Fifth Army Musketry School for Course.	
			2nd Lieut. E.J. Moir joined the Battalion for duty and was posted to "C" Company.	
			Baths at ST. JAN TER BIEZEN were allotted to Battalion and were used by all Companies and Headquarters during period 8 a.m. to 2 p.m. 170 men bathed per hour, and clean clothes were issued.	
			The following letter of appreciation was received from O.C., 5th Siege Battery:-	
			"I should like to place on record that the party of your Battalion under 2nd Lieut. W.F. Roper, attached "to my Battery from 3rd to 5th inst., has done excellent service in assisting 5th Siege Battery in the "recent Offensive, in bringing up Ammunition and helping the personnel to run forward the guns when dug in.	

A6045 Wt.W11442/M160 35,000 12/16 D.D.&L. Forms/C/2118/14.

Army Form C. 2118.

WAR DIARY
or
INTELLIGENCE SUMMARY. 11th (Service) Bn. Royal Fusiliers

(Erase heading not required.)

Place	Date	Hour	Summary of Events and Information	Remarks and references to Appendices
			"They have done very good work".	
			(Sgd) C.W. Langley, Major R.G.A.	
			Commanding 5th Siege Battery.	
			Captain R.M. Ford, M.C., was appointed Second-in-Command of the Battalion.	
			Authority for the following Officers to wear badges of higher rank was received :-	
			Lieut. E.L. Jones, M.C............ Acting Captain.	
			2nd Lieut. E.W. Ede............ Lieutenant.	
			[signature] Capt. & Adjt.	
			11th Bn. Royal Fusiliers.	

MAP REF.
FRANCE "B"
Sheet 27 N.W.
2nd.Ed.1/10,000

"OPERATION ORDERS" No.18.   Copy No....2....

S E C R E T

1. The Battalion will move tomorrow to C.7.c.8.8.

2. The Battalion will parade with the head of the column on starting point facing north ready to move off at 12-45.pm. in column of route.
Order of march;- Hd.Qrs, "D", "B", Drums, "A", "C" Coy's.
Starting point;- H.32.b.2.8.
Route;- H.20.d.1.3. - H.8.c.central - B.29.d.5.6. - La CLOUCHE - ESQUELBECQ Station.

3. First Line Transport will accompany the Battalion.

4. One Motor Lorry for the Battalion will report at G.30.c.2.6. at 12-30.pm. The Quartermaster will detail a guide to conduct Lorry to Quartermasters Stores.

5. Officers Kits and Baggage must be dumped at Coy.Hd.Qrs and Bn.Hd. Qrs.under a guard of 1 N.C.O. and 1 man (bad marchers) ready for collection at 11.am. The Transport officer will arrange to collect these Kits &c.and convey them to the Q.M.Stores. Officers Green Mess Boxes will be carried on the Cookers. Mess and Maltese Cart will report at Battalion Headquarters at same hour.

6. Lewis Gun Limbers will report to Coy.Hd.Qrs at 11.am. and after loading will rejoin and move with the 1st Line Transport.

7. Advanced Party consisting of one N.C.O per Coy and Headquarters, Transport, will report to Lieut.E.L.Jones at Battalion Headquarters at 6-30. this morning and proceed on Bicycles to Brigade Hd.Qrs, BUYSSCHEURE, where they will report to Staff Captain.
Each party will be provided with a Sheet 27.N.W. 1/20,000

8. Dress;- Full marching order - steel helmets will be carried under pack straps.

9. All waterbottles will be filled before leaving.

10. Rations. Haversack Ration will be carried on the man.
Dinners on arrival.
The unexpended portion of the days ration will be carried on the Cookers.

11. Reveille;- 7-30.am   Breakfast;- 8.am.
Sick Parade;- 8-30.am.

12. All billets will be left in scrupulously clean condition. Coy's will leave rear parties for this purpose. These parties on completion of their work will report to Cpl.Bentley at Bn.Hd.Qrs. and march to the new area.
All Wire ~~Netts~~ Beds will be left in billets.

13. Coy's will report arrival in new area giving map location if possible.

3rd.September 1917   Sd. O.C.Whiteman. Capt.
Issued at 3-15.am.   A/Adjutant 11th Bn.Royal Fusiliers.

Copies to:-   No.1 Adjutant.   No.9. O.C. "D" Coy.
               No.2.War Diary   No.10.R.S.M.
               No.3.War Diary   No.11.Cook Sgt.
               No.4.Spare.   No.12.Officers Mess
               No.5.Hd.Qr.Details.   No.13.Transport Officer
               No.6.O.C. "A" Coy.   No.14.Quartermaster
               No.7.O.C. "B" Coy.   No.15.Lewis Gun Sgt.
               No.8.O.C. "C" Coy.   No.16.Lieut.E.L.Jones.

TRAINING PROGRAMME.

11TH BN. ROYAL FUSILIERS.   -   PERIOD 9th - 15th September 1917.

DATE	TIME	NATURE OF TRAINING	LOCATION
SUNDAY. 9th	9 a.m. - 5 pm		
MONDAY. 10th.	10 am - 3 pm.	Battalion Attack Scheme.	I.1.a.
TUESDAY. 11th.	9 - 10 am. 10 - 10.30 am 10.30 - 11 am. 11 am - 1 pm. 2.30 - 3 pm.	Physical Drill and Bayonet Fighting. Musketry. Close Order Drill. New Attack Formation. Rifle Bombing. "A" and "B" Coys. will be Mopping-up Parties for 7th Bedfords.	L.1 - L.7.
WEDNESDAY. 12th	----	Trip to Seaside.	
THURSDAY. 13th.	----	Battalion Attack Scheme.	G.30.
FRIDAY. 14th.	9 - 10 a.m. 10 - 11 a.m. 11 am - 1 pm. 2.30 - 3 pm.	Physical Drill and Bayonet Fighting. Mopping-up Parties. Platoon Attack Scheme. Rifle Bombing and Musketry.	
SATURDAY. 15th.	9 - 10 a.m. 10 - 11 a.m. 11 am - 1 pm. ----	Physical Drill and Bayonet Fighting. Rapid Wiring. Company Attack Scheme. "C" and "D" Coys. will be mopping-up Parties for 7th Bedfords.	G.30.

REMARKS :-   Trained and Recruit Lewis Gunners under Lewis Gun Officer for instruction daily at Battalion Headquarters except when required for Company and Battalion Attack Scheme practices.
Trained and Recruit Signallers under Signalling Officer for instruction daily at Battalion Headquarters.
All Parades on Company Parade Grounds except where otherwise stated.
Location of Company Parade Grounds :-

"A" Company...C.13.a.8.8   "B" Company...C.1.d.
"C" Company...C.7.a.3.8   "D" Company...C.1.c.
Battalion Headquarters....B.12.d.9.8.

Lectures to Officers and N.C.O's. will be given during the week.
The use of the Prismatic Compass will be practised by Officers under Company arrangements.
The afternoons will be devoted to Games, etc. whenever possible.
Intensive digging will be practised daily.
Night Patrols will be carried out every evening under Company arrangements.
Times and locations to be sent to Orderly Room.
Bombs for Training purposes may be drawn from Quartermaster.

8th September 1917.

Capt.
A/Adjt.
for Lt-Col.
Commanding 11th Bn. Royal Fusiliers.

"OPERATION ORDERS" No.19.   Copy No..........

1. The Battalion will parade in column of route ready to move off from starting point at 9-30.am tomorrow, and march to rendezvous H.6.d.3.5.
   Starting point;- C.8.c.5.0.
   Order of march;- Hd.Qrs, "A", "B", Drums, "C", "D".
   Newly joined officers will march with their Coy's.
   Route;- C.8.c.5.0 - Cross Roads C.19.c.9.0. - C.25.b.2.6. ↓ FME DE HOAT HOF to H.6.d.3.5. (rendezvous)

2. Haversack Rations will be carried.   Dinners on return.

3. Dress :- Battle Order - Steel Helmets will not be worn.

4. Coy. Commanders and Captain A. Aley will report at Orderly Room at 8.30 a.m. - mounted - and will proceed in advance to rendezvous.

5. ATTACK SCHEME.   The enemy are holding a line running approximately through I.1.a.2.5 and I.1.a.8.2. with a support line running approximately through C.25.c.6.3 to I.1.b.2.9.
   The 11th Royal Fusiliers will attack this position with a "A" Coy. on the right, "B" Coy. on the left, "C" Coy. in support, and "D" Coy. in reserve.

   FIRST OBJECTIVE.   I.1.a.2.5 to I.1.a.8.2.

   FINAL OBJECTIVE.   C.25.c.6.3. to I.1.b.2.9.

   There will be a halt of 15 minutes on first objective. During this time Platoons must be re-organized ready for further advance. On reaching final objective, consolidation and preparations to meet counter-attack will immediately be made
   Mopping-up parties will be supplied by 2 Companies from another Battalion.   These parties will report to Coy. Commanders concerned at rendezvous.   Special
   The O.C. Mopping-up Party will garrison and consolidate various Strong Points shown on the ground.   Special attention will be paid to the flanks during the advance, in case Battalion on flanks should be held up.
   Flank Battalion represented by Signal Flags.
   Enemy will represented by the Drums and Pioneers.

   Forming up positions, First and Final Objectives, will be shown to Coy. Commanders on the ground.

   Barrage will be represented by 5 Signallers with flags.

   Battalion to be formed up by 11 a.m.

   Zero hour will be notified later.

   Opening of Barrage will be represented by drums.

   Rifles of Drums will be carried on limber.

   Tools, Rifle Grenades and Blank Ammunition will be issued at rendezvous.

The following parties will report at rendezvous to the undermentioned Officers:-

   Party representing Flank Battalions................. to Adjutant.

   Newly joined Officers............................... to Major Sulman.

   Battalion Observers................................. to Captain Meaker.

   "Enemy" (Drums and Pioneers)........................ to Captain Aley.

   "Barrage"... to Lieutenant Brookling.

Lewis Guns will be carried on Limbers under arrangements made by Lewis Gun Officer.

(SGD) O.C. WHITEMAN, Capt.
A/Adjt. 11th Bn. Royal Fusiliers.

11th Bn. FRANCE "OPERATIONS ORDER" No. 20.   Copy No...16....

INFORMATION. The enemy is holding a trench system as shown on map (German Front Line). Support Line (First Objective). Second Line (Final Objective).

INTENTION. The 11th Bn. Royal Fusiliers will attack this system with "A" Coy. on right, "B" Coy. on left, "C" Coy. in support and "D" Coy. in reserve.

OBJECTIVES. "A" and "B" Coys. will fight their way through to and consolidate Final Objective. On reaching Final Objective "A" Coy. will immediately push out strong patrols to seize and consolidate the high ground shown on line of exploitation. Patrols must then be pushed out in front of the line.
"C" Coy. will consolidate the First Objective. "D" Coy. will consolidate and garrison the original German Front Line Trench and will remain there as Battalion Reserve. This Coy. will not be used except under orders from Commanding Officer.

"MOPPING UP" PARTIES. Two Coys. of the 7th Bedfordshire Regiment, one to each Assaulting Coy., will provide "Area and Special Point" Moppers-up.
First line of Area Moppers-up will proceed to and mop-up and garrison Strong Points Area on line of West of railway.
Second line of Moppers-up will mop-up Area up to and including First Objective, garrisoning the latter and picketing Strong Points cleared till relieved by Special Point Moppers-up.
One group of Special Point Moppers-up will garrison each of Strong Points, B, C, D, E, F.
One Platoon of Special Point Moppers Up will garrison Strong Point "A"

FORMING UP. The Assaulting Coys. will form up on the line shown on Sketch Map in Nos. 1, 2 and 3 lines mixed up and forming one line.
The Area Moppers-up and one platoon of Special Point Moppers will form up in two lines. The Support Platoons and Lewis Guns of the Assaulting Coy. will form up in one line in rear of the Moppers-up.
The Support Coy. will form up in our old front line
The Special Point Moppers-up less one Platoon will form up in rear of the Support Coy.
The Reserve Coy. will form up in rear of the Special Point Moppers-up.
The Battalion will be formed up by 11 a.m.
Coy. Commanders will report by Runner to B.H.Q. when this is complete.
The Platoon Special Point Moppers up for the garrison of Strong Point "A" will form up behind the Area Moppers Up on the Right Flank of "B" Coy.

MACHINE GUNS. One Gun will move to Strong Points, "A", "B" and "D", as soon as these positions have been captured. One Gun will remain in reserve at Battalion Headquarters.

STOKES MORTARS. Two Guns will move to Strong point "A" as soon as the position has been captured.

BATTALION HEADQUARTERS. Battalion Headquarters will be situated at H.5.b.3.6. in old front line. An Advanced Battalion Signal Station will be established at Strong Point "A" as soon as First Objective has been taken.

CONSOLIDATION. Strong points will be constructed on the high ground at points Nos.1 and 2. These positions will be constructed by "A" and "B" Coy's respectively. A good amount of actual digging is expected consolidating the lines described under "Objectives"

Map Ref.
"B" Series
Sheet 27 N.W.
2nd Edition.
1/20,000.

Secret

"OPERATION ORDERS"

No. 21.

Copy No. 5.

Information	The enemy is holding a trench system as shewn on map (German Front Line). Support Line (First Objective) Second Line (Final Objective).
INTENTION.	The 11th Bn. Royal Fusiliers will attack this system with "C" Coy on the right, "D" Company on the left, "B" Company in Support and "A" Company in Reserve.
OBJECTIVES.	"C" and "D" Coy's will fight their way through to an consolidate Final Objective. On reaching Final Objective both Coy's will immeidately rush out strong patrols to seize ground shewn on line of exploitation. "B" Coy will move in close support to assaulting Coy's and if not used to reinforce them will halt at least 100 yards before the Final Objective. "A" Coy will move to the original German Front Line trench and remain there as Battalion Reserve. This Coy will not be used except under orders from Commanding Officer. The assaulting Coy will not halt on the First Objective, but keep close up to the barrage until it halts, and reorganise there.
MOPPING UP PARTIES.	Two Companies of the 7th Bedfordshire Regiment, one to each assaulting Coy will provide "Area and Special point" Moppers up. First line of Area Moppers up will closely follow assaulting Coy's and not proceed beyond strong points "C", "D", "E". Second line of Moppers Up will Mop up Area up to and including First Objective, garrisoning the latter and picqueting all strong points. One group of Special Point Moppers Up will garrison each of strong points "C", "D", "E". One platoon of Special Point Moppers Up will garrison strong points "A" and "B".
FORMING UP.	The assaulting Coy's will form up on the line shewn on sketch map Nos. 1, 2, and 3 lines mixed up and forming one line. The Area Moppers up form up in two lines. One platoon special point Moppers Up for the garrison of strong points "A" and "B" will form up behind the Area Moppers Up on the right flank of "C" Company. The Support platoons and Lewis Guns of the assaulting Coy's will form up in one line in rear of the Moppers Up. The Support Coy will form up in our old front line. The Special Point Moppers Up, less one platoon, will form up in rear of the Support Coy. The Reserve Company will form up in rear of the Special Point Moppers Up. The Battalion will be formed up by 11 a.m. Company Commanders will report by Runner to Battalion Headquarters when this is complete.
MACHINE GUNS.	Three Guns will move to the First Objective as soon as the position has been captured. One Gun will remain in Reserve and move with Battalion Headquarters.
STOKES MORTARS.	Two Guns will move to Strong Point "B" as soon as the position has been captured.
BATTALION HEADQUARTERS.	Battalion Headquarters will be situated at H.6.b.7.8. in old Front Line. An advanced Signal Station will be established in old German Front Line about I.1.c.2.5. as soon as First Objective has been taken.

CONTINUED.

ARTILLERY. Barrage will open 200 yards in front of our forming up position, and will move at the rate of 50 yards per minute.
Heavy standing Barrage will be on all known strong points, and will lift when the Shrapnel Barrage is within 200 yards of the Strong point.

ZERO HOUR. Zero hour will be 11-50.am.

Flank Battalions will be represented by a RED flag.

Enemy lines will be represented as follows:-
    OLD GERMAN FRONT LINE..........WHITE Flags.
    FIRST OBJECTIVE................BLUE Flags.
    FINAL OBJECTIVES...............RED Flags.
    LINE OF EXPLOITATION...........YELLOW FLAGS.

Barrage will be represented by "Drums".

Assaulting Coy's will carry 25% large tools. Support and Reserve Coy's 50% large tools.

Blank ammunition will be issued at rendezvous.

The following parties will report at rendezvous to the undermentioned Officers:-

    Party representing Flank Battalions..........O.C."A" and "B" Coy's.
    Barrage (Drums)..............................2nd.Lieut.H.L.Smedley.
    Mopping up Parties.(Coy.Commanders)..........Adjutant.
    "Enemy" (Coy.Commanders).....................Adjutant.
    Battalion Observers..........................Capt.E.E.Mosker.
    Stretcher Bearers............................Capt.J.C.Sale.
    Umpires.........Lieut.E.L.Jones.)
                  2nd.Lt.B.P.Webster.)......Commanding Officer.
                  2nd.Lt.D.G.Welch.)

Lewis Guns will be carried on Limbers under arrangement made by Lewis Gun Officer.

                                                              Capt.
                                                              A/Adjutant.

12th September.1917.   11th Bn.Royal Fusiliers.

Issued at 7.pm.   Copies to.   No.1. H.Q.54th Bde.
                                         No.2. H.Q.54th Bde.
                                         No.3. Commanding Officer
                                         No.4. Adjutant.
                                         No.5. War Diary.
                                         No.6. War Diary.
                                         No.7. O.C."A" Coy.
                                         No.8. O.C."B" Coy.
                                         No.9. O.C."C" Coy.
                                         No.10. O.C."D" Coy.
                                         No.11. Lewis Gun Officer.
                                         No.12. Signalling Officer.
                                         No.13. Quartermaster.
                                         No.14. O.C. 7th Bedfordshire Regt.
                                         No.15. O.C. 54th Machine Gun Coy.
                                         No.16. O.C. 54th Trench Mortar Batty.
                                         No.17. Transport Officer
                                         No.18. R.S.M.
                                         No.19. Office Copy.
                                         No.20. Spare.

Legend:
- Strong Point
- X—X— Forming Up Line
- ●—●— Coy Boundary
- First Objective
- Final Objective
- Line of Exploitation

German Front Line

X—X— LEFT COY   X—X— RIGHT COY
BATTN HQ
OLD FRONT LINE
(SUPPORT COY)
RESERVE COY

CONSOLIDATION. A good amount of digging is expected in the First and Final
Objectives.   The consolidation of the Final Objective will
take the form of a series of positions, not a continuous line.

ARTILLERY.   Barrage will open 200 yards in front of our forming up position,
and will move at the rate of 50 yards per minute.   There will
be a halt of 15 minutes on First Objective.   The barrage will
then move at the rate of 100 yards in 2 minutes.   During the
15 minutes halt the barrage will be 100 yards in front of First
Objective.
Heavy Standing Barrage will be on all known Strong Points, and
will lift when the Shrapnel Barrage is within 200 yards of the
Strong Point.

ENEMY.   Will be represented by 2 Companies of the 6th Northamptonshire
Regiment, wearing Steel Helmets or white cap-bands.

ZERO HOUR.   Zero hour will be 11.30 a.m.

GENERAL.   Flank Battalions will be represented by a RED flag.

Enemy lines will be represented as follows :-
    OLD GERMAN FRONT LINE......................WHITE flags.
    FIRST OBJECTIVE............................BLUE flags.
    FINAL OBJECTIVE............................RED FLAGS
    LINE OF EXPLOITATION.......................YELLOW flags.

Strong Points - All known Strong Points will be marked with a
Notice board.

Barrage will be represented by "Drums".

Assaulting Companies will carry 25% large tools.   Support and
Reserve Companies 50% large tools.   Tools will be carried on
limber and issued at rendezvous.
      Blank ammunition will be issued at rendezvous.
Lewis Guns will be carried on limbers under arrangement made by
Lewis Gun Officer.

The following parties will report at rendezvous to the
undermentioned Officers:-

Party representing Flank Battalions......O.C. "C" and "D" Coys.
Barrage (Drums)..........................R.S.M.
Mopping-up Parties (Coy. Commanders).....C.O.
"Enemy" (Coy. Commanders)................C.O.
Battalion Observers......................2nd Lieut. H.L. Smedley
Stretcher Bearers........................Capt. J. C. Sale.
Umpires.......Capt. E.R. Meeker.)
              Lieut. E.L. Jones.)......Commanding Officer.
              2nd Lt. D.C.Welch.)

18th September 1917.

                                              Capt.
                                              A/Adjutant.
                                         11th Bn. Royal Fusiliers.

Issued at   Copies to :-

          No. 1. H.Q. 54th Bde.   No. 13. Quartermaster.
          No. 2. H.Q. 54th Bde.   No. 14. O.C. 7th Beds. Regt.
          No. 3. Commanding Officer.   No. 15. O.C. 7th Beds. Regt.
          No. 4. Adjutant.   No. 16. O.C. 6th Northants. Regt.
          No. 5. War Diary.   No. 17. O.C. 6th Northants. Regt.
          No. 6. War Diary.   No. 18. O.C. 54th M.G.C.
          No. 7. O.C. "A" Coy.   No. 19. 54th T.M.B.
          No. 8. O.C. "B" Coy.   No. 20. Transport Officer.
          No. 9. O.C. "C" Coy.   No. 21. R.S.M.
          No. 10. O.C. "D" Coy.   No. 22. Office Copy.
          No. 11 Lewis G. Officer.   No. 23. Spare.
          No. 12 Signalling Officer.

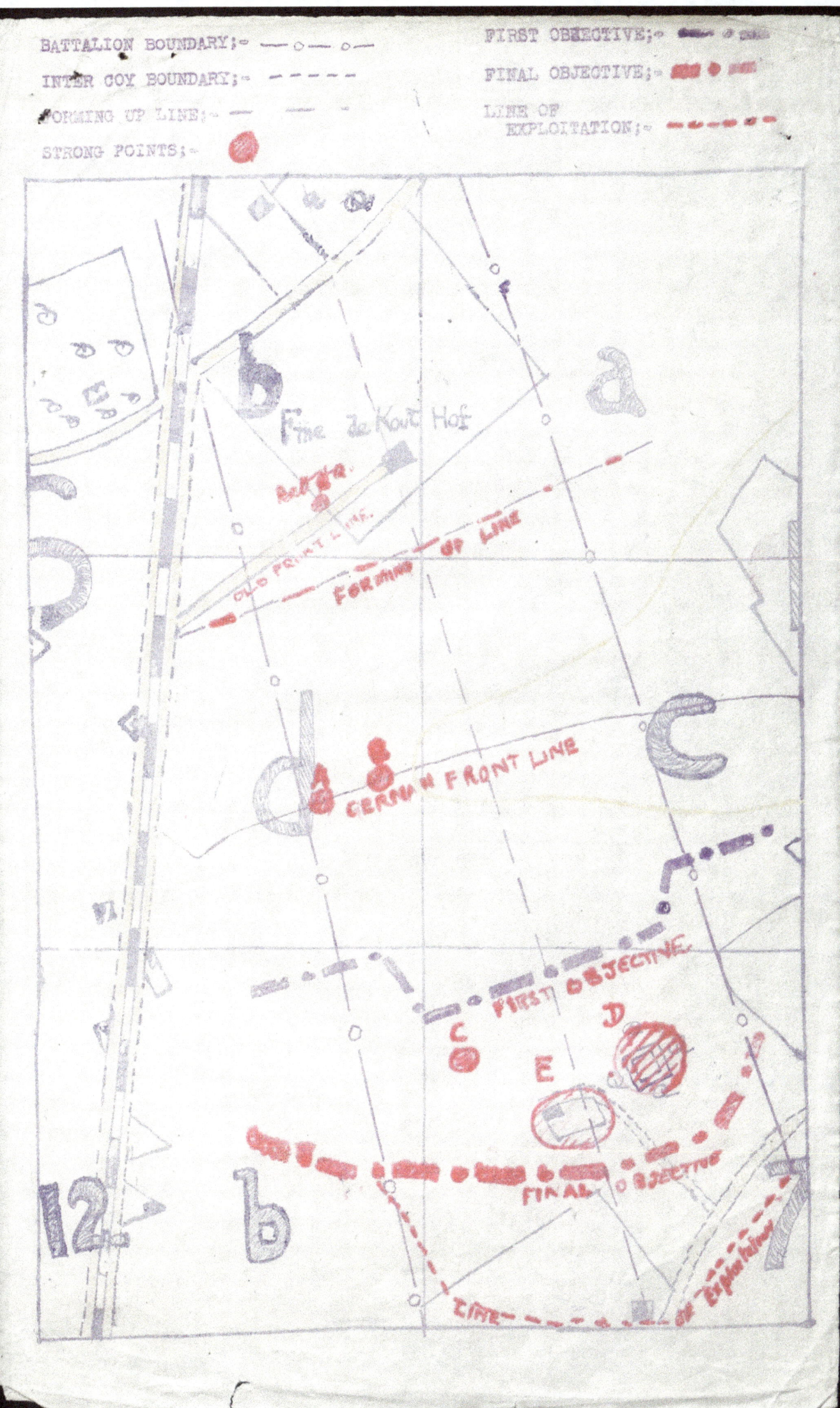

SECRET. OPERATION ORDER NO. 22.   Copy No. 4

Map Reference :-
Frame Sheet 2 7 N.W.
Edition 2.

MOVEMENT.	The 54th Infantry Brigade Group will be moving to the ST. JAN TER BIEZEN Area by train from ARNEKE tomorrow 22nd instant. The 11th Royal Fusiliers together with the 12th Middlesex and the 54th Machine Gun Company will proceed by train leaving at 2.30 p.m.
	The Battalion will parade ready to move as follows :-
	Order of March :- Hd.Qrs., "B", "C", Drums, "D", "A". Head of Column. Starting Point :- B.12.b.2.0.
	Time :- 11.30 a.m.
	Route :- From Starting Point via Forge C.25.b.1.5., Fme de Kout Hof, thence along East side of Railway to ARNEKE Station.
	"A" Coy. will join the Battalion at B.18.a.9.8.
	Dress :- Full Marching Order. Steel helmets will be carried in pack straps.
PARADE STATE.	Coys. will hand to the R.S.M. on parade, a State showing the number of Officers and other ranks actually entraining.
RATIONS, MEALS, &C.	Officers will carry haversack rations. Dinners will be cooked tonight, and with the unexpended portion of the day's rations, will be carried on the man. Water bottles will be filled tonight. Teas :- On arrival in new billets.
R.E. PLATOON.	The Officer and other ranks comprising this will parade and move with their respective Coys.
COOKS.	Each Coy. will detail one Cook to accompany the Coy. Cooker.
Officers' CHARGERS.	These will march with the Battalion to ARNEKE, when Pte Murray will be in charge of this party and be responsible for taking them to L.2.a.4.0. unless other destination is given at ARNEKE. Grooms will accompany Battalion and take over Chargers at ARNEKE.
ADVANCE PARTY.	An Advanced Party consisting off Lieut H.W. Broadling and the C.Q.M.Sgts., Cpl. Farley and one N.C.O. from the Transport will proceed by train leaving ARNEKE at 9 a.m. tomorrow morning.
BAGGAGE.	All Officers' Kits and Mess Stores of "B", "C" and "D" Coys. will be dumped at Q.M. Stores by 6.30 a.m. Officers' Kits and Mess Stores of "A" Coy. must be ready for removal by limber at 6 a.m. Hd.Qrs. Officers' Kits and Orderly Room Baggage will be dumped outside respective Billets for collection by limbers at 6.30 a.m. The Transport Officer will be responsible for sending limber to collect "A" Coy. and Hd.Qrs. Officers' Kits, etc. Coy. Commanders must please see there is no delay with Kits, etc. All Officers' Kits must be rolled as compactly as possible. The usual Mess Box will be carried on the Cooker. Drummers' Packs and Rifles will be dumped at Quartermaster's Stores by 6.30 a.m. Lewis Guns have been loaded today as per special orders from the Lewis Gun Officer. Lewis Guns will be drawn by Coys. from limber on arrival at new Billets. Cooking Signalling and Hd.Qrs. Detail/Equipment will be carried on the usual tool limber. This must be loaded up by 7.15 a.m.

CONTINUED.

2.

One Lorry will be detailed to report to Q.M. Stores. Quartermaster will detail Guide to report at a place to be notified later, to conduct Lorry to Stores (further instructions re Lorry will be given the Quartermaster as soon as available).
No Loaders will be detailed by Coys.

BILLETS. All Billets, etc. will be left scrupulously clean.
Coy. Commanders and Hd.Qrs. Details will report to A/Adjutant on parade that their Billets are clean.
All Tents will be left standing with the flies rolled up.
Coy. Commanders are reminded that no loose ammunition is to be left in Camp or Billets.

TRANSPORT. The Mess Cart and Maltese Cart will be at their respective Headquarters by 7 a.m.
Cookers are to be loaded ready to move off at 7 a.m.
The whole of the First Line Transport and Train Baggage Wagons will proceed by March Route under the Transport Officer.
All Transport must be ready to move off at 7.30 a.m.
"A" Coys' Cooker will join the Transport on the march at C.8.a.75.70 at 7.40 a.m. (This Cooker must not be late).
All Transport will be Brigaded and march under the orders of the Officer Commanding 152nd Coy. A.S.C. Starting Point :- LEDRINGHEM (I.3.a.1.7).
Time :- 9 a.m.
Transport will be drawn up along the main street in LEDRINGHEM ready to move off by this hour.
Transport of the 11th Royal Fusiliers will lead and will wait with the head of its Column at I.3a.3.9, facing South-west.
All other arrangements as to the order of march will be made by Officer Commanding 152nd Coy. A.S.C.

The entire Battalion Transport will move off at 7.30 a.m. to Starting Point (as above) via C.8.d.75.70 BUSCH HOUCK - LA MOTTE.

ARRIVAL IN NEW BILLETS. On arrival in new Billets Coys. will report arrival and if detached from Battalion Headquarters give Map Co-ordinate of Coy. Office.

(SGD) E.L.JONES, Lieut.
A/Adjt.
11th Bn. Royal Fusiliers.

21st September 1917.
Issued at 9.10 p.m.

Copies to :-
No. 1. C.O.
2. Adjutant.
3. War Diary.
4. War Diary.
5. O.C. "A" Coy.
6. O.C. "B" Coy.
7. O.C. "C" Coy.
8. O.C. "D" Coy.
9. Quartermaster.
10. Transport Officer.
11. Signalling Officer.
12. Lewis Gun Officer.
13. R.S.M.
14. Cpl. Farley.
15. Sgt. Greening.
16. Spare.

PROGRAMME OF TRAINING

11TH BN. ROYAL FUSILIERS ...... PERIOD 16TH - 22ND SEPTEMBER 1917.

DATE	TIME	NATURE OF TRAINING	LOCATION
SUNDAY 16-9-17	9.30.am From 10.30.am	Church Parade. Baths.	C.7.a. WORMHOUDT.
MONDAY 17-9-17.	9.am. to 10.am 10.am to 10.30. 10.30.am to 11. 11.am to 12. 12.noon to 1.pm 2.30. to 3.30.	Physical Drill and Bayonet Fighting. Musketry. Close order drill. New attack formation. Rifle Bombing. Rifle Bombing & Musketry for backward men.	
TUESDAY 18-9-17		Battalion attack scheme.	I.1.
WEDNESDAY 19-9-17.	9.am to 10.am 10.am to 11.am 11.am to 1.pm 2.30. to 3.30.	Physical Drill and Bayonet Fighting. "Mopping Up" parties. Platoon attack scheme. Rifle Bombing and Musketry for Backward men	
THURSDAY 20-9-17		Company attack scheme	I.1.
FRIDAY 21-9-17.	9.am to 11.am 11.am to 1.pm 9.am to 11.am 11.am to 1.pm 9.am to 10.am 11.am to 12. 12.noon to 1.pm 2.30. to 3.30.	Rapid wiring........"C" Coy. Forming up and Mopping up....."C" Coy. Forming up and Mopping up....."D" Coy. Rapid wiring........"D" Coy. Physical Drill and Bayonet Fighting.) Forming up and new attack formation.) for "A" Close order drill.) and "B") Coy's. Rifle Bombing and Musketry for backward men	Battn.Hd.Qrs. Battn.Hd.Qrs.
SATURDAY 22-9-17.	9.am to 11.am 11.am to 1.pm 9.am to 11.am 11.am to 1.pm 9.am to 10.am 10.am to 12.n. 12.n. to 1.pm 2.30. to 3.30pm	Rapid Wiring........"B" Coy. Forming up and Mopping up......"B" Coy. Forming up and mopping up......"A" Coy. Rapid wiring........"A" Coy. Physical Training and Bayonet Fighting. For "C" Forming up and New attack formation and "D" Close order drill Coy's Rifle Bombing and Musketry for backward men	Battn.Hd.Qrs. Battn.Hd.Qrs.

REMARKS.

Trained and Recruit Lewis Gunners under Lewis Gun Officer for instruction daily at Battalion Headquarters except when required for Company and Battalion attack schemes.

Trained and Recruit Signallers under Signalling Officer for instruction daily at Battalion Headquarters.

All parades on Company Parade Grounds except where otherwise stated.

Location of Company Parade Grounds:-
"A" Coy.........C.13.a.c.d.   "B" Coy............C.1.d.
"C" Coy.........C.7.a.b.d.   "D" Coy............C.1.c.
Battalion Headquarters.........B.12.a.c.d.

Lectures to Officers and N.C.O.'s will be given during the week.

The use of the Prismatic Compass will be practised by Officers under Coy arrangements.

The afternoons will be devoted to Games, etc., whenever possible.

Intensive digging will be practised daily.

Night Patrols will be carried out under Company arrangements. - Times and Locations to be sent to Orderly Room.

Bombs for Training purposes may be drawn from Quartermaster.

Battalion Observers under special instruction by Observation Officer.

PRACTISING LESSONS LEARNT FROM LAST WEEKS TRAINING AND DAILY BRIGADE REPORT.

O.C. Whiteman
Captain.
A/Adjutant, for
Commanding 11th Bn. Royal Fusiliers.

PROGRAMME OF TRAINING

11th BN. ROYAL FUSILIERS   PERIOD 24th – 29th September 1917.

DATE	TIME	NATURE OF TRAINING	LOCATION
MONDAY 24.9.17.	9 – 10 a.m. 10 – 10.30 a.m. 10.30 – 11 a.m. 11.10 – 12 noon. 12 noon – 1 p.m. 2.15 – 3 p.m.	Physical Training and Bayonet Fighting Musketry. Practice in Dummy Bomb Throwing. Close Order Drill. Intensive Digging. Musketry for backward men. Lecture by R.S.M. on Musketry to NCO's	
TUESDAY 25.9.17.	9 – 10 a.m. 10 – 10.30 a.m. 10.30 – 11 a.m. 11.10 – 12 noon. 12 noon – 1 p.m. 2.15 – 3 p.m.	Physical Training and Bayonet Fighting Gas Helmet Drill. Musketry. Practice in Dummy Bomb Throwing. Company Route March, with special attention to March Discipline. Musketry for backward men. Lecture by R.S.M. on Musketry to NCO's	
WEDNESDAY 26.9.17.	9 – 10 a.m. 10 – 10.30 a.m. 10.30 – 11 a.m. 11.10 – 12 noon. 12 noon – 1 p.m. 2.15 – 3 p.m.	Physical Training and Bayonet Fighting Musketry. Practice in Dummy Bomb Throwing. Close Order Drill. Intensive Digging. Musketry for backward men. Lecture by R.S.M. on Musketry to NCO's	
THURSDAY 27.9.17.	9 – 10 a.m. 10 – 10.30 a.m. 10.30 – 11 a.m. 11.10 – 12 noon. 12 noon – 1 p.m. 2.15 – 3 p.m.	Physical Training and Bayonet Fighting Gas Helmet Drill. Musketry. Practice in Dummy Bomb Throwing. Company Route March, with special attention to March Discipline. Musketry for backward men. Lecture by R.S.M. on Musketry to NCO's	
FRIDAY 28.9.15.	 2.15 – 3 p.m.	Battalion Route March Musketry for backward men.	
SATURDAY.	9 – 10 a.m. 10 – 10.30 a.m. 10.30 – 11 am. 11.10 – 11.45 a.m. 11.45 – 12.15 p.m. 12.15 – 1 p.m. 2.15 – 3 p.m.	Physical Training and Bayonet Fighting Practice in Throwing Dummy Bombs. Gas Helmet Drill. Close Order Drill. Musketry. Intensive Digging. Musketry for backward men	

REMARKS.
   ✓ Trained and Recruit Lewis Gunners will carry out Programme arranged by Lewis Gun Officer, except when required for Platoon or Company Attack Schemes
   ✓ Trained and Recruit Signallers will carry out Programme arranged by Signalling Officer.
   ✓ Lectures to N.C.O's. will be given during the week.
   ✓ The afternoons will be devoted to Games, whenever possible.
     Dummy Bombs for training purposes may be drawn from Quartermaster's Store
   ✓ Battalion Observers under special instruction by Observation Officer
     If suitable ground can be found, the above programme will be varied so that Platoon and Company Attack Schemes may be carried out.
     Practising lessons learnt from last week's training and daily Brigade Reports.

                                             Lieut.
                                             A/Adjutant.
                                           11th Bn. Royal Fusiliers.

OXO -

RIGHT FLANK BOUNDARY

SP.

LEFT FLANK BOUNDARY.

PROGRAMME OF TRAINING
11TH BN. ROYAL FUSILIERS......PERIOD 1ST - 7TH OCTOBER 1917

DATE	TIMES	NATURE OF TRAINING
SUNDAY	10.am	Church Parade.
MONDAY 2-9-17	9.am to 10.am 10.am to 11.am 11.am to 1.pm 2-15.pm to 3.pm	Physical Training and Bayonet Fighting Musketry. Platoon in attack. Musketry for backward men.
TUESDAY 3-9-17	9.am to 10.am 10.am to 11.am 11.am to 1.pm 2-15.pm to 3.pm	Physical Training and Bayonet Fighting Musketry. Company in "leap-frog" attack. Musketry for backward men.
WEDNESDAY 4-9-17	9.am to 10.am 10.am to 11.am 11.am to 12.noon 12.noon to 1.pm 2-15.pm to 3.pm	Physical Training and Close order drill Musketry. Action on reaching objective. March discipline and deployment. Musketry for backward men.
THURSDAY 5-9-17	9.am to 10.am 10.am to 11.pm 2-15.pm to 3.pm	Musketry. Battalion in the attack (leap-frog) Musketry for backward men.
FRIDAY. 6-9-17	9.am to 10.am 10.am to 11.am 11-15.am to 12.noon 12.noon to 1.pm 2-15.pm to 3.pm	Physical Training and Bayonet Fighting Musketry. March discipline and Artillery formation Close order drill. Musketry for backward men.
SATURDAY 7-9-17.	9.am to 10.am 10.am to 11.am 11-15.am to 1.pm 2-15.pm to 3.pm	Bayonet fighting and Close order drill. Musketry. Company in "leap-frog" attack. Musketry for backward men.

REMARKS - LOCATION &c.

All Officers and N.C.O's to visit Model Battle Field at A.30.c.
Company, and Platoon,Commanders Conferences, daily.
Lectures to Officers, and N.C.O's will be given during the week.
Trained and Recruit Lewis Gunners will carry out programme arranged
    by Lewis Gun Officer, except when required for Platoon or Company
    attack schemes.
Trained and Recruit Signallers will carry out programme arranged by
    Signalling Officer.
Battalion Observers will receive special instruction daily under
    Observation Officer.
Special classes for N.C.O's in Physical Training and Bayonet Fighting
    will be held under the Brigade Instructor.
Intensive Digging will be practised daily.
Night patrols will be sent out.
The afternoons will be devoted to games whenever possible.
Location of parade ground:- Tunnelling Camp.
    Brigade Training Area.

Lieut.
for Major.
Commanding 11th Bn.Royal Fusiliers.

29/9/17

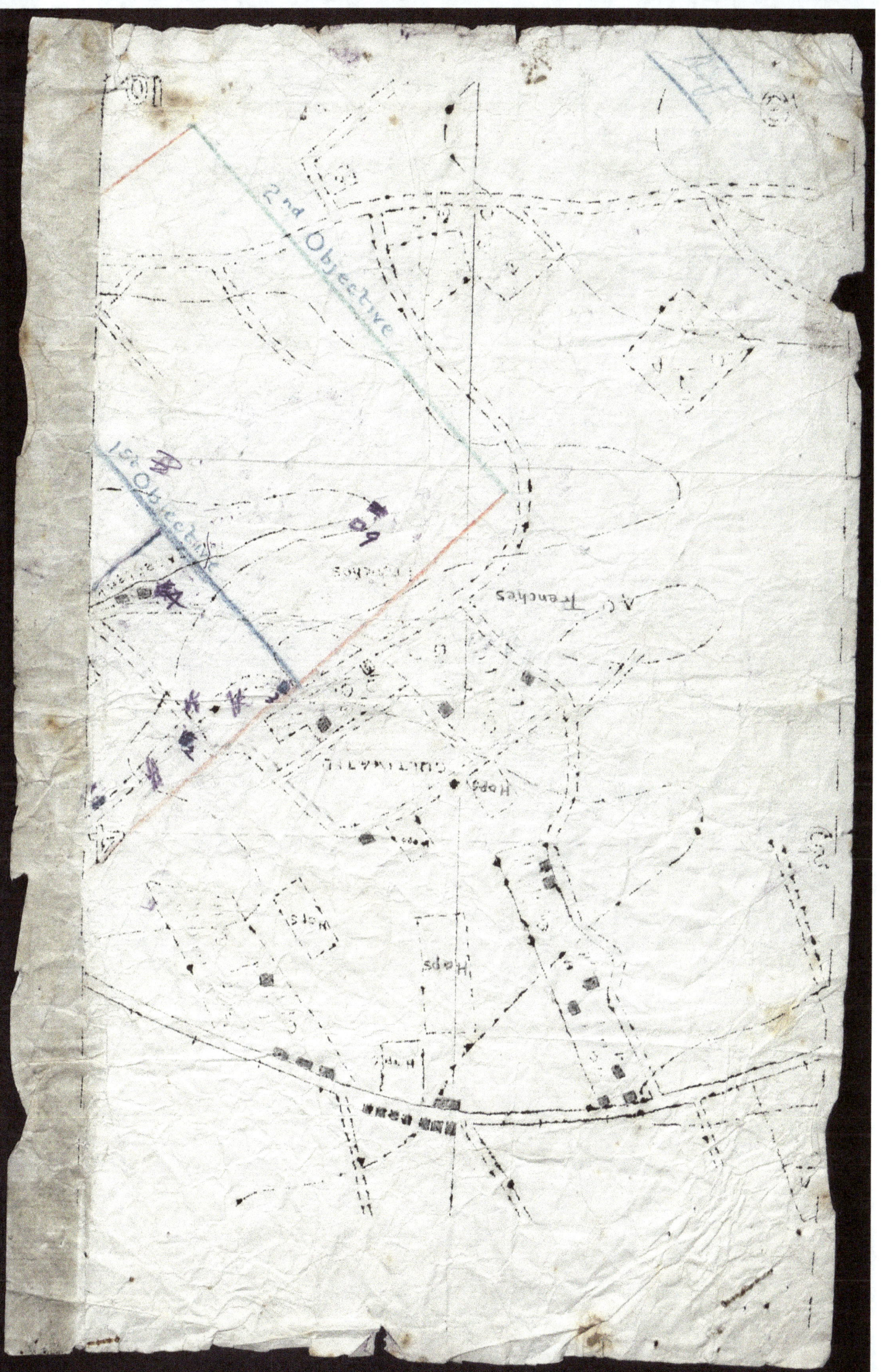

Army Form C. 2118.

11TH BATTALION,
THE
ROYAL FUSILIERS.

WAR DIARY
or
INTELLIGENCE SUMMARY.
(Erase heading not required.)

Place	Date	Hour	Summary of Events and Information	Remarks and references to Appendices
TUNNELLING CAMP	10/10/17		The Battalion carried out Training under Company Commanders arrangements which included Close order drill, Musketry and Physical Drill.	
-do-	11/10/17		"B" Echelon - consisting of specialists such as Reserve Company Sgt.Majors, Platoon Sergeants Lewis Gunners, and Signallers and Junior Officers proceeded to HOUTKARQUE for Training at the 18th Division Reinforcement Depot. 2nd.Lieut.W.Hornfeck proceeded on a Lewis Gun Course at the G.H.Q., Small Arms School, LE TOUQUET The following Casualties occurred to the Platoon attached to 80th Field Coy's Royal Engineers while doing work in the forward area;- 2 Other Ranks Killed, 6 Other Ranks Wounded. Training was carried out as on the 10th inst.	
-do-	12/10/17		Training of Battalion was carried out as per Training Programme (Copy attached) Operation orders giving Details of Scheme for this day are attached (No.26)	
-do-	13/10/17		Battalion Training was carried out as yesterday and the Scheme laid down in Orderation Orders No.26 was repeated. Strength of Battalion at this date;- 45 Officers 987 Other Ranks - 15 Officers were temporarily detached on Courses, employment etc, and 251 Other Ranks were away from Battalion on Courses Reinforcement Camp etc etc.	
-do-	14/10/17		Sunday. Battalion paraded for Divine Service at 10.am on the Football Ground adjoining Camp. Captain J.C.Sale M.C. (R.A.M.C) Medical Officer attached to the Battalion was awarded the DISTINGUISHED SERVICE ORDER for Gallantry and devotion to duty during the Operations against WESTHOEK RIDGE on the 10th August 1917. This day all Overcoats of the Battalion were fitted with tabs and buttons so that they could be worn short when men were in the line and so save the bottom of the coats getting muddy and wet. During this period 10th to 14th October 1917 at TUNNELLING CAMP the Battalion was fitted with Service Dress where necessary, Repairs to Boots and equipment was executed by the Regimental workshops.	
TRENCHES	15/10/17.		The Battalion proceeded to forward area by busses in accordance with Operation Orders No.27 (copy attached) 1st Line Transport moved independently to a spot at about B.28.b.5.5. Sheet 28 N.W. BELGIUM.	

Army Form C. 2118.

11th BATTALION.
THE
ROYAL FUSILIERS.

From: ....
Date: ....

WAR DIARY
or
INTELLIGENCE SUMMARY.
(Erase heading not required.)

Instructions regarding War Diaries and Intelligence Summaries are contained in F. S. Regs., Part II. and the Staff Manual respectively. Title pages will be prepared in manuscript.

Place	Date	Hour	Summary of Events and Information	Remarks and references to Appendices
TRENCHES	16/10/17		Battalion occupied CANE TRENCH at C.9.a. Sheet 28 N.W. BELGIUM. Casualties Other Ranks;- 1 Killed 3 XX Wounded 1 Wounded and died of wounds. 2nd Lieut.C.S.Knott was slightly wounded & remained at duty. The Battalion relieved the 10th Essex Regt.-53rd Infantry Brigade- on the night 16/17th in the front line- POELCAPPLE. Companies being distributed at V.19 Sheet 20 S.E.3 WESTROUSEEK. Casualties	
-do-	17/10/17 18/10/17		on 17th were Other Ranks;- 4 Killed, 16 Wounded 2 Shell Shock. Remained in the front line - Battalion Headquarters was at BULOW FARM - U.30.c POELCAPPLE Map. and were relieved by the 7th Bedfordshire Regiment on night 18/19th October 1917 and proceeded to CANAL Dugouts at C.26.a Sheet 28 N.W. BELGIUM. Casualties on 18th inst were Other Ranks:- 3 Killed 12 Wounded and 1 Wounded & Died of wounds.	
CANAL DUGOUTS	19/10/17 to 21/10/17		Remained in CANAL Dugouts and cleaned up as much as possible. The strength of the Battalion at this date was 45 Officers, 933 Other Ranks of these 22 Officers and 296 Other Ranks were away from Battalion on Courses, At Division Reinforcement Camp, etc etc... at 8-15.pm the Battalion moved up to CANE TRENCH Area as per Operation Orders No.29 (copy attached)	
TRENCHES	22/10/17 to 24/10/17		at 3.am on morning of 22nd inst the Battalion moved forward from CANE TRENCH Area to PHEASANT FARM at U.A - POELCAPPLE MAP , and acted as support Battalion to 10th Essex Regt - 53rd Bde.who attacked the BREWERY East of POELCAPPLE. This attack was very successful.- all objectives being gained and held. Battalion was called on to hold the positions taken - this operation was successfully accomplished. Casualties on 21st inst were Other Ranks 1 Killed, 4 Wounded, 1 Shell Shock. Casualties on 22nd inst were Other Ranks:- 2 Killed 29 Wounded 14 Shell Shock and Captain A.Aley wounded Battalion held the line.and late at night- from 7.pm, the Battalion was relieved and proceedd to YSER CANAL at C.26.c where Busses were waiting to convey Officers and men to DIRTY BUCKET CAMP at A.30.Central Sheet 28 N.W.BELGIUM. Casualties for the 23rd inst were Other Ranks:- 12 Killed 27 Wounded 2 Shell Shock. Casualties for the 24th inst were Other Ranks:- 1 Wounded.	
DIRTY BUCKET CAMP.	25/10/17. te 28/10/17		Battalion rested and cleaned up, service dress was refitted where required, unserveceable clothing being replaced by new. The Battalion was reinforced by 10 other ranks from the Base. on the 25th 4 Other Ranks reinforced the Battalion from Base. and 10 Other Ranks proceeded on Leave "A" & "B" Coy's had baths- the remainder of Battalions Baths were cancelled as no water was available. Coy's were at the disposal of their Commanders for training which was limited owing to lack of ground No.23707 Pte.Anderson proceeded to England as candidate for commission. Authority from 18th Division was received for Captain Ford.M.C. to wear badges of Major while acting	

A6945 Wt. W14422/M1100 350000 12/16 D. D. & L. Forms/C./2118/14.

Army Form C. 2118.

11TH BATTALION,
THE
ROYAL FUSILIERS.

WAR DIARY
or
INTELLIGENCE SUMMARY.
(Erase heading not required.)

Instructions regarding War Diaries and Intelligence Summaries are contained in F. S. Regs., Part II. and the Staff Manual respectively. Title pages will be prepared in manuscript.

Place	Date	Hour	Summary of Events and Information	Remarks and references to Appendices
PROVEN AREA	29/10/17		2 Other Ranks proceeded on Leave.	
	to		6 Other Ranks were sent to 54th Machine Gun Coy for special instruction in the use of the Vickers Gun	
	31/10/17		Captain G.S.Pearcy M.C. proceeded on Leave.	
			3 Other Ranks proceeded on Leave.	
			2 Other Ranks Reinforced the Battalion from Base.	
			On the 20th October 1917 No.6210 Pte.O'Neill J. and No.2100 Pte.Hurst.J. were awarded th MILITARY MEDAL for gallantry and devotion to duty whilst on a carrying fatigue for the Royal Garrison Artillery.	
			On the 20th October 1917 Captain E.L.Jones proceeded on Leave.	
			on the 17th October 1917 No.53088 B/C.Pitcher.H. proceeded to England as Candidate for Commission.	

Captain.
Adjutant.
11th Battalion Royal Fusiliers.

WAR DIARY
or
INTELLIGENCE SUMMARY.
(Erase heading not required.)

Army Form C. 2118.

11TH BATTALION,
THE
ROYAL FUSILIERS.

Place	Date	Hour	Summary of Events and Information	Remarks and references to Appendices
DIRTY BUCKET CAMP	25/10/17 to 28/10/17		2nd-in-Command to the Battalion. Major (Acting Lieut-Colonel) A.E.Sulman M.C. was promoted to Temporary Lieut-Colonel. The Strength of the Battalion at this date was:- 45 Officers, 834 Other Ranks. of these 9 Officers and 84 Other Ranks were away on Courses, Leave etc., etc.	
			2 Other Ranks proceeded on Course at the 18th Corps School - Lewis Gun Branch. Captain.R.R.Meeker assumed Command of "B" Coy this day. 2nd.Lieut.H.J.H.Saunders proceeded on Leave Coy's were at the disposal of their Commanders for Training. The Commanding Officer inspected Coy Organisation. The No.17 Platoon formed for work with the 80th Field Coy Royal Engineers were this day attached to "D" Coy. Lieut.H.W.Breckling was appointed 2nd-in-Command of "C" Coy this day.	
			2nd.Lieut.E.J.Meir proceeded to POPERINGHE to undergo a course in Anti-gas duties at the 5th Army Gas School. 3 Other Ranks proceeded on Leave. 3 Other Ranks proceeded to 18th Corps School for a Course in Signalling. 1 Other Rank proceeded to 54th Trench Mortar Battery to undergo instruction.	
PROVEN AREA	29/10/17 to 31/10/17		At 9-45.am the Battalion and 1st Line Transport proceeded by march route to P.2. Area (PROVEN) and occupied PICADILLY CAMP A.2o of 7 - Sheet 19. BELGIUM. (See Operation Orders No.30 copy attached) 1 Other Rank proceeded to G.H.Q. Lewis Gun School - Le TOUQUET for a Course. 5 Other Ranks proceeded on Leave. Authority was received for 2nd.Lieut.G.Tantrum to wear badges of higher rank - Lieutenant. 2nd.Lieut.G.W.Gibbs joined the Battalion this day for duty and was posted to "D" Coy.	
			4 Other Ranks joined the Battalion as reinforcements from Base. No.57992 Pte.Franklin and No.16997 Pte.North were tried by Field General Court Martial for "Absence without Leave" Notification was received that 14 days leave would now be given starting from 1st November 1917 instead of the 10 days as hereto.	

Copy of 54th Brigade Memo No.B.M.46 forwarded for information of Coy's
----

All Battalions.

   Units will make as soon as possible flags to denote during a battle, positions of Battalion, Coy and Platoon Hd.Qrs.

2.   The colours of the flags should be the same as those commonly used by units.

   11th R.Fusiliers..........Blue and Red.
   7th Bedfordshire Regt.....Yellow and Black
   6th Northants Regt........Blue with White letters
   12th Middlesex Regt.......Yellow and Red.

3.   It is suggested that the dimensions of Bn.Hd.Qrs flag be 2 foot square with letters R.F. Mx. etc.

   Coy H.Q. eighteen inches by 12 and cut;- 18"/ B / 12"

   Platoon with number on flag and cut;- 15" / 12"

4.   These flags will always be used in training.

                        Sd.   G.P.J.Cumberlege   Capt.
                              Brigade Major
                              54th Inf. Bde.

SECRET.   OPERATION ORDER NO. 24.   Copy No. 2

58TH BRIGADE SCHEME.

INTENTION. The Battalion will attack the First Objective with "A" Coy. on right and "C" Coy. on left.   "B" Coy. will "leap-frog" "A" and "C" Coys. and capture the Second Objective.
"D" Coy. will be Counter-Attack Coy.

FORMING UP. "A" and "C" Coys. will form up on line shown on attached Map.
"B" Coy. will form up at least 100 yards in rear of "A" and "C" Coys. and move at ZERO to a position 200 yards beyond forming up line.
"D" Coy. will form up in rear of "B" Coy. and move on orders from Battalion Headquarters.

BATTALION H.Q. Battalion Headquarters will be situated about L.4.d.6.8. and will move to Strong Point No. 4 on the capture of Second Objective.

M.G.C. and T.M.B. Machine Gun Company and Trench Mortar Battery will move into Valley about L.4.d.6.3. after the capture of Second Objective and await further orders.

MESSAGES. Negative and positive information must be constantly sent back.

GARRISON. All Troops detailed to capture Strong Points etc., must remain there as Garrison.

ENEMY. No Troops will be representing "Enemy".

BARRAGE. Barrage will be represented by Flags and will report to 2nd Lieut. H.L. Smedley at forming up line at 10.15 a.m.   He will be assisted by 2nd Lieut M. Taylor and 2nd Lieut W.F. Roper.

TOOLS. 50 per cent. Large Tools will be carried by "A", "C" and "B" Coys. These will drawn from the Quartermaster's Stores.

UMPIRES. Captain G.S. Pearcy, Lieut E.L. Jones and Lieut. B.P. Webster. These Officers will report Commanding Officer at rendezvous at 10.15 a.m Captain G. Dekin will report to O.C., 12th Middlesex Regiment at 9.15 am

OFFICERS. "A" and "B" Coys. will each detail three Officers and "C" and "D" Coys. two Officers, to report to Adjutant at 10.15 a.m.   These Officers will remain in all Strong Points and write a report on the manner in which the Strong Point was captured.
All Officers not detailed as above and not going into action will witness the Attack from the Shrine.   These Officers will march to forming up position with their Coys.

5th October 1917.   Capt.
Issued at 7.50 p.m.   Adjt.
                                                           11th Bn. Royal Fusiliers.

Copies to :-
1. Adjutant.
2. War Diary.
3. War Diary.
4. C.O.
5. O.C., "A" Coy.
6. O.C., "B" Coy.
7. O.C., "C" Coy.
8. O.C., "D" Coy.
9. Quartermaster.
10. Signalling Officer.
11. Assistant Adjutant.

SECRET.
OPERATION ORDER No. 25.   Copy No. 8

1. The Battalion (less Hd.Qr. Details and "D" Coy) will make a practice attack on the Brigade Training Area tomorrow October 2nd 1917.

2. The Battalion Frontage (about 400 yards) will be as indicated on the attached Map.

3. "A" Coy. will capture and consolidate a position corresponding with the blue line shown.
   "B" Coy. will "leap-frog" through "A" Coy. and capture the red line.
   "A" Coy. will consolidate under the barrage and according to the ground a series of positions corresponding with the red line.
   "C" Coy. will not move until the first Objective is taken.
   "D" Coy. (less 2 Platoons) is detailed as Counter Counter-Attack Coy and will be under the Command of 2nd Lieut. Hopkins. After the red line is captured "D" Coy. (less 2 Platoons) will move to the Farm "K", where they will remain awaiting Orders from the Battalion Commander.
   "C" Coy. will move 200 yards in rear of "B" Coy to the First Objective and will proceed when the final Objective is captured to the Farm marked "X" where they will remain awaiting Orders from the Battalion Commander.
   2 Platoons of "D" Coy. will be the "Enemy" and will be placed in position by the C.O.
   Captain Airy, commanding this portion of the Company will report to C.O. at the Shrine at 10.30 a.m.
   The "Enemy" will wear their hats reversed.

4. The Battalion will be formed up in Attack Formation ready to move at 11 a.m.
   Forming Points, etc., will be indicated by Notice Boards.

5. Coys. will indicate the position of their Headquarters during Battle by a Flag in accordance with letter D.M. 42 (Copy attached).

6. Zero hour will be notified on the ground.

7. **BARRAGE.**
   The Barrage will come down 100 yards in front of the forming-up line for 1 minute and will then proceed by bounds of 50 yards with 2 minutes halt between each bound.
   Barrage will be represented by Flags.
   The new setting of Barrage will proceed by bounds running 50 yards and then halting for two minutes.
   2nd Lieuts. W. Taylor and R.E. Killingbach will be on either Flank controlling the Barrage.
   6 Drummers will be detailed by R.S.M. to form Barrages. They will march with "F" Coy. to the ground.
   All Coys. to be as strong as possible.

2nd October 1917.

Issued at 9 p.m.   Copies to:-
1. C.O.
2. Adjutant
3. "A" Coy.
4. "B" Coy.
5. "C" Coy.
6. Lieut. E.L. Jones.
7. R.S.M.
8. War Diary
9. War Diary
10. Spare
11. Spare
12. Spare
13. Spare

Signed E. Agnew Lieut.

P.S. Barrage will halt for 10 minutes 100 yards beyond 1st Objective to enable C. Coy to move up.

SECRET. OPERATION ORDER No. 25. Copy No 15

INTENTION.   The Battalion will attack on a Four-Company Front and
              capture Objective as shown on attached Map, with "X"
              Battalion on its right and "Y" Battalion on its left.
              (both imaginary).
              Twelve hours after the capture of Objective, "O"
              Battalion and "P" Battalion (both imaginary)will leap-
              frog this line and capture a further Objective.

FORMING UP.   The Battalion will form up on the line shown on Map
              with "C" Coy. on right, "A" on left of "C", "B" Coy. on
              left of "A" Coy, "D" Coy. on left of "B".
              Battalion to be formed up by 10.45 a.m. Coys. will
              report to Battalion Headquarters when this is complete

ROLE of COYS. All Coys. will fight their way through to Objective and
              consolidate on that line.   All Strong Points, fortified
              Farms, etc., after capture will be garrisoned.

BARRAGE.   Will be represented by Flags.   The Barrage will open
              100 yards in front of the forming up line, and after a
              pause of one minute will advance by 4 @ yard bounds to
              about 100 yards beyond the Objective.
              There will be a halt of two minutes at each bound.
              Party representing the Barrage will report to 2nd Lieut.
              H.L. Smedley at 10 a.m.   He will be assisted by 2nd
              Lieuts. R.W. Gale and W.P. Rover.

BATTALION   Will be situated at Shrine and will move to Strong Point 7
HEADQUARTERS. after capture of the Objective.

M.G.C. & T.M.B. will both move to Strong Point 7 after capture of
              OBJECTIVE.
ZERO.   11 a.m.
ENEMY.   Each Coy. will detail 11 men to represent "Enemy". These
              men will report to Lieut. H.W. Brookling at 10 a.m.

STRONG POINTS. Will be marked by Notice Boards.   They are numbered on
              Map.

TOOLS.   50 per cent. large Tools will be carried by all Coys.
              These can be drawn from Q.M. Stores.

UMPIRES.   Captain Ford M.C., Captain Dekin, Captain Penroy,
              Captain Jones, Lieut. Webster.   These Officers will
              report to Commanding Officer at 10 a.m.

OFFICERS.   All Officers not going into action will report to Adjutant
              at 10 a.m.   These Officers will be required to write
              a Report on the manner in which Strong Points are captured

    8th October 1917.

                                                           Capt.
                                                           Adjt.
Issued at 4.30 p.m.   11th Bn. Royal Fusiliers.

    Copies to :-   1. C.O.   9. Quartermaster.
                     2. Adjutant.   10. Transport Officer.
                     3. 2nd-in-Cmd.   11. Signalling Officer
                     4. 54th Brigade. 12. Lewis Gun Officer.
                     5. 54th Brigade. 13. Assistant Adjutant.
                     6. "A" Coy.   14. War Diary.
                     7. "B" Coy.   15. War Diary.
                     8. "C" Coy.   16. "D" Coy.
                                      17. Spare.
                                      18. Spare.

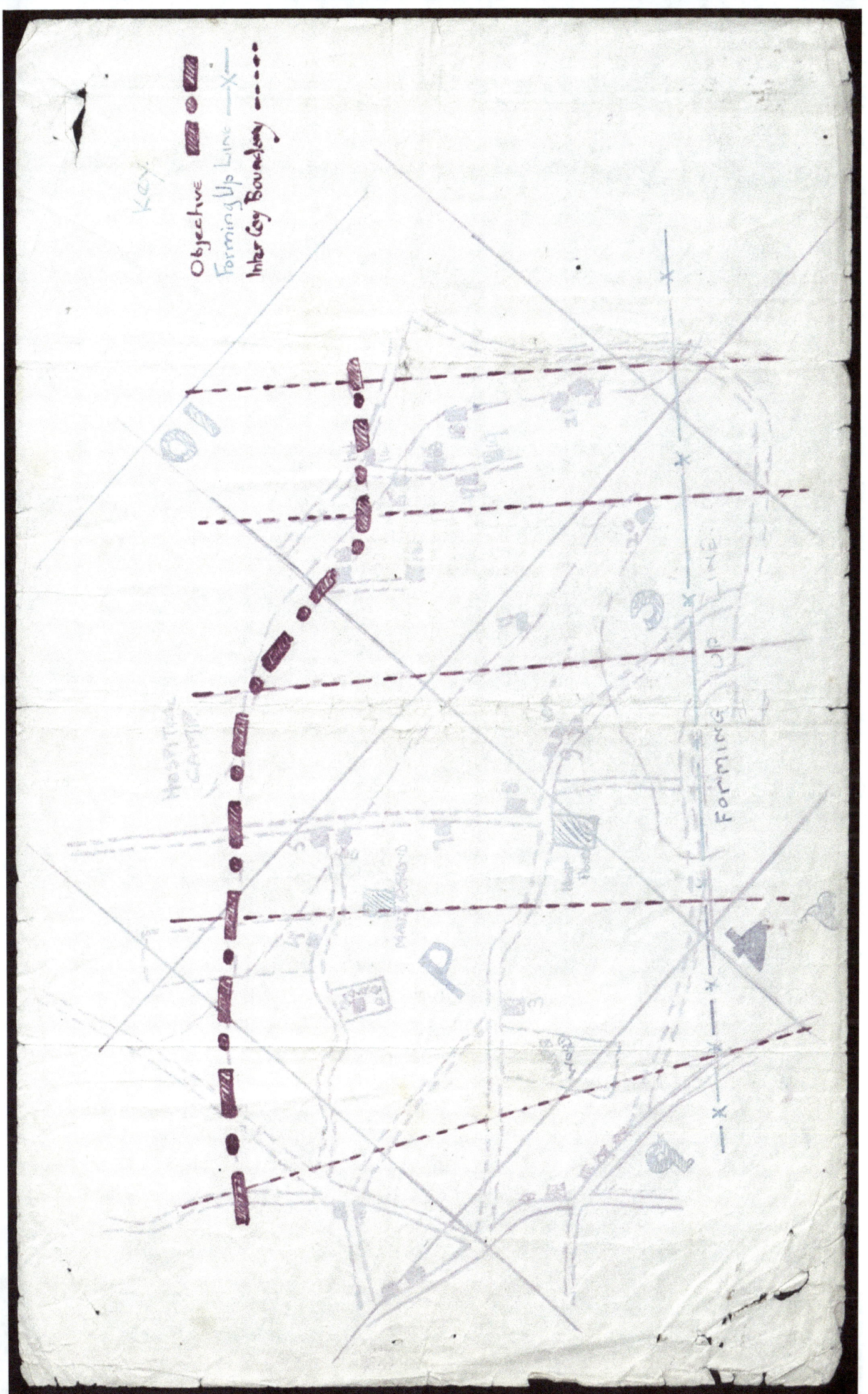

SECRET.   OPERATION ORDERS NO. 28.   Copy No. 15

BATTALION ATTACK SCHEME.

INTENTION. The Battalion will attack on a Four-Company Front and capture Objective as shown on Map attached.
"V" Battalion on its right and "W" Battalion on its left (both imaginary).
One hour after the capture of the Objective "X" and "Y" Battalions (imaginary) will "leap-frog" and capture further Objective.

FORMING UP. Coys. will form up as shown on Map in the following order :- "C", "A", "D", "B", with "C" Coy. on the right. Forming up to be completed by 10.30 a.m. Coys. will notify Headquarters by Runner when this is completed.
Inter-Company Boundaries as shown on Map.

ROLE OF COYS. They will fight their way through to and consolidate the Objective under a protective Barrage. Each Coy. must retain at least three Sections as a Reserve.

BATTALION HEADQUARTERS. Battalion Headquarters will be situated at V.15c.1.6. and move to V.16.c.9.7 after the capture of the Objective.

BARRAGE. The Barrage will be represented by Flags and will open 100 yards in front of the forming up line where it will remain for 1 minute and then move back by 50 yard bounds. There will be a halt of 2 minutes on each bound. The protective Barrage will come down 100 yards beyond Objective.
2nd Lieut. H.L. Smedley will be in charge of the Barrage and will assisted by 2nd Lieut. J.P. Turnbull and 2nd Lieut. M. Taylor.

GARRISON. All Farms and Fortified places will be garrisoned after capture.

TOOLS. 60 per cent. large tools will be carried by Coys. These will be drawn from the Quartermaster's Stores.

CARRYING PARTY. Carrying Party will report to 2nd Lieut. P.D. Benham at 10 a.m. at Battalion Headquarters. 2nd Lieut. Benham will make arrangements with Transport Officer to carry S.A.A., Bombs, Special Tins of Water, Lewis Gun Drums, etc., by Limber to Battalion Headquarters.

STRONG POINTS. Strong Points and fortified places other than those represented by actual buildings, will be marked by Notice Boards.

ZERO. Zero :- 11 a.m.

UMPIRES. Captain R.H. Ford, M.C., Captain C. Dakin, Captain G.S. Pearcy, M.C., Captain E.L. Jones, M.C. Lieut. B.P. Webster. These Officers will report to C.O. at 10 a.m.

11th October 1917.

Issued at 6.40 p.m.

                                                                    Capt.
                                                                    Adjt.

Copies to :-   11th Bn. Royal Fusiliers.

1. C.O.
2. Second-in-Command.
3. Adjutant.
4. 54th Brigade.
5. 54th Brigade.
6. Assistant Adjutant.
7. O.C. "A" Coy.
8. O.C. "B" Coy.
9. O.C. "C" Coy.
10. O.C. "D" Coy.
11. Lewis Gun Officer.
12. Signalling Officer.
13. Transport Officer.
14. Quartermaster.
15. War Diary.
16. War Diary.
17. 2nd Lieut. P.D. Benham.
18. Spare.

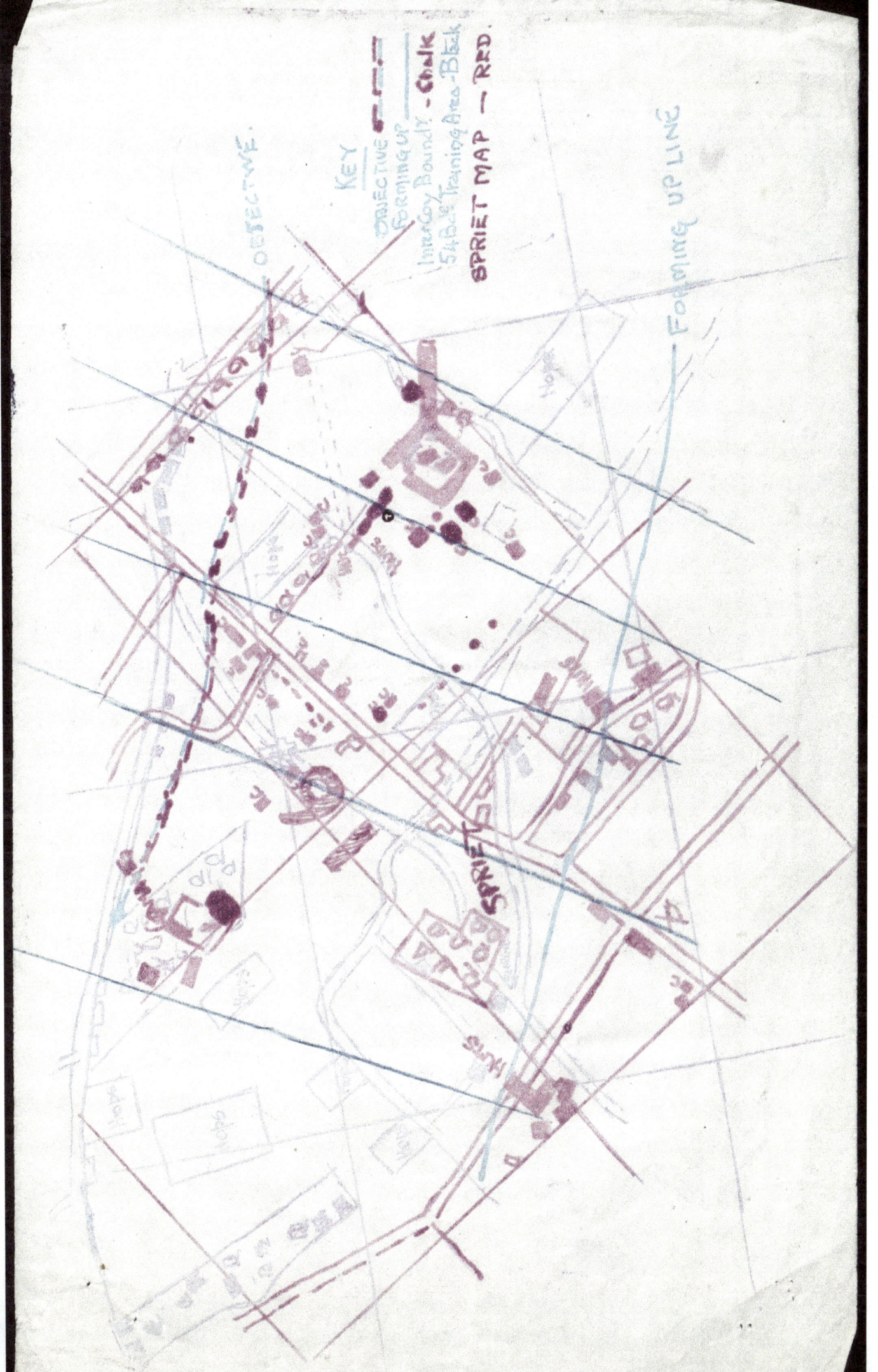

PROGRAMME of TRAINING.

11TH BN. ROYAL FUSILIERS. — **PERIOD 12th October - 19th October 1917.**

DATE	TIMES	NATURE OF TRAINING	LOCATION
FRIDAY 12.10.17.	Morning	Battalion Attack Scheme.	54th Bde. Area
SATURDAY 13.10.17.	Morning	Battalion Attack Scheme.	Ground W. of Camp.
SUNDAY 14.10.17.	10 a.m.	Church Parade.	
MONDAY 15.10.17.	9 a.m. - 1 p.m. / 2.30 - 4.30 pm.	Company Training. / Tactical Scheme for Officers and N.C.O's	53rd Bde. Area
TUESDAY 16.10.17.	Morning	Battalion Attack Scheme.	53rd Bde. Area
WEDNESDAY 17.10.17.		Brigade Attack Scheme.	
THURSDAY 18.10.17.	9 a.m. - 1 p.m. / 2.30 - 4.30 pm.	Company Training. / Tactical Scheme for Officers and N.C.O's	54th Bde. Area
FRIDAY 19.10.17.	Morning	Battalion Attack Scheme.	54th Bde. Area

REMARKS:- Lewis Gunners will carry out programme arranged by Lewis Gun Officer, except when required for Company or Battalion Attack Schemes.
Signallers will carry out programme arranged by Signalling Officer.
Battalion Observers will receive special instruction daily under Observation Officer.
The afternoons will be devoted to Games whenever possible.
Training will be carried out on Company Parade Grounds, except where otherwise stated.

11.10.17.

Capt.
Adjt.
for Lt-Colonel,
Commanding 11th Bn. Royal Fusiliers.

SECRET OPERATION ORDERS No. 27. Copy No. 4

DETAIL.	Orderly Officer tomorrow :-	2nd Lieut. J.P. Turnbull	
	Company on duty tomorrow :-	"C" Coy.	
	Reveille :- 6.30 a.m.	Breakfast :- 7 a.m.	
	Sick Parade :- 7.30 a.m.	C.O's. Orders :- Nil.	

MOVE. The 54th Infantry Brigade will relieve the 53rd Infantry Brigade in the line on the night 16/17th October.
The 11th Bn. Royal Fusiliers will relieve the 10th Essex Regiment.
Orders to be issued later.
The Battalion will embuss tomorrow and proceed to CANE TRENCH.

PARADE. The Battalion will parade under Company arrangements and embuss at 10 a.m. at the entrance of TUNNELLING CAMP on the PROVEN-POPERINGHE Road in the following order :-
Headquarters, "C", "D", "A" and "B" Coys.
Dress :- Battle Order.
Haversack Rations will be carried, water bottles will be filled before leaving present Camp.

ADVANCED PARTY. Advanced Party of not more than 5 per Coy. and Headquarters, will report to 2nd Lieut. H.L. Smedley at Orderly Room at 7.45 a.m. tomorrow morning. Coy. Officers' Mess Personnel should be included in this party.

BAGGAGE. All spare Kit, Packs and Blankets will be dumped outside Quartermaster Stores by 8 a.m., and conveyed by Lorry to Divisional Dump, Rue Tete d'Or, POPERINGHE.
The Quartermaster will arrange for transport of all Stores to Lorries.

BAGGAGE FOR FORWARD AREA. All Officers' Kits, etc. for Forward area, will be dumped at Coy. Officers' Mess by 8 a.m.

FIRST LINE TRANSPORT. AND OFFICERS' CHARGERS. Will move under Order of Battalion Transport Officer to Chateau des Trois Tours, after baggage has been loaded on Lorries.

COOKERS, WATERCARTS, AND LEWIS GUN LIMBERS. Will proceed to CANE TRENCH under the orders of Transport Officer

DETAILS. All Officers and other ranks not accompanying the Battalion into action will parade at 10 a.m. on Company Parade Ground under the orders of Captain R.N. Ford, M.C. and march to Divisional Reinforcement Camp, ROUTKERQUE.
This party will take with them rations for 16th inst.
Officers' Kits and Men's Blankets will be dumped on Company Parade Ground at 9.30 a.m.

REAR PARTY. Captain R.N. Ford, M.C. will detail one N.C.O. and 10 Other Ranks to clean up Camp after departure of Battalion.

CARRYING PARTY. Will parade under 2nd Lieut. P.D. Benham at 8 a.m. at Quartermaster's Stores to assist in loading and afterwards will parade with party proceeding to ROUTKERQUE.

BAGGAGE WAGONS. Transport Officer will arrange to return Baggage Wagons to Train on completion of the march.

16th October 1917.
Issued at 10.45 p.m.

Capt.
Adjt.
11th Bn. Royal Fusiliers.

Copies to :-

No. 1. C.O.	6. Asst. Adjutant.	11. Transport Officer.
2. Second-in-Command.	7. O.C. "A" Coy.	12. Quartermaster.
3. Adjutant.	8. O.C. "B" Coy.	13. Lewis Gun Officer.
4. War Diary.	9. O.C. "C" Coy.	14. Signalling Officer.
5. War Diary.	10. O.C. "D" Coy.	15. Sgt. Greening.
		16. Spare.

S E C R E T.   OPERATION ORDERS No. 29.   Coy No......

INTENTION.   The 11th Bn. Royal Fusiliers will be Counter-Attack
                    Battalion to 3d Brigade according to orders issued
                    to all concerned.

MOVE.   The Bn. will parade at 6.15 p.m. tonight and move to
                    CANE TRENCH Area, in the following order :-
                        "B", "D", "A", "C" HdQrs.
                    200 yards will be maintained between Platoons.

                    "A", "B", "C" and Headquarters will occupy same Area as
                    on the 18th inst.. "D" Coy. will be in trench
                    occupied by 12th Middlesex Regiment on the 18th inst
                    At 3 a.m. the Battalion will move to PHEASANT TRENCH
                    and ROSE TRENCH Area in the same order.
                    The following Area will be occupied by Coys.

                        "A" Coy.   Right PHEASANT TRENCH.
                        "B" Coy.   Right ROSE TRENCH.
                        "C" Coy.   Left PHEASANT TRENCH.
                        "D" Coy.   Left ROSE TRENCH.
                        HdQrs.   PHEASANT FARM.

WATER BOTTLES.   Will be filled before leaving present Area, and all
                    ranks must be reminded that it will probably have to
                    last all day.

RATIONS.   For the 22nd and 23rd will be carried on the man.
                    Rations and water for the 24th will be carried to Coy.
                    HdQrs. on the 23rd.

HOT MEALS.   Will be ready this evening at 7 p.m.

WATER.   Water for 23rd and 24th will be sent to Coy. HdQrs.
                    on preceding days.

BAGGAGE.   All Officers Kits and Blankets will be dumped at
                    Battalion Dump about 6.45.a.4.6 at 3 p.m. this
                    afternoon.
                    Coys. will send Guide to R.S.M. who will show position
                    of dump.

TOOLS.   50% Shovels will be carried. Men carrying these will
                    not carry Entrenching Tools and Helves
                    The Entrenching Tools and Helves will be dumped on Bn.
                    Dump by 3 p.m.

OFFICERS'   Will be placed on their Coy. Cookers by 7.30 p.m.
MESS KITS

BATTLE STORES.   Coys. will report to Orderly Room when all Battle
                    Stores have been issued to men.
                    All surplus Wire Cutters, etc. will be dumped on Bn.
                    Dump by 3 p.m.

RUM.   Will be carried forward under Coy. arrangements.

ARRIVAL IN   All Coys. will report arrival to Battalion Headquarters
CANE AND
PHEASANT AREAS.

21st October 1917.   Capt. & Adjt.
    Issued at 1.45 p.m.   11th Bn. Royal Fusiliers.

    Copies to :-   1. C.O.
                      2. Adjutant.   7. Lewis Gun Officer.
                      3. "A" Coy.   8. Signalling Officer
                      4. "B" Coy.   9. Transport Officer
                      5. "C" Coy.   10. Quartermaster
                      6. "D" Coy.   11. R.S.M.
                                               12. War Diary.
                                               13. War Diary

SECRET. OPERATION ORDERS NO. 30. Copy No......16....

Map Reference :-
Sheet 27.
BELGIUM & FRANCE.

DETAIL. Reveille :-   7 a.m.   Breakfast :-   7.30 a.m.
         Sick Parade :-   8 a.m.   C.O's. Orders :- To be notified
                                                          later.

INTENTION.   The 54th Brigade will move to P.2 (P ROVEN) Area tomorrow.

PARADE.   The Battalion will parade in column of route ready to march at 9.45 a.m.
             tomorrow.
             ORDER OF MARCH :-   Hd.Qrs, "A", "B", Drums, "C" and "D".
             STARTING POINT :-   The Baths.
             DRESS :-   Full Marching Order - Steel Helmets will be
                                 carried under Pack Straps.

             Two hundred yards will be maintain between Coys.

ROUTE.   CHemin MILITAIRE - CORNICE CROSS - A.10.a.2.0 - INTERNATIONAL CORNER -
             A.9.a.1.5. - thence via MILITARY ROAD WEST to F.10.d.9.2. - CROMBEKE
             ROAD.

FIRST LINE   Will accompany the Battalion. and Mess/Maltese Carts will report at
TRANSPORT.   9 a.m. to Headquarter Mess and Medical Inspection Room respectively.

RATIONS.   Will be carried on the Cookers.   Rations for the 30th inst., will be
             delivered in new Area.   Refilling Point for 30th - F.1.c.8.8, Sheet 27.

ADVANCED   Lieut. C. Tantram and 1 N.C.O. from "A" and "B" Coys. will report at
PARTY.   Brigade Headquarters at 7 a.m. tomorrow.   1 N.C.O. from Headquarters,
             "C" and "D" Coys. will report to Lieut. C. Tantram in New Area at 9.30 a.m.

MEALS.   Dinners on arrival.

BAGGAGE.   All Officers' Kits, Blankets, Mess Stores, etc., will be dumped at
             Quartermaster's Stores by 9 a.m.   1 N.C.O. per Coy. and Headquarters.
             will report to Quartermaster when all Baggage has been dumped.
             Officers' Green Mess Boxes will be carried on Coy. Cookers and loaded
             by 9 a.m.   Lorries for Kits and Blankets will arraive at Brigade
             Headquarters at 8 a.m. - Quartermaster will send a Guide to report to
             Lieut. Alcock at 8 a.m.

LOADING   Each Coy. will detail 2 men to report to Quartermaster's Stores at 8.45 am.
PARTY.

WATER   Will be filled before leaving present area.
BOTTLES.

REAR PARTY. Each Coy. and Headquarters will detail 4 Other Ranks to report to 2nd
             Lieut. R.E. Killingback at Orderly Room at 9.30 a.m.   This party will
             clean up the Camp and will not move off without permission of Lieut.
             Alcock, 54th Brigade Staff.

SANITATION. Coy. Commanders will be held personally responsible for the cleanliness
             of the Area occupied by their Coys.

28th October 1917.
Issued at 11 p.m.
                                                    Capt. Adjt.
                                        11th Bn. Royal Fusiliers.

Copies to :-
        No. 1. C.O.   No. 9. O.C. "C" Coy.
            2. 2nd-in-Command.   10. O.C. "D" Coy.
            3. Adjutant.   11. Quartermaster.
            4. Office.   12. Transport Officer.
            5. War Diary.   13. Signalling Officer.
            6. War Diary.   14. R.S.M.
            7. O.C. "A" Coy.   15. Spare.
            8. O.C. "B" Coy.   16. Spare.

WAR DIARY
or
INTELLIGENCE SUMMARY.
(Erase heading not required.)

Army Form C. 2118.

Place	Date	Hour	Summary of Events and Information	Remarks and references to Appendices
PICCADILLY CAMP.	1.11.17. to 3.11.17.		The Battalion carried out Training under Coy. arrangements. Captain G.S. Pearcy, M.C. and 8 Other Ranks proceeded on leave. 427 lbs. of Dripping were collected during October and used for making "Tommy" Cookers for use in the line, in addition to 156 lbs. despatched for Munition purposes. The XVIII Corps Commander sent hearty congratulations on the success of the Division on the 22nd ult., adding that this success was gained in spite of bad weather, bad mud and hot artillery fire, and that all concerned deserve great credit. 2nd Lieut. P.D. Benham took over temporary command of R.E. Platoon in absence of 2nd Lieut. T.A. Smith, in Hospital. All P.H. pattern Smoke Helmets were called in to Stores. Also Entrenching Tools, except one per Section. 2nd Lieut. M. Taylor and 7 other ranks proceeded to VOLKERINGKHOVE for Course at XVIII Corps School. Strength of Battalion :- 45 Officers, 831 Other Ranks.	
do.	4.11.17.		Church Parade was held at 10.30 a.m. on the ground adjoining the Camp. A lecture on Trench Discipline was given to all Coy. Officers and N.C.O's. 3 other ranks proceeded on leave.	
DE WIPPE CAMP.	5.11.17.		On the 5th inst. the Battalion and First Line Transport proceeded by March route to DE WIPPE Camp (BELGIUM Sheet 28 - A.11.b.2.4.) 3 other ranks proceeded on leave.	
do.	6.11.17.		The day was spent in cleaning huts, drains and ditches in the Camp and neighbourhood. A Court of Inquiry was held to enquire into and report upon the wounding of No. 7317, Pte. Holderness, M. 1 other rank proceeded on leave.	
do.	7.11.17.		Baths at RIVERDINGHE CHATEAU were allotted to the Battalion from 9 a.m. to 1 p.m. and were used by all Coys. and Headquarters. 1 other rank proceeded on leave.	
do.	8.11.17.		Training was carried out in accordance with Coy. arrangements. A Battalion Trench Mortar	

Army Form C. 2118.

WAR DIARY
or
INTELLIGENCE SUMMARY.
(Erase heading not required.)

Instructions regarding War Diaries and Intelligence Summaries are contained in F. S. Regs., Part II. and the Staff Manual respectively. Title pages will be prepared in manuscript.

Place	Date	Hour	Summary of Events and Information	Remarks and references to Appendices
DE LIPPE CAMP.	9.11.17.		Section was formed from 12 other ranks previously attached to 54th Trench Mortar Battery. They were transferred to "A" Coy. Captain E.R. Mesker and 2 other ranks proceeded on leave.	
			Training was carried out under Coy. arrangements. A Lecture on Trench Discipline was given to all Coy. Officers and N.C.O's. 2nd Lieut. R.B. Killingbeck and 7 other ranks proceeded to BOLLEZEELE for Trench Mortar, Lewis Gun and Bombing Courses at XIV Corps School.	
			The HOULTHOULST FOREST sector extending from FAIDHERBE CROSS ROADS to LES 5 CHEMINS, was reconnoitred by Officers from 7th to 9th inst. Strength of Battalion :- 45 Officers, 840 other ranks.	
TRENCHES.	10.11.17. to 13.11.17.		On the 10th inst. the Battalion proceeded by train from ONDANK to BOESINGHE and relieved the 10th Essex Regiment in the line South of HOULTHULST FOREST (BELGIUM Sheet 20 - U.5 and 6.). Copy of Operation Orders attached. Heavy rain fell whilst the Battalion were marching to the line and the troops arrived in the line in a very wet condition. Battalion Headquarters was at U.6.c.5.3. Details left out of action proceeded to SUTTON CAMP where Training was carried out.	
			Lieut. H.W. Brookling was appointed "Additional Captain" and authorised to wear the badges of such rank pending confirmation by higher Authority.	
			On the 10th inst. 1 other rank proceeded to Course at Fifth Army Musketry School. 5 other ranks proceeded on leave.	
			On the 11th November, 2 other ranks proceeded to VADENCOURT for Courses at Fifth Army Observing and Infantry School, and 5 other ranks proceeded on leave.	
			On the 12th November 1 other rank proceeded on leave and 5 other ranks on the 13th November. During their tour in the line the Battalion carried out a good deal of work on the Outpost and other positions, the work however being hindered by the waterlogged state of the ground and the extreme darkness at night. No movement was possible during the daytime. Hostile Artillery and Machine Guns were fairly active, and the Enemy used a large number of gas shells. The following casualties were suffered :-	
				Killed.	Wounded.	Gassed.
			11th November	4	2	-
			12th "	1	1	-
			13th "	-	7	18
			14th "	-	1	1

Army Form C. 2118.

WAR DIARY
or
INTELLIGENCE SUMMARY.
(Erase heading not required.)

Instructions regarding War Diaries and Intelligence Summaries are contained in F. S. Regs., Part II. and the Staff Manual respectively. Title pages will be prepared in manuscript.

Place	Date	Hour	Summary of Events and Information	Remarks and references to Appendices
			Lieut-Colonel A.V. Sulman, M.C. Wounded. 14th November. 2nd Lieut. E.G. Hanwell. Gassed. 15th " Owing to the wetconditions and the impossibility of movement except at night, a large number of men suffered with "Trench Feet", 85 other ranks being evacuated for that reason.	
BABOON CAMP.	14.11.17. to 16.11.17.		The Battalion was relieved in the line on the night of the 13/14th inst. by the 7th Bedfordshire Regiment. Owing to shelling the relief could not be completed until 4 a.m. The Battalion returned to BABOON CAMP where it remained in Support for three days. During this period the Battalion supplied a number of parties for carrying material to the front line trenches positions. Strength of Battalion :- 44 Officers, 704 Other Ranks. On the 14th inst. a F.G.C.M. at ELVERDINGHE CHATEAU for the trial of No. 225370 Pte T. Gibbs, charged with desertion. On the 16th inst. the Battalion returned to DE WIPPE CAMP, entraining from BOESINGHE to ONDANK. No. 58816, Pte Sansome, R.A., proceeded to England as candidate for commission. Between the 14th and 16th inst. 6 other ranks proceeded on leave. 3 Other Ranks proceeded to MERCKEGHEM for Bombing Course and 3 Other Ranks for Lewis Gun Course at VIX Corps School.	
DE WIPPE CAMP.	17.11.17.		Baths at ONDANK were allotted to the Battalion from 10 a.m. to 3 p.m. and clean clothing was provided. When not at the Baths the Coys. were engaged in cleaning up and re-organization. No. 12225, Sgt. Martin, S. was awarded a Bar to his Military Medal, and No. 63305 Pte Piper, C.J. and No. 26554, Pte Clark, A.W., were awarded the Military Medal, gallantry and devotion to duty in action. Conduct Sheets were checked by Captain G. Dakin.	
do.	18.11.17.		Voluntary Church Services were held near the Camp. 3 other ranks proceeded on leave and 2 other ranks proceeded to a Course at 19th Corps School, MERCKEGHEM. 2nd Lieut. W.A. Smith rejoined from Hospital and took over command of R.E. Platoon from 2nd Lieut. P.D. Benham.	
	19.11.17. to 20.11.17.		The Battalion was employed in constructing a Rifle Range and Bayonet Fighting Course, and in draining and sandbagging the huts in the Camp. On the 20th inst. 2nd Lieut. E.W. Clements and 4 other ranks proceeded to VAILBUREUX for Course at 5th Army Trench Mortar School. 1 other rank was	

A6915 Wt W14422/M180 350,000 12/16 D. D. & L. Forms/C./2118/14

Army Form C.2118.

WAR DIARY
or
INTELLIGENCE SUMMARY.
(Erase heading not required.)

Instructions regarding War Diaries and Intelligence Summaries are contained in F.S. Regs., Part II. and the Staff Manual respectively. Title pages will be prepared in manuscript.

Place	Date	Hour	Summary of Events and Information	Remarks and references to Appendices
	xxxxxxxx		sent for a month to work on a Farm near HERZEELE, and 8 other ranks proceeded to Base to return to England to work as Ploughmen	
	21.11.17.		Training was carried out during the morning and a party of 1 Officer and 33 other ranks was engaged on construction of new Transport Lines at ONDANK. A F.G.C.M. was held at ELVERDINGHE CHATEAU for the trial of No. 225370, Pte Gibbs, T., charged with Desertion, No. 15611 Pte Hagon, T., charged with Absence without Leave, No. 7449 Pte Wallace, W., charged with Disobedience, and No. 15833 Pte Underwood, C., charged with using insubordinate language. Gibbs was sentenced to 10 years P.S., sentence being suspended, Hagon was sentenced to 28 days F.P. No.1, Wallace was sentenced to 63 days F.P. No. 1, and Underwood was sentenced to 14 days F.P. No. 1. 2nd. Lieut. B.E. Beckett proceeded to PROVEN to attend an Intelligence Course at 9th Squadron R.F.C. 2nd Lieut. J. Ruxton proceeded on leave.	
TRENCHES.	22.11.17. to 25.11.17.		On the 22nd inst. the Battalion proceeded by train from ONDANK to BOESINGHE and relieved the 10th Essex Regiment in the line, South of HOUTHULST FOREST, taking over the same Sector as on 10th inst. (Copy of Operation Orders and Trench Instructions attached). Whilst on the way to the line the Adjutant (Captain O.C. Whiteman) was killed and 1 other rank wounded. During this tour in the line much work was done, partly under R.E. supervision, in improving the and consolidating the positions, and in putting out wire. Enemy's Artillery and Machine Gun fire was normal. The following casualties were sustained:- 2 other ranks wounded. Captain H.R. Mundey and Captain K.B. Michell rejoined the Battalion on the 23rd inst.	
CANAL BANK CAMP.	26.11.17. to 28.11.17.		On the night of the 25/26th inst., the Battalion was relieved by the 7th Bedfordshire Regiment, and returned to CANAL BANK Camp, where it remained in Reserve for 3 days, during which Carrying Parties were supplied for taking up material to the front line positions.	

Army Form C. 2118.

WAR DIARY
or
INTELLIGENCE SUMMARY.
(Erase heading not required.)

Place	Date	Hour	Summary of Events and Information	Remarks and references to Appendices
DE WIPPE CAMP	28.11.17. to 30.11.17.		On the 28th inst. the Battalion returned to DE WIPPE Camp, entraining from BOESINGHE to ONDANK.	
			On the 29th inst. the Battalion paraded for promulgation of sentence of 10 years P.S. by F.G.C.M. to No. 225370 Pte T. Gibbs, found guilty of Desertion. 8 other ranks proceeded on leave. Small working parties were found by the Battalion.	
			No. 50384 Pte Merrifield, L.G., proceeded to England as a candidate for Commission. 1 other rank proceeded to PROVEN for Course at 9th Squadron R.F.C. on use of Lewis Gun against Aircraft.	
			On the 30th inst. Training was carried out under Coy. arrangements. Captain H.J. Munday took over charge of "A" Coy. from Captain E.H. Cliff. Captain N.B. Michell took over charge and payment of "B" Coy. from Captain E.R. Meaker as from 29th inst.	
			Captain E.R. Meaker was transferred to "C" Coy as Second-in-Command and relinquished the rank of Acting Captain "whilst commanding a Coy", and was appointed Additional Captain as from the 29th inst.	
			Lieut. E.P. Webster reverted to the rank of 2nd Lieutenant with effect from 11.8.17, and was transferred to "D" Coy as 2nd Second-in-Command.	
			Lieut. E.W. Ide reverted to the rank of 2nd Lieutenant with effect from 12.8.17. Additional Captain H.W. Brookling reverted to rank of 1st Lieutenant as from 23.11.17. and 2nd Lieut. W. Hornbeck.	
			took over the duties of Lewis Gun Officer from 2nd Lieut. W. Hornbeck. Lieut. C. Tantram took over the duties of Acting Adjutant on 29.11.17. and 2nd Lieut. E.J Moir took over from Lieut. C. Tantram the duties of Regimental Signalling Officer. Strength of Battalion :- 44 Officers, 745 other ranks.	

9-12-17.

a/Capt
11th Royal Fusiliers

TRAINING PROGRAMME.

11th Bn. Royal Fusiliers.   -   Period 30th October to 3rd November 1917.

Date	Times.	Nature of Training.	Remarks.
31.10.17.	9 a.m. to 1 p.m.	Rifle Range and Musketry.	"A" Coy.
	9 - 10 a.m.	Close Order Drill, Platoon and Coy.)	"B", "C"
	10 - 11 a.m.	Musketry.)	and "D"
	11 a.m. - 12 noon.	Physical Training and Bayonet Fighting.)	Coys.
	12 - 1 p.m.	Rifle Bombing.)	
1.11.17	9 a.m. to 1 p.m.	Rifle Range and Musketry.	"B" Coy.
	9 - 10 a.m.	Close Order Drill, Platoon and Coy.)	"A", "C"
	10 - 11 a.m.	Musketry.)	and "D"
	11 a.m. - 12 noon.	Physical Training and Bayonet Fighting.)	Coys.
	12 - 1 p.m.	Rifle Bombing.)	
2.11.17.	9 a.m. to 1 p.m.	Rifle Range and Musketry.)	"C" Coy.
	9 - 10 a.m.	Close Order Drill, Platoon and Coy.)	"A", "B"
	10 - 11 a.m.	Musketry.)	and "D"
	11 a.m. - 12 noon.	Physical Training and Bayonet Fighting.)	Coys.
	12 - 1 p.m.	Rifle Bombing.)	
3.11.17	9 a.m. to 1 p.m.	Rifle Range and Musketry.	"D" Coy.
	9 - 10 a.m.	Close Order Drill, Platoon and Coy.)	"A", "B"
	10 - 11 a.m.	Musketry.)	and "C"
	11 a.m. - 12 noon.	Physical Training and Bayonet Fighting.)	Coys.
	12 - 1 p.m.	Rifle Bombing.)	

REMARKS:- Lewis Gunners will parade with their Coys. for Close Order Drill daily, at
9 a.m., except when the Coys. is on the Range.
Trained and Recruit Lewis Gunner will parade daily at 10.15 a.m. for special
instruction under Battalion Lewis Gun Officer.
The Rifle Range will be at the disposal of the Lewis Gun Officer every
afternoon and Monday morning 5.11.17.
Musketry Sergeant will report to Coy. Commanders on the Range daily at 9 a.m.
to assist in training.
Backward men will parade outside Orderly Room daily at 2.30 p.m. for an
hour's official instuction under the Musketry Sergeant.
Trained and Recruit Signallers will carry out programme arranged for by
Signalling Officer.

Capt. Adjt.
11th Bn. Royal Fusiliers.

PRELIMINARY OPERATION ORDERS No.31.

Copy No.........

INTENTION.	The 11th Battn. Royal Fusiliers will relieve the 10th Essex Regt in the Line tomorrow night.
MOVE.	The Battalion will proceed from OMDAM by train to BOESINGHE
PARADE GUIDES COY.SECTORS	Details will be issued later.
DETAILS LEFT OUT OF ACTION	Special Orders will be issued separately.
SURPLUS KIT.	i.e. Overcoats, Haversacks, caps etc, will be placed in sandbags marked distinctly with owners names, and dumped with Baggage.
BAGGAGE.	Blankets, Officers Kit, Mess Stores required for the line will be Dumped in "A" & "C" Coy's Huts - entrance opposite Bn.Qr.Mess by 9 am on a site marked by a notice board EMILE CAMP.
BAGGAGE FOR DETAILS LEFT OUT OF ACTION.	See Special Orders.
1ST LINE TRANSPORT & Q.M.STORES.	Less "A" and "B" Coy's Cookers and one Water Cart will stay at EMILE CAMP. "A" & "B" Coy's Cookers, one Water Cart will proceed to SUTTON CAMP under Sgt Cook after the Battalion leaves BOESINGHE.
LEWIS GUN LIMBERS.	will be loaded tonight and accompany Cookers to BOESINGHE where the Lewis Guns etc will be collected by Coy's.
RATIONS.	Three days Rations and one Tommy Cooker will be carried by each man also two filled water bottles Tea ration for the 10th will be carried on the man Coy Cookers will leave for BOESINGHE siding at 9-45.am Dinners will be ready by 1.pm.
WATER BOTTLES.	Both water bottles will be filled tonight.
RUM.	for the 11th will be carried by platoons in two Waterbottles under platoon commanders arrangements.
RIFLE OIL.	One pint bottle will be carried by section Commanders for his section
VERY PISTOL AMMUNITION.	will be issued on the scale - 4 Pistols and 48 rounds per Coy.
ENTRAINING STATE.	Coy's and Headquarters will render entraining state by 6.pm tonight.
SANITATION.	Coy Commanders will ensure that their Hutments etc., are left in a sanitary condition. Major R.M.Ford, M.C. will inspect Coy's lines at 9 am.

Captain
Adjutant.
11th Battalion Royal Fusiliers

COPIES TO:-

No.10 Quartermaster
No.11 Transport Officer
No.12 Signal ing Officer
No.13 Sgt
No.14 Gun Officer
No.15 T.M.Section

CONTINUATION OF PRELIMINARY OPERATION ORDERS
No.31

Copy No. 3

DETAIL	Detail for tomorrow:- Reveille:- 7.am. Breakfast:- 7-30.am. Sick Parade:- 7.am
PARADE.	The Battalion will parade on Coy Parade grounds to proceed to ONDANK STATION and move off in following order:- Headquarters, "B", "A", "C", "D". Headquarters will move at 8-40.am. Coy's will follow as above, maintaining an interval of 200 yards between Coy's. The Battalion will parade at BOESINGHE at 5-30.pm. Order of march will be issued later.
DRESS.	Packs will be worn slung. The second waterbottle, Jerkin and Rations will be carried in the Pack.
GUIDES	Guides on the scale of 1 per platoon and Coy Headquarters, 2 per Battalion Headquarters, will meet leading Coy's at 6.pm where CHARGES STREET Duckboards cross the LANGEMARK-BIXSCHOOTE Road at WIDENDRIFT
DISTRIBUTION OF COY'S	"B" Company......Right Forward Coy. "A" Company......Left Forward Coy. "C" Company......Right Support Coy. "D" Company......Left Support Coy.
LIAISON OFFICER	2nd.Lieut.G.M.Gibbs will report to French Battalion Commander by 4-30.pm at U.10.a.6.6. He will take his servant and Rations with him.
TRENCH STORES.	Coy's will take over all trench stores, Ammunition, S.O.S. Rockets etc., in the line and render return to Orderly Room by 6.pm on the 11th inst.
FRENCH ROCKET SIGNALS.	S.O.S.Rocket bursting simultaneously into three stars of any colour. - Lengthen Range - Rocket bursting into six stars of any colour.
COMPLETION OF RELIEF.	Coy's will inform Battalion Headquarters by Runner when Relief is Complete.

ALTERATIONS IN PRELIMINARY OPERATION ORDERS No.31.

BAGGAGE.	Blankets, Officers Kits, Mess Stores not required for the line will be dumped in "A" and "C" Coy's huts - entrance opposite Bn.Hd.Qrs Officers Mess by 9.am on a site marked by a notice board EMILE CAMP.
WHALE OIL.	*For Rifle Oil read* One pint bottle will be carried by Section Commanders for their Sections.
SANITATION.	Company Commanders will ensure that their Hutments etc are left in a sanitary condition. Major.E.V.Ford. M.O. will inspect Coy's lines at 8-15.am.
1ST LINE TRANSPORT.	1st Line Transport will move to EMILE Camp and pass DE WIPPE Corner at 10.am. Route:- BOESTEN - ELVERDINGHE

Sd. O.C.Whiteman Capt.
9-11-1917. Issued at 9-35.pm.   Adjutant 11th Bn.Royal Fusiliers.

COPIES TO:-
No.1. C.O.	No.2. 2nd-in-Comd.	No.3 Adjutant
No.4. Office	No.5 War Diary	No.6 War Diary
No.7. O.C."A" Coy	No.8. O.C."B" Coy	No.9. O.C."C" Coy
No.10.O.C."D" Coy	No.11.Quartermaster	No.12.Transport Officer
No.13.Signalling Offr.	No.14.Sgt.Greening	No.15.Lewis Gun Officer
No.16.N.C.O. T.M.Sec.	No.17 R.S.M.	No.18 & 19 Spare.

SPECIAL OPERATION ORDERS FOR DETAILS.
To go with Preliminary Operation Orders No.31.

DETAILS. Company Details left out of Action, Police, Drums, Trench Mortar Section &c.

O.C.DETAILS. Capt. E.H.Clark.

PARADE. Outside Battalion Headquarters Mess ready to move off at 11 a.m. and proceed to Sutton Camp (XXXXXXXXXX) (F.10.b.9.5.) Sheet 2/

ROUTE. INTERNATIONAL CORNER - SUTTON CAMP.

RATIONS. Rations for 10th will be carried on the man. Rations for 11th and after will be sent from EMILE Camp.

ADVANCE PARTY. One N.C.O. per Coy and H'qrs.will report to Capt.H.W.Brookling at Orderly Room at 10 a.m., proceed to SUTTON Camp and make arrangements for accommodation with Capt.Gadsden 6th. Northamptonshire Regiment.

BAGGAGE. Blankets,Officers kits &c & H'qrs.cooking utensils will be dumped on "A" & "C" Coy.hut, entrance opposite Battalion H'qrs.Mess on site marked with notice "SUTTON CAMP" by 10 a.m.

LOADING PARTY. N.C.O.i/c Trench Mortar Section will detail one N.C.O. and 4 men to load and accompany baggage to SUTTON Camp. This N.C.O. will report to the Quartermaster at 9 a.m.

OFFICERS MESS KITS. All Officers will arrange to take sufficient mess kit for themselves. This will be dumped with kit for SUTTON Camp.

OFFICERS MESS. A combined mess will be formed if possible on arrival in new area with Capt.H.W.Brookling as P.M.C.

SANITATION. Officer Commanding Details will arrange to leave behind 1 Officer 1 N.C.O. and 8 men to ensure that present camp is left in a scrupulously clean condition.

9-11-17.

Capt.
Adj.
11th.Bn.Royal Fusiliers.

Copies to:- No.1. C.O.
No.2. 2nd.in.Cmd.
No.3. Adjutant.
No.4. Office.
No.5. War Diary.
No.6. O.C. "A" Coy.
No.7. O.C. "B" Coy.
No.8. O.C. "C" Coy.
No.9. O.C. "D" Coy.

No.10. War Diary.
No.11. Quartermaster.
No.12. Transport Officer.
No.13. Signalling Officer.
No.14. Sgt.Greening.
No.15. Lewis Gun Officer.
No.16. N.C.O. T.M.Section.
No.17. R.S.M.
Nos.18 & 19 Spare.

TRAINING PROGRAMME

11th Battalion Royal Fusiliers................Period 19th - 21st November 1917.

DATE	TIMES	NATURE OF TRAINING	REMARKS.
MONDAY 19-11-1917	9.am to 1.pm	"A" Coy. Draining Camp and Sandbagging Huts. "B" Coy) Building Rifle Range. "C" Coy) "D" Coy..Construction Bayonet Fighting Course	
TUESDAY 20-11-1917	9.am to 1.pm 9.am to 10.am 10.am to 11.am 11am to 12noon 12 noon to 1.pm	Constructing Range and Bayonet Fighting Course Close order drill, platoon and Coy. Musketry. Physical Training & Bayonet Fighting Rifle Bombing.	Two Coy's. Two Coy's
WEDNESDAY 21-11-1917	9.am to 1.pm 9.am to 10.am 10.am to 11.am 11.am to 12.noon 12.noon to 1.pm 9.am to 1-30.pm	Constructing Range and Bayonet Fighting Course Close Order drill, platoon and Coy Musketry. Physical Training & Bayonet Fighting Rifle Bombing R.E.Working Party.	One Coy. One Coy. Two Coy's.

Remarks. Lewis Gunners will parade with their Coy's for close order drill
Trained and Recruit Lewis Gunners will parade daily p.m for special
    instruction under Battalion Lewis Gun Officer.
Musketry Sgt.will assist in construction of the Range daily at 9.am
Trained and Recruit Signallers will carry out programme arranged for
by Signalling Officer.

Captain
Adjutant
for Major.

18-11-1917.   Commanding 11th Bn.Royal Fusiliers.

Ref. Map. Sheet 28
N. BELGIUM.

OPERATION ORDERS No.32.

Copy No............

16

INTENTION.
1.
The 11th Bn.Royal Fusiliers will relieve the 10th Essex Regt.in the Line tomorrow night (22nd/23rd inst)

PARADE.
2.
The Battalion will parade on Coy parade grounds to proceed to ONDANK SIDING and move off in the following order;-
Hd.Qrs, "D", "C", "A" & "B" Coy's.
Hd.Qrs. will move off at 12-15.pm.   Coy's will follow as above maintaining an interval of 100 yards between Coy's.
The Battalion will detrain at BOESINGHE SIDING and remain there until paraded to move to the line under orders to be issued later.

ROUTE.
3.
HUNTER STREET - LANGEMARCK - BIXSCHOOTE ROAD - CLARGES STREET.

GUIDES.
4.
Guides on the scale of 2 per Bn.Hd.Qrs, 1 per Coy Hd.Qrs and 1 per platoon will meet the Battalion at the junction of CLARGES STREET with LANGEMARCK - BIXSCHOOTE Road at 6.pm.

INTER BATTN. BOUNDS.
5.
6 CHEMINS - COLOMBO HOUSE Road inclusive to Right Battalion U.6.a.05.80. - U.6.a.90.35. - U.6.a.85.60.

DISTRIBUTION OF COY'S.
6.
"D" Coy................Right Forward Coy.
"C" Coy................Left Forward Coy.
"A" Coy................In Support.
"B" Coy................In Reserve.

DETACHED POSTS.
7.
(1) S.O.S. Relay post VEE BEND.....Officer Commanding "B" Coy will detail 1 N.C.O. and 3 men to relieve similar post of 10th Essex Regt. on Coy relief.
(2) Liaison Post LASALLE FARM......The Signalling Officer will detail 2 runners to relieve similar post of 10th Essex Regt. by 4.pm.

LIAISON OFFICER.
8.
2nd.Lieut.Norman will relieve Liaison Officer at LOUVOIS FARM by 4-30.pm. He will take his servant and rations with him.

BAGGAGE.
9.
Blankets, Officers Kits, Mess Stores not   ; required for the line or Details Camp will be dumped in "Drums" Nissen Hut by 10-30.am.
Cpl.Ludwick, Pte.Giles and Morris (C Coy) will be in charge of this dump.
1 N.C.O. per Coy and Hd.Qrs.,will report to Quartermaster when all Coy & Hd. Qr. Baggage is dumped.

SPARE KIT.
10.
Spare Kit, Overcoats, Haversacks and Iron Rations of each man proceeding to the line will be packed in one sandbag, clearly marked, name,Coy, etc., in block capitals and dumped as above.

LORRIES.
11.
Lorries for conveyance of Quartermasters Stores will be at DE WIPPE Cross Roads at 8.am.   Quartermaster will arrange a guide to report there at 7-45.am to Lieut.Alcock.

FIRST LINE TRANSPORT
12
1st Line Transport will move to EMILE CAMP under orders of Brigade Transport Officer.   Starting Point:- DE WIPPE CAB. Time;- 9.am.
Order of march;- Regimental order.   200 yards between every 8 vehicles.

MEALS.
13.
Dinners:- and Teas at BOESINGHE - times to be notified later.

MESS CART.
14
Mess Cart will move independently to BOESINGHE SIDING.

COOKERS & WATER CARTS
15
"A" and "B" Coy's Cookers and both Water Carts will proceed to BOESINGHE SIDING and arrive there by 11-30.a.m.   "C" and "D" Coy's Cookers will accompany 1st Line Transport.

LEWIS GUNS
16
Lewis Gun Limbers will be loaded tonight and accompany Cookers to BOESINGHE SIDING where Lewis Guns will be collected by Coy's.

CONTINUED.

MULE PACK   Special Instructions will be issued separately.
TRAIN.
  17.
EMPTY PETROL Coy's will ensure that all empty Petrol Tins, Food Containers are placed
TINS.   on Ration Dump by 7.pm daily.
  18.

RATIONS.   The unexpended portion of tomorrows ration, one Tommy Cooker per man and
  19.   Rations for the 23rd and 24th inst will be carried on the man.

SOCKS.   Two pairs of socks will be carried on the man.
  20.
RUM.   Six Waterbottles of Rum per Coy and 3 for Hd.Qrs. for consumption on 23rd
  21   inst will be carried under Coy and Hd.Qr. arrangements.

WATER.   Two filled Waterbottles per Officer and man will be carried.
  22.
VERY PISTOLS. 4 per Coy and 12 rounds per pistol have been issued.
  23.
WIRE CUTTERS One large handled wire cutter each will be drawn by "C" and "D" Coy's, and
  24.   handed over on relief to "A" and "B" Coy's.
Saws.
  25.   2 Circular Saws will be carried by "C" Coy and 1 by "D" Coy, and handed
              over on relief to "A" and "B" Coy's.

REAR H.Q.   Rear Battalion Headquarters will be established at EMILE CAMP.
  26.
WADERS.   Arrangements for issue will be notified later.
  27.
COMPLETION   Coy's will inform Battalion Headquarters by Runner when relief is
OF RELIEF.   completed.
  28.

DETAILS   Special Orders issued separately.
LEFT OUT OF
ACTION

    Issued at 9-20.pm.   Captain.
    21st November 1917.   Adjutant.
                                    11th Bn. Royal Fusiliers.

         Copies to:-   No. 1. C.O.
                         No. 2. 2nd-in-Comd.
                         No. 3. Adjutant.
                         No. 4. Office.
                         No. 5. War Diary.
                         No. 6. War Diary.
                         No. 7. O.C. "A" Coy.
                         No. 8. O.C. "B" Coy.
                         No. 9. O.C. "C" Coy.
                         No.10. O.C. "D" Coy.
                         No.11. Signalling Officer.
                         No.12. Transport Officer.
                         No.13. Quartermaster.
                         No.14. R.S.M.
                         No.15. Sgt. Greening.
                         No.16. Spare.

SPECIAL OPERATION ORDERS FOR DETAILS

DETAILS. (A) Company Details left out of action Police, Drums, Trench Mortar Section, Officers Mess Staff, Courts Martial Witnesses, Candidates for Courses, Sick &c.will proceed to "H" Camp. Nominal roll will be issued to O.C.Details.

(B) Quartermasters Stores, Workshops, Pioneers, Post Corporal, Mess Sgt, Orderly Room Staff, Lewis Gun Sgt, C.Q.M.Sgts.& Storeman, Cooks will proceed to EMILE CAMP.

O.C.DETAILS. Capt.G.Dekin.

PARADE. "A"Details for "H"Camp will parade outside Guard Room ready to move off at 11 a.m. Route:- INTERNATIONAL CORNER. "H" CAMP.

"B"Details will move under orders of Quartermaster.

ADVANCE PARTY. One N.C.O.per Coy.& H'qrs.will report to Lieut.B.P.Webster at Orderly Room at 10 a.m.and proceed to "H" Camp. Lieut.B.P.Webster will report there to Lt.Colonel.Bridcutt DSO 18th.Middlesex Regiment who will allot accommodation.

BAGGAGE. "A"Details blankets, Officers Kits, Cooking Utensils, will be dumped in "A" & "C"Coy.hut entrance opposite B.H.Q.Mess on site Marked "H"Camp.by 10 a.m.

"B"Details blankets and Kit will be dumped at Q.M.Stores. by 9 a.m.

LOADING PARTY. N.C.O.i/c T.M.Section will detail one N.C.O. and 4 men to load "A"Details baggage, this N.C.O.will report to Quartermaster at 9-45 a.m.

OFFICERS MESS KITS. All Officers will take sufficient mess kit for themselves, this will be dumped with "A"Details Kit.

OFFICERS MESS. A combined mess will be formed if possible on arrival in new area. Lieut.B.P.Webster will be P.M.C.

SANITATION. O.C.Details will arrange to leave 1 Officer, 1 N.C.O. and 8 men to ensure present camp is left in a clean condition.

(Sd)O.C.Whiteman.
Capt.
Adj.

21-11-17.

11th.Bn.Royal Fusiliers.

Issued to all recipients of Operation Orders No 39.

WAR DIARY
or
INTELLIGENCE SUMMARY

Army Form C. 2118.

11 Royal Fusiliers

Place	Date	Hour	Summary of Events and Information	Remarks and references to Appendices
DE WIPPE CAMP. A.11.63.2. SHEET MAP BELGIUM 28 N.W.	1/12/17		Training was carried out in accordance with programme attached. 400 lbs of anything were collected from the Battalion during form and was used for making Tommy Cookers for use in the line	
	2/12/17		On 2nd instant Church parade was held in a YMCA hut near the camp. On 3rd instant training was carried out in accordance with programme attached. No. 6694 Cpl. I. Rydon was awarded a Bar to his Military Medal and No. 20512 Sergeant D. Bowen No. 6184 Pte S. B. Elliot and No. 58953 Pte W. D. Dunn were awarded Military Medals for gallantry and devotion to duty whilst in the HOUTHULST FOREST Sector.	
TRENCHES	4/12/17		On the 4 instant the Battalion proceeded by train from ONDANK SIDING to BOESINGHE and thence to the line South of HOUTHULST FOREST (BELGIUM Sheet 20 & 5+6) relieving the 10th Essex Regiment (C.O. Coy Operation, Trench Inundation Orders attached) Details left out of action proceeded to H tents. Two officers and 52 other ranks proceeded to ONDANK and remained	J.F.

WAR DIARY
or
INTELLIGENCE SUMMARY.
(Erase heading not required.)

Army Form C. 2118.

Place	Date	Hour	Summary of Events and Information	Remarks and references to Appendices
TRENCHES	4/12/17		Three weeks 15th instant working upon new transport lines. During the three days the Battalion has been on the line a great deal of transport work particularly	
	7/12/17		wiring was done. Whilst the last day the weather was extremely cold and the ground was frost bound. The following casualties were sustained:- 3 killed and 6 wounded.	
			Capt J Griffith was Court Martialled. On the 5th instant a Field General Court Martial was held for the trial of No. 4398 Pte W Reynolds which was adjourned for Medical evidence. On the night of the 7th/8th instant the Battalion was relieved by the 7th Bedfordshire Regt and proceeded to BOESINGHE, entraining thence to INTERNATIONAL CORNER where the Battalion detrained and marched to "H" Camp, where it arrived on the 8th instant.	
"H" CAMP	9th 11th		Battalion strength, 44 officers 972 Men. On the 9th inst 11 Other Ranks proceeded to the 19th Corps Works Battalion. On the 10th and 11th inst baths and clean clothing were provided for the Battalion at BOX CAMP. On the 10th inst a Court of Enquiry was	
A.10.A.O.2 Sheet Belgium 28 N.W.	10th 12th 14th		held to enquire into and report on the wounding of No. 4410 Pte W Wallace. The finding being that the wound was self inflicted	

Army Form C. 2118.

WAR DIARY
or
INTELLIGENCE SUMMARY.
(Erase heading not required.)

Place	Date	Hour	Summary of Events and Information	Remarks and references to Appendices
H Camp	1917 Dec		Training was carried out during the period 10th to 15th inst. Parades afternoon were	
	11th to 15th		paid to Musketry, and as a rifle range was exposed to the Camp the Battalion fired each day on the Range. Shooting competitions for fifteen & over took place at the Camp.	
			No. 16118 Pte Dwight T. was awarded the Military Medal, was not invested. Touring Parties were provided for New Transport Lines at ONDANK & in repairing the road leading to to Camp.	
			Hon Lieut & Quartermaster W S Meechan MC was promoted Hon Capt & Quartermaster as from 22-9-17 and Temp Lieut (A/Capt) E M Duff was promoted Temporary Capt as from 11-12-17.	
			On the 15th inst the P.B. Platoon returned to the Battalion. Battalion Strength: - 14 Officers 719 O.R.'s	
ROUSBRUGGE	Dec 16th to 22nd		The Battalion marched to ROUSBRUGGE as per operation orders attached. On arrival there Parade grounds had to be reconnoitred for & practising was carried out in accordance with programme attached. Working parties were provided for the construction of a 100 yards rifle range	

Army Form C. 2118.

WAR DIARY
or
INTELLIGENCE SUMMARY.

(Erase heading not required.)

Instructions regarding War Diaries and Intelligence Summaries are contained in F. S. Regs., Part II, and the Staff Manual respectively. Title pages will be prepared in manuscript.

Place	Date	Hour	Summary of Events and Information	Remarks and references to Appendices
ROUSBRUGGE	1917 Dec			
	16 to 22		All rifles were examined by the Brigade Armourer Sgt & all unsafe were condemned & were reissued in exchange for others.	
	Dec 20		Lieut Colonel A B Coleman MC proceeded to assume command of the Battalion at MERCKEGHEM & Capt HR Munday commander of "B" Coy proceeded to take command of a company with the same Battalion.	
			Major R M Ind MC assumed command of the Battalion.	
			Capt E H Cliff took over Pay & command of "A" Coy & Capt L Jones MC took over the duties of Acting Adjutant.	
	Dec 21		Lieut Colonel L L Cain DSO Lieut Colonel A B Coleman MC & Capt W B Whitehouse (Killed in action 22-11-17) appeared in London Gazette as "deserving of special" mention for distinguished & gallant services & devotion to duty."	Capt Sleigh not officer
	Dec 23		On the 23rd inst the Battalion paraded for Divine Service at ROUSBRUGGE	
	Dec 24 to 29		Training was carried out as per programme attached. The 24th 25th & 26th inst were observed as holidays with the exception of a short route march on the 26th.	
			Divine Holy Services were held on Christmas Day, & special arrangements were made	

Army Form C. 2118.

WAR DIARY
or
INTELLIGENCE SUMMARY.
(Erase heading not required.)

Instructions regarding War Diaries and Intelligence Summaries are contained in F. S. Regs., Part II. and the Staff Manual respectively. Title pages will be prepared in manuscript.

Place	Date	Hour	Summary of Events and Information	Remarks and references to Appendices
ROUSBRUGGE	1917 Dec			
	26th		for the comfort & funerals of the men of the Battalion. 30 parcels provided by Queen Alexandra's fund were despatched. A committee was formed to organise the year's work commencement of the Battalion.	
	27th		On the 27th inst. special instruction in wiring was given to Officers & other ranks Sappers by 2nd Lieut Field (50th Field Coy R E)	
	28th		On the 28th inst the Battalion was inspected by the Brigadier Commander & afterwards carried out a tactical scheme. Bombing, Lewis gun & Transport Competitions were held. Prizes being awarded to the winners.	
	29th		On the 29th inst field firing competitions were held. A Field General Court Martial was held on the 29th inst at ROUSBRUGGE for the trial of No 9637 Pte Bugele A.G. for refusing to obey an order when in the line. He was convicted & sentenced to 3 years P.S.	
	30th		On the 30th inst the Battalion paraded for Divine Service at ROUSBRUGGE	
	31st		On the 31st inst the Battalion was engaged in a tactical scheme & in musketry on the range.	

Army Form C. 2118.

WAR DIARY
or
INTELLIGENCE SUMMARY.
(Erase heading not required.)

Place	Date	Hour	Summary of Events and Information	Remarks and references to Appendices
RUSBRUGGE	1917 Dec		During the month 18 Officers & 78 O.R's proceeded on leave & 9 Officers & 17 O.R's proceeded on Courses to Schools of instruction	

W. H. Hincaey
2nd Lieutenant
an Adjutant
for Major
Commanding 11th Batt: Royal Fusiliers

SECRET.

OPERATION ORDERS NO. 33.

Copy No. 6

Ref. Map Sheet 28.
N.W. BELGIUM.

INTENTION. 1.	The 11th Bn. Royal Fusiliers will relieve the 10th Essex Regiment in the line tomorrow night (4/5th inst).
PARADE. 2.	The Battalion will parade on Coy. parade grounds to proceed to ONDANK SIDING and move off in the following order :- "B", "A", "C", "D" and Headquarters. "B" Coy. will move off at 1.15 p.m. Coys. will follow as above maintaining an interval of 100 yards between Coys. The Battalion will detrain at BOESINGHE SIDING and remain there until paraded to move off to the line under orders to be issued later. Time of departure approximately 8 p.m.
ROUTE. 3.	HUNTER STREET - LANGEMARCK - BIXSCHOOTE ROAD - CLARGES STREET.
GUIDES. 4.	Guides on the scale of 2 per Battalion Headquarters, 1 per Company Headquarters and 1 per Platoon will meet the Battalion at the junction of CLARGES STREET with LANGEMARCK - BIXSCHOOTE Road at 10 p.m.
DISTRIBUTION of COYS. 5.	"B" Coy................. Right Forward Coy. "A" Coy................. Left Forward Coy. "C" Coy................. In Support. "D" Coy................. In Reserve.
DETACHED POSTS. 6.	S.O.S. Relay Post VEE BEND... Officer Commanding "D" Coy. will detail 1 N.C.O. and 3 men to relieve similar post of 10th Essex Regiment on Coy. relief.
BAGGAGE. 7.	Blankets, Officers' Kits, Mess Stores not required for the line or Details Camp will be dumped in "Drums" Nissen Hut by 10.30 a.m. 1 N.C.O. and 2 men (to be notified later) will be in charge of this Dump. 1 N.C.O. per Coy. and Headquarters will report to the Quartermaster when all Coy. and Headquarters Baggage is dumped.
SPARE KIT. 8.	Spare Kit, Overcoats, Haversacks and Iron Rations of each man proceeding to the line will be packed in one sandbag, clearly marked :- Name, Coy. etc. in block capitals and dumped as above.
LORRIES. 9.	Lorries for conveyance of Quartermaster Stores will be at DE WIPPE CROSS Roads at 8 a.m. 1 Officer will be detailed later to report to Battalion Headquarters at 8 a.m. to guide Lorries to the different camps.
FIRST LINE TRANSPORT. 10.	First Line Transport will move to MICHEL FARM. Starting Point :- DE WIPPE CABARET. Time :- 9 a.m. Order of March :- Regimental Orders. 200 yards between every 8 vehicles.
MEALS. 11.	12 noon. Dinners :- Here at / Teas at BOESINGHE at 6.30 p.m.
MESS CART. 12.	Mess Cart will move independently to BOESINGHE SIDING.
COOKERS AND WATER CARTS. 13.	"A", "C" and "D" Coy's. Cookers and both Water Carts will proceed to BOESINGHE SIDING after Dinners. "B" Coy's. Cooker will accompany "A" Details to "H" Camp. The Regimental Transport Officer will detail one Water Cart to proceed to "H" Camp after Battalion leaves BOESINGHE.
LEWIS GUNS. 14.	Lewis Gun Limbers will be loaded tonight and accompany Cookers to BOESINGHE SIDING where Lewis Guns will be collected by Coys.
MULE PACK TRAIN. 15.	Special Instructions will be issued separately.
EMPTY PETROL TINS. 16.	Coys. will ensure that all empty petrol tins, Food Containers are placed on Ration Dump by 5.45 p.m. daily.

(1).

(2).

RATIONS. 17. — The unexpended portion of tomorrow's ration, 2 Tommy Cookers per man and rations for the 5th, 6th and 7th inst., will be carried on the man.

SOCKS. 18. — Two pairs of socks will be carried on the man.

RUM. 19. — Six waterbottles of Rum per Coy. and 3 per Headquarters for consumption on 5th inst., will be carried under Coy. and Headquarters arrangements.

WATER. 20. — Two filled Waterbottles per Officer and man will be carried.

VERY PISTOLS. 21. — 4 per Coy. and 12 rounds per pistol will be taken.

WIRE CUTTERS. 22. — One large handled wire cutter each will be drawn by "A" and "B" Coys., and handed over on relief to "C" and "D" Coys.

SAWS. 23. — 2 Circular Saws will be carried by "A" Coy and 1 by "B" Coy, and handed over on relief to "C" and "D" Coys.

REAR HEADQUARTERS. 24. — Rear Battalion Headquarters will be established at MICHEL FARM.

WADERS. 25. — Arrangements for issue will be notified later.

COMPLETION OF RELIEF. 26. — Coys. will inform Battalion Headquarters by Runner in writing when relief is completed.

DETAILS LEFT OUT OF ACTION. 27. — Special Orders issued separately.

ENTRAINING STATE. 28. — 2nd Lieut. K. L. Smedley, will report to a Representative of the 54th Brigade with Battalion Entraining State at 10 p.m. on ONDANK SIDING.

BRIGADE GUARD. 29. — Guard at Brigade Headquarters will dismount at 8 a.m. tomorrow.

3rd December 1917.
Issued at 9 p.m.

Lieut.
A/Adjt.
11th Bn. Royal Fusiliers.

Copies to :-

No. 1. C.O.
2. 2nd-in-Command.
3. Adjutant.
4. Office.
5. War Diary.
6. War Diary.
7. O.C., "A" Coy.
8. O.C., "B" Coy.
9. O.C., "C" Coy.
10. O.C., "D" Coy.
11. Signalling Officer.
12. Lewis Gun Officer.
13. Transport Officer.
14. Quartermaster.
15. R.S.M.
16. Sgt. Greening.
17. Spare.

SECRET.

TRENCH INSTRUCTIONS.

TO ACCOMPANY OPERATION ORDERS No. 33.

GAS ALARM RATTLES.

These will be drawn from BABOON CAMP Drying Room on the way up to the line on the following scale :- 2 per Battalion Headquarters, 1 per Company Headquarters and 1 per Platoon.

TRENCH WADERS.

An extra water bottle (empty) will be issued at BOESINGHE SIDING, prior to the Battalion moving forward.

O.C., Coys. will ensure that the second water bottle is filled as soon as possible from the Battalion Water Cart. Three Sandbags per man have been issued for use as under :-

1. For Spare Kit.
2. For wearing on the way up to the line from BOESINGHE SIDING.

TRANSPORT AND RATION ARRANGEMENTS.

The following arrangements will hold good during the forthcoming tour in the line, as regards Pack Animals bringing "Supplies, etc" up to the Line. Three Battalion Dumps will be established known as "A" Dump, "B" Dump and "C" Dump.
"A" Dump will be established at VEE BEND.
"B" Dump will be established at ROAD JUNCTION on OBTUSE BEND - FAIDHERBE Cross Road, 200 yards South of FAIDHERBE Cross Roads.
"C" Dump will be established on West of LOG HUT, 60 yards West of LES CINQUES CHEMIN Cross Roads.

The undermentioned supplies, etc., will be brought up on the night of 4/5th inst :-
    5 Hot Food Containers per Coy.
These will be dumped by Pack Transport as under :-
  At "A" Dump :-   1 Platoon "D" Coy. Hot Food Container (Two)
  At "B" Dump :-   Remaining Hot Food Containers mentioned above.
Hour of arrival at "A" Dump :-   As soon after 1 a.m. as possible.
O.C., "A", "B", and "C" Coys. will detail 3 men to be at Dump "B" at 1 a.m. to convey Hot Food Containers to their Coy. Headquarters.   O.C. Platoon, "D" Coy. at VEE BEND will detail a party of the same strength to be at Dump "A" at 12.50 am. This party will convey to "D" Coy. Headquarters Hot Food Containers for the remainder of the Coy.

The undermentioned "Supplies, etc" will be brought up on the night of the 5/6th inst :-
    5 Hot Food Containers per Coy.
    6 Petrol Tins Water)
    1 Petrol Tin Rum   ) per Coy & Bn. Hd.Qrs.
These will be dumped as under :-
At "A" Dump :-
    "D" Coy's. Hot Food Containers and Rum.
    "B" and "D" Coys' water.
At "C" Dump :-
    Remainder of supplies brought up.
Hour of arrival at "A" Dump :- As near 5 p.m. as possible.

O.C. Platoon at VEE BEND will detail 3 men to collect and carry Hot Food Containers to their Coy. To be at Dump "A" at 4.50 p.m. He will also arrange for the safe custody of "B" and "D" Coys' Water and Rum.

O.C.Coys. "A", "B" and "C" Coys. will each detail 3 men to be at Log Hut (Dump C) at 5 p.m. to carry Hot Food Containers and Rum to their respective Coy. Headquarters. They will afterwards return for the Coy's Water.

The undermentioned "Supplies etc" will be brought up on night of 6/7th inst :-
    5 Hot Food Containers per Coy.
    6 Petrol Tins Water)
    1 Petrol Tin Rum   ) per Coy and Bn. Hd.Qrs.
These will be dumped as under :-
At "A" Dump :-
    "B" Coy's. Hot Food Containers, Water and Rum.
At "C" Dump :-
    Remainder of above.
Hour of arrival :- As for night 5/6th inst.

(1).

- 2 -

O.C. "B" Coy. will detail 3 men to collect "B" Coy's Hot Food Containers, Water and Rum.   To be at "A" Dump at 4.50 p.m.
O.C. "A", "C" and "D" Coys. will detail 3 men to be at Log Hut (Dump C) at 5 p.m. to carry Hot Food Containers and Rum to their respective Coy. Hd.Qrs. They will afterwards return for their Coy's Water.

It is absolutely essential that the Pack Animals take back to the Transport Lines all empty Food Containers and Petrol Tins to ensure being able to get same sent up full on following nights.   Officers Commanding Coy's in forward area will therefore ensure that all their empty petrol tins and Food Containers are taken to "C" Dump as soon after dark as possible.   Similarly Officer Commanding Company at VEE BEND will take similar steps to have above named empty receptacles sent to "A" Dump.

The Regimental Transport Officer will also ensure that his animals do not return un-laden.

He will be responsible that all empty food containers and petrol tins at both "A" and "C" Dumps are taken back to the First Line Transport and handed over to the Quartermaster.

The Commanding Officer will hold Officers Commanding Coys. responsible that the following are brought out of the line on the Battalion being relieved in the forward area :-
(a). The extra Waterbottle.
(b). Waterproof Sheets.
(c). Waders.
(d). The Lewis Gun Magazines actually carried into the line by the Lewis Gun Teams.   This of course equally applies to the Inter-Coy. relief on night of 5/6th inst.

WHITE PARACHUTE FLARE - COUNTER ATTACK AEROPLANE SIGNAL.

These flares will be dropped only when 100 or more of the enemy are seen to actually advancing to attack.

S.O.S. RELAY POSTS.   Are established at VEE BEND, CANNES FARM, and U.26.d.7.6. In addition, Artillery concentration Light Signals have been established at the same points.
For the purpose of the above Signals, Battalion Sectors will be sub-divided into
No. 1.   Sub-sectors.
No. 2.   "   "
No. 3.   "   "
No. 4.   "   "

No. 1 Sub-sector is bounded on the E. by the point where front line crosses the main STADEN-YPRES Railway.
On# the W. by a S.W. and N.E. line drawn through V.1.a.9.1 and V.1.b.1.2.

No. 2 Sub-sector is bounded on E. by line mentioned in last line of above para.
On the W. by a S.W. and N.E. line drawn through U.6.d.1.4 and U.6.b.90.45.

No. 3 Sub-sector is bounded on E. by line mentioned in last line of above para.
On the W. by a S.W. and N.E. line drawn through U.5.d.5.4. and U.6.a.7.7.

No. 4 Sub-sector is bounded on E. by the line mentioned in last line of above para.
On the W. by a S.W. and N.E. line running through U.5.a.1.1. and U.5.a.7.7.

The object of the Signals is to bring a concentration of Artillery on to the Sector where the main attack has developed.
These signals will be sent up on the orders of front line Company Commanders, and will be repeated at Battalion Headquarters.

The Signals will be as follows :- and are to be taken in operation forthwith :-

No. 1 Sub-sector; 1 Red and 1 White Very Light (sent up in pairs until answered).
No. 2 Sub-sector; 1 Green Very Light (sent up until answered).
No. 3 Sub-sector; 1 Red Very Light (sent up until answered).
No. 4 Sub-sector; 1 Red and 1 Green Very Light (sent up in pairs until answered).

(continued)

- 3 -

S.O.S. LINES.
Until further orders, 18-pdr. S.O.S. lines will be :-
157th Brigade three batteries V.1.a.95.08 to U.6.b.80.34.
242nd Brigade one battery Road U.6.b.20.85 to O.36.d.25.20.
Two batteries O.36.c.5.0 to O.36.c.0.2. to O.35.c.9.0.
Remainder no change.   How: S.O.S. lines will be :-
242nd Brigade Road O.36.d.15.08. House O.36.d.05.05. Cross Roads
   O.35.c.92.68.

SALVAGE DUMPS.   These will be established at U.22.c.1.6., U.21.b.2.0, U.21.a.6.3.

TRENCH FEET.   The preliminary precautions against wastage through "Trench Feet, before going into the line, will be adhered to.   In addition, every N.C.O. and man will carry one pair of Trench Waders into the line; on arrival at his post, the garrison (less the sentry) will change their boots, socks and puttees, and put on a clean pair of socks and a dry pair of Waders. Similar action will be taken by the Support Companies.   The puttees worn marching up, will be placed in the pack, the boots being strapped or lashed on top.
Reserve Coys. will not put on their Waders until they are moved up in relief into the front line, where they will carry out the same procedure.

S.O.S.   The S.O.S. for the Second Army is - a Rifle Grenade bursting into stars "Red over Green over Yellow".

TRENCH STORES.   Coys. will render a list of Trench Stores taken over, to Headquarters as soon as possible after arrival.

S.O.S. GRENADES.   Will be taken over from outgoing unit.

THIS DOCUMENT MUST NOT BE TAKEN INTO THE FRONT LINE.

3.13.17.

Lieut.
A/Adjt.
11th Bn. Royal Fusiliers.

SPECIAL OPERATION ORDERS FOR DETAILS.

DETAILS. (1). "A" Details left out of action - Coys. (less "B" and "D"), Police, Drums, Officers' Mess Staff, Courts-Martial Witnesses, Candidates for Examination Courses, Sick, etc., will proceed to "H" Camp. Nominal Roll will be issued to O.C., "A" Details.

(2). "B" Details :- Quartermaster's Stores, Workshops, Post Corporal, Mess Sgt., Orderly Room Staff, Lewis Gun Sgt., C.Q.M.Sgts., Storemen, Cooks, will proceed to MICHEL FARM.

"C" Details. (3). The Details in (1) of "B" and "D" Coys. together with Pioneers, will be employed under Captain E.L. Jones, M.C., who has been issued with separate instructions. This Party, Strength approximately 52 O.R's will be accommodated at A.6.c.9.3.
The above mentioned will parade outside Battalion Headquarters at 2 p.m. tomorrow.
2nd Lieut. E.F. Atterbury will accompany the party.
The Quartermaster will arrange for 1 Cook with the necessary utensils to accompany this party, and also for a Water Cart to pay two Daily visits from MICHEL FARM.

O.C. "A" DETAILS. Captain C.S. Pearcy, M.C.

PARADES. "A" Details for "H" Camp will parade outside Guard Room ready to move off at 2.30 p.m. Route :- INTERNATIONAL CORNER, "H" CAMP.
"B" Details will move under orders of Quartermaster.

ADVANCE PARTY. 1 N.C.O. per "A" and "C" Coys. and Headquarters will report to Captain E.H. Cliff at Orderly Room at 1.15 p.m. and proceed to "H" Camp. Captain E.H. Cliff will report there to O.C., 54th Brigade Details, who will allot accommodation.

BAGGAGE. "A" Details' Blankets, Officers' Kits, Cooking Utensils, will be dumped in "A" and "C" Coys' hut - Entrance opposite Battalion Headquarters Mess on site marked "H" Camp by 10 a.m.
"B" Details' Blankets and Kits will be dumped at Quartermaster's Stores by 9 a.m.
"C" Details will carry their own full Kit and Blankets.

LOADING PARTY. O.C., "A" Details, will detail 1 N.C.O. and 4 men to load "A" Details' Baggage. This N.C.O. will report to Quartermaster's at 9.45 a.m.

OFFICERS' MESS KITS. All Officers will take sufficient Mess Kit for themselves; this will be dumped with "A" Details' Kit.

OFFICERS MESS. A combined Mess will be formed if possible on arrival in new area. Captain E.H. Cliff will be P.M.C.

SANITATION. O.C., "C" Details will arrange to leave 1 Officer, 1 N.C.O. and 8 men to ensure present Camp is left in a clean condition.
This Officer will render a Report in writing to O.C., "B" Details, at MICHEL FARM.

3.12.17.

Lieut.
A/Adjt.
11th Bn. Royal Fusiliers.

Issued to all recipients of Operation Orders No. 53.

S E C R E T. OPERATION ORDERS No. 54. Copy No. 7

INTENTION. 1.	The 54th Infantry Brigade will move to new Training Area near HARINGHE tomorrow.
MOVE. 2.	The 11th Bn. Royal Fusiliers will move to new Camp by road passing INTERNATIONAL CORNER at approximately 10.35 a.m.
PARADE. 3.	The Battalion will parade on New Camp Road. Head of Column on main road ready to move off at 10.15 a.m. Order of March :- Headquarters, "A", "B", "C" and "D". "Drums" will march in rear of "A" Coy. A distance of 100 yards will be maintained between Coys. and between "D" Coy. and Battalion Transport. A distance of 500 yards will be maintained between Battalions. Trench Mortar Section will march under Headquarters.
ROUTE. 4	MILITARY ROAD and POPERINGHE - DUNKERQUE Road.
FIRST LINE TRANSPORT. 5.	First Line Transport will move 100 yards in rear of rear Coy. Mess Cart and Maltese Cart and Cookers will join on main road.
REAR PARTY. 6.	All Coys. and Headquarters will detail 4 Other Ranks to report to 2nd Lieut. H.J.H. Saunders at Orderly Room at 9 a.m. to clean up Camp. This Officer will render a Certificate to Orderly Room on arrival at new Camp to the effect that the Camp and Horse Lines were left scrupulously clean. This party will meet similar party of 7th Bedfordshire Regiment at 2 p.m. at INTERNATIONAL CORNER and march to new Area under orders of Senior Officer.
BAGGAGE. 7	Blankets rolled in bundles of TEN will be dumped on main road near E.F.C. by 8.15 a.m. Officers' Kits and Mess Stores at 9 a.m. in same place. 1 N.C.O. per Coy. and Headquarters will report to Quartermaster when all Kit has been dumped. O.C., "C" Coy. will detail two N.C.O's. and 20 men to report to Quartermaster's Stores at 8.5 a.m. This party will move Quartermaster's Stores to dump
RATIONS. 8.	Dinners on arrival.
LORRIES. 9.	Three Lorries will be available for the Battalion. They will report at INTERNATIONAL CORNER at 8 a.m. Quartermaster will detail Guide to meet them.
CAMP FURNITURE. 10.	No Camp Furniture or Tents will be removed from present Area.
DRESS. 11.	Battle Order less Steel Helmets. Packs with steel helmets and jerkins under pack straps will taken under Coy. arrangements to dump near E.F.C. on main road by 8.15 a.m. Waterproof Sheets will be carried on the belt.
SANITATION. 12.	Coys. will ensure that the area is left in a scrupulously clean condition. Lines will be inspected by the Commanding Officer at 9.50 a.m.

15th December 1917.

Lieut.
A/Adjt.
11th Bn. Royal Fusiliers.

Issued at 7.45 p.m.

Copies to :-
- No. 1. C.O.
- 2. 2nd-in-Command.
- 3. Adjutant.
- 4. Asst. Adjutant.
- 5. Office.
- 6. War Diary.
- 7. War Diary.
- 8. O.C., "A" Coy.
- 9. O.C., "B" Coy.
- 10. O.C., "C" Coy.
- 11. O.C., "D" Coy.
- 12. Signalling Officer.
- 13. Lewis Gun Officer.
- 14. Quartermaster.
- 15. Transport Officer.
- 16. R.S.M.
- 17. Sgt. Greening.
- 18. Spare.

PROGRAMME OF TRAINING.

First Week.

MONDAY 17.12.17.

Organization Parade...........)	"A" Coy........ 9.15 a.m.
C.O's. Inspection.............)	"B" Coy........ 10 a.m.
)	"C" Coy........ 11 a.m.
)	"D" Coy........ 12 noon.

The whole of Headquarters, including
Transport personnel, but excluding
animals and vehicles....................... 2 p.m.

Bayonet Fighting and)	"C" and "D" Coys... 9 - 10 a.m.
Physical Training...........)	"A" Coy............ 10 - 11 a.m.
	"B" Coy............ 11 a.m. - 12 n.

Arms and Close Order Drill..)	"D" Coy........ 10 - 11 a.m.
Saluting....................)	"A" Coy........ 11 a.m. - 12 noon
	"B" & "C" Coys. 12 a.m. - 1 p.m.

Afternoon. Lectures to Platoon Commanders on Leadership and value of
Training during next few weeks. Discussion and explanation
of second day's Training.

R.S.M. takes N.C.O's. in Arms Drill.... 2 - 3 p.m.

TUESDAY 18.12.17.

Inspection..................................)
Bayonet Fighting and Physical Training..) 9 - 10 a.m.
Musketry................................. 10 - 11 a.m.
Arms Drill............................... 11.15 a.m. - 12 noon.
Close Order and Open Section Drill......)
Saluting................................) 12 noon - 1 p.m.

Afternoon. Lectures to Platoon Commanders on Outposts (telling off
Picket) See Div.HQ.........

R.S.M. takes N.C.O's. in Guard Mounting and Duties. 2 - 3 p.m.

WEDNESDAY 19.12.17.

Inspection..................................)
Bayonet Fighting and Physical Training..) 9 - 10 a.m.
Musketry................................. 10 - 11 a.m.
Demonstration of Outposts (telling off
Pickets................................. 11.15 a.m. - 12 noon.
Close Order and Open Section Drill......)
Saluting................................) 12 noon - 1 p.m.

Afternoon. Demonstration to Platoon Commanders of Siting Defensive
Positions.

R.S.M. takes N.C.O's. in Saluting, Cane and
Communication Drill.................................. 2 - 3 p.m.

THURSDAY 20.12.17.

Inspection..................................)
Bayonet Fighting and Physical Training..)
Close Order and Open Section Drill......) 9 - 10 a.m.
Saluting................................)
                                          10 - 11 a.m.
Wiring ("A" and "B" Coys.)................ 11 a.m. - 1 p.m.
Rifle Grenade and Bomb Practice, ("C"
and "D" Coys.)............................ 11 a.m. - 12 noon.
Musketry, ("C" and "D" Coys.)............. 12 noon - 1 p.m.
Lewis Gun Sections ("C" and "D" Coys.)
digging Lewis Gun position under Lewis
Gun Officer............................... 11 a.m. - 1 p.m.

Afternoon. Lectures to Platoon Commanders on Platoon in Attack,
vide S.S.135, 143 and J.600.

R.S.M. take N.C.O's. in Saluting (Cane Drill).. 2 - 3 p.m.

- 2 -

FRIDAY 21.12.17.

        Inspection..............................)
        Bayonet Fighting and Physical Training.) 9 - 10 a.m.
        Route March (Demonstration)............)
        March Discipline.......................) 10 - 11 a.m.
        Wiring ("C" and "D" Coys................. 11 a.m. - 1 p.m.
        Rifle Grenade and Bomb Practice, ("A"
        and "B" Coys)............................ 11 a.m. - 12 noon.
        Musketry ("A" and "B" Coys.)............. 12 noon - 1 p.m.
        Lewis Gun Sections ("A" and "B" Coys.)
        digging Lewis Gun position under Lewis
        Gun Officer.............................. 11 a.m. - 1 p.m.

Afternoon.   Football, etc.
        Company Conferences on work for next day and progress
        made during week.

SATURDAY 22.12.17.

        Inspection..............................)
        Bayonet Fighting and Physical Training.) 9 - 10 a.m.
        Open Section Drill.....................)
        Arms Drill on the move.................) 10 - 11 a.m.
        Musketry (Tests to discover weakness).
        Failures to be put back for special
        instruction.............................. 11.15 a.m. - 1 p.m.

Afternoon.   Football, Running, etc.
        Company Conferences on following week's work.

REMARKS.   Lewis Gunners will parade with Platoons for Lectures and Open
        Section Drill.   At other times they will parade under
        Lewis Gun Officer.

        Trained and Recruit Signallers and Runners will carry out programme
        arranged by Battalion Signalling Officer.

Night Work.

        One fine night during week will be selected by Officers
        Commanding Coys. to practice Officers and N.C.O's. in
        marching by Compass.

18.12.17.

                                            Lieut.
                                            A/Adjt.
                              11th Bn. Royal Fusiliers.

TRAINING PROGRAMME.

11th Bn. Royal Fusiliers. — Period 23 - 29.12.17.

Date.	Time	Particulars.
SUNDAY.		Church Parade.
MONDAY.	Morning.	Battalion Route March.
	Afternoon.	Foot Inspection.
	Evening. 7.p.m.	Marching on Compass Bearings for Coy. Officers
TUESDAY.		Christmas Day.
WEDNESDAY.	Morning.	Short Battalion Route March or Rally by Companies at a point to be notified.
THURSDAY.	Morning.	
	9 - 11 a.m.	"A" Coy. Firing on the Range.
	9 - 10 a.m.	"C" Coy. Wiring.
		"D" Coy. Musketry Instruction.
	10 - 11 a.m.	"D" Coy. Wiring.
		"C" Coy. Musketry Instruction.
	11 - 1 p.m.	"B" Coy. Firing on the Range.
	11.15 a.m. - 1 pm.	"A", "C" and "D" Coys. Close Order and Open Section Drill and Games.
	9 - 11 a.m.	"B" Coy. ditto.
FRIDAY.	9 - 11 a.m.	"C" Coy. Firing on the Range.
	9 - 10 a.m.	"B" Coy. Musketry Instruction.
		"A" Coy. Wiring.
	10 - 11 a.m.	"B" Coy. Wiring.
		"A" Coy. Musketry Instruction.
	11 am - 1 pm.	"D" Coy. Firing on the Range.
	11.15 am - 1 pm.	"A", "B" and "C" Coys. Close Order and OPEN Section Drill and Games.
	9 - 11 a.m.	"D" Coy. ditto.
SATURDAY.	9 am - 1 pm.	Lewis Guns. Firing on the Range.
	9 - 10 a.m.	"D" Coy. Wiring.
		"A", "B" and "C" Coys. Extended Order Drill.
	10 - 11 a.m.	"C" Coy. Wiring.
		"D" Coy. Extended Order Drill.
		"B" Coy. Close Order Drill.
		"A" Coy. Musketry and Games.
	11 am - 12 noon.	"B" Coy. Wiring.
	11.15 am - 12 noon	"A", "C" and "D" Coys. Close Order Drill.
	12 noon - 1 p.m.	"A" Coy. Wiring.
		"B", "C" and "D" Coy. Musketry and Games.

REMARKS.

On Monday, Thursday and Friday afternoons from 2 to 3 p.m., all N.C.O's. will parade under the R.S.M. for instruction in Guard Mounting and Duties, and Close Order Drill.

On Thursday and Friday afternoons small Tactical Scheme for all Officers. (Details later).

Specialists. Lewis Gunners will train as such under Coy. L.G. Sgts. except when (a) when firing on the Range, (b) Close Order Drill is detailed) and (c) Battalion Route March on Monday. Signallers will train as such under the Signalling Officer.

The above is subject to alteration if found necessary.

22.12.17.

Major.
Commanding 11th Bn. Royal Fusiliers.

11th (S) Batn. ROYAL FUSILIERS.

Army Form C. 2118.

WAR DIARY
or
INTELLIGENCE SUMMARY
(Erase heading not required.)

28.F.
(20 mats)

Place	Date	Hour	Summary of Events and Information	Remarks and references to Appendices
HARINGHE AREA	1918 Jany 1st	10.0ᵃ	New Years Day was kept by the Battalion. D.B. Ogilvie was Champion Piper to the Battalion being at "D" place in the 2nd Army piping competition. Coys Coy arrangements. The Chief Engineer visited the Coys & Transport details for the 3rd inst. Training movement order by all Coy issued. Capt. E. Robin was ordered to investigate & report & return [to?] R. Services to that of Captain on arrival case of hunting [supervisor?] of Coy & duty of R. Service [management of?] Army Wing & Long [Eckleigher?] & two flying aircraft. 3 ORs were wounded. On the 2nd inst the Battalion [proceeded?] by	
DE WIPPE	Jany 4th / Jany 5		Route march to DE WIPPE CAMP (Copy [Special?] orders "400 attached) Battalion Strength 43 officers & 703 OR. On the 4th inst not parading across [?] sent inward boy diarrhoea. The R.E. [?] provided the [?] Lach Coy P.S. on the 5th inst the Battalion proceed to [Devonshire?] Coy Hust & [?] inst went into clean clothing are provided to the Battalion at ONDANK. [Lieuts?] E Robin & T. [Hicks?] were wounded in the building [?] of [personnel?] service in the field. 6th & 9th inst the Bn [strength?] in training	

Army Form C. 2118.

WAR DIARY
or
INTELLIGENCE SUMMARY
(Erase heading not required.)

Instructions regarding War Diaries and Intelligence
Summaries are contained in F. S. Regs., Part II.
and the Staff Manual respectively. Title pages
will be prepared in manuscript.

Place	Date	Hour	Summary of Events and Information	Remarks and references to Appendices
	1918		accidently killed as a result of a collision between two aeroplanes in one of which he is to have been an unconscious flight. Major F. Dean M.C. assumed command of the Battalion. On the 7th, 8th, 9th inst. firing was carried out under Coy arrangements. Bivouacs permanent to the prevention of trench feet there was administered. On the 8th inst. wire patrols in the presence of the Battalion were commenced. Fresh rations being carried in replacement of those being consumed by component of L Coy at time of visit. Brigadier assumed pay command was awarded to No 477199 Sgt Hugg H.W. The Meritorious Service Medal was awarded to No 477199 Sgt Hugg H.W. Late Orderly Room Clerk.	
LINE	10th Jan		On the 10th inst. the Battalion supported from ON DANK to BOESINGHE & from there proceeded to the Left Battalion sector of HOUTHULST FOREST (Belgium Sheets V5 & 6) relieving the 7th Royal West Kent Regiment (55th Brigade) in the line. Details not required in the line proceeded to DUBLIN CAMP (copy Operation Orders No. 37 attached) During the 4 days the Battalion was in the line a front account of work was done in wiring & strengthening the	
	14th Jan			

A0915 Wt W11422/M1160 350,000 12/16 D. D. & L. Forms/C./2118/14.

Army Form C. 2118.

WAR DIARY
or
INTELLIGENCE SUMMARY.
(Erase heading not required.)

Instructions regarding War Diaries and Intelligence Summaries are contained in F. S. Regs., Part II. and the Staff Manual respectively. Title pages will be prepared in manuscript.

Place	Date	Hour	Summary of Events and Information	Remarks and references to Appendices
	1918		The position & all available details of the line were explained in carrying up instructions to the proposa. The following casualties were sustained 10 O.R's killed & 5 O.R's wounded accompanied by 2nd Lt Snee ful Between Sergts 40 Officers & 702 O.R's 14/18.	
			On the 14th inst the Battalion was relieved in the line by the 7th Yorkshire Regt and proceeded to BABOON CAMP where they were in reserve to the Brigade. On the night of the 15/16th inst the Battalion preceded by the night 16/17th inst provided carrying parties & on the night 17/18th inst The Battalion (less 1 coy) was in front of the front line in support of the Royal Scots 2nd Lieut F Ansbury being wounded by M.G. fire. This was the only casualty sustained in spite of very heavy M.G. fire.	
BABOON CAMP				
			On the 18th inst the Battalion was relieved at BABOON CAMP and returned to DE WIPPE CAMP where it remained until the 19th inst. Battalion Church of England service 2nd Lieut W Rogers	
DE WIPPE. McGa			at BOESINGHE & proceeded to ONDANK. From there to DE WIPPE CAMP where	
			The 19th inst was spent in cleaning hut & equipment	

WAR DIARY or INTELLIGENCE SUMMARY

Army Form C. 2118.

(Erase heading not required.)

Place	Date	Hour	Summary of Events and Information	Remarks and references to Appendices
	1918			
			Assumed command of the Battalion T.M. Selwyn. B the 20th inst. the Battalion	
			paraded for Divine Service. Baths & clean clothing being provided.	
			21st Lieut H.J.H. Saunders took over the duties of I.O. Officer. From the 21st to	
			23rd inst. training was carried out in accordance with programme	
			issued from Brigade (copy attached). On the 24th inst. Lieut Col. M Chalmers M.C.	
			moved from Brigade & resumed command of the Battalion. Lieut Col. 33rd inst.	
			an inspection of Lewis Box Respirators was made by the Brigade	
			Gas Officer. Battalion Strength 38 Officers 669 O.R. 27/1/18	
LINE	25th Jan		on the 25th inst. the Battalion entrained at LONDANK & proceeded to BOISINGHE relieving	
	26 Jan		from there to the line (Left Batln sector South of HOUTHULST FOREST) relieving	
			the 7th Royal West Kent Regiment. Details left out of action proceeded	
			to Lower Bakoon Camp (Belgian Camp) (Copy of operation order attached)	
			The Battalion remained in the line from the 25th to 28th inst. during this	
			tour much work was done in the way of improving temporary strong points,	
			the positions occupying these were made habitable & suitable shelters	
			for the night. On the 28th/29th Inst. the three left posts of the Battalion were	

WAR DIARY
or
INTELLIGENCE SUMMARY

Army Form C. 2118.

Place	Date	Hour	Summary of Events and Information	Remarks and references to Appendices
	1918		clearly between our own & a joint-post" was wirer wired at the rear on	
			of the left flank of the Battalion with the Right flank of the 51st Division	
			The following casualties were sustained 3 O.R. wounded	
			During the two hours in the line enemy shelling was considerably less	
			than that experienced during the previous week	
LOWER BADOON CAMP	27th Jan		Bn. relieved by the 26/27th Bn. The Battalion was relieved by the 7th Bedfordshire Bn.	
	28th Jan		and proceeded to LOWER BADOON CAMP where it remained in support	
			being relieved by the 96th Bde.	
EMILE CAMP	29th/30th Jan		Bns. had dinner and lunch and was provided for the Battalion at CAMP	
			and ELVERDINGHE CHATEAU	
			BANN. On 10.25 a.m. the Battalion proceeded to EMILE CAMP & remained	
HEIDEBEEK	30th Jan		there until 11.30 a.m. when proceeded by route march to HEIDEBEEK	
CAMP			CAMP near CROMBEKE (Belgium) distance about 19 x 10 kilometres (Copy appendix	
CROMBEKE	31st Jan		Orders "C" attached) Battalion strength 37 Officers + 860 O.R. on the	
			29th inst Lieut A.P.Webster arrived for + assumed of A. Coy. On the	
			31st inst. Capt Rees at the disposal of Coy. Commander for training up +	
			organisation during the month 7 Officers + 59 O.R. proceed on leave +	
			3 Officers + 74 O.R. proceeded to Courses of instruction	
			6th February 1918	
			[signature] Col. O.M. Argm	
			11th Royal Irish Fus.	

SECRET.   ORDER No. 35.   Copy No...... 4

                                           move
1. The 54th Brigade will be in Reserve and will move tomorrow from the HARINGHE
   Area to the BOESINGHE 3 Area.   Order of March :- 54th Brigade Headquarters,
   6th Northamptonshire Regiment, 11th Royal Fusiliers, 12th Middlesex Regiment,
   7th Bedfordshire Regiment, 54th Machine Gun Company.

2. The 11th Royal Fusiliers will move to DE WIPPE CAMP.   Time :-   9 a.m.
   Starting Point :- Cross Roads at W.23.d.9.4.
   Order of March :- "D", Hdqrs, "C", Drums, "A", "B". T.M.B.will march with Hdqrs.
   Route :- via CROMBEKE, CROMBEKE - POPERINGHE Road to INTERNATIONAL CORNER to
   DE WIPPE.
   Distances to be observed on the march :- Between Coys. 100 yards; between
   Battalions 500 yards.
   Battalion will move in column of fours.   "A" and "B" Coys. will join the
   Battalion at the road junction W.18.d.8.1.
   Dress :- Fighting Dress, wearing steel helmets.
   Caps will be placed by Coys. in sandbags and dumped with packs.

3. Lieut. H.W. Brookling will be mounted and will ride on ahead of the Battalion
   to warn Traffic Control, and see that proper distance between the Unit in front
   is maintained.

4. An Advance Party of C.Q.M.Sgts. from each Coy. and Headquarter Details and 1
   N.C.O. from the Transport will report to 2nd Lieut. E.C. Simmons at 7.30 a.m. at
   Q.M. Stores.   They will proceed to DE WIPPE, and arrange for billetting the
   Battalion.   The Hut next to that in which the Drums are billetted will be kept
   for "Pediculria".   This party may proceed by "Lorry jumping".

5. Officers' Kits and Mess Stores will be dumped by 7.15 a.m. as under :-
   "A" and "B" Coys. outside Coy. Offices.   "C", "D" and Hdqrs. outside Q.M.
   Stores.   These articles must be loaded by 7.30 a.m. sharp.
   Orderly Room boxes, etc. will be dumped at Q.M. Stores by 7 a.m.
   The Mess Cart will be at Headquarter Mess at 7.15 a.m.
   The following will be dumped by 7 a.m. as under :-
   Blankets rolled in bundles of 10, together with men's packs.
   "A" and "B" Coys. outside Coy. Offices.   "C", "D" and Hdqrs. outside Q.M. Stores.
   Hdqrs. Cooking Apparatus will be loaded by 7.30 a.m. on the limber detailed by
   the Transport Sergeant.
   Officers' Green Mess Boxes will be carried on Coy. Cookers.
   2 Lorries for blankets and 1 for packs have been asked for - further details
   will be issued later.

6. Loading Parties will be found as under by :-
   "A" Coy..... 1 N.C.O. and 7 men.
   "B" Coy..... 1 N.C.O. and 7 men.
   O.C. "B" Coy. will detail 1 N.C.O, who will be responsible for loading the Kits
   and Mess Stores by 7.30 a.m.
   "C" Coy..... 1 N.C.O. and 20 men to report to Q.M. at Q.M. Stores at 7 a.m.
   The Q.M. will find Guard for blankets, packs, etc. dumped at "A" and "B" Coys'
   Lines.

7. Lewis Guns, Signalling Apparatus and Stokes Guns will be loaded tonight under
   the supervision of respective Officers.

8. Each Coy. and Hdqrs. Details will detail 3 men (and "C" Coy. 1 N.C.O.) to report
   to 2nd Lieut. E.F. Atterbury at Q.M. Stores at 9 a.m.   The duty of this party
   is to clean the billets after the Battalion has moved out. This party will not
   move off till the Acting Staff Captain is satisfied that the billets are clean.

                              (continued)

9. Transport :- The First Line Transport including Cook Carts will be brigaded will move under the orders of the O.C., 152 Coy. A.S.C.
Starting Point :- As above.   Time :- 8 a.m.
Order of March :- 152 Coy. A.S.C., 8th Northamptonshire Regiment, 54th Machine Gun Coy., 11th Royal Fusiliers, 12th Middlesex Regiment, 7th Bedfordshire Regiment.
100 yards distance between Transport of Units will be maintained.
Destination of Transport :-   OMDANK Transport Lines.
The Maltese Cart will report at Medical Inspection Room at 7 a.m.
  etc.

10. Coys. will notify arrival in new billets to B.H.Q.

11. All billets must be left clean.

12. No Camp furniture will be removed from present Area.

                                               (Sgd)   E.L. JONES, Capt.
                                                                      A/Adjt.
                                           11th Bn. Royal Fusiliers.

3rd January 1918.
Issued at 6.15 a.m.

Copies to :-
	1. C.O.	10.	Signalling Officer.
	2. Adjutant.	11.	Lewis Gun Officer.
	3. Office.	12.	Quartermaster.
	4. War Diary.	13.	Transport Officer.
	5. War Diary.	14.	R.S.M.
	6. O.C. "A" Coy.	15.	Cook Sergeant.
	7. O.C. "B" Coy.	16.	Spare.
	8. O.C. "C" Coy.	17.	O.C. Advance Party.
	9. O.C. "D" Coy.	18.	Spare.

SECRET.   OPERATION ORDERS No. 37.   Copy No. 6

Intention. The 11th Bn. Royal Fusiliers will relieve the 7th Royal West Kent Regiment in the line tomorrow night (10/11th January 1918). The Battalion will parade on Coy. Parade Grounds to proceed to and entrain at ONDANK SIDING, and move off in the following order :- "D", "A", "B", "C" and Headquarters.

Parade. "D" Coy. will move off at 11.30 a.m. Coys. will follow as above, maintaining a distance of 100 yards between each other. The Battalion will detrain at BOESINGHE SIDING and remain there until 3 p.m. The Battalion will be ready to move off to the Front Line in the following order :- "D" Coy will leave the siding at 3 p.m. sharp and proceed by the CLARGES STREET Route, "A" Coy. Headquarters, "B" Coy. and C Coy.

Guides. Two per Battalion Headquarters. One per Coy. Headquarters and one per Platoon will meet the Battalion at BOESINGHE SIDING.

Distribution of Coys.
"D" Coy........ Right Forward Coy.
"A" Coy........ Left Forward Coy.
"B" Coy........ In Support.
"C" Coy........ In Reserve.

Detached Posts. The Coy. at VEE BEND will take over and man the S.O.S. Relay Post at VEE BEND. Strength :- 1 N.C.O. and 3 men. This Post will be handed over on Inter-Coy. Relief.

Baggage. Officers' Kits, Blankets and Mess Stores not required for the line will be dumped in the old Q.M. Stores by 10 a.m. Cpl. Rosewell, "C" Coy. and 1 man (to be detailed later) will be in charge of this Dump.
Spare Kits, Overcoats and Haversack of each man proceeding to the line will be packed in one sandbag clearly marked :- Name and Coy. &c. in BLOCK capitals, and dumped as above by 10 a.m. 1 N.C.O. per Coy. and Headquarter Details will report to the Quartermaster when all Coys. and Headquarters' Baggage is dumped.

First Line Transport. First Line Transport will not move.

Meals. Dinners on arrival at BOESINGHE SIDING. "B", "C" and "D" Coy. Cookers will proceed to the Siding and have Dinners ready by 1 p.m. Hot Tea will be served at 2.15 p.m. "A" Coy. Cooker will proceed to DUBLIN CAMP.
The Mess Cart will proceed to BOESINGHE SIDING with Lunch for Headquarters Mess and also all Coy. Messes. The Mess Sgt. will be responsible for arranging this.

Water Carts. Both Water Carts will move to BOESINGHE SIDING with the Cook Carts. Cookers and Water Carts will return to Transport Lines.

Lewis Guns. Lewis Gun Limbers will be loaded by 10 a.m. tomorrow and accompany Cookers to BOESINGHE SIDING where Lewis Guns will be collected by Coys. Twelve Drums per Gun will be taken. Eight Drums per Gun will be taken over in the line from the Royal West Kents, receipt being given by Coy. Commander. On production of this receipt by the Royal West Kent Regiment to the Quartermaster, he will hand over in exchange for the receipt the number of drums the receipt was given for.

Wirecutters, Very Pistols & Periscopes. Four 1" Pistols and 12 rounds 1" White Ammunition 6 Wirecutters and 6 pairs Wiring Gloves will be issued to each Coy. 2 Periscopes will be at B.H.Q. for Coys. if needed. The R.S.M. will carry 1-1½" Very Pistol.

(continued)

Rations.	The unexpended portion of tomorrow's rations, one "Tommy" Cooker per man and rations for the 11th and 12th inst., together with Iron Rations will be carried on the man. Further "Tommy" Cookers will be issued later.
Socks.	Two Pairs Socks will be carried on the man.
Rum.	Five Water Bottles per Coy. and 4 for B.H.Q. will be issued for consumption on the night of 10/11th inst.
Sandbags.	Four Sandbags per man will be issued.
Circular Saw	One Circular Saw will be issued to each Front Line Coy.
Empty Petrol Tins and Hot Food Containers.	Coys. will ensure that all empty Petrol tins and Food Containers are returned to Quartermaster each night.
Water Bottles.	To be filled before leaving BOESINGHE SIDING.
Rear Headquarters.	Rear Battalion Headquarters will be at the Transport Lines. 2nd Lieut. H.L. Smedley will be in charge.
Waders.	Arrangements for issue will be notified later.
Completion of Relief.	Coys. will inform Battalion Headquarters by Runner in writing when Relief is completed.
Entraining State.	Coys. will render to Orderly Room by 11 a.m. to-morrow Entraining State.
White Smocks	The Quartermaster will issue these to the two Front Coys. and the Support Coy.
Mufflers.	The Quartermaster will distribute 160 of these equally among Coys.
JERKINS.	Jerkins will not be worn but will be carried in the pack - Waterproof Sheet under the flap of the pack.
Inter-Coy. Relief.	The Circular Saws and White Smocks will be handed over when Inter-Coy. Relief takes place

DETAILS LEFT OUT OF ACTION.

All Details left out of action will parade at 10 a.m. under 2nd Lieut. E.W. Ede, who will march them to DUBLIN CAMP, where he will report to the Camp Commandant.
Officers' Kits for this Camp will be dumped outside the Orderly Room by 10 a.m.
The Transport Officer will detail one Limber to take these Kits to the new Camp.
Other Ranks will move in full marching order carrying their blankets.
The Mess Sergeant will arrange and be responsible for the Officers' Mess at DUBLIN CAMP

Lieut. C. Tantram will be in charge of the Details.
O.C. Coys. and Headquarter Details will render to Orderly by 9 a.m. a Nominal Roll of those proceeding to DUBLIN CAMP.

(continued)

SUPPLIES.

Dump. The following arrangements hold good during the forthcoming tour in the line, as regards animals bringing supplies, etc. up to the line :-

Two Battalion Dumps will be established known as "A" Dump "B" Dump :-

"A" Dump will be at VEE BEND.
"B" Dump will be at Road Junction on OBTUSE BEND - FAIDHERBE Cross Roads, 200 yards South of FAIDHERBE Cross Roads.

The undermentioned supplies will be brought up on the night of 10/11th inst.:-
Five Hot Food Containers per Coy. These will be dumped by Pack Transport as under :-
At "A" Dump, Five Hot Food Containers.
At "B" Dump, the remainder.
Hour of arrival at "A" Dump approximately 10 p.m.
O.C., "B" Coy. will detail 3 men to be at "B" Dump at 10 p.m. to convey Hot Food Containers to their Coy. Headquarters.
O.C. Coy. at VEE BEND will detail 3 parties each of 1 N.C.O. and 3 men to meet the Pack Train at VEE BEND. These parties must be ready at 9.45 p.m.
O.C. Coy. will post a Sentry to watch for arrival of Pack Train. The Sentry will turn out the above parties so that the Pack Train is not kept waiting.
O.C. Coy. at VEE BEND will detail an Officer to superintend the distribution.

(a). One party will convey the five Food Containers to "C" Coy. Headquarters from A Dump.
(b). One party will proceed with Pack Train to "B" Dump and carry the five Hot Food Containers to "A" Coy. Headquarters.
(c). One party will proceed with Pack Train to "B" Dump and carry the five Hot Food Containers to "D" Coy. Headquarters.

ON THE NIGHT 11/12th inst.

Five Hot Food Containers per Coy.
One Petrol Tin Rum per Coy.
Water if required.
One Petrol Tin Rum for B.H.Q.
Coys. will detail the same parties to carry as detailed for the night 10/11th inst., except that the times will be as under :-
Time of arrival at "A" Dump..... 5.30 p.m.
Sentry to be posted at 5.15 p.m. to watch for Pack Train and warn Carrying Parties to turn out immediately the Transport arrives.
B Coy's party to be at B Dump at 5.40 p.m

ON THE NIGHT 12/13th inst.

Five Hot Food Containers per Coy.
One Petrol Tin Rum per Coy.
One Petrol Tin Rum for B.H.Q.
Rations for consumption on 13th and 14th inst.
Carrying Parties for these will be detailed later.

ON THE NIGHT 13/14th inst.

Five Hot Food Containers per Coy.
One Petrol Tin Rum per Coy.
One Petrol Tin Rum for B.H.Q.
O.C. "A" Coy. will detail 1 N.C.O. and 3 men to be at "B" Dump at 5.40 p.m. to carry Containers and Rum to their Co Headquarters.
O.C. Coy. at VEE BEND will detail three parties each N.C.O. and 3 men. These parties will work as fo

(continued)

ON THE NIGHT 13/14th (contd).

    (a). This Party will convey the five Food Containers and Rum to "D" Coy. Headquarters.
    (b). This party will accompany the Pack Train to "B" Dump and convey Food and Rum to "B" Coy. Headquarters.
    (c). This party will accompany the Pack Train to "B" Dump and convey food and rum to "C" Coy. Headquarters.
O.C. Coy. at VEE BEND will detail an Officer to supervise the distribution.
The Rum for Battalion Headquarters will be left at B.H.Q. by the party carrying to the Support Coys. Headquarters.

Liaison Officer. O.C. Coy. at VEE BEND will detail one Officer to act as Liaison Officer, to report at B.H.Q. at 11 p.m. tomorrow.

Gas Rattles. Coys. will take over all Gas Rattles in the line, and unless otherwise order they will be retained.

A.A.Mountings. Anti-Aircraft Mountings will be handed over.

Trench Stores. Coys. will render to B.H.Q. as soon after Relief as possible list of Trench Stores taken over.

Discipline. As far as is possible all men must be shaved and washed. "Pedicuria" will be continued in the line, as explained at Coy. Commanders' Conference today.

Transport. The Transport Officer will detail 1 Limber to report at Orderly Room at 10.30 a.m. tomorrow to remove Orderly Room Boxes, etc. to Transport Lines. The Limber detailed to take Officers' Kits to DUBLIN CAMP will, on the way back to the Transport Lines, call for Headquarters' Cooking Utensils.

Sanitation. The Camp must be left in a clean condition. The Orderly Officer will report to the Adjutant at 11 a.m. that the lines are clean.

AMENDMENTS.

White Smocks must be treated with the greatest possible care. If snow is on the ground at the time of the Inter-Brigade Relief, White Smocks will, as far as the supply is available, be worn by all personnel proceeding to and from the Outpost Line and main line of resistance.
Smocks will be issued with preference to the Front Line Coys. and to those who have to visit the Outpost Lines.
Should Thaw set in, the suits will be collected and kept as dry and clean as possible and the Staff Captain will arrange to withdraw them from the line.

ROUTE.-(Amendment).
The Battalion will move from BOESINGHE SIDING by WIDJENDRIFT Road as far as WIDJENDRIFT and then by CLARGES STREET.

                                                    Capt.
                                                    A/Adjt.

9th January 1918.
Issued at 9 p.m.
                        11th Bn. Royal Fusiliers.

Copies to :-
No. 1.	C.O.	No. 7. O.C. "B" Coy.	13. Cook Sgt.
2.	Adjutant.	8. O.C. "C" Coy.	14. L.G.O.
3.	Office.	9. O.C. "D" Coy.	15. R.S.M.
4.	War Diary.	10. Quartermaster.	16. O.D.H.Q.Det.
5.	War Diary.	11. Transport Offr.	17 - 20
6.	O.C. "A" Coy.	12. Signalling Offr.	Spares.

Reference Dress for March tomorrow.
The following articles will be carried in the Haversack :-

    Iron Rations.
    Holdall.
    Cleaning Kit.
    1 pair Socks.
    Towel.
    Soap.

The Canteen will be carried under the Haversack straps.
The unexpended portion of the days rations will be carried in the Canteen.

SECRET.   ADMINISTRATIVE INSTRUCTIONS TO ACCOMPANY ORDERS NO.38.

The following arrangements hold good during the forthcoming tour, as regards animals bringing up supplies &c to the line.

Two Battalion dumps will be established known as "A" dump & "B" dump. "A" dump will be at VEE BEND.
"B" dump will be at road junction on OBTUSE BEND- FAIDHERBE CROSS ROADS 200 yds. south of FAIDHERBE CROSS ROADS.- a notice board marked "B"

The men will prepare for themselves and drink hot tea between 5 & 6 a.m. Rum will be issued between 5 & 6 a.m. Hot soup will be brought up each evening and issued between 8 & 9 p.m.

The undermentioned supplies will be brought up on the night of the 24/25th Jan.1918. All supplies will be brought up by limber as far as "A" dump.

        5 Drying drums.
        5 Hot food containers per Coy.
        2 Hot food containers for B.H.Q.
        Hour of arrival at "A" dump approximately 8 p.m.

O.C. "D" Coy. will detail the following parties:-

(1)   1 N.C.O. and 3 men to carry from "A" dump hot food containers to "A" Coy. H'qrs.
(2)   1 N.C.O. and 3 men to carry from "A" dump hot food containers to "B" Coy. H'qrs.
(3)   1 N.C.O. and 3 men to carry same to .C. Coy. H'qrs.
(4)   1 N.C.O. and 3 men to carry same to "D" Coy. H'qrs.
(5)   2 men to carry same to Battalion H'qrs.

These parties are to be ready by 7-45 p.m.
O.C. "D" Coy. will post a sentry at 7-45 p.m. to watch for the arrival of the transport. Immediatley it arrives he will turn out the above 5 parties.

O.C. "D" Coy. will detail 5 men to carry the 5 Drying Drums together with the necessary "Tommy" Cookers from "A" Dump to the forward Coys' Headquarters as follows :-
        2 to "C" Coy.
        2 to "B" Coy.
        1 to "A" Coy.
O.C. "D" Coy. will detail an Officer to superintend distribution at "A" Dump.

ON NIGHT 25/26TH INST.
There will be 5 Hot Food Containers with Soup and 1 Petrol Tin with Rum for each Coy. and 2 Hot Food Containers and 1 Tin Rum for B.H.Q.
The Limber containing these will arrive at VEE BEND at 7.30 p.m. The same parties will be told off as above for the same duties. Sentry to be posted at 7.15 p.m.
The party detailed for carrying the Drying Drums will not be required for this night.
Charcoal for B.H.Q. will also be sent up this night - 1 man to be detailed by O.C. "D" Coy. to carry this from "A" Dump to B.H.Q.

Gum boots have been issued this day as follows to :-
"A" Coy............... 59 pairs.   "B" Coy.............. 59 pairs.
"C" Coy............... 63 pairs.   "D" Coy.............. 9 pairs.
Coy. Commanders will ensure that their men bring these numbers out of the line when relieved.

All hot food containers are to be returned to "B" dump by each Coy. by 6 p.m. each night. O.C. "D" Coy. will send parties to bring the hot food containers which Coys. have dumped at "B" Dump, back to "A" Coy. These must be at "A" Dump before 7 p.m. each evening.

                        (Sd) E.L. Jones. Capt. A/Adj.
                        11th. Bn. Royal Fusiliers.

SECRET. OPERATION ORDER No. 38. Copy No. 5

Intention. The 11th Bn. Royal Fusiliers will relieve the 7th Royal West Kent Regiment in the line tomorrow night (24/25th Jan.)

Parade. The Battalion will parade on Coy. Parade Grounds to proceed to and entrain at ONDANK SIDING.
Time ;- 12.15 p.m.
Order of March ;- Hdqrs. "C", "B", "D", "A".
Dress ;- Fighting Dress (Packs slung), Jerkins, socks and gum boots in pack. Jerkins will not be worn.
Coys. will maintain 100 yards distance between each other.
The Battalion will detrain at BOESINGHE SIDING and remain there till 3 p.m.
The Battalion will be ready to move off to the front line in the following order :-
Details Later

Route ;- Corduroy ROAD to WIDJENDRIFT ROAD, then via CLARGES STREET

Entraining State. Coys. will render Entraining State to Orderly Room by 11 am tomorrow.

Disposition of Coys.
Coys
"C" Coy...... Left Forward Coy.
"B" Coy...... Right Forward Coy.
"A" Coy...... Support Coy.
"D" Coy...... Reserve Coy.

Guides. Guides on the scale of 2 per Battalion Headquarters, 1 per Coy. Headquarters and 1 per Platoon, will meet the Battalion on CLARGES STREET where the track leads to LUVOIS FARM at 5.30 p.m.
The Royal West Kents will also send 1 Guide for each Post to the same place, at same time.

Completion of Relief. Will be reported by wiring Coy. Commander's name To B.H.Q.

Detached Posts. "A" Coy. will detail 1 N.C.O. and 3 men to take over the S.O.S. Relay Post at VEE BEND. This party will report to Brigade Major, Brigade Headquarters, FIFTEEN WOOD, at 11 am. 24th inst. Great care must be exercised that the duties of this Post are fully understood.

First Line Transport. First Line Transport will not move.

Baggage. Officers' Kits, Blankets and Mess Stores not required for the line, will be dumped in the old Q.M. Stores by 10 a.m. 1 N.C.O. and 1 man (to be detailed later) will be in charge of this dump. Cap
Spare Kits, Overcoats, and Haversack of each men proceeding to the line will be packed in one Sandbag clearly marked with name and Coy. etc. in BLOCK CAPITALS, and dumped as above at 10 a.m.
1 N.C.O. per Coy. and Hdqrs. Details will report to the Quartermaster when all Coys. and Hdqrs' Baggages is dumped.

Meals. Dinners on arrival at BOESINGHE SIDING. "B", and "D" Coy. Cookers will proceed to the SIDING and have Dinners by 1.15 p.m. Hot Tea will be served at 2.15 p.m.
"C" Coy. Cooker will proceed to DUBLIN CAMP.
The Mess Cart will proceed to BOESINGHE SIDING with Lunch for Hdqr. Officers and also Coy. Officers. The Mess Sergeant will be responsible for arranging this.
"A" Coy. Cooker will proceed to Transport Lines.

Water. Both Water Carts will move to BOESINGHE SIDING with the Cook Carts. All Water Bottles will be filled before leaving this point. Cookers and Water Carts will return to Transport Lines

(2).

Lewis Guns and Drums.	Details regarding these will be issued later.
Wirecutters, etc.	8 Wirecutters and 6 pairs Wiring Gloves also 4 - 1" Pistols and 12 rounds 1" White Ammunition will be issued to each Coy. 2 Periscopes will be at B.H.Q. for Coys. if needed. 1 Circular Saw will be issued to each Front Line Coy. The R.S.M. will carry one 1½" Very Pistol.
Rations.	To be carried on the man ;- (a). Unconsumed portion of day's rations. (b). Two days' rations. (c). Iron Rations. (d). Two Water Bottles.
Socks.	Each man will carry three pair of socks.
Gum Boots.	Arrangements for issue will be notified later.
Gas Rattles.	Will be issued by the Quartermaster to Coys, 1 to each Platoon and Coy. Hdqrs, 2 to B.H.Q.
Rum.	5 Water Bottles per Coy. and 4 for B.H.Q. will be issued for consumption on the night 24/25th inst.
Notice Board.	The Quartermaster will have two Notice Boards prepared ;- 1 marked "A" Dump, the other "B" Dump. "A" Coy. will be responsible for carrying these up and erecting them at the spot where the dump will be established
Drying Drums.	The Quartermaster will prepare 5 Drums (Drying) and provide two "Tommy" Cookers with each. Arrangements for Transport will be notified later.
Discipline.	As far as is possible all men must be shaved and washed.
Inter-Coy. Relief.	On night of 25/26th there will be an Inter-Coy. Relief :- "D" Coy relieves "B" Coy. - "B" Coy. relieves "A" Coy. "A" Coy. relieves "C" Coy. - "C" Coy. to VEE BEND. The Circular Saw will be handed over when Inter-Coy. Relief takes place.
Empty Petrol Tins and Food Containers.	Coys. will ensure that all empty Petrol Tins and Food Containers are returned to the Quartermaster each night.
Trench Stores.	Coys. will render to B.H.Q. as soon after Relief as possible, list of Trench Stores taken over.
Sanitation.	The Camp must be left in a clean condition. The Orderly Officer will report to the Adjutant at 11 a.m. that the lines are clean.
Rear Battalion Headquarters.	Will be at Transport Lines.
Liaison.	O.C. C. Coy. will detail 2nd Lieut. G. Norman to report at B.H.Q. at 10 p.m. on night 24/25th inst. to act as Liaison Officer.

23rd January 1918.
Issued at 1.30 p.m.

Barnes
Capt. A/Adj.
11th Bn. Royal Fusiliers.

Copies to ;-
No. 1. C.O.
No. 2. 2nd-in-Command.
No. 3. Adjutant.
No. 4. Office.
No. 5. War Diary.
No. 6. War Diary.
No. 7. O.C. "A" Coy.
No. 8. O.C. "B" Coy.
No. 9. O.C. "C" Coy.
10. O.C. "D" Coy.
11. Quartermaster.
12. Transport Officer.
13. Signalling Officer.
14. Sgt. Greening.
15. L.G.O.
16. R.S.M.
17 - 19 Spares.

SECRET.   ADDENDA TO OPERATION ORDERS NO. 38

Day Positions. During daylight only the posts shown on map "A" (day disposition) will be occupied and the strength of these positions is shown on scale already issued. This number on each post will on no account be exceeded.
<u>This operation does not apply to the picquet line.</u>
At dawn 25th.Jan.1918.the men to be withdrawn from front line posts will be accommodated as follows:-
"B"Coy. in 5 Chemins post and EGYPT WEST.
"C"Coy. in UCKFIELD post and SUEZ post.

Gum Boots. Every N.C.O. and man in front line and support Coys. will wear gum boots while holding their respective positions. On relief ankle boots will be worn. Runners only will wear ankle boots in the line. Officers will be held directly responsible that this order is obeyed by every N.C.O. and man.
"B"Coy. will, on inter Coy.relief, hand over sufficient boots to supply "D"Coy. with required number.

Inter-Company Relief. On night of 25/26th. support and counter attack Coys. will relieve front line Coys. as follows:-
"D"Coy. will relieve "B"Coy. in right sector.
"B"Coy. will relieve "A"Coy. in support.
"A"Coy. will relieve "C"Coy. in left sector.
"C"Coy. will then move to VEE BEND as counter attack Coy.
"D"Coy. will start from VEE BEND at 9 p.m.

BAYONETS. These will not be fixed in front line posts.

No. 4 Post. This post will be moved to a position on or at the s of the MARESCHAL FARM ROAD, so as to be able to f down the road.
"B"Coy. will effect this on night 24/25th.

Hot Soup. On night 25/26th.inst."D"Coy. will carry soup up to Coy.H'qrs. as detailed before inter Coy relief starts.

S.O.S.Relay Post. This post found by "A"Coy. will do this duty during the whole period the Battalion is in the line.

Work. Work programmes must be carried out with the least possible interruption by relieving Coys.

On completion of relief second night Coys. will report to B.H.Q. over the wire using Coy.Commander's name as code word.

Pass words. First night........ RUXTON. ("A"Coy.)
Second night....... MICHELL. ("B"Coy.)
Third night........ BROOKLING. ("C"Coy.)

<u>AMENDMENTS TO OPERATION ORDERS NO. 38.</u>
O.C."D"Coy. will arrange for the carrying up and fixing of the notice board for "A"dump.
2nd.Lieut.G.Norman will not report to B.H.Q. as ordered.
2nd.Lieut.G.W.Gibbs will report to B.H.Q. at 10 p.m. on night 24th.Jan.to act as liaison Officer.

(Sd) E.L.Jones.
Capt.A/Adj.
11th.Bn.Royal Fusiliers.

23-1-18.

SECRET.   ORDERS FOR DETAILS LEFT OUT OF   Copy No.....
                    ACTION.

Details left out of Action will be divided into two parties :-

(X) 60 men under 2nd Lieut. B.H. Beckett will be accommodated
    at LOWER BABOON CAMP (Nominal Roll is attached hereto).

(Y) Remainder of Details will proceed to DUBLIN CAMP and be
    under the command of Lieut.Col R.Turner D.S.O. 6th.
    Northamptonshire Regiment, who will allot accommodation
    and supervise training.

All "Y" Details will parade at 10 a.m. under Capt.G.S.Peaxy MC.
who will march them to DUBLIN CAMP where he will report to the
Camp Commandant. All ranks will move off in full marching
order carrying their blankets. Major G.Dekin M.C.will be in
command of these details.

All "X"Details will parade under 2nd.Lieut.B.H.Beckett and will
proceed with the Battalion to ONDANK SIDING following behind
"A"Coy.
On arrival at BOESINGHE they will have their dinners and then
proceed to LOWER BABOON CAMP. "X"Details will parade in full
marching order.
All blankets for the "X"Details will be dumped outside Orderly
Room by 10 a.m. in a separate dump. The Transport Officer will
detail one limber to be at Orderly Room by 11 a.m. to load up
and take these blankets to LOWER BABOON CAMP, where 2nd.Lieut.
B.H.Beckett will arrange to collect them.
"B"Coy.Cooker will proceed to LOWER BABOON CAMP instead of
returning to Transport Lines as previously ordered,and cook for
"X"Details. Rations will be sent up daily.
One Water Cart will supply water daily to these details.

The Maltese Cart will report to Medical Inspection Hut at 10 am.

One limber will report to Orderly Room at 11 am.to collect
Orderly Room boxes &c.

XXXXXXXXXXXXXXXXXXXXXXXXXXXXXXXXXXXXXXXXXXX
The Mess Sgt.will be responsible for arranging for the Messing
of the Officers at DUBLIN CAMP.

                                    (Sd) E.L.Jones.
                                         Capt.A/Adj.
23-1-18.   11th.Bn.Royal Fusiliers.

ADDENDA TO OPERATION ORDERS NO.38.
Lewis Guns. will be carried by Lewis Gunners. At least 12 Lewis Gun Drums
    will be carried up by each Lewis Gun Team. The Q.M. will send
    up by limber on the first night 8 drums per gun,total 128.
    O.C."D"Coy. will detail parties to carry these as under:-
    One party of one N.C.O. & 4 men to carry 32 drums from "A"dump
    to "A"Coy.H'qrs. and three similar parties to carry 32 drums
    each to "B" "C" & "D"Coys.respective H'qrs.
VICKERS GUNS. The Vickers Gun Section will pack by 10 a.m.,their gun in a
    limber which will be proceeding to VEE BEND night of 24/25th.
    Jan.1918. The section will collect their gun from VEE BEND
    & carry it to B.H.Q. During the tour in the line the section
    will be at AJAX HOUSE with Battalion H'qrs.
    The Bn.Lewis Gun Sgt will proceed to
    the line with this limber and be   (Sd) E.L.Jones.Capt.A/Adj.
23-1-18 responsible for the Vickers Gun and   11th.Bn.Royal Fusiliers.
    also the distribution of the Lewis
    Gun Drums.

No. 305.

All Coys.

PRIORITY OF WORK ON RELIEF FROM THE LINE.

19.1.18.   Baths.

20.1.18.   Interior Economy, and cleaning arms and equipment.

21.1.18.   Interior economy. cleaning arms and equipment and
           reorganization.

22.1.18.   Physical Training, short route march not exceeding
           4 miles.   Reorganization, interior economy,
           cleaning arms and equipment.

23.1.18.) Musketry.
  to) Strong Point attack by platoons.
24.1.18.) Rifle Grenade firing.
           Close Order Drill.

Lewis Gunners - special training under Lewis Gun Officer.
Signallers.   -   "   "   "   Signalling Officer.
Painting of Transport Wagons.
Inspection Signallers of Battalions 24.1.18.

19.1.18.
                                     Capt.
                                     A/Adjt.
                   11th Bn. Royal Fusiliers.

SECRET.   ORDER NO. 44.   COPY No........

MAP SHEETS 19 S.E. 27 N.E. and 28 N.W.

1.   The Battalion will move to HEIDEBEEK CAMP (X.20.b.central.),
     CROMBEKE AREA tomorrow.
     The Battalion will parade in line on the road ready to move off
     at 8-50 a.m.
     Order of march:-   H'Qrs. "D" "A" Drums "B" "C".
     Drums will march with and in rear of "A" Coy.
     Dress:-   Battle Order as explained. Box Respirator in the "Alert"
               position. Puttees must have trouser lap of 3½ inches.
     A distance of 100 yds. will be maintained between Coys. when on the
     march.

2.   Route:-   EMILE CAMP, ELVERDINGHE, DROMORE CORNER, D° WIPPE,
               INTERNATIONAL CORNER, A.2.a.37, F.F.10.d.9.4, CROMBEKE,
               HEIDEBEEK CAMP.

3.   Haversack Rations to be carried. These are to be drawn from the
     C.Q.M.Sgts. tonight.

4.   Two lorries for blankets and one lorry for packs are allotted to
     the Battalion. The Quartermaster will send a guide to
     ZOMMERBLOOM CABARET at 8 am. 30th.Inst for these.

5.   Officers kits, mess boxes and blankets will be dumped near guard
     room at 8 am.
                                    below straps
6.   Packs(marked) with steel helmets/will be dumped at the cross roads
     behind the spot marked "SALVAGE DUMP" by 7-15 am. Coys. will be
     marched to and from this dump. Map location of Dump B.9.c.9.3.
     Each Coy. will detail one "light duty" man to act as a guard over the
     Company's packs. This man will take the whole of his equipment
     with him when he goes to the dump. He will march up with his Coy.

7.   Lewis Guns have been loaded on limbers today.

8.   Loading Party. Each Coy. will detail 4 men, H.Q.Details 4 men,
     and "D" Coy. 1 Sgt. to report to the Quartermaster at the blanket
     dump at 8 am.
     2nd.Lieut.J.R.Cruikshank will have charge of this party. They will
     remain behind to clean the camp after the Battalion has moved out.
     This party will not move off until the Assistant Staff Captain is
     satisfied the camps are clean.
     In spite of this party being left behind Coys. will make every
     effort to leave their lines in a clean condition.

(2)

9. An advanced party consisting of 2nd.Lieut. [ ] [   ] & 5 C.Q.M.Sgts. will proceed on bicycles to the new camp and arrange for billetting the Battalion. This party will parade outside Orderly Room at 7 am. and march to DE WIPPE CABARET where they will procure bicycles and then ride to their destination. The Transport Officer will detail one N.C.O. to proceed with this party to arrange the Transport Lines &c.

10. The Mess Cart and Maltese Cart will report to the H.Q. and Medical Inspection hut respectively. They must leave EMILE CAMP by 8 am and arrive at WETHERBY CAMP in time to move with First Line Transport.

11. "B" & "D" Coy. cookers will prepare breakfast for the Battalion and proceed with the G.S. Wagons. Horses for these will report at 8-30 am.
"A" & "C" Coy. cookers will rejoin First Line Transport tonight.

12. Breakfast water and all water bottles will be filled tonight. Water Carts to return to First Line Transport tonight.

13. First Line Transport will be Brigaded and will march under the orders of O.C. 159 Coy. A.S.C.
Order of march:- 159 Coy.A.S.C. - 54th.Bde.H'qrs. - 11th.Royal Fusiliers. - 7th.Bedfordshire Regt. - 12th.Middlesex Regt. - 6th.Northamptonshire Regt. - 54th.M.G.Coy. - 80th.Field Coy.R.E.
Starting point:- DE WIPPE CORNER.
Time:- 8 am.
Destination:- HEYDEBEEK CAMP.
Route:- As for March given above. 150 yds. distance between Transport will be maintained.
All Officers charges will XXXX be at EMILE CAMP at 8-30 am.

14. Arrival in new billets will be reported to Orderly Room at once.

[signature]
Capt. & Adjt.
11th. Bn. Royal Fusiliers

CO-1-18.
Issued at 7 pm.

Copies to :-
1. C.O.
2. 2nd. in Command.
3. Adjutant.
4. Office.
5. War Diary.
6. War Diary.
7. O.C. "A" Coy.
8. O.C. "B" Coy.
9. O.C. "C" Coy.
10. O.C. "D" Coy.
11. Quartermaster.
12. Transport Officer.
13. Lewis Gun Officer.
14. Signalling Officer.
15. Cook Sgt.
16. R.S.M.
17-20. Spares.

REMARKS :-

The keynote of this series of training will be :-

(a) Training in discipline.
(b) Training of section and platoon commanders, who must be forced to actually perform the executive.
(c) Development of smartness, and improvement in the turn out.
(d) Obtaining men's closest attention, by enforcing strictest discipline, so as to prepare their minds to received advanced instruction in the field.
(e) Raising the morale of the troops by keen games in the afternoons, amusements in the evening.

Platoon commanders must be educated to take greater interest and pride in their platoons. They must be encouraged to work up their platoons, so as to be the smartest and best platoon in the Battalion. Leather equipment must be taken to pieces, scoured, soaped and polished, web scoured and treated with blanco. The lanyard, pipeclayed, will be worn over the left shoulder. Platoon Commanders can well afford to spend a little money on their platoons, so as to help purchase cleaning materials; Regimental funds can also help. Great attention is to be given to the care of clothing, grease must be removed - hot water and soda will be found useful, brown paper and a hot iron, petrol if available. The self-respect and pride in themselves will be developed if the men are made to keep themselves smart and tidy; waste is also avoided. Officers, especially junior Officers, must be particular about their own personal turn out. Commanding Officers will deal severely with any officers who, by their personal turn out and appearance do not set a right example for their men to mould themselves upon.
Work must be short, sharp and to a definite end. Every scrap of energy must be put into the work by Officers, who will exact the maximum amount from the men. Slackness and slovenliness is the worst class of training. Movements must be made crisp and sharp. When an Officer is called by his senior he will double up, not walk; the same applies to N.C.O's. and men who are called by Officers. Energy and vitality must permeate all training.

31.1.18.

Capt. A/Adjt.
11th Bn. Royal Fusiliers.

Army Form C. 2118.

WAR DIARY
or
INTELLIGENCE SUMMARY.
(Erase heading not required.)

11th R.Dns

Place	Date	Hour	Summary of Events and Information	Remarks and references to Appendices
HEIDEBEEK CAMP	1st/2/1918		On the 1st & 2nd inst. training was carried out in accordance with programme. (Copy attached) Battalion Strength — 37 Officers 664 ORs.	
CROMBEKE AREA			On the 3rd inst. the Battalion paraded for Divine Service in Camp, a special service for Intercession having also been held at WAAYENBERG Camp. On the 4th inst. training was carried out in accordance with programme. (Copy attached). Special instruction was given to # junior officers in arms & close order drill. The Divisional Commander presided at the pitton of the Lys Star to 15 ORs of the Battalion in the presence of representatives from all ranks in the Brigade (Copy of this attached). 2nd Lieut. E. Campbell joined the Battalion for duty & was posted to "B" Coy. On the 5th inst. the Battalion paraded in fighting order & was inspected by the Commanding Officer. Special attention being directed to the cleanness & fit of equipment & clothing. A Divisional Fair (Re-opened Chemises) on account of bad weather) was held near OEST-CAPPELL, a number of men from the Battalion were conveyed there in lorries. On the 6th & 7th inst. training was carried out under Coy. arrangements and	SS F. (28 total)
BELGIUM 4 FRANCE Sheet 19x 20 Bright				

WAR DIARY or INTELLIGENCE SUMMARY

Army Form C. 2118.

Place	Date	Hour	Summary of Events and Information	Remarks and references to Appendices
			instruction in Musketry was given to junior Officers, on the Lewis Gun by Lt Thompson assisted by a number of "C" Coy, on the 8th inst Coy were at the disposal of Coy Commanders. Battalion Strength 38 Officers 670 O.Rs. On 10th inst the Battalion paraded at 5-15 am & marched to PROVEN where it entrained with Transport and leaving PROVEN at 4-10 am arrived at NOYON (FRANCE Sheet 70p 0 E) at 9 p.m. from NOYON the Battalion proceeded by route march to BEHERICOURT (Sheet 70 E 17) when it was billeted (Copy of Operation Orders 70 A attached). On the 11th & 12th inst Coys were at the disposal of Coy Commanders for cleaning up & training. Special attention being given to musketry & firing on Range. Special instruction in Musketry was given to Junior Officers.	
BEHERICOURT			On the 12th inst 3 Officers & 220 O.Rs. (all being drawn from the attached 1st Bn Royal Fusiliers) joined & were posted to the Battalion as reinforcements. On the 13th inst the Battalion proceeded by route march to CAILLOUEL (Sheet 70 E E12) when it remained in billets for 2 days (Copy Operation Orders 70 b attached). On the 14th inst Coys were	

Army Form C. 2118.

WAR DIARY
or
INTELLIGENCE SUMMARY.
(Erase heading not required.)

Instructions regarding War Diaries and Intelligence Summaries are contained in F.S. Regs., Part II. and the Staff Manual respectively. Title pages will be prepared in manuscript.

Place	Date	Hour	Summary of Events and Information	Remarks and references to Appendices
			At the disposal of Coy Commanders for information parades Musketry firing on range was carried out. Major K.D.H. GWYNN D.S.O. joined the Battalion for duty on 13th inst & assumed duties of 2nd in Command. The Belgian CROIX de GUERRE was awarded to the following officers & O.R's of the Battalion viz. Lieut H.W. BROOKING. No 15815 C.S.M. BAILEY A. & No 9861 Pte GILES E. Such decorations being awarded for gallantry & devotion to duty when in the line.	
CLASTRES	15th to 26th Feby		On the 15th inst the Battalion proceeded by Route March to CLASTRES (square sheet 66c & 93 B) where it was billeted in D'ITAME CAMP on Coy (C) being billeted at JUSSY (66°M15) A Coy proceeded three to a machine Gun Course & on return proceeded to England for a machine gun course. On leave Major K.D.H. Gwynn D.S.O. assumed the temporary command of the Battalion. Battalion Strength 30 officers 672 O.R's. From the 16th to 26th inst inclusive the Battalion (less "C" Coy) was employed in running a shoot line of defence in the neighbourhood of ESSIGNY-LE-GRAND (Sheet 66c & H) The work principally consisted in digging trenches	

A8945 Wt W14422/M1180 339,000 12/16 D.D.&L. Forms/C./2118/16.

WAR DIARY
or
INTELLIGENCE SUMMARY.

(Erase heading not required.)

Army Form C. 2118.

Place	Date	Hour	Summary of Events and Information	Remarks and references to Appendices

Making strong points & digging out & working & was carried out under the supervision of the 79th Field Coy R.E. The work was done in daylight without interference from enemy artillery, & no casualties were sustained.

During this period "C" Coy were employed in rigging a cable from the same locally under the supervision of the O/C 11th Divisional Signal Coy R.E. Wiring Party Tables to work carried out by "A" "B" & D Coys during this period are attached. Training was carried out by Specialists not engaged in working according to attached Reference.

On the 18th inst. Lewis N.C. Os winners at Matthew & Wilcox joined Bn Battalion as reinforcements. By the 21st R 22nd & 23rd not both were accepted to the Battalion at REMIGNY & JUSSY (Sheet 66. M & N) by the 21st inst two Battalion Reinforcements were formed up for anti-aircraft work, the intention being that two Lewis Guns should always be mounted & prepared to deal with enemy aircraft. On 21st inst all the Battalion Lewis Guns were inspected by Major McGlashan DSO Battalion Sheykh .... Officers RFC Bn the 23rd inst 10.5 E.R. Joined

WAR DIARY
or
INTELLIGENCE SUMMARY.
(Erase heading not required.)

Army Form C. 2118.

Instructions regarding War Diaries and Intelligence Summaries are contained in F. S. Regs., Part II. and the Staff Manual respectively. Title pages will be prepared in manuscript.

Place	Date	Hour	Summary of Events and Information	Remarks and references to Appendices
CAILLOUEL			The Battalion on reinforcement. On the 26th inst the Battalion proceeded by route march to CAILLOUEL (Shet 70 F Est) where it was billeted. (Copy of march table forwarded). Major N.A.H. Bryan DSO proceeded to a conference at 5th Army Infantry School & Major G Dixon MC assumed command of the Battalion. On the 27th & 28th inst. Coys treated the disposal of Coy Commanders for cleaning equipment & organisation. Baths were provided for the Battalion at CAILLOUEL. At 11-30 am. on 28th inst. the Battalion was ordered under 15 minutes notice to leave their billets for the line in the event of an enemy attack developing on the Corps front. In the evening the order was cancelled. (Copy enclosed going in case of alarm attached). Recce Reconth of Officers & 72 O.Rs. proceeded on leave. 11 officers & 89 O.Rs. proceeded on Courses at School of Instruction.	

Signed [signature]
Lieut. Colonel,
Comdg. 11th (Service) Bn. Royal Fusiliers

PROGRAMME OF TRAINING.

11th Bn. Royal Fusiliers – Period 1st to 7th February 1918.

Day	Activity	Time
FRIDAY. 1.2.18. All Coys.	Inspection by O.C. Coy. Close Order Drill by Platoons.	9 – 9.30 a.m.
"	Physical Training and Bayonet Fighting.	9.30 – 10 a.m.
"	Fitting Equipment and Packing Kits – Fighting Order.	10 – 11 a.m.
"	Cleaning Kits and turn-out.	11 a.m. – 12 noon.
"	Musketry.	12 p.m. – 1 p.m.
	Afternoon.	Football Match R.Fus. v Bedfords.
SATURDAY. 2.2.18. All Coys.	Marching and Saluting. Organization of Sections in a Platoon.	9 – 9.30 a.m. / 9.30 – 10.30 am.
"	Physical Training and Squad Drill by Sections.	10.30 – 11.30 a.m.
"	Packing Kits – Marching Order.	11.30 a.m. – 12.30 pm.
"	Musketry.	12.30 – 1 p.m.
	Afternoon.	Football – Inter-Coy. Matches.
MONDAY. 4.2.18. All Coys.	Close Order Drill by Platoons and Coys.	9 – 10 a.m.
"	Kit Inspection by Platoons.	10 – 11 a.m.
"	Guard Mounting.	11 a.m. – 12 noon.
"	Interior Organization.	12 – 1 p.m.
	Afternoon.	Football.

NOTE:— Speed in turning out will be practised and enforced at all parade changes.

For Tuesday, Wednesday and Thursday the above programme will be repeated, except that on Feby 7th, there will be a Battalion route march from 11 a.m. to 1 p.m.

Specialists. Signallers and Runners will be trained under Regimental Signalling Officer, according to programme submitted to Commanding Officer.
Stretcher Bearers will train every day under the Medical Officer.
Lewis Gunners will train under the Lewis Gun Officer.

SECRET.   ORDER NO. 49.   Copy No..... 6

1. The Battalion will entrain on Feby 9th,1918 on train No.15 scheduled to leave PROVEN at 4.40 and due to arrive at NOYON at 18.40 same day.

2. The Battalion will parade in the Big Square in Camp, ready to move off at 2.15 a.m.(9th instant) in the following order;- HQrs. "A" ,"C", "B" & "D" Coys. Dress;- Full marching order, overcoat and jerkin in the pack. Blanket rolled and placed round the pack horse-shoe shape. Steel Helmets will be carried under pack straps. Each man will carry only one blanket.
   ROUTE TO PROVEN;- CROMBEKE - ROUSBRUGGE Road to CROSS ROADS in X.19.D. thence due South to PROVEN Station.
   100 yards distance will be maintained between Coys.
   Connection will be maintained forward.

3. The Transport Officer and 1 Officer to be detailed by O.C.Coys and H.Q.Details will reconnoitre in daylight the route and the approach to the station and also the entraining facilities.

4. Two cyclist orderlies to be detailed by O.C.HQ.Details will reconnoitre in the daylight on the 8th instant the way to PROVEN Station and find the R.T.O's office there.
   These 2 orderlies, with bicycles, will report to the Orderly Room at 12.30 a.m. on the 9th instant for orders.

5. O.C.Coys and H.Q.Details and Transport Officer will forward to Orderly Room by 2.p.m. Feby 8th, a marching out state, shewing number of Officers, men, animals, G.S.Limbered G.S. and two wheeled wagons & bicycles.

6. An unloading party consisting of Capt.N.B.Micheal, 2 Officers and 100 Other Ranks will report on arrival at NOYON to the R.T.O. The party will wait at the detraining station till last train of Brigade Group has arrived.
   Capt.J.N.Beasley M.C. will make arrangements to billet this party near the station.
   O.C."B" & "D" Coys will each detail 1 Officer and 50 Other Ranks to compose this party. The Q.M. will arrange rations and cooking for this party.

7. SUPPLY ARRANGEMENTS.
   (a). All units will move with their supply and baggage wagons in same train.
   (b). Men and animals will carry their rations for consumption on the 9th. Rations for the 10th and 11th will be carried on supply wagons.
   (c). Water Carts will travel full. All water bottles will be filled before 8 p.m on the 8th instant.

8. TRANSPORT ARRANGEMENTS.
   (a) Animals will be watered before entrainment.
   (b) Head ropes must be provided for tying up animals in the truck.
   (c) Animals will be un-harnessed; harness stacked in the middle of the truck. Two men must travel in each truck.
   (d) Buckets for watering horses will be taken to water en route.

                                                          continued.

9. The train will halt for 1 hour at TINCQUES where:-
    1. Horses will be fed and watered
    2. Hot tea will be made for the men. Boiling water will be ready on arrival of train. The Q.M. will arrange to supply the tea, milk, sugar &c.
    3. A buffet canteen is open for officers and men.
    The Q.M. will arrange for dixies for making tea to be available.

10. O.C. "A" & "D" Coys will each detail a piquet to consist of 1 Sergnt and four O.R's. The duties of this piquet will be to prevent men leaving the train without permission during halts.
    "D" Coy piquet will be at that end of the train nearest the Transport
    "A" Coy piquet will be at the other end of the train.
    All doors on the right hand side of the train must be kept closed.

11. Three lorries have been asked for for the Battalion. The Q.M. will detail 1 Guide to report to Lieut. E.D. Alcock. M.C. at Bde. HQrs at CROMBEKE at 2.45 p.m. on the 8th instant. These lorries will do two journies if necessary.

12. REAR PARTY. O.C. "C" Coy will detail 1 Officer and 15 Other Ranks to be a rear party. Duty, to clean up the camp after the Battalion has moved out. This party will not move off until Lieut. E.D. Alcock, M.C. is satisfied that the Camp has been left scrupulously clean. This party will leave PROVEN on Train No. 17 (in which the 7th Bedfordshire Regt. will travel) at 10.40 a.m. on the 9th inst. They should be at the Station one hour before the train is due to leave. This party will arrive at NOYON at 0.40 a.m. on the 10th inst. They will carry their Rations for the 9th and 10th inst. The Officer in charge of this party will be responsible for handing over the Camp Warden all Stoves, Stove Piping, Tables, Forms, etc. Complete list to be forwarded to Orderly Room by 10 a.m. 11th inst.

13. Battalion personnel will report 1 hour before departure of train. Transport will arrive at Entraining Station three hours before departure of train. Entrainment to be completed half-hour before schedule time for departure.

14. On arrival at PROVEN Station the Transport Officer will report to the R.T.O. and to Captain V.D. Corbett (18th Middlesex Regiment), Brigade Representaive.
    No troops will be permitted to enter that Station yard until permission has been obtained from the R.T.O.

15. The Q.M. will arrange for surplus practice ammunition and bombs to be sent to the Area Commandant, CROMBEKE. Complete list to be sent to Orderly Room by 10 a.m. 11th inst.

16. O.C. "A" Coy. will detail the following parties :-
    (a) Loading party of 1 N.C.O. and 12 men to report to Q.M. at Q.M. Stores at 2 p.m. on 8th inst.
    (b) Guard of 1 N.C.O. and 3 Other Ranks to report to Q.M. Stores 2.45 p.m. on 8th inst. This party will proceed after reporting at PROVEN Station where they will act as a Guard over articles which will be dumped there.

17. All Lewis Guns and Drums will be loaded on the limbers by 6 p.m. 8th inst.

                                                        continued.

18. The Maltese cart will report to the Medical Inspection Room at 2 p.m.

19. The Mess Cart will report at HQ.Mess at 10.30 p.m. 8th instant.
The Mess Sergt. will be responsible for having this loaded ready to move off with the Transport at 12.15 a.m. 9th instant.
The Mess Sergt. will be responsible that proper arrangements are made for Officers' meals during the journey. Any mess stores required during the journey may be carried on the Coy Cookers.

20. Tea will be provided for the Battalion at 11 p.m. on the 8th inst.

21. O.C.Coys/ AND TRANSPORT will report in writing arrival in new billets.

22. All Coys and HQ.Details and Transport will render to Orderly Room by 12 noon 8th inst., complete list of all stoves, stove piping, table forms &c. in their possession.

23. The R.S.M. will carry some white chalk for marking carriages.

24. Capt. G.S.Pearcy M.C. is detailed to act as Brigade Detraining Officer. The Q.M. will arrange to carry a tent and get this erected at NOYON station on arrival there.

25. The undermentioned will be dumped on the road near the Medical Insp. Room at the times given on 8th instant:-

    Orderly Room Boxes &c...........................by 2.30 p.m.
    All blankets (other than the one to be carried on the man) rolled neatly and tightly in bundles of 10 .... by 2 p.m.
    The following will be dumped outside Q.M.Stores at times stated:- Officers Kits.........................8.5 p.m.
    All Coy Mess Stores, Boxes &c..........10.30 p.m.
NOTE:- Officers Kits have been badly packed lately. They are loosely rolled and take up more room than is really necessary. Articles have fallen out. Valises must be tightly rolled and securely fastened.

7.9.18.
Issued at :-

(Sd) E.L.JONES, Captain.
A/Adjutant 11th Bn. Royal Fusiliers.

Copies to :-

1. C.O. 2. 2nd-in-Command. 3. Adjutant.
4. Office. 5. War Diary. 6. War Diary.
7. O.C."A" Coy. 8. O.C."B" Coy. 9. O.C."C" Coy.
10. O.C."D" Coy. 11. Quartermaster. 12. Transport Officer.
13. L.G.Officer. 14. H.Q.Details. 15. R.S.M.
16. Cook Sgt. 17..18..19..20 Spares.

SECRET   ORDER No. 43.   Copy No......5

FRANCE.
   ST.QUENTIN 18.
Scale 1/100,000

1. The Battalion will move tomorrow to CAILLOUEL.

2. Time will be notified later.

                                            (Drums with
3. Order of March :- Hdqrs., "A", "B", Drums, "D","C") in rear of
   Transport will move with and in rear of the Battalion("B" Coy.)
   Coys. will move at 100 yards distance.
   Transport will move 200 yards in rear of Battalion.

4. ROUTE:- Via Main NOYON - CHAUNY Road.   Distance approx. 7 miles.

5. DRESS:- Full Marching Order, Overcoat and Jerkin in the pack,-
          Waterproof Sheet under the flap of the pack, Steel
          Helmets will be carried under pack straps.

6. All blankets will be carried by Lorries.
   The following will be dumped by all Coys. at Q.M. Stores by 10 a.m.
   tomorrow :-
          Officers' Kits and Mess Stores.
          All blankets neatly rolled in bundles of 10.
   Hdqr. Officers' Kits, Orderly Room Boxes, etc., and blankets of
   Head Quarter Details (neatly rolled in bundles of 10) will be
   dumped in the yard adjacent to Orderly Room by 10 a.m.

7. Lewis Guns will be loaded by 10 a.m. under the supervision of the Lewis Gun Sergeant.

8. Coys. will be ready to move off by 11 a.m. unless otherwise
   notified.

9. Coy. Commanders will ensure that all billets will be left in a
   clean condition.

                              (Sgd) E.L.JONES, Capt. A/Adjt.
                                    11th Bn. Royal Fusiliers.
19th February 1918.
Issued at 7.30pm.

Copies to :- 1. C.O.   11. Quartermaster.
             2. 2nd.in.Command.   12. Transport Officer.
             3. Adjutant.   13. LG.Officer.
             4. Office.   14. O.C. Hdqr.Details.
             5. War Diary.   15. R.S.M.
             6. War Diary.   16. Cook Sgt.
             7. O.C. "A" Coy.   17. Spare.
             8. O.C. "B" Coy.   18. Spare.
             9. O.C. "C" Coy.   19. Spare.
            10. O.C. "D" Coy.   20. Spare.

SECRET.   Copy No..........
                    ADDENDA TO ORDER NO. 43.

1. The Battalion will be formed up on the road by 11 a.m. with the head of the column at the gateway leading to Orderly Room.

2. Order of March :- Hdqrs., "A", "B", Drums (to march with and in rear of "B" Coy.) "C", "D", 19th Fusiliers, Transport. Distances will be maintained as stated in warning order.

3. The 19th Bn. Royal Fusiliers will parade under their Senior Sergeant on the Parade Ground of the Coy. to which they are attached, and then form up into one Coy. in the square at 10.45 am. The Officers from the 19th Bn. Royal Fusiliers will report to Major G. Dekin, M.C. at 10.45 a.m.

4. 2nd Lieut. W.A. Spence will report to Capt. G.N. Beasley, M.C. at the Area Commandant's Office, BETHANCOURT at 10 a.m. 13th inst. when Billets will be allotted to him.   2nd Lieut. W.A. Spence will take a bicycle.
The 5 C.Q.M.Sgts. will proceed on bicycles direct to CAILLOUEL and meet 2nd Lieut. Spence at the Church there at 10.30 a.m.

5. The Maltese/Carts will report respectively to the Medical Inspection Room and Headquarter Mess at 10 a.m. They must be ready to move with the Transport.

6. The blankets of the 19th Bn. Royal Fusiliers will be tied in bundles of 10 and dumped separtely at Q.M. Stores by 10 a.m.

7. Two Lorries will report to Bn. HQ. at 10 a.m. tomorrow. The Coy. on duty will detail a Loading Party of 1 N.C.O. and 15 other ranks to report to the Q.M. at 9.45 a.m. at Q.M. Stores.

8. Dinners will be on arrival in new rea; teas 5 p.m.

9. All Waterbottles will be filled before moving off. Water Carts to move filled.

10. Coys., Hdqr.Details and Transport will report in writing to Orderly Room arrival in new area.

11. All Coys.and Hdqr.Details will arrange for a Foot Inspection in the afternoon.

12. The Bn. will move on 14th inst. to CLASTRES.

13. All afternoon parades are cancelled for 13th inst.

                                   (Sgd) E.L.JONES, Capt. A/Adjt.
12.9.18.   11th Bn. Royal Fusiliers.
 Issued at 12.5 p.m. to
   All recipients of O/43.

Order No. 44.   Copy No.

1. The Battalion will move tomorrow to CLASTRES.

2. The Battalion will be formed up in line on the road with the head of the column at the MAIRIE by 12.30 p.m. in the following order,
    HQrs. "D" "A" Drums "B" "C" Transport. Drums to march in rear of and with "A" Coy.

3. Route:- To be notified later.

4. Dress:- Full marching order, overcoat and jerkin in pack, waterproof sheets under the flap of the haversack and steel helmets under pack straps.

5. Distances to be maintained on the March:-
       100 yards between Coys, 200 yards between last Coy & Transport.
       If the Battalion moves east of JUSSY, 200 yards between platoons must be maintained.

6. Baggage:- Two lorries have been asked for.
       Coys and Headquarters details will dump their blankets, neatly tied in bundles of 10, at the Q.M. Stores by 8 a.m.
       Officers' Kits and Mess Stores will be dumped at the same place by 9 a.m.
       Lewis Guns will be dumped by 10 a.m. at Signalling Dept.

7. One N.C.O. from each Coy and HQ. Details will report to the Q.M. when all his Coy's articles are dumped.

8. A loading party of 1 N.C.O. and 10 O.R's will be detailed by the Coy on duty to report to the Quartermaster at XXXX.a. The Q.M. will advise Coys the time he requires them by.

9. An advanced party consisting of 2nd.Lieut. W.A.Spence and the XXX the C.Q.M.S's together with 1 N.C.O. from the Transport will report at the Orderly Room at 8 a.m. tomorrow to proceed on bicycles to CLASTRES and arrange the billeting.

10. All water bottles will be filled before moving off. Water Carts to move filled.

11. The cookers and mess carts will report at the Battal Orp. Room at Headquarters and respectively at 12 noon. They must be ready to move off under with the Transport.

12. Dinners:- will be at 11.30 a.m. Teas on arrival in new area.

13. All billets must be left in a clean condition.

14. The Coy Orderly Officer will report to the Adjutant 1 hour before that fixed for moving off, that they are clean.

15. All Coys.and Details, Q.M. & Transport will report in writing arrival in new area.

16. All Officers' chargers will be required.

17. Packs and steel Helmets will be carried by lorry from NEUFMAUCOURT On arrival at Cross Roads L1 F.14.a. the Battalion will halt and packs will be taken from equipment, Coy & HQr. dumps will be formed. The haversack will from this spot, be carried on the back. Coys are reminded that packs should be clearly marked.

                                          (Sgd). E.L.Jones, Captain
                                          A/Adjutant 11th Bn.

SECRET.   ORDER NO. 41.   Copy No. 17

1. The Battalion will move on February 28th 1918 to CAILLOUEL
   Time :- 9.30 am.
   Starting Point :- Road Junction G.35.c.9.6.
   Order of March :- Hdqrs., "B", "A", Drums, "D", "C"., First Line Transport.
   The Drums and "C" Coy. will join the Battalion as it passes JUSSY.
   The Drums falling in behind "A" Coy. "C" Coy. will fall in behind "D" Coy.
   The Battalion is due to pass the Brigade Starting Point, M.15.c.c.
   at 10 a.m.
   Route :- From CLASTRES through JUSSY, FAILLOUEL, VILLEQUIER AUMONT, COMMENCHON, BETHANCOURT.
   Dress :- Full Marching Order. Caps will be worn. Steel Helmets under pack straps.
   Coys. will maintain 100 yards distance between each other.
   The Transport will move 200 yards in rear of the last Coy.

2. O.C., "C" Coy. will arrange for his Coy. to be ready to join the column as it passes "C" Coy's. billets. All troops at JUSSY (except the Drums who will march as above) will parade and move with "C" Coy.

3. The 11th Royal Fusiliers Trench Mortar Section will proceed with the Battalion to CAILLOUEL, and from there will be sent on to CREPIGNY where they will join the other T.M.B. Sections during the afternoon of the 28th inst. They will form a special wing of the Brigade School.
   O.C., Brigade School will be responsible for billetting, rationing, discipline, etc. but Captain R. Knight, M.C. will be responsible for the technical training.
   The Quartermaster will arrange for this Section's Guns and blankets to be delivered at CREPIGNY.

4. The Middlesex section of the 54th T.M.B., now attached to this Battalion, will report to the 6th Northamptonshire Regiment before 9 am. 28th inst. The 6th Northamptonshire Regiment being responsible for moving this section to CREPIGNY.

5. All Trench Mortar Sections will proceed to CREPIGNY rationed to 28th inst. Rations for consumption 29th inst. and onwards will be drawn by the Brigade School.

6. All Officers' Kits, Orderly Room Boxes, Mess Boxes and Stores will be dumped near the Q.M.Stores by 9.30 am.
   Blankets and all other baggage to be placed near the road opposite the Regimental Guard at 9.30 am.

7. All blankets must be neatly rolled in bundles of 10 and labelled Boards for Coys. and Hdqrs. and Q.M.Stores respectively will mark the dumping places.
   One N.C.O. from each Coy. and Hdqr.Details to report to the Q.M.Stores when all Coy. baggage is dumped.
   The Coy. on duty will detail a Loading Party of 1 N.C.O. and 30 men to report to Q.M. at Q.M.Stores at 7.30 a.m.
   The whole of the baggage of JUSSY detachment will be dumped alongside the Main road, JUSSY, in front of Brigade Headquarters by 7.30 am.
   A Loading Party to be detailed by O.C., "C" Coy., if Lorry arrives before departure of detachment - 1 N.C.O. and 3 men to take charge of dump till loaded.

8. Details as to Lorries will be notified later.

   The Maltese and Mess Carts will report to the Medical Inspection Room and Hdqr. Mess respectively at 9.30 am. They must be loaded ready to accompany the First Line Transport.

                                                    continued

The Transport will move with the Battalion. It will leave GLASTRES at 8 a.m. and join the Battalion at JUSSY. It must arrive at JUSSY so as to join the column and pass the Starting Point (N.19.c.5.5) at 10 a.m. as verbally explained to the Transport Sergeant.

All Camp Stores and Furniture will be left intact and camp must be left scrupulously clean.
The Coy. on duty will detail a Rear Party of 1 officer and 10 other ranks to remain behind to thoroughly clean the Camp. When this is done they will proceed to JUSSY and pick up a party of 1 N.C.O. and 9 men detailed by O.C. "C" Coy. to clean "C" Coy's Camp. The whole party will then be marched independently to CAILLOUEL.

Advanced Party has proceeded to CAILLOUEL today to arrange billets etc.
Major G. Dakin, M.C. will join the Battalion at CAILLOUEL and assume command.

All Water Bottles will be filled before moving off. Water Carts will travel full.
Dinners will be on arrival in new Area.

All Officers' Chargers will be required.

O.C. Coys. and Hdqrs. Details and Transport will report in writing arrival in new Area.

25.9.18.
Issued at 3.45 pm.

(Sgd) E.L.JONES, Capt. A/Adjt.
11th Bn. Royal Fusiliers.

Copies to :- 1. C.O.
2. Adjutant.
3. War Diary.
4. War Diary.
5. Office.
6. O.C. "B" Coy.
7. O.C. "C" Coy.
8. O.C. "A" Coy.
9. O.C. "D" Coy.
10. Quartermaster.
11. Transport Officer.
12. O.C. H.Q. Details.
13. L.G.O.
14. R.S.M.
15. Cook Sgt.
16. Spare.
17. Spare.

WA5g

Working Party for 14/2/18

Party No.	Party	Strength		Tools	Rendezvous	Time	Task	Remarks
		Off.	O.R.					
1	D				Junction of Amiens rd & G. rd.	9am	Wiring	Length to W.T. end O. Stormy Pk.
2	B			do.	do.	9am	do	Work on Church Keep
3	A			do.	do.	9am	do	Work on T Keep

Note: The distribution is subject to alteration by 19th Field Coy R.E. H.Q. (Laventie Pl.)

15/2/18

E L Jones
Capt & Adjt

WP/1343

Bombing parties to parade as follows:-
B. Bombing attacks Dec 14-15

Appx. A/A 031
"1st Royal Fusiliers"

Party No	Coy Finding Party	Strength	Tools	Rendezvous	Time	Guides From	Remarks
1	"A"	One Company	As before	Cross Roads H.19.a.1.6. being 200 yds about 200 yds by junction road	9 am	79 Field Coy R.E.	Work the Strong Point at H.9.C.2.6. 1 Coy to work on dump + to carry up bombs to strengthen dugout
2	"D"	One Company	do.	nearest from TOSSY POINT LIZERKOLLES to ESSONY	9 am	do.	½ Coy on Strong Point at H.13.6 around CHURCH on H.7.b. and H.7.C. wiring
3	"B"	One Company	do.	MAP LOCATION to seen at ORDERLY ROOM Opera	9 am	do.	One Strong Point around Church, Wiring and strengthening existing dug outs.
4							Dumps:– As the dumps are undesirable for Coys to camp so parking Coy to look out dumps

NOTE:– Parties to come to these positions in small parties, units Coys as much as possible.
Each to lay forth straight on ahead and to ????? to parade well 84 breakfast. First Coy Open ?????s
To talk. Roads known. Shot Islands for ?????ers ??? ??????s ammunition
???? Shot Islands for Netherlands rifle barrels & ball ?????? ammunition will panel ?????? to Casta??.

SAA will have places and brasses finished.

No. 1587

WORKING PARTY TABLE — 18-2-15

Today	Working Party	General F.S.	Tools	Ammunition	Time mass from	Time	Remarks
1	M.P. Fat Finisher Party	Transport	As Engineer Park H.Q. R.E.	Engineer Park H.Q. R.E.	7 pm	Working Party H.Q. R.E.	Worn K.D. around chest
2	do A Coy	do	do	do	7 pm	do	Coat T Webb belt
3	do D Coy	do	do	do	7 pm	do	Temple M Young O's Army Boots

NOTE.— The above is subject to modification in the event of interference of the weather.

O/C Royal LANDON. M.E. 774 Field Coy R.E.

11-2-15

PROGRAMME OF TRAINING.

11th Bn. Royal Fusiliers.   19th February 1918.

	First day.	Second day.	Third day.	Fourth day.	Fifth day.	Sixth day.

8 am. to 2.30pm approximately. — Companies on Working parties for 41st Brigade. During the morning the Lewis Gunners detailed for Anti-Aircraft Guns, clean all Guns, Spare parts, and also have training in Immediate Action and Stoppages.

4.30 to 5.30 pm — Lewis Gunners training, chiefly in Immediate Action and Stoppages.

Signallers. — When not on Working parties :-

    8.55 to 10.30 a.m.   Flag Drill and Physical Training.

    10.30 am to 12 noon.   Visual, Flag and Shutter.

    12 noon to 1 p.m.   Buzzer.

    4.30 to 5.30 p.m.   Lamps, Visual.

Scouts, Snipers & Observers. — In the daytime :-

    Reconnoitring Line.

In the evening :-

    Practise Patrol Work and Fighting Patrols.
    Marching by Compass and Lectures.

GAS DRILL FOR ALL COYS. IS HELD DURING THE AFTERNOON.

Major.
Commanding 11th Bn. Royal Fusiliers.

W.P. 22.

WORKING PARTY TABLE for Xxght 19/2/18.

Party No.	Unit finding party.	Strength Offr.	Strength O.R.	Tools	Rendezvous	Time	Guides from:	Remarks.
1	11th Royal Fusiliers. *B*		One Company	As before.	Crucifix at G 18 d	9 a.m.	79th Field Co.R.E.	½ Coy. to complete "W" Strong Point. ½ Coy. to complete "Y" Strong Point.
2	do. *A*		One Company	do.	do.	9 a.m.	do.	½ Coy. to complete "O" Strong Point. ½ Coy. to complete "T" Strong Point.
3	do. *D*		One Company	do.	do.	9 a.m.	do.	1 Coy. to work on "KEEP" around Church.

Note: The above distribution is only an estimate and may be altered by Lieut. LANDON, M.C., 79th Field Coy., R.E. as required.

WP25.

Working parties 20/2/18

Party No.	Working party	Strength Off.	Strength O.R.	Tools	Rendezvous	Time	Guides from	Remarks.
1	"D"		On coy.	As before	Junction of road & Ct. q. 18d.	9am	79 Field Coy R.E.	Complete "W","Y" and "O" Strong Points.
2	"B"		do.	do	do	9am	do	Work on "Church" Keep
3	"A"		do	do	do	9am	do	Work on "T" Keep.
Note.	*This distribution is subject to alteration at the discretion of 79 Field Coy R.E. (Lieut Landon R.E.)							

19/2/18

(sd) E L Jones
Capt A/Adjt.

No. 1587.

WORKING PARTY TABLE for 21-2-18.

Party No.	Unit finding party	Strength & No.R	Tools.	Rendezvous.	Time	Guides from.	Remarks.
1	11th Royal Fusiliers B Coy	One Company	as before.	Crucifix on road G.18.D.	9 a.m.	79th Field Coy R.E.	Work on "Keep" around church
2	do A Coy.	do	do	do	9 a.m.	do	Work on "T" Strong Point
3.	do D Coy.	do	do	do	9 a.m.	do	Complete "W", "Y" and "O" Strong Points
NOTE.	The distribution of No 3 party is subject to alteration at the discretion of Lieut LANDON. M.C. 79th Field Coy R.E.						

20-2-18.

Capt a/adj
11th Bn Royal Fusiliers

WORKING PARTY TABLE for 22/2/18.

W.Pay......

Party No.	Unit finding party.	Strength Off; O.R.	Tools	Rendezvous	Time	Guides from:	Remarks.
1	11th Royal Fusiliers	One Company	As before.	Crucifix on road at G 18 d.	9 a.m.	79th Field Co.R.E.	Work on "Keep" around Church.
2	do.	do.	do.	do.	9 a.m.	do.	Work on "T" Strong Point.
3	do.	do.	do.	do.	9 a.m.	do.	Complete "O" and "Y" Strong Points.

No. 1685.

Working Party Table for 23-2-18.

Party No.	Company finding Party.	Strength	Tools.	Rendezvous	Time	Guides from.	Remarks.
1	B Coy.	1 Coy.	As before.	Crucifix on Q.18.d. road	9 a.m.	49 Field Coy R.E.	Took on "Reef" around Church
2	A Coy.	1 Coy.	do.	do	9 a.m.	do.	Took on "T" and Z Strong Points
3	D Coy.	1 Coy.	do.	do	9 a.m.	do.	Complete "O" and "Y"
	NOTE.			No 3 Party may be relieved if one Company is unnecessary. If so those not required for "O" and "Y" should be distributed between "Z" and "Church"			

22/2/18.

Captain
A/Adjutant
11th Royal Fusiliers

WORKING PARTY TABLE for 24/2/18.   No 1762.

Party No.	Work	Strength	Tools	Rendezvous	Time	Guides from	Remarks
1	Wiring party. 11th Royal Fusiliers B Coy	One Company	As before.	Sucker Company at rendezvous	9 AM	Sucker Company at rendezvous	Water KEEP'd around Church
2	do A Coy	do	do	do	9 AM	do	1 Enter T and Z Shoystints
3	do D Coy	do	do	do	9 AM	do	Complete O and Y Shoy Dads

NOTE: The 11th Royal Fus. will arrange between 4 Coy's as to above WORKS at 9 AM.
to carry out the tasks and supervise the work generally.

23-2-18.

[signature]
Capt' 9/4/4
11th Royal Fusiliers

No 1822

WORKING PARTY TABLE for 25-2-18.

Party No	Front finding Party	Strength	Tools	Rendezvous	Time	Guides from	Remarks
1	4th Battalion Royal Fusiliers B Coy	As before	As before	Shelter Bay cross roads	9 a.m.	Under Coy arrangements	As in Working Party Table of yesterday
2	do A Coy	do	do	do	9 a.m.	do	do
3	do D Coy.	do	do	do	9 a.m.	do	do

24-2-18.

Capt & Adjt
4th Bn Royal Fusiliers

SENLIS
20000

from the left of
TORRENS.
W.21.A

54th Inf.Bde.
18th Div.

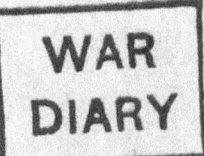

11th BATTN. THE ROYAL FUSILIERS.

M A R C H

1 9 1 8

Army Form C. 2118.

17th Battalion Royal Fusiliers WAR DIARY
INTELLIGENCE SUMMARY
(Erase heading not required.)

Place	Date	Hour	Summary of Events and Information	Remarks and references to Appendices
CHILGROVE	1/3/18		Battalion remained in Training at Chilgrove	
	3		Lieut G.H. LEE, M.C., 2nd Lieut W.T. FRANCIS joined the Battalion from the 16th B: Royal Fusiliers were posted to A Coy	
	5		Draft of 27 O.R. joined the Battalion	
	7		Lieut M.N. BROOKING authorised to wear badge of Captain pending confirmation. Acting rank Capt E.R. MEAKER to hospital 2nd Lieut T.J. LAWRENCE to ENGLAND sick	
	9		Support Tube cases into use at Upper	
	10		Lieut G.H. LEE assumed command of "B" Coy. 1 O.R. accidentally killed	
	11		ARA Competition commenced on Range	
	14		Lieut Y.C.M. CORNISH to ENGLAND for 6 months Tour of duty Capt C.Y. KATTENBACH joined from 12th B: Royal Fusiliers	
	15		2/Lieut B.H. BECKETT to ENGLAND on Transfer to R.F.C.	
	16		2/Lieut M.A. SMITH to 20 O.B. C.R.E. (probation) for Permt. Field Coy. R.E.	
	18		2/Lieut N.G. BRYANT, E.S. CLAYTON to ENGLAND on Transfer to M.G.C.	

WAR DIARY
or
INTELLIGENCE SUMMARY.
(Erase heading not required.)

Army Form C. 2118.

Place	Date	Hour	Summary of Events and Information	Remarks and references to Appendices
CAILLOUEL	19/3/18		Draft of 30 OR. joined the Battalion	
			From information given by prisoners Great German attack expected on the 20/21st. Battalion now in Corps & Army Reserve.	
	20	3pm	Battalion ordered to stand to ready to turn out.	
	21	4.15 am	German attack commenced. Thick mist. Very still.	
		12 noon	Battalion rec'd the Faillouel Wood. Details moved to Caillouel	
		3 pm	Wood rec'd that Battle Zone penetrated & Lombay Ridge & Wood falling. Situation obscure. Battalion with 8th Northants ordered to counter attack gaps in trenches running from Lizerolle - Mortiescourt.	
		8pm	This accomplished having joined up with cavalry details on left flank.	
		10pm	Orders received to move back to Tergnier where would be moved to Tergnier bridgehead, with troops of mixed detachment & M.G. on left & 18th on right to depth on a one company front. A.B.C.D. During portion during the day. Right to Railway Bridge. 7th Bedfords on right. 6th Northants in support on Railway Embankment.	
	22	Dawn	Battalion formed up on caren bank LH. left resting on Quarry and	

Army Form C. 2118.

WAR DIARY
or
INTELLIGENCE SUMMARY.
(Erase heading not required.)

Instructions regarding War Diaries and Intelligence Summaries are contained in F. S. Regs., Part II. and the Staff Manual respectively. Title pages will be prepared in manuscript.

Place	Date	Hour	Summary of Events and Information	Remarks and references to Appendices
NEAR TOSSY	22	12 noon	Enemy fired solid repeat effort to cross canal began. Bridges had not been effectively destroyed.	
		3 pm	General attack along the whole line. CAPT C.R. MICHELL killed.	
		6 pm	Enemy penetrated the canal bank in places in position held by 7th BEDFORDS. 6TH NORTHANTS moved to counter attack. Line re-established. Remainder of Bn and 7th BEDFORDS – 6TH NORTHANTS firmly established at Railway Bridge. Whole Brigade front covered. Left flank from TOSSY left obscure. B+C Coys moved up in close support f A Coy. On canal bank with D Coy in wood French showed behind canal.	
TOSSY	23/22 night		Enemy made determined effort to cross canal & sharp fighting took place on front with parties which had renetrated these were repulsed. 141 TH DIVN	
	23	Dawn	Enemy forced TOSSY Bridgehead after strong attacks in force (this uncertain at time)	
		6 am	freed away from canal bank. Battalion freed off canal bank by flank fire from TOSSY while Battalion took up 'B' Coy's position.	
		8.20 am	It became evident that 14TH Divn on left had been driven right in and	

A6945. Wt. W11432/M1160. 35M,000. 12/16. D. D. & L. Forms/C./2118/14.

WAR DIARY
INTELLIGENCE SUMMARY
(Erase heading not required.)

Army Form C. 2118.

Place	Date	Hour	Summary of Events and Information	Remarks and references to Appendices
		6.30 am	Bn left [illegible] The Bn. was then definitely committed by 3/Lt Hon. W. MEDLEY who clearly wanted to withdraw a portion of [illegible] without the orders ahead the situation was grave & together with other established the first line. The enemy had penetrated the line between left Bn depot & 1 mile and had HALNAT WOOD. our patrols & orders & intimate & Brigade was ordered to fall back to FRERE-FAILLOUEL line.	
	23	11 am	this returning from close contact with the enemy who were opening the 3 Bn. for fire & left flank was more difficult operation to carry well covered by REDFORDS & [illegible] the night first also some episode. The enemy pressing closely in large numbers & [illegible] of our own arms & over some were unable to get back under the heavy MG fire from 5th Hur & Capt H.V. BROOKING was severely wounded and cut off after retiring with The greatest gallantry throughout the action. During the day the enemy artillery opened assisted by him	

Army Form C. 2118.

WAR DIARY
or
INTELLIGENCE SUMMARY.
(Erase heading not required.)

Instructions regarding War Diaries and Intelligence Summaries are contained in F. S. Regs., Part II. and the Staff Manual respectively. Title pages will be prepared in manuscript.

Place	Date	Hour	Summary of Events and Information	Remarks and references to Appendices
	23rd		Aircraft who were present in great numbers and flying very low, kept up heavy and accurate bombardment of our lines	
		6.30 pm	General withdrawal by stages to VILLEQUIER-AUMONT covering lines, been being heavy the whole way.	
CAILLOUEL	23/24	12 m	Remainder of Bn with the Brigade withdrew to CAILLOUEL where they rested for night	
	24th	10 am	The Batt. reorganised with 3 companies, making HQrs a fighting Coy. Bdes took up a line from CAILLOUEL northward to the ridge & wood D'AUTRECOURT. Royal Fusiliers in support on the CREPIGNY - D'AUTRECOURT Ridge. The 113 line Regt d'Infanterie were attached to the Batt. continuing our line northwards	
	25th	6 am	Batt. withdrawn to the GRANDRU spur, held this forming a defensive flank to the cavalry	
		12 noon	At about midday the Batt. withdrew to ridge crossing BEAUGIES-UGNY which was being held by the French. after a short rest the Batt was ordered to take up a position in the South side of the	

WAR DIARY or INTELLIGENCE SUMMARY

Army Form C. 2118.

Place	Date	Hour	Summary of Events and Information	Remarks and references to Appendices
BABOEUF	25th	3pm	NOYON-CHAUNY CANAL Bn in debunking in Wood near the Beafords & Frasiers were ordered to retake BABOEUF to over the withdrawal of the French. Rather in rear the Beafords were on the left and the Frasiers on the right and the 2 Bns were on a complete to succeed. The 2 Bns. were crowded forward and d/after the The Bn. village. the NORTHANTS were in support and moved to the line of the attack moved forward and entered to the line of the TOM do the NOYON canal. the French guns being withdrawn under cover of darkness. the Bn & Withdrew to the new line held by SALENCY and the Bde crossed the canal the south bank and marched to the area about CALONNE. the Bn D & A HQRS	
AUDIGNICOURT	26th	2am		
	27th	noon	move to cave at AUDIGICOURT. Bde moved to ST AUBIN in billets to Reserve to the 58th Divn.	
	28th	9am	Rested	
	29th	9am	Dr ASHLEY of USA joined Battn. as M.O. (attached)	

Army Form C. 2118.

WAR DIARY
or
INTELLIGENCE SUMMARY.
(Erase heading not required.)

Instructions regarding War Diaries and Intelligence Summaries are contained in F. S. Regs., Part II. and the Staff Manual respectively. Title pages will be prepared in manuscript.

Place.	Date	Hour	Summary of Events and Information	Remarks and references to Appendices
BOYES	30th Jan		Battn. moved to NANTEUIL for entraining. French lorries employed. The Battn. trained AMIENS to BOVES.	
GENTELLES	31st	9 am	Move to GENTELLES. Found huts at HANGARD destroyed	

O Anderson Lt Col
Comm'g 4th Glos Regt
10 April 1918

S E C R E T.   11th Bn. The Royal Fusiliers.

Copy No... 6.

Reference Map :-   MOVEMENT ORDER No. 1.
AMIENS Sheet 17.

----

1. The Battalion will move today to BOUTILLERIE.

2. The Battalion will form up in column of Route facing West outside Billets, ready to move off at 2 pm.
   Order of March :-   Headquarters, "X" Coy, "Y" Coy.
   Interval between Coys :-   50 yards.

3. Dress :-   Battle Order, Steel Helmets, Blankets en banderolle over right shoulder.

4. Transport will be brigaded and pass Starting Point (THE CHURCH, BOVES) at 3.40 pm.   Each Coy. will arrange for Guides to meet Cookers, etc., at BOUTILLERIE.

5. All Officers' Valises and Mess Kit will be stacked outside Headquarters Mess at 1.30 pm.

6. Orderly Room Boxes will be picked up outside Orderly Room at 1.30 pm.

7. Coy. Commanders will report their Coys. in billets on arrival in new Area.

9th April 1918.

Capt. A/Adjutant,
for Lieut.Colonel.
Commanding 11th Bn. The Royal Fusiliers.

Issued at 12 noon.

Copies to :-

1. C.O.
2. 54th Brigade Headquarters.
3. "X" Coy.
4. "Y" Coy.
5. "Z" Coy.
6. War Diary.
7. War Diary.
8. Office.
9. Quartermaster.
10. R.S.M.
11. Spare.
12. Spare.

IF A MOVE BY BUS ORDERED.

Embussing Point : n Head of Convoy at Northern entrance to BETHANCOURT on GUIVRY - BETHANCOURT Road.

TRANSPORT OFFICER AND QUARTERMASTER.

If a move by bus is ordered, First Line Transport will proceed in its own time.
First Line Transport will be brigaded and will be divided into two Echelons :- "A" and "B".

"A" Echelon.	"B" Echelon.
All G.S. Wagons.	1 Water Cart (full)
1 Water Cart (full)	Officers' Mess Cart.
Maltese Cart.	Four Kitchens.
All Pack Animals.	

"A" Echelon (under 2nd Lieut. R.W. Gale, 11th Royal Fusiliers) will proceed along routes laid down above, according to which Sector the Brigade is being despatched.
Immediately the order to move is received two Mounted Orderlies will be despatched at once to Brigade Headquarters. These Orderlies will go forward with Brigade Headquarters and will be employed as liaison between Brigade Headquarters and "A" Echelon of First Line Transport. The Transport Officers will be responsible for despatching these two Orderlies.
Position of "A" Echelon Park will be arraged by Brigade Headquarters.
After Units have moved forward First Line Transport will be controlled by Brigade
"B" Echelon (less 7th Bedfordshire Regt., who will remain at ROUEZ) under Captain and Quartermaster W.S. Minchin, M.C., will be brigaded and remain at CAILLOUEL.
Captain Minchin will be in telephonic communication at the present Brigade Headquarters.

STOKES, LEWIS AND MACHINE GUNS.

Transport Officer to note clause under this heading.

GENERAL NOTES.

All requirements for S.A.A., etc. to be notified direct to Battalion Headquarters.

(Sgd) E.L. JONES, Capt. A/Adjt.
11th Bn Royal Fusiliers.

ACTION TO BE TAKEN IN THE EVENT OF "STAND-TO" ORDER BEING REC.

1. Limbers will be packed.

2. Men will be kept in their billets.

3. Rations issued.

4. Water bottles will be filled.

5. An Officer to be near the telephone to receive instructions from Brigade Headquarters.

6. One Tool Limber to report to Captain Knight at Trench Mortar Battery Headquarters, CREPIGNY, with two day's rations and feed. Captain Knight to billet drivers and find accommodation for horses.

MOVE BY EITHER ROUTE MARCH OR BUS.

1. All personnel to be left out of action to be with "B" Echelon at CAILLOUEL.

2. Dress :- Fighting Order with the usual amount of S.A.A. carried on the man.

3. Surplus Kits :- This must be stacked in some selected billet by small rear party, whose duty will be to collect it.

4. Lewis and Machine Guns:- All Lewis and Machine Guns and Lewis and Machine Gun Limbers will accompany the troops to Embussing Point. These Limbers will rejoin "A" Echelon of Front Line Transport after handing over their guns, belt boxes or drums. If the move is made by March Route, Limbers will proceed with Battalion and rejoin "A" Echelon after disposing of their guns.

5. Tools:- Large Picks and Shovels will be issued to the men as the move would probably be carried out by bus.

6. Maps :- 66c)
           66d) Or S.W. and N.W.
           70d)

           70e
           ST. QUENTIN.

The above must be carried by all Officers.

SECRET.   PRELIMINARY ORDERS.   Copy No. 10.

1.   The Battalion may be ordered to move either to the:-

      (a) NORTHERN SECTOR (CLASTRES - MONTESCOURT area).

            Route :- BETHANCOURT - COMMENCON, UGNY-le-GAY, LA NEUVILLE -
                     CUGNY - FLAVY-le-MARTEL, JUSSY.
                     Battalion Area A, B, C. (Tracing X).
                     Brigade Headquarters :- G.35.c.8g. West side of
                     Railway.

      (b) CENTRE SECTOR (BOIS VIEVILLE - LIEZ Area).

            Route :- BETHANCOURT - COMMENCHON, VILLEQUIER-AUMONT -
                     FAILLOUEL - FRIERES FAILLOUEL, MENESSIS - CANAL
                     BRIDGE, M.31.c. LIEZ.
                     Battalion Area A, B, C. (Tracing Y).
                     Brigade Headquarters:- M.31.b.7.5.

      (c) SOUTHERN SECTOR (AUTREVILLE - PIERREMANDE Area).

            Route :- Road junction MAREST - DAMPCOURT - L.2.c.8.8 -
                     MANICAMP - CANAL BANK - L.23.b. - Road junction
                     L.10.c. - BICHANCOURT - AUTREVILLE.
                     Battalion Area A, B, C. (Tracing Z).

      Lettering on Tracings refers to :- "A" - Royal Fusiliers.
                                         "B" - Bedfords.
                                         "C" - Northants.

                     BRIGADE IN CORPS RESERVE.

1.   PIERREMANDE - AUTREVILLE.

2.   LIEZ - BOIS de VIEVILLE.

3.   MONTESCOURT - CLASTRES.

      The Brigade may be called upon :-

            (a) To carry out a deliberate and organized counter-attack.

            (b) To man positions in the Battle Zone.

(1)

54th Inf.Bde.
18th Div.

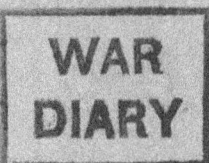

11th BATTN. THE ROYAL FUSILIERS.

A P R I L

(1.4.18   to   1.5.18)

1 9 1 8

Army Form C. 2118.

WAR DIARY
or
INTELLIGENCE SUMMARY.
(Erase heading not required)

Place	Date	Hour	Summary of Events and Information	Remarks and references to Appendices
GENTELLES	Apr19 1st. am.		2nd.Lieut.E.J.Moir rejoined the Battalion. Taking over S.O. 2nd.Lieut.F.A.Leatherland rejoined the Battalion. 11th.Royal Fusiliers & 7th.Bedfordshire	
	2nd.		Regiment ordered to move to HANGARD village and attack the high ground to the East of it. Intense enemy Artillery and M.G.fire prevented the attack developing and the Battalion was ordered back to GENTELLES. 2nd.Lieut.G.Normen died of wounds. 2nd.Lieuts.J?Ruxton and W.Collings wounded.	
	3rd.		Rested in GENTELLES and reorganised.	
	4th.	2 am.	One Coy.plus one extra Lewis Gun Team moved up in support to the 6th.Northamptonshire Regiment	
		3 pm.	This detachment returned.	
BOIS DE HANGARD.	5th.	6-30 pm.	Battalion ordered to Counter Attack north of BOIS DE HANGARD the enemy having been reported in occupation of the wood. After crossing very heavy ground, the Battalion occupied a gap in the front line held by the 53rd. and 55th.Bdes. The 10th.Essex Regiment came up on the right flank later linking up the Battalion with the 54th.Bde. in the HANGARD line. Battalion under orders of the G.O.C. 53rd.Bde. No.12217 R.S.M.Frost G was wounded.	
	6th.	4 am.	Relieved by the 19th.Australian Regiment.and moved to billets at BOVES.	
BOVES.		2 pm.	The Battalion moved to billets at BOVES.	
	7th.	9 am.	The Battalion rested. Baths and clean up. Capt.E.L.Jones M.C. from leave, assumed command of amalgamated "C" & "D" Coys.	
	8th.	3-15 am.	The Battalion"stood to" for expected enemy attack. "Stand down" 9-30 am.	
	9th.	2 pm.	Moved to billets at BOUTILLERIE.	
BOUTILLERIE.	10th.	9am.	The Battalion rested. Clean up.	
	11th.	9 am.	Coy.Training.	
	12th.	9 am.	C.O's Inspection. Training.	
	13th.	4 am.	The Battalion ready to "Stand to".	
		2-30pm.	Tactical scheme for Officers & N.C.O's.	
	14th.	9-30am.	Church Parade. Baths allotted to Battalion.	
	15th.	9 am.	Coy.Training. "A" & "B" Coys moved into new billets.	
	16th.		2nd.Lieut.S.W.Collings rejoined from Hospital. and 282 C.R's joined Battalion & were posted to Coys. The Battalion reorganised in four Coys and H.Q.Details.	
	17th.	9-30am.	Battalion parade. Training.	
	18th.	9-30am.	Battalion parade & inspection by C.O. Training.	
ST.ACHEUL.	19th.	11am.	The Battalion moved to new billets at ST.ACHEUL. Move completed by 12 noon.	
	20th.	9 am.	Battalion parade and Coy.training. 2nd.Lieut.S.W.Collings killed. 2nd.Lieut.C.Campbell seriously wounded Capt.W.S.Minchin M.C. & 2nd.Lieut.S.W.Collings killed. 2nd.Lieut.C.Campbell seriously wounded by shell near b1 1let. 2 O.R's killed and 2 O.R's wounded.	

Army Form C. 2118.

WAR DIARY
or
INTELLIGENCE SUMMARY.

(Erase heading not required)

Instructions regarding War Diaries and Intelligence Summaries are contained in F. S. Regs., Part II. and the Staff Manual respectively. Title pages will be prepared in manuscript.

Place	Date	Hour	Summary of Events and Information	Remarks and references to Appendices
ST.ACHEUL	21st.	10am.	The Battalion paraded for divine service, dismissed owing to hostile shelling. The Brigade Commander presented parchments. 2nd.Lieuts.P.D.Benham,J.P.Turnbull,C.Roberts,F.G.Dale, R.M.MacNaughton,T.Adshead,W.Fairbank and 8 O.R's joined the Battalion.	
	22nd.	9am.	Brigade Field Day on ground S.W. of CAGNY.	
		3pm.	The Battalion returned to billets.	
	23rd.		Lieut.Musson,G.E. and 2nd.Lieuts.A.B.Stowell,C.F.Wixcey,G.E.T.H.Evans,H.Nicholas joined the Battalion.	
	24th.	9 pm.	"A" & "B" Coys.billet shelled 8 O.R's killed and 4 wounded.	
		4 am.	"Stand TO". The Battalion left billets 7 am.proceeding by AMIENS-LONGUEAU road as far as LONGUEAU and thense by track to point south of wood in M.32.d.(Ref.Sheet 62D)where Artillery formation was adopted. "A" & "B" Coys.being in front, and "C" & "D" Coys in support.	
		11 am.	Battalion took up position in trenches on the Western side of wood. Later Battalion was ordered to move up to position South of BOIS DE GENTELLES and "dig in". A great number of gas shells fell in vicinity and Box Respirators became necessary.	
		2-30 pm.	Battalion ordered to take over trenches cutting BOIS DE GENTELLES-DOMART ROAD at point 2000 yds.S.E. of BOIS DE GENTELLES.	
		8 pm.	Battalion releived by French XX Tirailleurs and Coys proceeded according to orders to concentration point on high ground N of BOIS DE GENTELLES.	
	25th.	1pm.	Coys march back independently to camp situated on high ground S.W. of CAGNY.	
		6-30am.	Battalion left camp and moved to N.of CAGNY later position was taken up on sunken road E.of BOIS DE BLANGY.	
	26th.		Battalion remained in position taken up on previous day.	
	27th.		Battalion moved to billets at BELLOY ST LEONARDS in busses.(picking up details on BOVES-CAGNY Road) arriving 10-30 pm.	
BELLOY ST LEONARDS.	28th.		The Battalion rested. Clean up.	
	29th.		The Battalion carried on with Coy Training.	
	30th.		Coy.training.	
	May. 1st.		Lieut.Colonel.A.E.Stilman M.C.proceeded on leave.	

Major.
Commanding 11th.Bn.The Royal Fusiliers.

WAR DIARY
INTELLIGENCE SUMMARY
(Erase heading not required.)

Army Form C. 2118.

11th Royal Sussex

Instructions regarding War Diaries and Intelligence Summaries are contained in F.S. Regs. Part II. and, the Staff Manual respectively. Title pages will be prepared in manuscript.

Place	Date	Hour	Summary of Events and Information	Remarks and references to Appendices
	6.5.18.		Battalion Transport to CONTAY. The Battalion left BELLOY ST.LEONARD and proceeded to WARLOY by 'bus.	
	7.5.18.		Battalion took over from 15th London Regiment. Line from E.2.a.9.0 to E.8.a.5.0.(Sheet 62d N.E.) Craters blown in ALBERT - AMIENS Road. Except for desultory shelling situation quiet. Captain and Adjutant C.V. WATTENBACH proceeded on leave. Lieut. G.F. Musson, Assistant Adjutant, took over duties.	
	8.5.18.		Slight shelling during day. Situation quiet.	
	9.5.18.		Moderate Barrage by our guns at 4.5 am. Except for a few Gas Shells at D.6.central, Situation quiet.	
	10.5.18.		Operations commenced on Left 9 am. Enemy work at Post at E.8.b. No Other Enemy movement. Aircraft. Moderate activity on both sides, during day.	
	11.5.18.		Fairly heavy shelling of Front Line and Posts during day. T.M. Shells on PIONEER TRENCH. Enemy activity at Post E.8.b. Enemy Aircraft active.	
	12.5.18		Small Parties of Enemy seen on road E.11.a and d.	
	13.5.18.		Battalion relieved by 6th London Regiment at 12.15 am. 13.5.18. and proceed to bivouac at C.18.central.	
	14.5.18.		2nd Lieut. A.J.MOORAT ("C" Coy) and A.G.POWELL ("A" Coy) joined the Battalion from R.T.C. Acting Captain E.L. JONES, M.C. to be Temporary Captain dated 31.10.17.	
	15.5.18.		Lieut. A.W. Savours assumed 2nd-in-Command of "B" Coy.	
	16.5.18.		Lieut.Col. A.E. Sulman, M.C. rejoined from Leave. The Battalion took over from 7th Bedfordshire Regiment in LAVIEVILLE Line from D.15.b.1.2. to D.22.a.5.9. with Coy. in support at D.15.a.7.2. (Sheet 62d N.E.).	
	17.5.18.		Battalion took over from Royal West Kent Regiment (Brigade Counter-Attack Battalion) in Line D.11.d.4.1. to D.17.c.9.0. (Sheet 62d N.E.).	
	18.5.18.		Enemy Artillery lively round D.11.a. and D.17.d. (Sheet 62d N.E.) 5 O.R's. killed and 6 O.R's. wounded.	
	19.5.18.		Situation quiet. LAVIEVILLE shelled intermittently throughout the day.	
	20.5.18.		Gas Shells (about 20 blue cross) dropped in D.11.d.central at 10.45 pm.	
	21.5.18.		Situation quiet. 3 bombs dropped from E.A. at D.17.a.5.3. at 10.15 pm.	
	22.5.18.		2nd Lieut. P.D. BENHAM admitted to Hospital. Blue Cross Gas Shells dropped round D.11.d. central and in Valley D.23.a and b. (Sheet 62d N.E.).	
	23.5.18.		Battalion carried out practice Counter-Attack at 10.15 pm., from Line held, to Support Line running D.18.b.9.1. to E.13.a.6.8. Situation quiet.	
	24.5.18.		Battalion relieved by 23rd London Regiment at 12.30 am. and proceeded to C.20.b. in Bivouacs Enemy shelled from D.10.15 pm. at D.11.d. and along ALBERT-AMIENS Road, D.17.b.9.9.,	

Army Form C. 2118.

WAR DIARY
or
INTELLIGENCE SUMMARY.
(*Erase heading not required.*)

Instructions regarding War Diaries and Intelligence Summaries are contained in F. S. Regs., Part II. and the Staff Manual respectively. Title pages will be prepared in manuscript.

Place	Date	Hour	Summary of Events and Information	Remarks and references to Appendices
BEHENCOURT WOOD.	25.5.18.		to D.16.d.1.8 (Sheet 62d N.E.). 2nd Lieuts. S.R.HUGHES and R.S. BURLEY and Other Ranks arrived from R.T.C. 18th Divisional Wing. 2nd Lieut. T. Adshead rejoined Battalion from Hospital. 2nd Lieuts. W. Ross and G.E.T.H. Evans rejoined Battalion from Lewis Gun Course, LE TOUQUET. 2nd Lieuts. H.W. Measures, W. Hornfeck and E.W. Ede, M.C. (Additional) to be Acting Captains whilst commanding Companies dated 7.4.18.	
	26.5.18.		Re-organization under Company Commanders.	
	27.5.18.		Captain and Adjutant C.V. Wattenbach rejoined Battalion from Leave. Working Party of 4 Officers and 400 Other Ranks under Capt. E.E. Ede, M.C. to WARLOY. A few shells in vicinity of Camp 12 midnight to 2 am 28.5.18.	
	28.5.18.		Inspection of Lewis Gunners from Line by B.G.C. 54th Infantry Brigade.	
	29.5.18.		Working Party under Capt. W. Hornfeck. Inspection of First Line Transport at 9 am. by B.G.C. 54th Infantry Brigade. 2nd Lieut. C. Roberts rejoined from 4th Army School. Commanding Officers' Conference at B.H.Q. 11 am. Sixtyxx.	
	31.5.18.		Battalion took over from 6th London Regiment Line from V.28a.b. to U.23.c. Relief complete 5.30 pm.	
	1.6.18.		Barrage by our guns to assist operations on the Left 3.30 to 4.45. Situation quiet. Two apparent dumps set alight at 9.50 pm. True Bearing 150° from B.H.Q.	
	2.6.18.		About 300 Gas and H.E. Shells sent over 3.30 to 4.45 . on SENLIS and Battalion position. Heavy shelling on Battery B.16.c. and U.22.a.(retaliation). Situation quiet.	

9th June 1918.

[signature]
Lieut.Colonel.
Commanding 11th Bn. The Royal Fusiliers.

Army Form C. 2118.

WAR DIARY
of
INTELLIGENCE SUMMARY.
(Erase heading not required.)

11th Battalion,
The Royal Fusiliers

Instructions regarding War Diaries and Intelligence Summaries are contained in F. S. Regs., Part II. and the Staff Manual respectively. Title pages will be prepared in manuscript.

Vol 3 F (3 sheets)

Place	Date	Hour	Summary of Events and Information	Remarks and references to Appendices
LINE.	June. 3 1918.		Battalion took over front line from 10th Bn.Essex Regiment. Relief completed 12.30 a.m. 4.6.18.	
	4th.		Battalion moved from Right Battn.Headquarters in W.25.a.8.5. (MELBOURNE TRENCH) to Left Battn. Headquarters at W.19.b.5.6. (occupied by 2nd Bn.Bedford Regt.)	
	5th.		Patrol sent out to examine enemy's wire &c., from W.21.b.6.5. No hostile forces encountered. Situation quiet.	
	6th.		Battalion "Stood to" 11.45 p.m. - dawn in anticipation of Boche raid. Companies warned and counter-attack dispositions arranged. All quiet during night.	
	7th.		"B" Company went back to HENENCOURT to practice for operation. "A" Company.6th Bn.Northampton- shire Regiment took over.	
	8th.		"A" and "C" Companies returned to HENENCOURT to practice wiring and digging. Map made of Boche wire. "D" Company took over front line of whole Brigade Sector.	
HENENCOURT WOOD.	9th.		Battalion Headquarters and "D" Company relieved by 2nd Battn.Bedford Regiment, and returned to HENENCOURT WOOD. Assault rehearsed 4.30 p.m. & 10 p.m. Enemy plane down in rear of lines 4.30a.m.	
	10th.		2 Officers and 135 O.R's from R.T.C. (Digging and Wiring party) Rehearsal 11.30 a.m. Hon.Lieut. & Quartermaster G.H.Manley reported for duty. 11.45 p.m. Battalion took over old line from 2nd Bn.Bedford Regiment. Relief completed 12.20 a.m. 11th June.	
	11th.		Wire cutting by Artillery. Proposed minor operation with 35th Division cancelled.Situation quiet.	
	12th.		Two fighting patrols from Battalion unable to obtain identification. Bombing raid on QUARRY by 10th Bn.Essex Regiment. Major and Company Commanders(U.S.A.) attached to Battalion for instruction.	
	13th.		Battalion relieved in Left Sector by 7th Bn.Buffs. Relief completed 12.30 a.m. 14th.	
	14th.		Battalion proceeded to WARLOY in billets.	

Army Form C. 2118.

(2)

WAR DIARY
or
INTELLIGENCE SUMMARY.
(Erase heading not required.)

Instructions regarding War Diaries and Intelligence
Summaries are contained in F. S. Regs., Part II.
and the Staff Manual respectively. Title pages
will be prepared in manuscript.

Place	Date	Hour	Summary of Events and Information	Remarks and references to Appendices
WARLOY.	June. 17th.		2nd Lieut.F.L.Moody returned from leave. Major W. Hurnybun joined Battalion for duty.	
	19th.		Major K.D.H.Gwynn D.S.O., returned from leave.	
LINE.	20th.		Battalion relieved 7th Bn. Queens in RIGHT SECTOR.&"B" Company, 7th Bn.BUFFS., in SWAN TRENCH. Relief completed 1.35 a.m. 21.6.18. 2nd Lieut.E.J.Moir to Hospital.	
	21st.		Visibility bad. SWAN TRENCH shelled by our Artillery. Lieut.R.P.Tinsley to 111.Corps Infantry School.	
	22nd.		2nd Lieut.G.F.Boyce to R.T.C. and Taken on Strength. Few 5.9's in Valley W.19. Wire cutting by 6" Newtons all day. Patrol out from "B" Coys.front line to examine enemy wire. Gas Projectors discharged on ALBERT 12 midnight. Considerable T.M., and Artillery activity. 2nd Lieut.W.A.Smith proceeded on Leave.	
	23rd.		2nd Lieut.C.G.Rowe to England for Signalling Course. DUNSTABLE. Patrol out 5 p.m. - 6.45 p.m. to examine enemy wire. Aerial activity increased. Shelling medium throughout day.	
	24th.		Considerable shelling along all parts of Battalion Sector. "B" Company ration party, 2 killed and 1 wounded. Night misty and visibility poor.	
	25th.		Wet and misty till 9.30 a.m. Two British Planes down in flames W.13.c. South of MILLENCOURT. Situation quiet and shelling moderate.	
	26th.		Carrying party of about 250 for wire and L.T.M. ammunition at night. Situation quiet. Patrol out to wire in W.21.d.1.3.-2.8.	
	27th.		ALBERT shelled with shrapnel at intervals all day. Large working and carrying parties to Front Line in evening. British Plane down South of ALBERT 8.30 p.m.	

Army Form C. 2118.

WAR DIARY
or
INTELLIGENCE SUMMARY

(Erase heading not required.)

Place	Date	Hour	Summary of Events and Information	Remarks and references to Appendices
LINE	29th June.		Battalion relieved by 6th Bn.Northamptonshire Regiment and moved to Brigade Reserve, taking over from 2nd Bn.Bedford Regiment. Relief completed 2.30 a.m. **30th** June.	
	30th.		Minor operation by 2nd Bn.Bedford Regiment and 6th Bn.Northamptonshire Regiment in conjunction with XIIth Division on left. Operations started 9.35 p.m. All Objectives gained. Battalion supplied 3 Officers and 120 O.R's digging party for Communication Trench to Boche front line.	
	1st July.		Counter-Attacks at 2.15 a.m. and 9 p.m. repulsed.	
	2nd.		2 a.m. Boche Counter-Attack repulsed. Situation quiet during day. 9.15 p.m. Boche barrage compelled our men to withdraw from newly won positions to old front line, which we hold. Artillery lively all day. Advance party returned from HENENCOURT WOOD 12 midnight.	

9.7.1918.

Major.
Commanding 11th Battalion. The Royal Fusiliers.

SECRET.   **11TH BN. THE ROYAL FUSILIERS.**   Copy No... 3

Reference :-
Map SENLIS   ORDER No. 9.
1/20,000

1.   The 54th Infantry Brigade will carry out an Operation on night of 11/12th June 1918 in conjunction with and on the right of the 105th Brigade.

2.   The 11th Bn. The Royal Fusiliers will attack, capture and hold the enemy trench shown on the map issued to Coys., as the Second Objective.

3.   Map "A" shows Final Objective to be consolidated in YELLOW.
        Wire to be put out in BLUE.
        Blocks to be constructed by filling in the trench for 30 yards in BROWN.
        Trenches to be cut in BROWN.
        Forming up Line First Wave in RED.
            ditto   Second Wave in GREEN.
        Leap Frog Line in WHITE.

4.   "B" Coy. will form First Wave and capture First Objective.
        "D" Coy. will Leap Frog on WHITE Line and capture Second Objective.

5.   Covering Parties will remain out until 2 am. when they will withdraw to YELLOW Line.

6.   First Wave will commence MOVING forward directly the artillery barrage opens at Zero.
        Second Wave will follow after an interval of half a minute.
        The Digging, Wiring and Carrying Parties will move as soon as the White Lights are thrown up from First Objective, or rifle fire shows the attack has got sufficiently far ahead.

7.   The details as to Strength, Disposition, Route and Roles of the various columns have been issued to Coys. In order to avoid the hostile barrage on our Front Line, the Communication trench will be cut commencing at W.21.b.7.1., and the party will work back towards our Line. 2nd Lieut. Dale will lay a tape from our Front Line, and his men following behind him as soon as the attack goes forward. The German trench requires deepening about W.21.b.7.1.

8.   L.G.O. will arrange for 4 L.G's. to be dug in and camouflaged about SHELLHOLE TRENCH W.21.b.5.9. They will have Posts for anti-aircraft work and WILL repel counter-attack.

9.   Lieut. Savours will be responsible for providing Covering Parties for Diggers and Wirers from W.21.b.9.7. to W.21.b.7.1.
        L.G's. will be employed to assist the Covering Parties.

10.   Watches will be synchronized over the 'phone at 7 pm. 11th inst.

11.   The S.O.S. is that in use by the Third Army - GREEN over RED over GREEN. The S.O.S. of the Fourth Army will be taken into use after dawn on 13th inst.

12.   The Officer Commanding No. 10 Column will keep the closest liaison with the Officer Commanding Right Column, 4th Bn. North Staffordshire Regiment.

13.   Coys. will be formed up on their tapes half an hour before Zero.   Zero notified later.
        Reports to B.H.Q. that forming up is complete will be wired by using Coy. Commander's names as code word.

(1).

(2).

14. Officers Commanding "B" and "D" Coys. are responsible for seeing that, after capture of Front and Support Lines of enemy trench, are linked up at W.21.b.8.8.

15. The Digging Party of 75 men will withdraw at 2 am and occupy our old Front Line from W.21.b.4.4. to W.21.b.0.3., i.e:- the right leg of the HAIRPIN.

16. "A" and "C" Coys. on completion of Wiring, and at 2 am in any case, will withdraw to and occupy SHELL HOLE TRENCH and act as immediate counter-attack troops under the Commanding Officer's orders.

17. O.C. "A" and "C" Coys. will dispose the men thinly in SHELL HOLE TRENCH. The defence of the trench will be the Lewis Gun batteries.

18. The positions selected must, however, be governed by the necessity of having a good compact body of troops with which to counter attack, should it be necessary to do so on the YELLOW LINE.

19. The various Light Signals will be :-

(a). Capture of Objectives - A series of White Lights thrown up.
(b). Artillery Support.- A series of Green Lights.
(c). Lengthen Range - A series of Red Lights.
(d). S.O.S. - In event of enemy counter attack.
(e). Aeroplanes - Rifle laid on Parapet in lines of four, two yards between rifles and ten between groups - Aeroplane will ask by Klaxon.

20. Communication - One Loop Set.

One Power Buzzer and two Lamps will go forward under orders Signal Officer. These will be established as near as possible to Coy. Hdqrs.

The greatest efforts will be made to get information back as to the progress of the raid and subsequent action by the enemy.

21. The Carrying Party will establish its Dump, of Water, Bombs, L.G. Magazines and S.A.A. about W.21.b.8.8.

22. The Battalion will be relieved on night of 12/13th inst.

Lieut.Colonel.
Commanding 11th Bn. The Royal Fusiliers.

10th June 1918.
Issued 7 pm. by Runner.

Copies to :-
1. 54th Infantry Brigade.
2. Commanding Officer.
3. Adjutant.
4. "A" Coy.
5. "B" Coy.
6. "C" Coy.
7. "D" Coy.
8. O.C.4th Bn. N. Staffordshire Regt.
9. S.O.
10. M.O.
11. I.O.
12. L.G.O.
13. Lieut. Dale.
14. Lieut. Fairbanks.
15. War Diary.
16. War Diary.
17. R.S.M.
18. Spare.
19. Spare.
20. Spare.

WAR DIARY
or
INTELLIGENCE SUMMARY.

(Erase heading not required.)

Instructions regarding War Diaries and Intelligence
Summaries are contained in F. S. Regs., Part II.
and the Staff Manual respectively. Title pages
will be prepared in manuscript.

Army Form C. 2118.

11 RF

Place	Date	Hour	Summary of Events and Information	Remarks and references to Appendices
HÉNENCOURT	5 July		Battalion relieved in Reserve Line (MELBOURNE TR, CAREY TR MURRAY TR) & Front line (SWAN TR, by units of 15th Brigade & proceeded to bivouacs W of HÉNENCOURT WOOD relieving 8th E. SURREYS Relief completed 1.30 am. 2/Lieut A.E. BANTS rejoined the Battn from leave.	
	7	"	Major K.D.H. Swayne DSO assumes command of the Battalion vice Lt. Col Pulman M.C. to England 7.7.18.	
	9	"	"Practice Battle Positions" received 9 pm. Brigade moved accordingly. Returned to bivouacs 10.30 pm.	
	12	"	Battalion relieved by 17th LONDONS & proceeded to by bus GUENEMÉCOURT. Taking over billets of 1/5th LONDON Regt. Corps in billets 11.30 pm. Divisional rest started.	3h F (contd)
GUÉNEMÉCOURT	13	"	Programme of training issued by Brigade for period of rest.	

Army Form C. 2118.

WAR DIARY
INTELLIGENCE SUMMARY.
(Erase heading not required.)

Place	Date	Hour	Summary of Events and Information	Remarks and references to Appendices
GUEDECOURT	July		Capt. P. Baker joined Batty. for duty, assumed command of "D" Coy. vice A/Capt. MEASURES	
	2 July		A/Capt. Measures reverts to rank of 2/Lieut on ceasing to command a Company.	
	29 July		Both Coys. sent out a/c F. from our wounders from 60th Bn. A.I.F. at 1.10 - 16.	
			b/two [illegible]	
1.10.c.30	"		Relief completed & two other [illegible] to FREHENCOURT Cops. company's camp.	
	30/31 July		Battalion relieved 33rd + 54th Australian Battns in line. J.30. 31. 36 B. H.Q. at J.30.c.F.8. Remainder trees at ROUND WOOD. C.25.6.	

Maurice Creek C
Capt. and Adjt.
11th Battalion The Royal Fusiliers.

54th Inf. Bde.

18th Division

11th BATTALION

ROYAL FUSILIERS

AUGUST 1918

11th Battn ROYAL FUSILIERS

WAR DIARY for the period 1st to 21st

AUGUST, 1918, APPARENTLY MISSING.

11th Bn. Royal Fusiliers

54 71/6 M 34

35.F. (extract)

Army Form C. 2118.

WAR DIARY
or
INTELLIGENCE SUMMARY.
(Erase heading not required.)

Instructions regarding War Diaries and Intelligence Summaries are contained in F. S. Regs., Part II. and the Staff Manual respectively. Title pages will be prepared in manuscript.

Place	Date	Hour	Summary of Events and Information	Remarks and references to Appendices
Railway Embkmt. S of ALBERT	22/8/18	1 a.m.	At 1 a.m. the Battalion attacked in conjunction with the 6th NORTHANTS, on our right, enemy's positions E of the ANCRE. The crossing of the ANCRE was carried out under extreme difficulty owing to the marshy state of the ground on either side of the river. We carried the first objective and reorganised. 2 Lt. W.H. MEASURES and 2 Lt. V.H. BARRELL were killed. BELLEVUE FARM was captured at about 11 a.m. and our final objective reached at about 1 p.m. During the operation we inflicted heavy casualties on the enemy besides taking 300 prisoners and several M.G's. Lt. R.P. TINSLEY 2 Lts. O. MORRISS, N.J. LILLINGTON, F.G. DALE, and F. ASHMORE were wounded.	
ANCRE	23/8/18		The 2nd. BEDS. attacked through our position and we withdrew to a defensive line running S. of BELLEVUE FARM.	
	24/8/18	2 p.m.	At 2 p.m. the Battalion took up a position in E.11 b.d. & c. (Ref. SENLIS 1/20.000) D.Coy were shelled during the night.	
	25/8/18		The Battalion were ordered to move up to BOTTOM WOOD E of FRICOURT. At 5 p.m. in conjunction with the 7th. BUFFS, on our left and the 12th. Div. on our right attacked high ground in front of MONTAUBAN. Enemy put up a stubborn resistance and we were unable to gain our objective that night.	
	26/8/18		At dawn we continued the attack and gained our final objective at about 6 p.m. Letter of congratulation received from Army (4th) on the magnificent way in which we forced the crossing of the ANCRE.	
	27/8/18		The Battalion was relieved in the line by the 53rd. Bde. and we withdrew to CATERPILLAR VALLEY & MONTAUBAN areas.	
	28/8/18		Battalion took up a position in MARLBORO' WOOD.	
	29/8/18.		Battalion received orders to proceed to trenches E. of TRONES WOOD. During the evening we were ordered to assemble in SAVERNAKE WOOD, and arrived there about 2 a.m.	
	30/8/18		The Battalion attacked in conjunction with the 6th. NORTHANTS on our left and the 22nd. LONDON REGT. on our right. Our objective was the road running N & S in RANCOURT. We attacked PRIEZ FARM and were met with very heavy M.G. and rifle fire. The Farm was found to be strongly held by the enemy, supported by a M.G. Coy. Capt. E.W. EDE was killed close to the Farm. The position was extremely obscure and the enemy finding our left flank uncovered was able to work round our flank and inflicted fairly heavy casualties on us. We eventually reached a line running from T 29 c 4.3. to B 5.c. 9.9. thence along trench to B.5 b 9.2. and B.6 c 2.9. During the night we withdrew to SAVERNAKE WOOD where the Battalion rested. 2 Lts. R.M. McNAUGHTON, E.A.S. PITMAN, C.L. STURROCK,	

Army Form C. 2118.

WAR DIARY
or
INTELLIGENCE SUMMARY.
(Erase heading not required.)

Instructions regarding War Diaries and Intelligence Summaries are contained in F. S. Regs., Part II. and the Staff Manual respectively. Title pages will be prepared in manuscript.

Place	Date	Hour	Summary of Events and Information	Remarks and references to Appendices
	31/8/18		2 Lt. H. HIGGINBOTHAM were wounded. A letter of congratulation was received from the Divisional Commander on the magnificent way the Battalion fought since the operations commencing 22/8/18.	

Total Prisoners captured since the 22/8/18 4 Officers 450 O.R's.
Total Casualties for period 22.8.18. to 30.8.18
  Officers :- 3 Killed.
        10. Wounded.

Other Ranks:- 33 Killed.
      228 Wounded.

Lieut. Colonel.
Commanding 11th. Bn. The Royal Fusiliers.

From O/C "D" Coy.   Aug: 9/1918

To: The Adjutant.
    11th R. F.

For your information, please:

Counter-Attack night of 6/7th Aug 1918.

When "D" Coy arrived in position. North Hants at first reported they knew nothing about the Scheme. A few minutes before the time I had ordered my men to be in the open, a message was received thro' 2Lt Fairbank & L/Cpl E. G. Hudson that N. Hants were ready to go at appointed time.

O/C "B" Coy asked advice re going over as he had discovered no one on his Left for 300 x. I said I was going if N. Hants were there & I received no orders to the contrary. Finally I sent definite message we were all ready.

Previous to this I made clear again to all personally
(1) How they would move.
(2) How flanks were to be protected.
(3) What we were responsible for.
(4) On reaching objective to stop C.T. in advance to prevent Bombing by the enemy.

We went forward & reached the objective though heavy mist delayed us slightly.

N. Hants on my right appeared to advance well but suddenly disappeared. Did my best to get in touch again.

Reached objective.

Caught a prisoner in a funk hole.

Captured a Machine Gun killing 2 men.

Before we had formed a block, the Enemy bombed from a C.T. on left.

Formed Squad under Sergt. Best & inflicted casualties, turning them back using our own bombs & the enemy's.

Then found trouble on my right but (L/Cpl Day's) L. Gun disposed of those until put out of action & bomb supply failed.

2/.

The enemy bombed heavily & sniping & M.G. fire caused trouble. I sent back runner for bombs, also Sgt Best. All available bombs from Lt Measures & reserves.

Finally bombed out & fell back to shell holes & another trench where fire steps were at once made.

B. Coy occupied this line & we were too crowded. Again bombed on the left. Passed back further bombs until exhausted & got men out of trench & crawled out in small groups.

Finally I was left with a few men of B & D. Coys. & N.C.O's in slit.

Crawled as far as possible but Germans put up barrage, M.G. fire & T.M. & continual sniping.

Remained in slit with the above & another officer of "B" Coy giving directions to men where to go.

Brought back one L.G. complete, & one out of action.

Did all I could in the way of signals but Very lights were not good, cartridges not even fitting the pistol. They should be kept in some other kind of wrapper in my opinion. Signals were given to Aeroplane when all seemed hopeless. As far as I remember I got back at approx: between 4.30 p.m. & 5.30 p.m.

P. Baker. Capt
O/C "D" Coy.

The Adjutant.

B.550

Oct. 3rd. 1918.

54.th. Inf. Bde. Hqrs.

54/18

Herewith War Diary for month ending 30th. Sept. 1918.

[signature]

Asst. Adjt.
11th. Batt. Royal Fusiliers

Army Form C. 2118

WAR DIARY
or
INTELLIGENCE SUMMARY.
(Erase heading not required.)

Instructions regarding War Diaries and Intelligence Summaries are contained in F.S. Regs., Part II. and the Staff Manual respectively. Title pages will be prepared in manuscript.

56 F. (copies)

Vol 9

Place	Date	Hour	Summary of Events and Information	references to Appendices
Combles	1/9/18		The Battalion left SAVERNAKE WOOD and took up a defensive position E. of COMBLES. D Coy in trench running from FREGICOURT N to T 23 b.5.3. B Coy., from T 23 d 5.4. A & C Coys., in sunken road at T 22 d.7.5.	
	2/9/18.		Battalion remained in these positions.	
	3/9/18.		Battalion proceeded during the evening to camp W. of COMBLES at T 20 Central. Programme of training made out.	
	4/9/18.		General Training. Games in afternoon.	
	5/9/18.		-do-	
	6/9/18.		-do-	
	7/9/18.		-do- Battalion bathed in COMBLES.	
	8/9/18.		Sunday. Church parade.	
	9/9/18.		General Training.	
	10/9/18.		-do-	
	11/9/18.		-do-	
	12/9/18.		-do-	
	13/9/18.		-do-	
	14/9/18.		-do- Bathing in BERNAFAY WOOD.	
	15/9/18.		-do-	
	16/9/18.		C.O's conference on pending attack by this Battalion. Battalion marched to SUGAR FACTORY in LONGUEVAL to watch 2nd.Bedfords and 6th. Northants carry out a demonstration attack through LONGUEVAL assisted by 5 tanks. Warning order received that Battalion would move to the Battle Zone on the 16th. Battalion and Coy. Commanders left at 9 a.m. by lorry to reconnoitre the sector over which we should attack. The Battalion embussed at LEUZE WOOD at 10a.m. and proceeded to MXXXXX MOISLAINS. On debussing the Battalion fell out on the side of the road and a german land mine exploded wounding 2Lt. MOIR E.J. and 23 O.R's. The Battalion marched to AIZECOURT - le - BAS where they bivouaced.	
	17/9/18.		Final conference on plan of attack and all arrangements completed. Companies left AIZECOURT le- BAS area at 6.30p.m. and proceeded to the W. of SAULCOURT where they rested.hot tea was sent up at 11.30.p.m.Coys then moved up to their assembly positions at 12.30 a.m.	
	18/9/18.		Coys. were reported in position for the attack at 3.10a.m. and attacked the enemy's positions at 5.20.a.m. assisted by tanks and a very heavy barrage.We met with stubborn enemy resistance W. of the Village of RONSSOY. Cont'd	

Army Form C. 2118.

WAR DIARY
or
INTELLIGENCE SUMMARY.
(Erase heading not required.)

Instructions regarding War Diaries and Intelligence Summaries are contained in F. S. Regs., Part II. and the Staff Manual respectively. Title pages will be prepared in manuscript.

Place	Date	Hour	Summary of Events and Information	Remarks and references to Appendices
	18/9/18		Continued. Enemy's feild guns were firing atnpoint blank range. B Coy. captured one of the guns. Several prisoners were captured by us. Our line at 8 p.m. ran roughly F 16 c 3.0. - F.15 d 2.9. F 16 c 3.8. - F 15 b 5.5. C Coy captured 2 field guns. Capt. G.E. CORNABY was wounded (since reported died of wounds) whilst trying to reorganise his Coy.	
	19/9/18		The Battalion remained in the positions gained the previous day. They were intermittently heavily shelled during the day and night. At 6.30.p.m. O.C. B Coy. sent a message that the enemy were massing opposite our front. The S.O.S. was sent up which was repeated all along the line. No enemy attack however developed owing to our intense barrage put down on enemy's forming up ground.	
	20/9/18.		Battalion remained in their positions. Cap t. P.BAKER, 2nd. Lt. W.H.MEASURES and 2nd Lt. W.ROSS awarded the M.C. for gallantry during operations on the 8th Aug.1918.	
	21/9/18.		Message received from Bde. to hold ourselves in readiness to move up at ½ hour's notice. Orders were eventually received for C & D Coys to be attached to the 2nd. BEDFORDSHIRE REGT. for operations. A.& B. Coys. moved to BASSE BOULOHNE SOUTH. 2Lt. F.M.HEWITT went down with Shellshock.	
	22/9/18.		At C & D Coys.formed up for the attack on road running from F.23 c 6.8. - F 23 d 3.5. and advanced towards their objectives (12 midnight 21/22nd)They were instructed to pick up an isolated post of the 2nd. Bedfords. on our left. These two Coys. took POT LANE - capturing about 20 prisoners- but could not advance further owing to heavy M.G.Fire. Bombing blocks were established in POT LANE and in POT TRENCH and awaited further instructions. These came that they were to attack at 3 p.m. with a barrage lasting 10 mins. on the strong point in DUNCAN AVENUE, straighten our line and that a Coy. of 2nd. Beds. would bomb up the trench. No barrage fell as arranged so they waited until 3.30 p.m. when they engaged the enemy's M.G's putting 2 out of action. This caused the enemy to retire and we advanced capturing the post with several prisoners. This position was immediately consolidated. Later the S.O.S. was sent up causing the barrage to fall on our positions. Our casualties through this were fairly heavy. At 1 .a.m. 23rd. The Battalion was relieved in the line and withdrew to the QUAERY W.of Ste.EMILIE.	
	23/8/19		Coys. reorganised and cleaned up generally. At 3.P.m. Battalion moved to billets in MURLU.	
	24/9/18 25/9/18 26/9/18		Battalion cleaned up and rested. General Training. The Divisional Commander addressed the Battalion and congratulated them on the splendid fighting spirit shown during the recent fighting.	
	27/9/18. 28/9/18		Conference on pending operations. Reorganisation. Battalion received orders to proceed to GUYENCOURT. They moved off at 3.45 a.m. and were	

WAR DIARY
or
INTELLIGENCE SUMMARY.
(Erase heading not required.)

Army Form C. 2118.

Place	Date	Hour	Summary of Events and Information	Remarks and references to Appendices
	28/9/18.		Continued.	
	29/9/18.		reported in position by 7 a.m., where they bivouaced. The Battalion received orders to move at 7.p.m. to LEMPIRE where they arrived at 9.30.pm. Battalion moved up to their forming up positions for the attack at 3.a.m. and were in position at 3.50.p.m. ZERO 5.50.a.m. The Battalion attacked in conjunction with troops of the 12th.Div. on left and the 6th. Northants on right. All objectives were captured and held by 10.a.m. The 107th Battalion (American Bde.) were observed to fall back to positions about 300 yards in rear of our troops. At the same time the enemy counterattacked on our front leaving about 25 prisoners in our hands. Measures were then immediately taken to protect our flanks with M.G.'s of the 18th M.G.Batt. and T.M. support. Our casualties were fairly heavy. 2nd. Lt. W.ROPER was killed. Our artillery on several occasions during the operations fired short inflicting casualties on our men. At 6.30.p.m. the enemy was observed to have pushed round the left flank of the 8th BUFFS. (12 Div) M.G. support was sent up and also 2 Coys of 55th.Bde. to safeguard our flank. Quiet during the night. Day's casualties approx. 125. At 9.30 a.m. message received that all artillery fire on W. side of CANAL was to cease. Patrols were sent into VENDHUILE and reported that the village was clear of the enemy. At 1.30 p.m. D.Coy. was sent forward into VENDHUILE with orders to occupy W.side of bridge over the Canal. A. B. & C. Coys followed at 2.15p.m. Message received from D. Coy. That they were in the village but that they could not get forward owing to our own guns firing on us. At 2.30 p.m. D.Coy. sent a message that they would have to withdraw if our fire was not stopped. 2nd.Lt. B.R.HUGHES was killed by one of our own shells. D.Coy. reported that they were in position with A. B.&C Coys. in rear at 5.30.p.m. Casualties 3 Officers and 62 O.R's. Orders for relief came through at 7.p.m. that the 2nd. Beds. would relieve the Battalion and that we were to withdraw to RONSSOY WOOD, where we arrived at 4.15 a.m.	
	30/9/18.			

Major, Commdg.,
11th. Batt. The Royal Fusiliers.

ORDERS FOR THE PRESENTATION OF THE "1914" STAR.

1. The Divisional Commander has kindly consented to present the ribbon of the above medal to men of 54th Infantry Brigade Group on 4th inst. at 10 a.m.

2. Two Companies each of 3 Officers and 80 other ranks will represent the 11th Bn. Royal Fusiliers.

3. Parade at 9.40 a.m. 4th inst. on Parade Ground of 19th Middlesex Regiment (as per Map handed Capt. N.B. Michell).

4. The Divisional Commander will be received with the General Salute on arrival on the Parade Ground. The Band of the 19th Middlesex Regiment will play the Salute.

"A" and "C" Coys. will each detail 40 other ranks made up into one Coy. of two Platoons under Lieut. H.W. Brookling
"A" and "C" Coys. will each detail one Platoon Officer.
"B" Coy. will detail 5 0 other ranks and "D" Coy. 30 other ranks to be made up into one Company of two Platoons, each to parade under Capt. G.S. Pearcy, M.C.
"B" and "D" Coys. will each detail one Platoon Officer.

The above will parade in the Big Square ready to move at 8.50 a DRESS :- Drill Order.
Captain N.B. Michell will be in charge of the party.

The undermentioned will parade in the Big Square under RSM. FROST. ready to move off at 8.50 a.m.:-

		No. 19917 RSM FROST, G.			
No. 8963	Sgt. Berry,	H.	No. 7864	Pte Coxall,	F.
13957	L/C Burchett,	J.	177	Pte Booty,	M.
15 670	Pte Sweeney,	T.	1565 6	Pte Taylor,	W.
359	Sgt Murphy,	D.	8884	Cpl Diggins,	A.
8800	Pte Jarrett,	W.	8971	Pte Christmas,	F.
9449	Pte Norman,	C.	9701	Sgt Whare,	W.
11565	Sgt Love,	W.	9636	Pte Darby,	A.

This party will report to the Staff Captain on the Parade Ground at 9.40 a.m. RSM Frost will hand to the Staff Captain a Nominal Roll of men to receive ribbons.

Capt. A/Adjt.
11th Bn. Royal Fusiliers.

3.9.18.

SECRET.   ORDER   Copy

All Coys.
Headquarters.
Quartermaster.
Transport Officer.

           In the event of an Order to move the Battalion will
parade on the road between the MAIRES MAIRIE and the Church.
Head of Column at MAIRIE.
Order of March :-   "A", "B", "C", "D" and HdQrs.
                                  D   C
Transport in rear.
           All Officers' Chargers will be required and must be
ready.
           All Mess Stores, will be packed and left here.
           Q.M.Stores and Workshops will remain.
           All baggage, Officers Valises, Kits and Blankets will
be dumped and also any other baggage.
           All C.Q.M.Sgts. will remain with all their Coy. Offrs.
baggage packed.
           All Water Bottles to be filled at once.
           Water Carts to be ready to move forward full.
           The Canteen will remain here.
           2nd Lieut. Swence will be in charge of the Orderly
Room.

20.6.15.   Capt. & Adjt.
                                            11th Bn., Royal Fusiliers

NARRATIVE OF OPERATIONS

carried out by

11TH BN. THE ROYAL FUSILIERS,

From 29th Sept. 1918 to 30th Sept.1918, inclusive.

1.	The Battalion formed up in assembly positions at 03.50 on the 29/10/18. There was little shelling but a fairly sustained machine-gun fire from the enemy. The Battalion, with the 6th Northamptonshire Regiment on the right, followed closely the attack of the 1/107th American Infantry battalion. At Zero - 05.50 - the attack commenced; there was some confusion among the American troops who had been late in getting into position. It was also reported that the Tanks were late in taking up the attack. Our barrage was somewhat thin and scattered, and a smoke barrage on our left put down by our own artillery, of which the Battalion had not been warned, added considerably to the difficulties of maintaining direction. The American infantry began to move over to the right of the objective before the completion of the attack, with the result that this Battalion and the 6th Northamptonshire Regiment were obliged to occupy the objective immediately, some of the "mopping up" being inevitably neglected. At 10.30 messages were received that all Coys. were on their objective and were consolidating.

Shortly after this the 1/107th American Infantry Battalion were observed to fall back into a position about 300 Yds. in rear on the right, under the influence of a counter-attack which left 20 prisoners in the hands of "C" Coy. Royal Fusiliers, and this withdrawal exposed the right flank of the Brigade. After due consideration with O.C. 6th Northamptonshire Regiment and O.C. 2/105 American Infantry Battalion, the following measures were adopted to protect this flank:-

"C" Coy. 6th Northamptonshire Regiment re-inforced their flank with one platoon, and the 2/105 American Infantry Battalion detached 3 Coys. for immediate support to the 1/107th American Infantry Battalion.

"B" Coy. 18th Machine-gun battalion (British) pushed up guns to cover this flank, and the 54th T.M.B. (British) arranged to give protective fire in case of need.

The enemy attack never materialized and our line held good, with the exception of MACQUINCOURT TRENCH on the right. (This, however, was not on the front of this Battalion).

As the result of an attempt to move forward Battalion Headquarters casualties were incurred through enfilade machine-gun fire directed from a derelict American tank which was apparently occupied by one of the enemy.

Demoralisation of our own troops, caused through our own artillery fire directed on to our foremost positions, was considerable, notwithstanding the efforts to divert same and the accurate information which was sent back to the Brigade as to the exact line and frontage held by the Battalion. Reports from one of the Coys. of this Battalion are attached with reference to this. Many casualties were suffered this way.

At 18.30 the enemy was observed endeavouring to "trickle" men round the left flank of the 6th Buffs (12th Division). Machine guns were moved up to cover this flank and two companies of the 7th Queens - 55th Brigade - were pushed forward to safeguard this flank. This operation, which was carried out late in the afternoon, met with apparent success.

The remainder of the night was quiet. The day's casualties were about 50 all told. There was considerable enemy fire on our immediate supports, and the TOMBOIS VALLEY was constantly subjected to gas shelling.

On the following day - 30/9/18 - our battle patrols along the whole of our front, which were pushed forward, reported the situation quiet. The harassing machine-gun fire which was encountered from the high ground on the right during the previous day had practically ceased, undoubtedly owing to the capture of GUILLEMONT FARM by the Australians troops on the previous evening.

In the afternoon word was received that American troops well on the right had moved forward considerably. Patrols were then sent on to VENDHUILE from our Battalion and the Village was reported clear of the enemy, with the exception of a few snipers and one or two machine-guns hidden in the ruins.

At 13.30 "D" Coy. Royal Fusiliers was sent forward with orders to occupy the West side of the Canal covering the Bridgeheads in VENDHUILE due East of the Church. The remaining 3 Coys. followed behind at intervals, eventually taking up positions in depth through the Village. Battalion Headquarters had them moved forward to TINO TRENCH on the North of the TOMBOIS ROAD. At 14.15 a message was received from "D" COY. that they were in the Village but could not move forward owing to our own artillery fire. (Before entering the Village it was definitely stated that NO artillery fire would be directed on the Village). At 14.30 a message was received that "D" Coy. would have to withdraw if our fire was not lifted. Coys. again lost several men through this, including 2/Lt. Hughes commanding "D" Coy, who was killed. At 17.15 messages were received that all Coys. were in position.

During our occupation of VENDHUILE our aeroplanes flew over and dropped bombs on our positions, fortunately with no loss to our troops. The day's casualties were 26 all told. Enemy shelling was practically Nil during this operation, but towards 20.00 was heavy on areas immediately in rear of our forward system.

3.   Orders for relief came through at 1900, the 2nd Battalion of the Bedfordshire Regiment relieving the Royal Fusiliers by 23.30 with no casualties to this Battalion, which then withdrew to bivouacking area near RONSSOY WOOD.

Major
Commanding 11th Bn. The Royal Fusiliers

"A" Form — Army Form C. 2121 (In pads of 100.)
MESSAGES AND SIGNALS.

No. of Message..........

Prefix......Code......m.	Words	Charge.	This message is on a/c of :	Recd. at......m.
Office of Origin and Service Instructions	Sent			Date............
Confidential	At.........m.		..............Service.	From............
	To...........			By............
	By...........		(Signature of "Franking Officer")	

TO — All Coys. + HQ

Sender's Number.	Day of Month.	In reply to Number.	AAA
B.556	4		

The attached is passed
for your information,
please.

OC A Coy — Whs
OC B — A.
OC C — PAH.
OC D — B.P.4.
OC HQ — WW7

Please pass in above order, HQ to return to O.Room

From ....
Place — Mountrail
Time ....

The above may be forwarded as now corrected   (Z)

Censor. — Signature of Addresser or person authorised to telegraph in his name — Capt / Adjt

* This line should be erased if not required.

Order No. 1625 Wt. W3253/ P 511 27/2 H. & K., Ltd. (E. 2634).

Army Form C. 2118.

WAR DIARY
or
INTELLIGENCE SUMMARY.
(Erase heading not required.)

Instructions regarding War Diaries and Intelligence Summaries are contained in F. S. Regs., Part II. and the Staff Manual respectively. Title pages will be prepared in manuscript.

11RF — B930 — Vol 9

87.F. (2 sheets)

Place	Date	Hour	Summary of Events and Information	Remarks and references to Appendices
Ronssoy.	1/10/18.		The Battalion remained in RONSSOY WOOD.	
	2/10/18.		The Battalion marched from RONSSOY WOOD to NURLU and embussed to RAINNEVILLE.	
	3/10/18.		The Battalion carried out reorganisation and training in accordance with Training programme.	
	4/10/18.		—do—	
	5/10/18.		Lt.Col.A.de P. Kingsmill was attached to the Battalion.	
	6/10/18.		The Battalion paraded for Divine Service at 09.45.	
	7/10/18.		The Battalion carried out training as per Training programme.	
	8/10/18.		—do—	
	9/10/18.		—do—	
	10/10/18.		—do—	
	11/10/18.		—do— (There was a Lecture for Officers at PIERREGOT	
			—do— (by the Divisional Gas Officer.	
	12/10/18.		The Battalion paraded at 09.30 to march to the Sports Ground. The Sports commenced at 11.00.	
	13/10/18.		The Battalion paraded for Divine Service at 10.45.	
	14/10/18.		The Battalion paraded for Route March at 09.15. The route taken was out to MOLLIENS-AU-BOIS, then home.	
	15/10/18.		The Battalion carried out training as per Training programme.	
	16/10/18.		—do—	
	17/10/18.		All Officers attended a Lecture at PIERREGOT by Lieut.Col. A.W.H. James, M.C. R.A.F. The Battalion leaves rest area and entrains at POULAINVILLE for ROISEL. Arrive in billets at AIZECOURT-LE-BAS at 04.00 18/10/18.	
	18/10/18.		The Battalion embussed at 13.30. for forward area - SERAIN arriving at 19.00. The Battalion was in close billets. 2/Lieut. W. Ross rejoined from Leave.	
	19/10/18.		The Battalion marched to MAUROIS arriving at 16.30 in close billets. 2/Lieut. C.H. Fisher joined B.H.Q.	
	20/10/18.		The Battalion moved up to LE CATEAU as support. Battle Surplus remained ELLINCOURT. Relieved 5th Connaught Rangers. Two O.R's casualties.	
	21/10/18.		2/Lieut. C.G.Rowe rejoined the Battalion from course. 2/Lieut. H.J. Poole joined the Battalion. Intermittent shelling of Town - casualties nil.	

Army Form C. 2118.

WAR DIARY
or
INTELLIGENCE SUMMARY.
(Erase heading not required.)

Instructions regarding War Diaries and Intelligence Summaries are contained in F. S. Regs., Part II. and the Staff Manual respectively. Title pages will be prepared in manuscript.

Place	Date	Hour	Summary of Events and Information	Remarks and references to Appendices
Le Cateau.	22/10/18.		Continued. The Town was intermittently shelled all day. The Battalion moved up to a position of assembly on W. side of Railway Embankment from K.23.c.1.3. to K.29.	
	23/10/18.		At Zero plus 4 minutes the Battalion moved along the Railway Embankment, under the railway bridge over the stream, and advanced in artillery formation in rear of the 2nd. Bedfordshire Regt. who were to capture the first objective. The enemy put down a heavy barrage on the bridge but our casualties were not unduly heavy. Our barrage was particularly good. The Battalion got away well to time, but were delayed in reaching their objective owing to the 2nd. Bedfordshire Regt. not pushing forward to their own objective. We reached the second objective at Zero plus 280 minutes without undue opposition. The enemy's artillery was by this time negligble. Here we captured 11 Field guns. At Zero plus 360 minutes the 55th Infantry Brigade leapfrogged through us and went forward to their own objectives. Battalion Headquarters then moved to FOREST in a cellar where 12 prisoners were captured. A copy of the Report on Operations is attached.	
	24/10/18.		In the early hours of the 24th. the Battalion moved forward into BOUSIES and formed up about 100 yds. in front of the road running from F.28.d.2.3. to F.28.a.0.5. At Zero - 04.10 - plus 10 minutes, the Battalion moved forward in rear of the 6th Northamptonshire Regt., who were to capture the first objective. The enemy's artillery was also weak and very scattered, but he was using a good deal of gas. Our barrage opened rather short and weak. At Zero plus 70 minutes we leapfrogged through the 6th Northamptonshire Regt., and pushed forward. Heavy machine-gun fire was encountered from a strong point in a Sunken Road at F.17.d.1.5. Our Tank came to our assistance, however, and knocked out the post. Several officers became casualties at this point. Capt. B. Webster, Capt. W. Hornfeck, and Lieut. G. Tyler were wounded. 2/Lieuts. F. Lyons, C. Macklin and F. Garner were gassed. The four Companies then came under the command of Lieut. E. Moody, who pushed forward again till held up by machine gun fire from the high ground at F.18.a.4.0. During the morning our artillery put down a heavy barrage on the positions occupied by our men, and forced them to Retire. We suffered very heavy casualties from this source. No further move was made till about 19.00, when the Battle was formed into three battle patrols which pushed forward and established themselves on the road running from F.11.b.2.3. to F.12.a.0.0.	

Army Form C. 2118.

WAR DIARY
or
INTELLIGENCE SUMMARY.
(Erase heading not required.)

Place	Date	Hour	Summary of Events and Information	Remarks and references to Appendices
Bousies.	25/10/18.		Continued. The Battalion was relieved at about 11.00 by the Essex Regt. - 55th Infantry Brigade. The Battalion came back to billets at BOUSIES, and moved to LA FAYTE FARM during the afternoon.	
	26/10/18.		2/Lieut. H.J. Poole and 2/Lieut. E. Partridge joined the Battalion at LA FAYTE FARM.	
	27/10/18.		2/Lieut. J.W. Hayes went to Hospital.	
	28/10/18.		The Battalion relieved the 7th Queens - R.W. Surrey Regt. - at ROBERSART. 3 O.R's casualties during the relief. The day was fairly quiet. There was intermittent shelling of the Village with "pip-squeaks".	
	29/10/18.		At about 10.00 an old French woman came into our lines from PREUX-AU-BOIS. She was 84 years of age and seemed to be in the last stage of exhaustion. All the information we could get from her was the fact that the night before the Boche had taken away her family, leaving her alone, whereupon she started wandering in the hope of reaching our line. She was evacuated in the usual way. The Battalion was relieved in the afternoon by the 2nd. Bedfordshire Regt., and came back to cellars in BOUSIES in reserve.	
	30/10/18.		The Battalion remained in these positions.	
	31/10/18.		There was intermittent shelling during the night, the enemy using some gas.	
			-do-	

10.11.18.

[signature]

Lieut. Colonel,
Commanding 11th Batt. The Royal Fusiliers.

Army Form C. 2118.

WAR DIARY
or
INTELLIGENCE SUMMARY.
(Erase heading not required.)

Instructions regarding War Diaries and Intelligence
Summaries are contained in F. S. Regs., Part II.
and the Staff Manual respectively. Title pages
will be prepared in manuscript.

Place	Date	Hour	Summary of Events and Information	Remarks and references to Appendices
ROBERSART.	1/11/18.		Relieved the 2nd. Bedfordshire Regiment in the Line.	
	2/11/18		In the Line - situation quiet. Final preparations for attack.	
	3/11/18		Took over Brigade front. Final preparations for attack made.	
	4/11/18		A composite Coy. consisting of "C" & "D" Coys. attacked, in conjunction with the 6th Northamptonshire Regt. and 2nd. Bedfordshire Regt., the enemy positions in PREUX-AU-BOIS. A heavy protective barrage was put down and 1 Tank allotted to us. A Field Gun, firing over open sights, was also attached to us. Zero:- 0615 hours.	
	5/11/18		The Battalion remained in Reserve.	
	6/11/18		The Battalion marched out from PREUX-AU-BOIS to LE CATEAU into billets.	
	7/11/18		Companies were at the disposal of Coy. Commanders for cleaning up kit, etc.	
	8/11/18		A Battalion parade was ordered but was cancelled owing to the inclement weather.	
	9/11/18		Battalion parade, and Coys. at the disposal of Coy. Commanders for re-organising and training.	
	10/11/18		The Battalion paraded for Divine Service at 0900. During the morning we received notification that President POINCARE was to visit the Town. A Guard of Honour was formed from the 11th Bn. The Royal Fusiliers. and the 6th Northamptonshire Regt., and the massed bands of the 2nd. Bedfordshire Regt., 2nd. Bedfordshire Regt. and the 6th Northamptonshire Regt., played the Guard of Honour up to the Maire's House, where they halted. The President was due to arrive at 1600 hours, but at 1645 he had not appeared, so the Guard of Honour and the Bands marched back.	
	11/11/18.		At 0800 hours news was received that hostilities on the Western Front would be suspended at 1100 hours. The Regimental Band formed up outside Battalion Headquarters at 1100 hours and sounded the "Cease Fire".	
	12/11/18		The Battalion formed up for Commanding Officer's parade at 0900 hours. The Commanding Officer then gave out the News regarding the cessation of hostilities, and dismissed the parade. The remainder of the day was a holiday. 2nd. Lieuts. G.F. Boyce and G.V. Treglow joined the Battalion. The Battalion formed up for Commanding Officer's parade at 0900 hours, but owing to an order being received to stand by for moving, the parade was dismissed after the Commanding Officer's inspection. The Battalion paraded again at 1200 hours in full marching order for inspection by the Commanding Officer. During the afternoon a message was received to the effect that the Battalion would move the next day (13 th inst.) between 0700 and 0800 hours.	
	13/11/18		The Battalion moved off on the march to SERAIN at 0830. The order of march in the Brigade was as follows:- 2nd. Bedfordshire Regt., 6th Northamptonshire Regt. and the 11th Battalion The Royal Fusiliers. The Battn. arrived at SERAIN at 1230 hours. Difficulty was experienced in obtaining accommodation for the whole Battalion, but with the aid of the Brigadier-General, fresh billets were obtained during the afternoon.	
	14/11/18		The Battalion paraded for Commanding Officer's inspection at 0930. This was followed by Ceremonial drill, arms drill and Battalion drill. 2nd.Lieut. B.H. Beckett returned from XIII Corps School. Lieut. G.E.T.H. Evans returned from Leave.	

Army Form C. 2118.

WAR DIARY
or
INTELLIGENCE SUMMARY.
(Erase heading not required.)

Instructions regarding War Diaries and Intelligence Summaries are contained in F. S. Regs., Part II. and the Staff Manual respectively. Title pages will be prepared in manuscript.

Place	Date	Hour	Summary of Events and Information	Remarks and references to Appendices
SERAIN	15/11/18		The Battalion paraded for Commanding Officer's inspection at 0950, followed by Ceremonial drill and general training.	
	16/11/18		Parades were carried out as on Friday the 15th. During the morning, a Draft of 81 Other Ranks reported.	
	17/11/18		The Battalion paraded for Brigade Thanksgiving Service at 1045 hours on the parade ground of the 5th Northamptonshire Regt. Major J. Hole M.C. was appointed Battalion Salvage Officer.	
	18/11/18		The Battalion paraded at 0830 under Major J. Hole M.C. for Salvage work in the area allotted to us. Lieut. V.C.M. Cornish joined the Battalion.	
	19/11/18		The Battalion carried out Salvage work as on the 18th. Brig.-Gen. L.W. de V. Sadleir-Jackson rejoined the Brigade.	
	20/11/18		The Battalion carried out Salvage work as on the 19th.	
	21/11/18		The Battalion, less "C" Coy., paraded at 0930 hours for inspection by the Commanding Officer. "C" Coy. carried out Salvage work at Brigade Dump. 2nd.Lieut. P. Lyons rejoined the Battalion from Hospital.	
	22/11/18		The Battalion carried out Salvage work, "A" & "D" Coys. being attached to the Machine Gun Corps. "B" & "C" Coys. worked on the Brigade Dump. A Football Match was played in the afternoon, between "B" Coy. 11th Battalion the Royal Fusiliers and "C" Coy. 6th Northamptonshire Regt., the Royal Fusiliers winning, by 10 Goals to 2.	
	23/11/18		The Battalion carried out Salvage work at the Brigade Dump, with the exception of 2 N.C.O's and 24 men from each Coy., who paraded for rehearsal of Torch-light Tattoo at 0900 hours. Major. J. Hole M.C. acted as President on a Court Martial. 2nd.Lieut. H.J.H. Saunders returned from Leave. Capt. H.L.Smedley and 2nd.Lieut. P.C. Kebbell returned from PARIS Leave. The Torch-light Tattoo was postponed indefinitely.	
	24/11/18		The Battalion paraded at 1100 hours for Brigade Church Service which was held on the parade ground of the 6th Northamptonshire Regt; the Brigadier attended.	
	25/11/18		The Battalion paraded at 0830 hours and marched to the Brigade parade on the ground of the 6th Northamptonshire Regt. The Brig.Gen. inspected the Brigade and gave Ceremonial drill. Capt. W.A. Smith M.C. went on Leave to U/K.	
	26/11/18		The Battalion paraded at 0900 hours for inspection by the Commanding Officer, which was followed by Ceremonial drill. Coys. then went on Salvage work. 2nd.Lieuts C. Lennon, D.E. Price, E.G. Susans, F.W. Turner and J.J. Paisley joined the Battalion from England. 2nd.Lieut. J.W. Hayes rejoined from Hospital.	
	27/11/18		Coys. paraded at 0815 hours for close order drill. The Battalion paraded at 0950 hours for inspection and Ceremonial drill by the Commanding Officer. At 1100 hours Coys. were dismissed to carry on Salvage work. Major. W. Hunnybun and Lieut. A.E. Benti returned from Leave. Capt. H. Tantrum and Capt. P.A. Hope went away on Leave to PARIS.	

Army Form C. 2118.

WAR DIARY
or
INTELLIGENCE SUMMARY.
(Erase heading not required.)

Instructions regarding War Diaries and Intelligence Summaries are contained in F.S. Regs., Part II. and the Staff Manual respectively. Title pages will be prepared in manuscript.

Place	Date	Hour	Summary of Events and Information	Remarks and references to Appendices
SERAIN	28/11/18.		A Divisional Review rehearsal was held on ground N.E. of SERAIN. The Battalion paraded at 0830 hours and marched on markers at 0915 hours. The Division was drawn up on a line running from U.15.c.19 to U.10.b.5.2. (reference Map Sheet 57B - 1/40,000), facing S.E. Brigadier-General L.W.de V. Sadleir-Jackson D.S.O. was in command of this parade. Lieut.Colonel Percival - 2nd. Bedfordshire Regt. - was in command of the 54th Infantry Brigade. Ceremonial drill was carried out, and the Division "marched past". Heavy rain fell throughout the parade.	
	29/11/18		Coys. paraded at 0815 hours for close order drill. The Battalion paraded at 0945 hours for inspection and Ceremonial drill by the Commanding Officer. 2nd.Lieuts. E. Robbins, R.F. Pettitt and F.G. Walford joined the Battalion from U/K.	
	30/11/18.		Parades were carried out as on the 29th inst. A Brigade Cross-country race took place during the afternoon, which was won by the 2nd. Bedfordshire Regt.	

8.12.18.

Lieut. Colonel,
Commanding 11th Bn. The Royal Fusiliers.

Report on Operations
carried out by the 11th Bn.
The Royal Fusiliers
from Oct.23rd to Nov. 4th 1918.

OPERATION ON OCTOBER 23rd.   Orders given to Company Commanders - See Battalion Order No 19 of the 22nd October, No.1 Copy of which was sent to 54th Brigade. Copy of this enclosed herewith.

NARRATIVE.

The Battalion formed up at 20 hours on the 22nd Oct. behind the Railway Embankment at K.23.c.1.3. and K.29.Central, in the following order:- C.D.B.A. Coys.

At Zero plus 5 minutes C. Coy. moved forward through the Railway Bridge, crossing the stream by footpath on E. side of the Embankment, in artillery formation in rear of the 2nd Bedfordshire Regt, A,D and B. Coys. following at close intervals.

The enemy put down a heavy barrage round the Bridge causing a number of casualties, but otherwise his barrage was weak.

Only one of the Tanks allotted to us was met at the point agreed upon K.23.a.6.5; the other was not seen. This Tank did remarkably fine work, moving forward with its allotted Coy. (B) through the first objective, in spite of the fact that it was fired on at close range by 2 Field guns and had to engage several machine-gun nests which should have been already dealt with by the preceeding Tanks and Infantry. It afterwards accompanied this Coy. to within 200 yds. of our final objective, and only returned when nearly run out of petrol. The Officer in charge shewed great determination, and although his Tank was pierced in several places by armour-piercing bullets, rendered the greatest assistance throughout the attack.

Shortly after starting to move forward, D. Coy. was slightly held up by machine gun posts at K.24 Central, which had evidently been overlooked by the preceeding Infantry; here 2nd Lieut. J.J.LAWRENCE was killed. The post was rushed and the occupants taken prisoners.

The attack proceeded up to time as far as the road running through K.18.b. and L.13.a. This road was evidently mistaken by the 2nd. Bedfordshire Regt. as their first objective, and the Battalion should have passed through the front line of the 2nd Bedfordshire Regt. to continue the attack to our final objective.

C. Coy, moving forward encountered Orchards about L.7.d.1.8, and thinking the 2nd Bedfordshire Regt. to be on their right objective, took this as their objective and proceeded to clear up this district.

D. Coy. moving off to the Right were held up for some time by the enemy's Field guns at point-blank range near the CEMETERY, but on the arrival of the Tank with B. Coy. were enabled to push forward. Here 2 Field guns were captured. They reached a position about L.8.a. Central and were here held up by heavy machine-gun fire from the Right.

B. Coy., with the Tank, still keeping with the barrage, pushed straight forward to within 200 yds. of their final objective, capturing 5 Field guns in the Orchards in L.2.c. They suffered heavy casualties on both flanks during the latter part of the advance, and having no troops on either side of them, were compelled to fall back to the Orchards in L.2.Central. Here touch was gained with D. Coy., who then moved forward to a position along the edge of Orchard in L.3.c.1.1.

A. Coy. in the meantime had moved forward to its allotted position, and took over the position vacated by D. Coy. These are the positions occupied when the 55th Brigade leapfrogged through us at Zero plus 360. Touch had been gained on both flanks.

At Zero plus 360 Batt. Hdqrs. took up their position in a house a L.7.c.8.7. C. & A. Coys. were then moved forward in support of B. & D who had gone forward to their objectives with the 55th Brigade - C. Co taking up a position in the Orchards at L.2.c., and A. Coy. being moved up to a position in close support to D. Coy. in the Orchards behind L'EPINETTE FARM.

One Coy. of the 2nd Bedfordshire Regt. also moved up and took over the BROWN LINE.

The Battalion remained in these positions for the rest of the day

OPERATIONS ON OCTOBER 24th.

The 6th Northamptonshire Regt. to take the 1st objective from F.16.d.6.4. to F.29.a.7.5. The 11th Bn. The Royal Fusiliers, in conjunction with the 2nd Bedfordshire Regt., to leapfrog through the 6th Northamptonshire Regt., and capture the 2nd objective - the ENGLEFONTAINE-ROBERSART ROAD.

At Zero minus 15 the Battalion formed up about 100 yds. in front of the road running from F.28.d.2.3. to F.28.a.0.5.

At Zero plus 10 minutes the Battalion moved forward in artillery formation in rear of the 6th Northamptonshire Regiment.

Our barrage was weak and short, and inflicted several casualties on us; Capt. W. Hornfeck was wounded. The enemy's artillery was also weak and scattered, but he was using a fair amount of gas.

At Zero plus 70 we leapfrogged through the 6th Northamptonshire Regt. and pushed forward. Little resistance was encountered until we came under heavy machine-gun fire from a strong point in the SUNKEN RD at F.17.d.1.5. Here C. Coy. was held up until the arrival of a Tank which at once came to our assistance, and driving straight down the SUNKEN ROAD, succeeded in knocking out the post. This was done under heavy artillery fire at close range, and it is extremely doubtful if w could have got forward at all without this Tank's assistance.

By this time the following Officers had become casualties:-
Capt. B. Webster, Capt. W. Hornfeck, Lieut. G. Tyler,
2/Lieuts. C. Macklin, F. Lyons and F. Garner.

The four Companies were then rather mixed up, but succeeded in pushing forward to the high ground in 17 D. where they were again held up by machine-gun fire from the high ground in 18A. & C. and severe flank machine-gun fire from the direction of RENUART FARM. They then fell slightly back behind the crest of the hill.

The positions of the Coys. were now as follows:- A. Coy. F.17.c.9.2. C. Coy. F.17.c.7.8. B. & D. Coys. in close support in Orchards behind stream running through F17C.

The enemy here made a counter-attack but was driven back by our fire with fairly heavy casualties.

We were now in touch with the 2nd Bedfordshire Regt. on the Right and the Argyle & Southern Highlanders on the Left.

At about 10.15 a barrage was put down on our Front line by our own heavies. The shooting was extraordinary accurate; many casualties were inflicted and the line was compelled to withdraw to the Orchards in front of BOUSIES WOOD.

At 11.15 the remainder of A. & C. Coys. moved forward to their original positions.

At 19.00 battle patrols pushed forward. The enemy having withdrawn we succeeded in establishing ourselves on the road running through F.11.d. & F.18.a.

We were relieved in the early hours of the 25th by the 10th Essex Regt.

The Battalion moved to BOUSIES, and in the afternoon to LA FAYTE FARM.

OPERATIONS ON NOVEMBER 4th 1918.

An attack was made on the morning of the 4th inst., in conjunction with the 2nd Bedfordshire Regt. and the 6th Northamptonshire Regt. We formed a composite Company consisting of C. & D. Coys.

At Zero minus 2 hours C. & D. Coys. formed up at A.13.d.3.7. to A.13.d.1.9. At Zero plus 30 Coys. moved off by platoons across Sunken Road at A.13.b.7.2. facing South - platoons in the line in extended order, one platoon and Hdqrs. in rear. Capt. H. Tantram took command of the Right flank and Lieut. C. Patridge the Left flank. Composite Coy. under the command of Capt. P. Hope.

At Zero plus 113 our barrage opened, rather wide of the mark and we suffered a few casualties. Tank No. 9196, which was detailed to assist us in our attack, joined us by this time and moved forward with us at Zero plus 118 minutes. It assisted us in breaking through two hedges but after crossing the stream, moved off to the Left to engage a reported enemy post and broke down. Beyond engaging the enemy with the 6 pdr. gun it was of no further use to us. The Company then experienced great difficulty in breaking through the hedges but picked up a dozen prisoners from a post on the Left flank.

We encountered little enemy artillery fire and it became increasingly difficult to keep touch along the line. The line was then held up by M.G. fire from positions on the road at A.20.a.2.8. and A.20.a.5.6. The remaining platoon was brought up and a party was sent along to the Cross Roads to deal with them from the flank.

We suffered several casualties and our position became serious. A message from Capt. Hope was received at 10.00 to that effect.

Pte. D. Sale pushed straight forward, regardless of all danger, with his Lewis gun and knocked out the enemy M.G. at A.20.a.2.8.

We then pushed on to the road and took about 30 prisoners from this position. Another 30 were brought out of the position at A.20.a.5.6. By this time our numbers were reduced to 20 men, and we pushed on down the main road and through the Orchard on the E. side of the road.

We took several large batches of prisoners from the houses and positions along the road and in the Orchard, numbering over 100 including 5 Officers.

We then pushed on over the Cross Roads and established touch with the Inniskillings at A.26.a.6.7. and with our A. Coy.

A post was established at A.20.c.8.3. and sent a patrol to gain touch with the 2nd. Bedfords on our Left. By this time the Village had been cleared of the enemy.

Lieut. Colonel.
Commanding 11th Bn. The Royal Fusiliers

SECRET.   Copy No. 12.

Key Map sheet.   11TH. BN. THE ROYAL FUSILIERS.
57B. 1/40,000 and   Order No. 19.
special Maps issued.

IMFORMATION.   At an hour and date to be notified later, the 54th Brigade, in
1.   conjunction with other Brigades and Divisions on the Right and Left will attack
       the Enemy's positions N.E. of LE CATEAU.

INTENTIONS.   On the attack on the 54th Brigade front the 2nd Bedfordshire Regt
2.   will take the first objective, the 11th Royal Fusiliers will leapfrog and
       take the 2nd objective - boundaries and objectives as given verbally.
       The 98th Inf. Brigade will attack on the left of 54th Brigade, and the 53rd
       Brigade on the right. The 4th Bn Kings Liverpool Regt taking the 2nd objective
       on the left of the Royal Fusiliers and the 6th Batt Berkshire Regt on the right.

APPROACH -   The Battalion will form up behind the Railway embankment from K.23.c.1.3.
FORMATIONS. to K.29 central, in the following order:- C.D.B.A, with head of "C" Coy
3.   at bridge at K.23.c.1.3. they will be in position by 20.00. Two Coys of the
       2nd Bedfordshire Regt will be formed up behind the embankment from Bridge
       K.23.c.1.3. to the FOREST ROAD. As soon as the rear of these two Coys have
       crossed the Railway, "C" will advance along the embankment, until their tail
       has crossed the bridge and then they will then advance in Artillery formation,
       parallel to the FOREST ROAD. "D", B and "A" will flank follow them in turn.
       On reaching the road running from K.18.b. to K.13.a. coys. will form up with
       the Left of their Coys. on the left boundary of the Brigade, and follow the
       2nd Bedfordshire Regiment as closely as possible to their objective. As soon as
       the 2nd Bedfordshire Regt. have seized their objective, "C" Coy. will advance
       and form up as near as possible to the protective barrage, "B","D" & "A" Coys.
       foeming up behind them. On the barrage lifting, Coys. will immediately proceed
       to the areas as allotted to them verbally, keeping as close to the barrage as
       possible.

COMPASS   The advance throughout will be carried out on a general bearing of 55 degr
BEARING. degrees Magnetic. There will be a 40 minute halt on the first objective.
4.   The Rpyal Fusiliers' objective will be reached at Z plus 200, the first objective
       at Zero plus 100. The probable time of start will be Zero minus 28.
       The 55th Infantry Brigade will leapfrog from the Royal Fusiliers at Zero plus 320.

ARTILLERY.   The attack will be carried out under a barrage advancing at the rate of
5.   100 yds. in 4 minutes. There will be approximately 1 gun to 3 0 yds. on the
       Brigade front. The attack on the first objective will be carried out under an
       additional barrage by Trench Mortars and Machine Guns. One section - "B" Coy.
       18th Machine Gun Battalion - will follow "D" Coy. to its objective.

TANKS.   It is probable that only one Tank will accompany the Battalion. This
6.   will proceed along the Left Boundary as far as the ORCHARD in L.2.c. and will
       strike across through L'EPINETTE Orchards with "D" Coy. A Supply Tank will dump
       ammunition, water and rations at about L.2.d.0.0. O.C. "A" Coy. will detail a
       guide to meet this Tank at S.E. edge of Copse in K.30 central at 11.00 on Z day,
       and guide the Tank to final destination. Should a second Tank be available it will
       proceed to the ORCHARD S.E. of the FOREST with "B" Coy.

COMMUNICATIONS   Communications, liason, and signal scheme will be carried out as issued.
& SIGNALS. "B" Coy. willdetail one platoon to advance on their Left flank and take up a
7.   position on the objective at F.26.d.3.0. They should keep in close touch with the
       4th King's Liverpool Regt. O.C. "D" Coy. will detail one section to operate on
       their Right flank and establish liason post with the 6th Berkshire Regt. at L.3.d.
       1.. The S.O.S. signal for the 54th Brigade is Green over Red over Green.
       S..ess signal is 2 White Very Lights in quick succession.

CONTACT   R.A.F. Contact Patrols will be answered by flares and electric torches
PATROLS. flashed by Officers. These will only be used by Front line troops. Contact
8.   planes will call for flares on the Royal Fusiliers final objective at 06.15.
       Watches synchronised at 22.30 at B.H.Q. which will be situated at Railway
       Embankment at about K.23.c.2.0. Counter-attack patrol will be in the air from
       dawn onwards. Should a counter-attack develop, this patrol will drop white
       parachute lights immediately over the attacking troops.

REPORTS R.A.P. 9.	Battalion H.Q. will follow the advance to the first objective and will take up a position near the cemetry in.L.7.c.8.8. All reports and prisoners will be sent here. R.A.P. will be situated near Batt. H.Q.	
CAPTURED GUNS. 10.	Location of Guns and Howitzers captured will be notified immediately to B.H.Q.	
ACKNOWLEDGE. 11.		

DISTRIBUTION
ISSUED AT.

                                                                                             Capt. & Adjt.
                                                                       for Lieut Colonel.

1.   54th Brigade.   Commanding 11th Bn The Royal Fusiliers
2,3,4&5.   All Coys.
6.   Adjt. for C.O.
7.   Lt. Fisher, I.O.
8.   M.O.
9.   R.S.M.
10.   Sigs.
11.   File.
12.   War Diary.
13.   -do-
14.   Spare.

Report on Operations
carried out by the 11th Bn.
The Royal Fusiliers
from Oct. 23rd to Nov. 4th 1918.

OPERATION ON OCTOBER 23rd.   Orders given to Company Commanders - See Battalion Order No 19 of the 22nd October, No.1 Copy of which was sent to 54th Brigade. Copy of this enclosed herewith.

NARRATIVE.

The Battalion formed up at 20 hours on the 22nd Oct. behind the Railway Embankment at K.23.c.1.3. and K.29.Central, in the following order:- C.D.B.A. Coys.

At Zero plus 5 minutes C. Coy. moved forward through the Railway Bridge, crossing the stream by footpath on E. side of the Embankment, in artillery formation in rear of the 2nd Bedfordshire Regt, A,D and B. Coys. following at close intervals.

The enemy put down a heavy barrage round the Bridge causing a number of casualties, but otherwise his barrage was weak.

Only one of the Tanks allotted to us was met at the point agreed upon K.23.a.6.5; the other was not seen. This Tank did remarkably fine work, moving forward with its allotted Coy. (B) through the first objective, in spite of the fact that it was fired on at close range by 2 Field guns and had to engage several machine-gun nests which should have been already dealt with by the preceeding Tanks and Infantry. It afterwards accompanied this Coy. to within 200 yds. of our final objective, and only returned when nearly run out of petrol. The Officer in charge shewed great determination, and although his Tank was pierced in several places by armour-piercing bullets, rendered the greatest assistance throughout the attack.

Shortly after starting to move forward, D. Coy, was slightly held up by machine gun posts at K.24 Central, which had evidently been over looked by the preceeding Infantry; here 2nd Lieut. J.J.LAWRENCE was killed. The post was rushed and the occupants taken prisoners.

The attack proceeded up to time as far as the road running through K.18.b. and L.13.a. This road was evidently mistaken by the 2nd. Bedfordshire Regt. as their first objective, and the Battalion should have passed through the front line of the 2nd BedfordshireRegt. to continue the attack to our final objective.

C. Coy, moving forward encountered Orchards about L.7.d.1.8, and thinking the 2nd Bedfordshire Regt. to be on their right objective, took this as their objective and proceeded to clear up this district.

D. Coy. moving off to the Right were held up for some time by the enemy's Field guns at point-blank range near the CEMETERY, but on the arrival of the Tank with B. Coy. were enabled to push forward. Here 2 Field guns were captured. They reached a position about L.8.a. Central and were here held up by heavy machine-gun fire from the Right.

B. Coy., with the Tank, still keeping with the barrage, pushed straight forward to within 200 yds. of their final objective, capturing 5 Field guns in the Orchards in L.2.c. They suffered heavy casualties on both flanks during the latter part of the advance, and having no troops on either side of them, were compelled to fall back to the Orchards in L.2.Central. Here touch was gained with D. Coy., who then

-1-

moved forward to a position along the edge of Orchard in L.3.c.1.1.

A. Coy. in the meantime had moved forward to its allotted position, and took over the position vacated by D. Coy. These are the positions occupied when the 55th Brigade leapfrogged through us at Zero plus 360. Touch had been gained on both flanks.

At Zero plus 360 Batt. Hdqrs. took up their position in a house a L.7.c.8.7. C. & A. Coys. were then moved forward in support of B. & D who had gone forward to their objectives with the 55th Brigade - C. C taking up a position in the Orchards at L.2.c., and A. Coy. being moved up to a position in close support to D. Coy. in the Orchards behind L'EPINETTE FARM.

One Coy. of the 2nd Bedfordshire Regt. also moved up and took over the BROWN LINE.

The Battalion remained in these positions for the rest of the day

OPERATIONS ON OCTOBER 24th.

The 6th Northamptonshire Regt. to take the 1st objective from F.16.d.6.4. to F.29.a.7.5. The 11th Bn. The Royal Fusiliers, in conjunction with the 2nd Bedfordshire Regt., to leapfrog through the 6th Northamptonshire Regt., and capture the 2nd objective - the ENGLEFONTAINE-ROBERSART ROAD.

At Zero minus 15 the Battalion formed up about 100 yds. in front of the road running from F.28.d.2.3. to F.28.a.0.5.

At Zero plus 10 minutes the Battalion moved forward in artillery formation in rear of the 6th Northamptonshire Regiment.

Our barrage was weak and short, and inflicted several casualties on us; Capt. W. Hornfeck was wounded. The enemy's artillery was also weak and scattered, but he was using a fair amount of gas.

At Zero plus 70 we leapfrogged through the 6th Northamptonshire Regt. and pushed forward. Little resistance was encountered until we came under heavy machine-gun fire from a strong point in the SUNKEN R at F.17.d.1.5. Here C. Coy. was held up until the arrival of a Tank which at once came to our assistance, and driving straight down the SUNKEN ROAD, succeeded in knocking out the post. This was done under heavy artillery fire at close range, and it is extremely doubtful if could have got forward at all without this Tank's assistance.

By this time the following Officers had become casualties:-
Capt. B. Webster, Capt. W. Hornfeck, Lieut. G. Tyler,
2/Lieuts. C. Macklin, F. Lyons and F. Garner.

The four Companies were then rather mixed up, but succeeded in pushing forward to the high ground in 17 D. where they were again held up by machine-gun fire from the high ground in 18A. & C. and severe flank machine-gun fire from the direction of RENUART FARM. They then fell slightly back behind the crest of the hill.

The positions of the Coys. were now as follows:- A. Coy. F.17.c.9.2. C. Coy. F.17.c.7.8. B. & D. Coys. in close support in Orchards behind stream running through F17C.

The enemy here made a counter-attack but was driven back by our fire with fairly heavy casualties.

We were now in touch with the 2nd Bedfordshire Regt. on the Right and the Argyle & Southern Highlanders on the Left.

At about 10.15 a barrage was put down on our Front line by our own heavies. The shooting was extraordinary accurate; many casualties were inflicted and the line was compelled to withdraw to the Orchards in front of BOUSIES WOOD.

At 11.15 the remainder of A. & C. Coys. moved forward to their original positions.

At 19.00 battle patrols pushed forward. The enemy having withdrawn we succeeded in establishing ourselves on the road running through F.11.d. & F.18.a.

We were relieved in the early hours of the 25th by the 10th Essex Regt.

The Battalion moved to BOUSIES, and in the afternoon to LA FAYTE FARM.

OPERATIONS ON NOVEMBER 4th 1918.

An attack was made on the morning of the 4th inst., in conjunction with the 2nd Bedfordshire Regt. and the 6th Northamptonshire Regt. We formed a composite Company consisting of C. & D. Coys.

At Zero minus 2 hours C. & D. Coys. formed up at A.13.d.3.7. to A.13.d.1.9. At Zero plus 30 Coys. moved off by platoons across Sunken Road at A.13.b.7.2. facing South - platoons in the line in extended order, one platoon and Hdqrs. in rear. Capt. H. Tantram took command of the Right flank and Lieut. C. Ratridge the Left flank. Composite Coy under the command of Capt. P. Hope.

At Zero plus 113 our barrage opened, rather wide of the mark and we suffered a few casualties. Tank No. 9196, which was detailed to assist us in our attack, joined us by this time and moved forward with us at Zero plus 118 minutes. It assisted us in breaking through two hedges but after crossing the stream, moved off to the Left to engage a reported enemy post and broke down. Beyond engaging the enemy with the 6 pdr. gun it was of no further use to us. The Company then experienced great difficulty in breaking through the hedges but picked up a dozen prisoners from a post on the Left flank.

We encountered little enemy artillery fire and it became increasingly difficult to keep touch along the line. The line was then held up by M.G. fire from positions on the road at A.20.a.2.8. and A.20.a.5.6. The remaining platoon was brought up and a party was sent along to the Cross Roads to deal with them from the flank.

We suffered several casualties and our position became serious. A message from Capt. Hope was received at 10.00 to that effect.

Pte. D. Sale pushed straight forward, regardless of all danger, with his Lewis gun and knocked out the enemy M.G. at A.20.a.2.8.

We then pushed on to the road and took about 30 prisoners from this position. Another 30 were brought out of the position at A.20.a.5.6. By this time our numbers were reduced to 20 men, and we pushed on down the main road and through the Orchard on the E. side of the road.

We took several large batches of prisoners from the houses and positions along the road and in the Orchard, numbering over 100 including 5 Officers.

We then pushed on over the Cross Roads and established touch with the Inniskillings at A.26.a.6.7. and with our A. Coy.

A post was established at A.20.c.8.3. and sent a patrol to gain touch with the 2nd. Bedfords on our Left. By this time the Village had been cleared of the enemy.

                                        Lieut. Colonel.
                            Commanding 11th Bn. The Royal Fusiliers

SECRET.   Copy No. 2

Ref.Map Sheet.   11TH. BN. THE ROYAL FUSILIERS.
57B. 1/40,000 and   Order No. 19.
special Maps issued.

INFORMATION.   At an hour and date to be notified later, the 54th Brigade, in
   1.   conjunction with other Brigades and Divisions on the Right and Left will attack
              the Enemy's positions N.E. of LE CATEAU.

INTENTIONS.   On the attack on the 54th Brigade front the 2nd Bedfordshire Regt
   2.   will take the first objective, the 11th Royal Fusiliers will leapfrog and
              take the 2nd objective - boundaries and objectives as given verbally.
              The 98th Inf. Brigade will attack on the left of 54th Brigade, and the 53rd
              Brigade on the right. The 4th Bn Kings Liverpool Regt taking the 2nd objective
              on the left of the Royal Fusiliers and the 6th Batt Berkshire Regt on the right.

APPROACH -   The Battalion will form up behind the Railway embankment from K.23.c.1.3.
FORMATIONS.   to K.29 central, in the following order:- C.D.B.A, with head of "C" Coy
   3.   at bridge at K.23.c.1.3. they will be in position by 20.00. Two Coys of the
              2nd Bedfordshire Regt will be formed up behind the embankment from Bridge
              K.23.c.1.3. to the FOREST ROAD. As soon as the rear of these two Coys have
              crossed the Railway, "C" will advance along the embankment, until their tail
              has crossed the bridge and then they will then advance in Artillery formation,
              parallel to the FOREST ROAD. "D", B and "A" will follow follow them in turn.
              On reaching the road running from K.18.b. to K.13.a. coys. will form up with
              the Left of their Coys. on the left boundary of the Brigade, and follow the
              2nd Bedfordshire Regiment as closely as possible to their objective. As soon as
              the 2nd Bedfordshire Regt. have seized their objective, "C" Coy. will advance
              and form up as near as possible to the protective barrage, "B","D" & "A" Coys.
              forming up behind them. On the barrage lifting, Coys. will immediately proceed
              to the areas as allotted to them verbally, keeping as close to the barrage as
              possible.

COMPASS   . The advance throughout will be carried out on a general bearing of 55 deg
BEARING.   degrees Magnetic. There will be a 40 minute halt on the first objective.
   4.   The Royal Fusiliers' objective will be reached at Z plus 200, the first objective
              at Zero plus 100. The probable time of start will be Zero minus 28.
              The 55th Infantry Brigade will leapfrog from the Royal Fusiliers at Zero plus 320.

ARTILLERY.   The attack will be carried out under a barrage advancing at the rate of
   5.   100 yds. in 4 minutes. There will be approximately 1 gun to 3 0 yds. on the
              Brigade front. The attack on the first objective will be carried out under an
              additional barrage by Trench Mortars and Machine Guns. One section - "B" Coy.
              18th Machine Gun Battalion - will follow "D" Coy. to its objective.

TANKS.   It is probable that only one Tank will accompany the Battalion. This
   6.   will proceed along the Left Boundary as far as the ORCHARD in L.2.c. and will
              strike across through L'EPINETTE Orchards with "D" Coy. A Supply Tank will dump
              ammunition, water and rations at about L.2.d.0.0. O.C. "A" Coy. will detail a
              guide to meet this Tank at S.E. edge of Copse in K.30 central at 11.00 on Z day,
              and guide the Tank to final destination. Should a second Tank be available it will
              proceed to the ORCHARD S.E. of the FOREST with "B" Coy.

COMMUNICATIONS Communications, liason, and signal scheme will be carried out as issued.
& SIGNALS.   "B" Coy. willdetail one platoon to advance on their Left flank and take up a
   7.   position on the objective at F.26.d.3.0. They should keep in close touch with the
              4th King's Liverpool Regt. O.C. "D" Coy. will detail one section to operate on
              their Right flank and establish liason post with the 6th Berkshire Regt. at L.3.d.
              1.2. The S.O.S. signal for the 54th Brigade is Green over Red over Green.
              Success signal is 2 White Very Lights in quick succession.

CONTACT   R.A.F. Contact Patrols will be answered by flares and electric torches
PATROLS.   flashed by Officers. These will only be used by Front line troops. Contact
   8.   planes will call for flares on the Royal Fusiliers final objective at 06.15.
              Watches synchronised at 22.30 at B.H.Q. which will be situated at Railway
              Embankment at about K.23.c.2.0. Counter-attack patrol will be in the air from
              dawn onwards. Should a counter-attack develop, this patrol will drop white
              parachute lights immediately over the attacking troops.

-2-

REPORTS   Battalion H.Q. will follow the advance to the first
R.A.P.   objective and will take up a position near the cemetry
  9.   in.L.7.c.8.8. All reports and prisoners will be sent here.
           R.A.P. will be situated near Batt. H.Q.

CAPTURED   Location of Guns and Howitzers captured will be notified
GUNS.   immediately to B.H.Q.
 10.

ACKNOWLEDGE.
 11.

DISTRIBUTION
ISSUED AT.

                                                                              Capt. & Adjt.
  1.   54th Brigade.   for Lieut Colonel.
  2,3,4&5.   All Coys.   Commanding 11th Bn The Royal Fusilier
  6.   Adjt. for C.O.
  7.   Lt. Fisher. I.O.
  8.   M.O.
  9.   R.S.M.
 10.   Sigs.
 11.   File.
 12.   War Diary.
 13.   -do-
 14.   Spare.

Army Form C. 2118.

WAR DIARY or INTELLIGENCE SUMMARY.

(Erase heading not required.)

11 RF

Place	Date	Hour	Summary of Events and Information	Remarks and references to Appendices
SERAIN.	1/12/18		Sunday. Brigade Church Parade.	
	2/12/18		A Divisional review took place at SERAIN. Lt. Gen. R.P. Lee, G.O.C. 18th Div. inspected and Division marched past.	
	3/12/18		Companies proceeded to ELINCOURT for baths.	
	4/12/18		Lt. Col. Gwynn addressed the Battalion. Companies were afterwards marched to the SERAIN-ELINCOURT road to see the King drive past. The Battalion lined both sides of the road and cheered lustily. The King alighted and walked along the lines accompanied by the Prince of Wales and his Staff.	
	5/12/18		Companies carried out Salvage.	
	6/12/18		Companies carried out Salvage, less A Coy.	
	7/12/18		Companies carried out Salvage.	
	8/12/18		Church Parade. Steeplechase in the afternoon.	
	9/12/18		Salvage carried out.	
WALINCOURT.	10/12/18		The Battalion moved to WALINCOURT at 14.00, arriving at 15.00. Billets very good.	
	11/12/18		Battalion cleared up Billets and surroundings.	
	12/12/18		Battalion Inspection by C. O.	
	13/12/18		Battalion Inspection by C. O. Games in afternoon.	
	14/12/18		Brig. Gen. S. Jackson inspected Billets.	
	15/12/18		Brigade Church Parade.	
	16/12/18		Lt. Col. Guy Blewitt D.S.O. M.C. assumed command of the Battalion vice Lt. Col. Gwynn D.S.O. who proceeded to Divisional Reception Camp.	
	17/12/18		Salvage carried out. Games in the afternoon.	
	18/12/18		Salvage carried out. Games in the afternoon.	
	19/12/18		Salvage carried out. Games in the afternoon.	
	20/12/18		Salvage carried out. Games in the afternoon.	
	21/12/18		Salvage. Mr. S. C. Turner, representative of the Battalion in England, arrived on a visit.	
	22/12/18		Brigade Church Parade.	
	23/12/18		Holiday. Football competition.	
	24/12/18		Holiday. Games and Battalion concert in evening.	

Army Form C. 2118.

WAR DIARY
or
INTELLIGENCE SUMMARY.
(Erase heading not required.)

Instructions regarding War Diaries and Intelligence Summaries are contained in F. S. Regs., Part II. and the Staff Manual respectively. Title pages will be prepared in manuscript.

Place	Date	Hour	Summary of Events and Information	Remarks and references to Appendices
WALINCOURT.	25/12/18		Xmas Day. Mens' Dinner at 14.00. Brig. Gen. S. Jackson wished the men a happy Xmas and a prosperous New Year. Each man received a penknife from Mr. Turner. Officers' Dinner at night.	
	26/12/18		Holiday. Steeplechase and games.	
	27/12/18		Salvage carried out. Games.	
	28/12/18		Salvage. Address on demobilization by Mr. Turner.	
	29/12/18		Brigade Church Parade.	
	30/12/18		Salvage. Capt. C.V. Wattenbach and Lieut. H.J. Saunders mentioned in despatches.	
	31/12/18		New Year's Eve. Officers' Dinner.	

9.1.19.

Guy Slewitt
Lieut. Colonel,
Commanding 11th Bn. The Royal Fusiliers.

WAR DIARY
INTELLIGENCE SUMMARY

Army Form C. 2118.

Confidential

11 R F(S) Bn 12

Place	Date	Hour	Summary of Events and Information	Remarks and references to Appendices
WALINCOURT	1/1/19		Salvage.	
			Children's Concert organised by Battalion (Address read by Mayor of WALINCOURT)	
	2/1/19		Salvage and Games	
	3/1/19		Salvage	
	4/1/19		4 men of Battalion demobilised.	
			Lt. Turner left the Battalion for England and received a hearty send-off.	
	5/1/19		Salvage. 10 Other Ranks demobilised.	
			Church Parade. Nickleclass in afternoon.	
	6/1/19		6 men left for Demobilization	
	7/1/19		Salvage and Games	
	8/1/19		ditto	
	9/1/19		ditto	
	10/1/19		ditto	
	11/1/19		ditto	

Army Form C. 2118.

WAR DIARY
or
INTELLIGENCE SUMMARY.
(Erase heading not required.)

Place	Date	Hour	Summary of Events and Information	Remarks and references to Appendices
WALINCOURT	12/1/19		Battalion Church Parade.	
	13/1/19		Ltr-men demobilized - Games in afternoon	
	14/1/19		Cadres - Battalion Concert in evening (great success)	
	15/1/19		Cadres and Games	
	16/1/19		Inter Platoon Football Competition	
	17/1/19		Cadres and Games	
	18/1/19		Coy's at disposal of Coy Commanders.	
			Capt H. L. Needley demobilized - Lt Colonel C.G. Kelly, DSO joined the Bn.	
	19/1/19		Brigade Church Parade	
	20/1/19		Cadres and Games.	
	21/1/19		Lectures and Games.	
	22/1/19		Cadres	
	23/1/19		Commanding Officers' Inspection	
	24/1/19		Cadres	
	25/1/19		Inspection of Billets.	
	26/1/19		Brigade Church Parade - Brigade Dance	

Army Form C. 2118.

WAR DIARY
or
INTELLIGENCE SUMMARY.
(Erase heading not required.)

Instructions regarding War Diaries and Intelligence
Summaries are contained in F. S. Regs., Part II.
and the Staff Manual respectively. Title pages
will be prepared in manuscript.

Place	Date	Hour	Summary of Events and Information	Remarks and references to Appendices
WALINCOURT	24/1/19		Ceremonial Practice	
	28/1/19		Inspection by Commanding Officer	
	29/1/19		Brigade Ceremonial Practice for presentation of Union Flags	
	30/1/19		Commanding Officers Inspection for presentation of Union Flags	
	31/1/19		Brigade Ceremonial Practice for presentation of Union Flags	

W. Mills, Lieut. Colonel.
Commanding 11th Bn. The Royal Fusiliers

11 RF
Vol 13
41 F.
(Jones)

WAR DIARY
~~INTELLIGENCE~~ SUMMARY.
(Erase heading not required.)

Army Form C. 2118.

Instructions regarding War Diaries and Intelligence Summaries are contained in F. S. Regs., Part II. and the Staff Manual respectively. Title pages will be prepared in manuscript.

Place	Date	Hour	Summary of Events and Information	Remarks and references to Appendices
WALINCOURT (France)	1/2/19		Colours by Corps Commander	
	2/2/19		Inspection of Billets by Brigadier-General	
	3/2/19		Church Parade – Brigade Dance	
	4/2/19		Inspection by Commanding Officer	
	5/2/19		Inspection of Billets by Commanding Officer & Baths	
	6/2/19		Inspection by Commanding Officer	
	7/2/19		Demobilization Inspection	
	8/2/19		200 Other Ranks and 10 Officers warned for Army of Occupation	
	9/2/19		Party for Army of Occupation equipped	
	10/2/19		Church Parade	
	11/2/19		Inspection by Commanding Officer	
	12/2/19		Inspection of Draft – Games	
	13/2/19		Draft for Army of Occupation equipped	
	14/2/19		15 men demobilized	
	15/2/19		Inspection and Games	
	15/2/19		Inspection of Billets by Commanding Officer	

Army Form C. 2118.

WAR DIARY
~~INTELLIGENCE SUMMARY~~
(Erase heading not required.)

Place	Date	Hour	Summary of Events and Information	Remarks and references to Appendices
WALINCOURT (France)	16/2/19		Church Parade Gams.	
	17/2/19		Kit Inspection of Draft.	
	18/2/19		Commanding Officer & Officers to Brussels Ball	
	19/2/19		General Training and Games	
	20/2/19		ditto	
	21/2/19		ditto	
	22/2/19		Inspection by the Commanding Officer	
	23/2/19		Church Parade	
	24/2/19		Inspection by Commanding Officer. Reorganise into 2 Coys.	
	25/2/19		Coys. at disposal of Coy Commander	
	26/2/19		ditto	
	27/2/19		ditto	
	28/2/19		Inspection	

Arthur Townshend
Captain
Commanding 12th Royal Sussex

Army Form C. 2118.

WAR DIARY
or
INTELLIGENCE SUMMARY.
(Erase heading not required.)

Instructions regarding War Diaries and Intelligence Summaries are contained in F. S. Regs., Part II. and the Staff Manual respectively. Title pages will be prepared in manuscript.

Place	Date	Hour	Summary of Events and Information	Remarks and references to Appendices
Wallncourt	March 1		The Commanding Officer inspected the Battalion billets.	
	2		The Battalion paraded for Divine Service under Capt. W.Smith. Summer time comes into force.	
	3.		Coys. at the disposal of Coy. Commanders.	
	4.		The Battalion bathed at MALINCOURT.	
	5.		Coys. carried out drill and recreational games in the morning.	
	6.		The Battalion carried out a route march to ESNES.	
	7.		A working party was supplied for loading ammunition at LONGSART DUMP.	
	8.		The Commanding Officer inspected the Battalion billets.	
	9.		Church Parade.	
	10.		Coys at the disposal of Coy. Commanders during the morning.	
	11.		The Commanding Officer inspected A & B Coys.	
	12.		The Battalion carried out a Route March to MALINCOURT.	
	13.		Coys. at the disposal of Coy. Commanders.	
	14.		Coys carried out 1 hours close order drill. Lecture by Commanding Officer.	
	15.		The Commanding Officer inspected billets.	

Army Form C. 2118.

WAR DIARY
or
INTELLIGENCE SUMMARY.
(Erase heading not required.)

Instructions regarding War Diaries and Intelligence
Summaries are contained in F. S. Regs., Part II.
and the Staff Manual respectively. Title pages
will be prepared in manuscript.

Place	Date	Hour	Summary of Events and Information	Remarks and references to Appendices
Malincourt	16.		Church Parade.	
	17.		The Battalion bathed at MALINCOURT.	
	18.		Coys. at the disposal of Coy. Commanders.	
	19.		A & B Coys. carried out a Route March to MALINCOURT.	
	20.		Coys. carried out 1 hour's close order drill and recreational games.	
	21.		Coys. at the dispsal of Coy. Commanders. Special Order by Brig. Gen BORRETT C.M.G.,D.S.O. Commdg. 18th Div. " Today the 18th Div. "as such, ceases to exist. The G.O.C. wishes to thank all officers, N.C.O's "and Men who have passed through the Division for their dyal support under "all circumstances.	
	22.		The Commanding Officer inspected the Battalion billets.	
	23.		Church Parade.	
	24.		The Battalion bathed at FLINCOURT. A Coy carried out a Kit Inspection of all ranks proceeding to the Army of Occupation.	
	25.		All ranks proceeding to the Army of Occupation were ordered to stand to and await instructions. The Commanding Officer addressed them in the Factory.	
	26.		Working party. The Draft detailed for the Armies of Occupation left for CAMBRAI en route for COLOGNE to join the 26th Bn. The Royal Fusiliers.	
	27.		The complete Cadre strength of the Battalion paraded for inspection.	
	28.		Lt.Col. G.F.Miller rejoined from leave.	
	29.		Major A.L.P.Girdler proceeded on leave.	
	30.		Church Parade.	
	31.		15 O.R.'s demobilised.	

A/Adjt. 11.Bn.The Royal Fusiliers.

WAR DIARY
or
INTELLIGENCE SUMMARY.
(Erase heading not required.)

Army Form C. 2118.

11 R F
SEP 15

H.S.F.
(2 sheets)

1919

Place	Date	Hour	Summary of Events and Information	Remarks and references to Appendices
April	1.		The Battalion moved to billets in SELVIGNY.	
	2.		Awaiting orders for cadre to proceed to ENGLAND.	
	3.		2 Officers and 9 O.R's proceeded to 26th. Bn. The Royal Fusiliers. Cologne.	
	4.		Games in the afternoon.	
	5.		-do-.	
	6.		Cadre paraded for Divine Service.	
	7.		Games in afternoon.	
	8.		Cadre bathed. Capt. W.A.Smith proceeded on leave.	
	9.		2 Officers and 5 O.R's proceeded to 26th. Bn. The Royal Fusiliers.	
	10.		Games.	
	11.		-do-.	
	12.		-do-.	
	13.		Church Parade & C.O's Inspection of billets.	
	14.		Recreational Games.	
	15.		Lieut A.E.Benti proceeded on leave.	
	16.		Recreational Games.	

Army Form C. 2118.

WAR DIARY
or
INTELLIGENCE SUMMARY.

(Erase heading not required.)

Place	Date	Hour	Summary of Events and Information	Remarks and references to Appendices
April	17.		Recreational Games.	
	18.		Church Parade (Good Friday.) Major A.L.P.Girdler returned from leave.	
	19.		Recreational Games.	
	20.		Cadre paraded for Divine Service.	
	21.		Audit Board assembled for the purpose of auditing the Bn. Accounts.	
	22.		Recreational Games.	
	23.		-do-.	
	24.		-do-.	
	25.		Madcaps Concert Party at LIGNY.	
	26.		Lieut. G.F.Boyce and 5.O.R'S proceeded to COLOGNE.	
	27.		Church Parade.	
	28½.		The Cadre bathed at LIGNY.	
	29.		Lieut A.E.Banti rejoined from leave.	
	30.		Recreational Games.	

Major.

Commanding 11th. (S) Bn. The Royal Fusiliers.

www.ingramcontent.com/pod-product-compliance
Lightning Source LLC
Chambersburg PA
CBHW080804010526
44113CB00013B/2325